Freud's Russia

History of Ideas Series
Paul Roazen, Series Editor

Brother Animal, Paul Roazen
Celebrations, William M. Johnston
Character and Opinion in the United States, George Santayana
Cultural Theory and Psychoanalytic Tradition, David James Fisher
Doctors and Their Patients, Edward Shorter
Encountering Freud, Paul Roazen
Fathers and Children: Andrew Jackson and the Subjugation of the American Indian, Michael Paul Rogin
Free Associations, Ernest Jones
Freud's Russia: National Identity in the Evolution of Psychoanalysis, James L. Rice
Freud, Women, and Society, J.O. Wisdom
Helen Deutsch, Paul Roazen
The House of the Prophet, Louis Auchincloss
The Necessity of Choice, Louis Hartz, edited, compiled, and prepared by Paul Roazen
On the Shoulders of Freud: Freud, Lacan, and the Psychoanalysis of Phallic Ideology, Roberto Speziale-Bagliacca
Oswald Spengler, Stuart H. Hughes
The Psychotherapy of Everyday Life, Peter Lomas
The Public Philosophy, Walter Lippmann
Sexuality, War, and Schizophrenia, Victor Tausk
Sigmund Freud, Helen Walker Puner
Sigmund Freud as a Consultant, Edoardo Weiss
The Therapeutic Process, the Self, and Female Psychology, Helene Deutsch
Women's Bodies, Edward Shorter

Freud's Russia

National Identity in the Evolution of Psychoanalysis

James L. Rice

Transaction Publishers
New Brunswick (U.S.A.) and London (U.K.)

Copyright © 1993 by Transaction Publishers, New Brunswick, New Jersey 08903

Library of Congress Catalog Number: 92-31244
ISBN: 1-56000-091-0
Printed in the United States of America

Library of Congress Cataloging-in-Publication Data

Rice, James L.
    Freud's Russia : national identity in the evolution of psychoanalysis / James L. Rice.
        p.   cm. — (History of ideas series)
    Includes bibliographical references and index.
    ISBN 1-56000-091-0
    1. Freud, Sigmund, 1856-1939. 2. National characteristics, Russian. 3. Dostoyevsky, Fyodor, 1821-1881 — Psychology. 4. Authors, Russian—Psychology. 5. Psychoanalysis and literature.
    I. Title. II. Series: History of ideas series (New Brunswick, N.J.)
BF109.F74R523 1992
150.19'52—dc20   92-31244
                                                                            CIP

In Memoriam

Herman Bennett Rice
1906-1976

Leo B. Arey
1913-1989

Lincoln Mason Knox
1938-1981

Have you ever seen a foreign newspaper after it has passed through Russian censorship at the frontier? Words, sentences, whole clauses are blacked out, so that the rest becomes unintelligible. A Russian censorship of this sort occurs in psychoses and produces the apparently meaningless deliria.

—Freud to Fliess, 22 December 1897

Issachar's perpetual torment was that he could not decide whether he was a Jew or an Egyptian; through revealing to him the mysteries of the divine wisdom, Ptamose solved the question for him: the deeper Issachar studied them, the clearer he saw that the god-man, Osiris, who had been slain, and He of Whom the prophets of Israel had said: "He has poured out His soul unto death and made intercession for the transgressors" were one and the same Messiah.

—Merezhkovsky, *Akhnaton, King of Egypt*

Contents

Acknowledgments		ix
Introduction		1
1.	Vaterlandslosigkeit	9
2.	Physician to the Tsar	25
3.	Counterfeit Rubles	43
4.	Russian Material	67
5.	The Wolf-Man—Analysis Interminable	93
6.	Dostoevsky in Freud's World	123
7.	Russische Innerlichkeit	159
8.	"Dostoevsky and Parricide"	177
9.	Ein Stock mit zwei Enden	201
Epilogue: Back to Barbarism		223
Photo Essay		151
Bibliography		237
Index		283

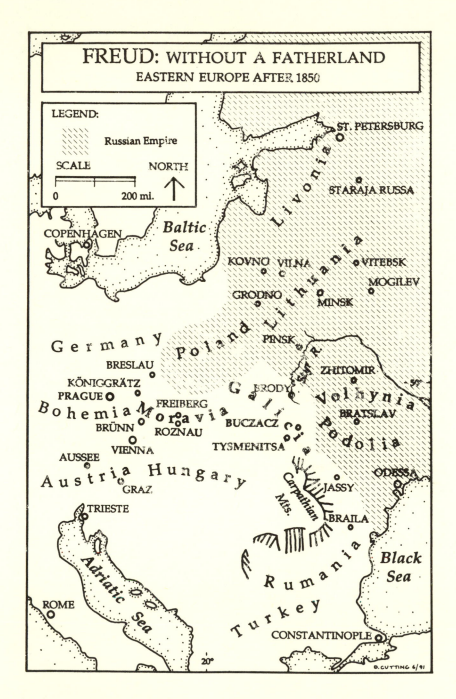

FREUD: WITHOUT A FATHERLAND
EASTERN EUROPE AFTER 1850

LEGEND:

Russian Empire

SCALE   NORTH

0   200 mi.

ST. PETERSBURG

STARAJA RUSSA

COPENHAGEN   *Baltic Sea*

Livonia

KOVNO   VILNA   VITEBSK

GRODNO   MOGILEV

MINSK

G e r m a n y   *Poland Lithuania*

PINSK

BRESLAU

KÖNIGGRÄTZ   *Galicia*   ZHITOMIR

PRAGUE   BRODY   *Volhynia*

FREIBERG   BRATSLAV

B o h e m i a   M o r a v i a   BUCZACZ   *Podolia*

BRÜNN   ROZNAU

TYSMENITSA

VIENNA

AUSSEE   ODESSA

A u s t r i a   H u n g a r y   *Carpathian Mts.*   JASSY

GRAZ

TRIESTE   BRAILA

Adriatic Sea   *Black Sea*

R u m a n i a

ROME   T u r k e y

CONSTANTINOPLE

20°

D.CUTTING 6/91

Freud without a Fatherland: After 1850

Acknowledgments

Parts of this study have been presented in various forums—the University of Oregon German Faculty Seminar (1975); the World Congress of Slavic and East European Studies III, Washington, D.C. (1985); the Conference on Russian Literature and Psychoanalysis at the University of California, Davis (1987); annual meetings of the North American Dostoevsky Society, AATSEEL, in San Francisco (1988 and 1991); the Seventh International Dostoevsky Symposium, Ljubljana, Slovenia (1989); Dartmouth College (1990)—and in my publications listed in the Bibliography (1982, 1985, 1989).

Debts large and small are owed to the following persons, some no longer among the living, who kindly helped at various moments in the research: Karen Achberger, Michael Amberger, Chester and Sabra Avery, Ralph and Eva Black, Ralph Black Jr., Clifford BreMiller, Roy Brener, Joseph Brodsky, Ronald Bulatoff, George W. Butterworth III, Catherine Clay and Alan Cresswell, Norma Comrada, Daniel B. Cosgrove, Lawrence N. Crumb, David Cutting, Theodore Draper, Stanislav Dzhimbinov, Kurt R. Eissler, Alan Elms, Alexandre M. Etkind, Efim Etkind, Mrs. Achilles Fang, Daniel Field, Hans F. Fink, Stanley Fish, Joseph and Rachel Fiszman, Gene D. Fitzgerald, Thomas V. Foster, Jr., Carolyn O. Frost, Peter Gay, Toby Gelfand, Sanford Gifford, T. Givón, Walther Hahn, Michael Heim, Barbara Heldt, Jean Laves Hellie, Michael Jones, David Joravsky, Mark Kanzer, Edward Kasinec, John Kerr, R. Alan Kimball, James Kludt, E. James Lieberman, Magnus Ljunggren, Lev Loseff, Patrick J. Mahony, Robert Mann, Jeffrey M. Masson, Nicholas Meyer, Martin Miller, John N. Mundall, Aleksandr Murinson and family, Nadine Natov, Paul Olum, Elliott Oring, Daniel Rancour-Laferriere, Thomas Roberts, Nathan Rosen, Gary Rosenshield, Richard J. Rosenthal, Michael Shapiro, Richard Sheldon, Peter J. Swales, Diane E. Thompson, Saul Toobert, George and Maggie Vinnedge, Winthrop Wetherbee, Dennis and

Heide Whelan, Ron Whistance-Smith, Irving Wohlfarth, Richard S. Wortman, Yosef Hayim Yerushalmi, and Liudmila Zagorskaia. Many others should be on this list, but a memory that fades over the years has failed to retain their identity.

My special thanks to Caryl Emerson, Hugh McLean, and Ellendea Proffer for reading the manuscript, giving advice, and offering encouragement. To Lev Loseff, for his kind words on the Voice of America Russian Program and elsewhere. Also to Paul Roazen for his example, for patient assistance at many turns, and for helping the book find its way into print. And to my colleague of a quarter century, Wolfgang Leppmann, for personal and professional support, for high spirits that made things easier, and for persuading me not to leave this project to the Germanists.

Sponsoring and assisting institutions include the University of Oregon Graduate School; the National Endowment for the Humanities; the Oregon Humanities Committee; the American Council of Learned Societies; the Harvard University Russian Research Center; the University of Oregon Library Reference and Interlibrary Loan Services; the Lenin Library Reference Section (Moscow); Sigmund Freud Copyrights (Wivenhoe, England); Pacific Rim University; and O.K.O. International.

And, of course, Ruth, Laura, Janet Fern, and Mirabel—my mother, wife, and daughters—first, last, always.

Introduction

All old friendships and relationships presented themselves to me once again and silently received the death-blow. (My fantasy still lives in Russian history.)

—Freud to his fiancée, 28 April 1885

Freud's Russia was, among other things, his family's homeland. His forefathers, like Dostoevsky's, lived for generations in the region that became Russian Lithuania, core of the Imperial Russian Pale of Jewish Settlement. His mother grew up in Odessa, where her brothers prospered and Freud's grandmother lived to great old age.

Recently it has been learned that Freud had dozens of kinfolk living on Russian terrain.[1] His father and cousins traveled to Odessa on business, not to mention Uncle Josef, who went to prison in Austria for trading in counterfeit rubles. Patients who were probably relatives came to Freud across the Russian border from Volhynia Province (the city of Zhitómir) before the turn of the century. By that time one of his Odessa cousins was married to a doctor, a likely entrée for psychoanalysis into the Russian medical community.

Freud's mother, his main link to the Odessa clan, served him as family historian when he wrote *The Interpretation of Dreams* (1900), and he visited her weekly in Vienna until her death in 1930. Freud's most famous patient, the Wolf-Man, was a Russian Orthodox Christian from Odessa, whose family physician, Moshe Wulff, became Freud's favorite analyst in Russia. After the Revolution, Wulff served as president of the Moscow Psychoanalytic Society until 1927, when its end was in sight.

1

As one may gather from this thumbnail sketch, Freud's Russia was to some extent a family affair and a personal matter, not just a purely political and figurative concept.

On the other hand, the Russian Empire, remote and outlandish, was long notorious in the West for its tyranny, aggression, pogroms, sedition, nihilism, terrorism, revolution, and finally—as Freud echoed the commonplace phrase, with ever deepening irony—the "Bolshevik experiment." Waves of Russian émigrés, among them medical students, revolutionaries, and impoverished *Ostjude*, were highly visible in Freud's Viennese world. But his first close contact with the Russian Orthodox intelligentsia occurred much earlier, when he studied with Charcot, who was himself a consulting physician to the tsar. Freud's best friends in Paris were two Russian doctors, one an assistant to the eminent Bótkin, the other destined to become Russia's leading neuropathologist. In these relationships we can observe Freud's first efforts to diagnose the Russian national character.

After the turn of the century, the Russian psyche was frequently on the agenda of the Vienna Psychoanalytic Society. The minutes summarize papers and discussions dealing with Russian Jewish patients, Russian terrorists, and several works of Dostoevsky, whose great vogue in the Germanic world began in 1906. In Freud's correspondence with Jung (1906-14), we find casual remarks about Russian patients and colleagues, sometimes embellished in comic stereotypes that further delineate Freud's Russia.[2] In these years, Freud's circle admitted diverse and remarkable figures from Russia, such as the Russophile millionaire Max Eitingon (a native of Mogilev), Sabina Spielrein from Rostóv-na-Donú, Lou Andreas-Salomé from Petersburg, and Trotsky's comrade Adolf Joffe, a patient of Adler's who contributed to the Russian psychoanalytic literature. Trotsky himself took an interest in the movement in the years before World War I, and became its only defender among the Soviet leadership, no doubt a factor in the early demise of Russian psychoanalysis after Trotsky's political defeat and exile. Freud was never acquainted with Trotsky, but was keenly aware of his presence in the Café Central.

In January 1910, Freud began to treat Sergei Pankeev, the Wolf-Man. That same year he received a gift subscription to the splendid Munich edition of Dostoevsky. Pankeev's memoirs reveal that passages from the great novelist were discussed with Freud in their analytic sessions. By 1920, the Russian writer and Russian patient had fused, in Freud's understanding, into a single Russian personality type.

A major task of my work has been to demonstrate this interplay between Freud's most famous clinical history and his view of Dostoevsky, as revealed in "Dostoevsky and Parricide" and other sources.

Freud's approach to Dostoevsky is both medical and cultural. It must be regarded both in the light of medical history, specifically the changing differential diagnosis of epilepsy and hysteria, and as a unique yet characteristic contribution to the Dostoevsky criticism of Freud's day. The Germanic literature on Dostoevsky, already massive in those days but not quite overwhelming in its bulk, is conveniently catalogued in a dissertation by Theoderich Kampmann, *Dostojewski in Deutschland*, published in 1930. I review the material that seems to bear most closely on Freud, following leads from his library inventories, footnotes, correspondence, and his general reading habits—for example, his abiding admiration for the historical novels and essays of Dmitri Merezhkovsky.

Dostoevsky was hailed by many, including Freud's postwar friend Stefan Zweig, as the greatest modern explorer of psychic depths. For this reason alone the Father of Psychoanalysis regarded him with profound ambivalence. And in Freud's world, Dostoevsky came to be known not only as the prophet of Russian revolution but also as a universal seer of human destiny. This reception somewhat impeded Freud's inclination to analyze Dostoevsky as a specifically Russian (archaic) type like the Wolf-Man.

The medical aspect of Dostoevsky was also complicated by Freud's ambivalence. On the one hand, the hereditary "neuropathological taint" recognized by Freud in his own immediate family included a case of epilepsy, the *morbus sacer* of Dostoevsky. On the other hand, the self-destructive obsessive neurosis Freud found so significant in Dostoevsky—compulsive gambling—had a fatal parallel in Freud's own behavior: smoking. But these stigmata may also have unconsciously contributed to their personal rapport, which Freud most clearly acknowledged in his praise of Dostoevsky's great intellect directed against religion. When Freud speculates about Dostoevsky's pathology, albeit with reservations, modern readers understandably may object.[3] But on problems of faith, Freud read Dostoevsky with better perception than many readers of our day. Seeking to mediate between Freud and Dostoevsky, we inevitably confront the vexed question of Dostoevsky and the Jews, and in turn the issue of Freud's Jewish identity. Some speculation on these problems is offered, with special attention to a book in Freud's library: *Die Beichte eines Juden in Briefen an Dostojewski*, by Leonid Grossman.

Prior studies of "Dostoevsky and Parricide" generally see it as a text in a vacuum, apart from Freud's other works. The history of its composition reveals that Freud set aside the draft, and after close reading of the "Grand Inquisitor" legend in *The Brothers Karamazov*, wrote *The Future of an Illusion* (1927). The subject and dialogic design of this famous essay are in direct response to the "Grand Inquisitor," a fact only once noted in passing by Freud's personal physician, Max Schur.[4] Skeptical allusions to "the Russian experiment" remind us that Freud's philosophical thought here, as usual, is linked to great events in current history, and his ironic reference to *Russische Innerlichkeit* (Russian introspective depths) directly echoes the opening passage of "Dostoevsky and Parricide," wherein Russian national character is exemplified by Ivan the Terrible. We conclude that "Dostoevsky and Parricide" belongs in Freud's series of publications on national psychology, including *Totem and Taboo*, *Beyond the Pleasure Principle*, *The Future of an Illusion*, *Civilization and Its Discontents*, *New Introductory Lectures to Psychoanalysis*, and *Moses and Monotheism*. Each of these major works incorporates significant Russian material—even the last, as we undertake to demonstrate in due course.

Freud's authorized biography by Ernest Jones suggests a "north-south" polarity in his psyche, symbolized by Prague and Rome in a famous series of dreams. Indeed, he spoke Czech as a second language in childhood and once planned to make his career in Prague.[5] Roman antiquities and travel to Rome were passions that he cherished and fulfilled. Several excellent psychohistorical studies explore this pattern, and one of the best, by Carl Schorske, was a major inspiration to begin the present work.[6] But in these contributions one is troubled by the fact that all seems quiet on the eastern front. Freud's lost fatherland lay beyond the Russian border and symmetrically to the west: in the Spain of the Inquisition, whimsically transformed in the

Spanish cult of Freud's youth. This polarity is equally important for his identity. Freud once suggested as a dominant theme of his dreams, in need of suppression, *Vaterlandslosigkeit*, meaning lack of a fatherland, lack of patriotism, and above all (and ironically) his Jewish identity as it would be slurred by bigots. Yet, paradoxically, one of the most striking features of *The Interpretation of Dreams* is that the author did not suppress but positively flaunts his Jewish identity. Our exploration of Freud's Russia may logically begin by considering Freud's concept of *Vaterlandslosigkeit* at home in Vienna and abroad, in the history of his family, and in the limited freedom of his dreams.

To recapitulate, this book is about Freud's Russian background, his Russian colleagues and patients, the impact of Russian history on his thought, the reception of Dostoevsky in his world, and Freud's personal involvement with Dostoevsky. An effort is made to defend Dostoevsky against Freud's post mortem, to mediate between Freud and Dostoevsky, and to establish their mutual empathy. Here nothing is done to psychoanalyze Dostoevsky himself, nor the genesis and design of his fictions.[7] As Freud once remarked to Stefan Zweig, Dostoevsky "cannot be understood without psychoanalysis—i.e., he isn't in need of it because he illustrates it himself in every character and every sentence."[8] Thus, as we have suggested elsewhere, the great value of psychoanalysis to readers of Dostoevsky is that it may help us see the obvious.

It may be necessary to add that what was obvious to Dostoevsky is by no means obvious to most of his readers. A case in point is Wittgenstein's rereading *The Brothers Karamazov* "an extraordinary number of times."[9] In an earlier book, *Dostoevsky and the Healing Art*, we have presented a medical history of the subject that ought to help avoid many routine errors. Another aspect of our general topic which is only touched upon here is the abortive history of psychoanalysis in Russia, which we note chiefly in its feedback to Freud at key moments. Capable investigators have applied themselves to this theme in recent years.[10]

By chance, a famous Russian fairy tale, "Mária Morévna," summarized in a footnote to Jung's "Phenomenology of the Spirit in Fairy Tales," signaled the way to my career in Russian literary history. While Jung remained opaque, Freud later offered some comforting therapeutic speculations, memorably "Mourning and Melancholia."

Twenty years ago, *The Wolf-Man by the Wolf-Man* presented intriguing Russian material, shrouded in mystification worthy of Freud's favorite Conan Doyle. Freud himself remained mainly in the shadows, or so it seemed, until the publication of his correspondence with Jung (in 1974). There he stood forth no longer as a dry collector of Jewish anecdotes but as a sympathetic wit in his own right. These letters admit us to the backstage mysteries of Freud's intimate professional life, and at times to the darker interior of his domestic and private existence. They also made me laugh aloud with Freud— perhaps, I would like to think, a measure of that "far-reaching psychical conformity" that shared laughter betokens.[11] This vivid sense of Freud's personality remained with me when I reread *The Interpretation of Dreams*, which now seemed invested with a familiar voice and multifarious design, as previously it had not. The book now appeared an ethnic self-affirmation, a historically precocious model for being (in the spirit of Joyce), and least of all a clinical method. In this spirit, Freud encouraged me to get on with the work. As for those who have a bone to pick with Freud for failing to heal the world, for grievous lapses in his art, probably they should lodge their complaint with the medical profession at large. Once our bodies betray us, so that we need a doctor's help, a certain resentment is only human. "Exactly what do we mean when we say, man is mortal? Obviously it's not a compliment."[12]

Notes

1   Marianna Krüll, *Freud and His Father*, pp. 234-35.

2   James L. Rice, "Russian Stereotypes in the Freud-Jung Correspondence."

3   The clinical picture of epilepsy has changed considerably since Freud wrote his essay on Dostoevsky. Meanwhile, documentation of Dostoevsky's medical history has also greatly improved. Dostoevsky's psychiatric symptoms have been reported in cases of temporal lobe epilepsy, a diagnostic category suspected but not yet proven in Freud's time. See Owsei Temkin, *The Falling Sickness*; Fabio Cirignotta, "Temporal Lobe Epilepsy with Ecstatic Seizures"; P.H.A. Voskuil, "The Epilepsy of Fyodor Mikhailovich Dostoevsky"; Norman Geschwind, "Dostoievsky's Epilepsy"; James L. Rice, "Dostoevsky's

Medical History: Diagnosis and Dialectic"; James L. Rice, *Dostoevsky and the Healing Art.*

4   Max Schur, *Freud, Living and Dying*, p. 404.

5   Ernest Jones, *The Life and Work of Sigmund Freud*, vol. 1, p. 331; Sigmund Freud, *The Complete Letters of Sigmund Freud to Wilhelm Fliess*, p. 423.

6   Carl E. Schorske, "Politics and Patricide in Freud's Interpretation of Dreams"; Kenneth A. Grigg, "All Roads Lead to Rome"; William J. McGrath, "Freud as Hannibal"; Stanley Rothman and Phillip Isenberg, "Sigmund Freud and the Politics of Marginality."

7   Elizabeth Dalton, *Unconscious Structures in "The Idiot"*; Susan C. Fischman, "Sigmund Freud and the Case of the Underground Man"; Louis Breger, *Dostoevsky*; James L. Rice, "Psychoanalysis of 'Peasant Marei': Some Residual Problems."

8   Sigmund Freud, *The Letters of Sigmund Freud*, p. 333.

9   James L. Rice, "Psychoanalysis of 'Peasant Marei," p. 259; Norman Malcolm, *Ludwig Wittgenstein*, p. 52.

10   Alex Kozulin, *Psychology in Utopia*; Martin Miller, "Freudian Theory Under Bolshevik Rule: The Theoretical Controversy During the 1920s"; Martin Miller "The Theory and Practice of Psychiatry in the Soviet Union"; Martin Miller, "The Origins and Development of Russian Psychoanalysis"; Magnus Ljunggren, "The psychoanalytic breakthrough in Russia"; A.I. Belkin, *Rossiiskii psikhologicheskii vestnik*; Daniel Rancour-Laferriere, "Freud Returns to Russia." See also James L. Rice, "Russian Stereotypes in the Freud-Jung Correspondence."

11   Sigmund Freud, *Jokes and Their Relation to the Unconscious*, p. 151.

12   Woody Allen, "My Speech to the Graduates," p. 58.

Freud family tree

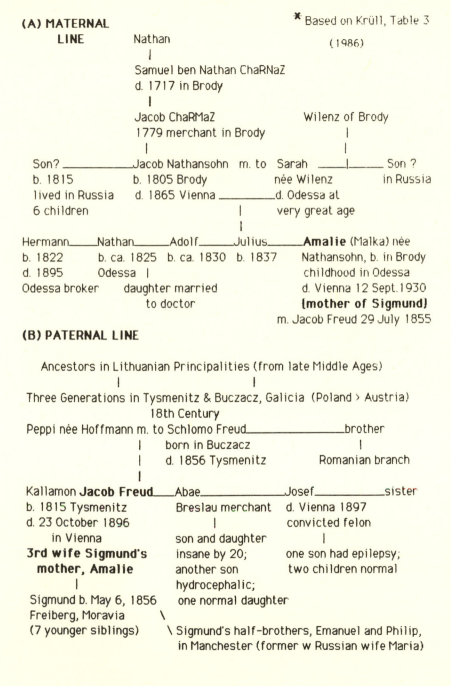

(A) MATERNAL LINE

✱ Based on Krüll, Table 3 (1986)

Nathan
|
Samuel ben Nathan ChaRNaZ
d. 1717 in Brody
|
Jacob ChaRMaZ   Wilenz of Brody
1779 merchant in Brody |
| |
Son?——————Jacob Nathansohn m. to Sarah ——|—— Son ?
b. 1815   b. 1805 Brody   née Wilenz   in Russia
lived in Russia d. 1865 Vienna———————d. Odessa at
6 children | very great age
                              |

Hermann——Nathan——Adolf——Julius——**Amalie** (Malka) née
b. 1822   b. ca. 1825 b. ca. 1830 b. 1837   Nathansohn, b. in Brody
d. 1895   Odessa | childhood in Odessa
Odessa broker   daughter married   d. Vienna 12 Sept.1930
                 to doctor   **(mother of Sigmund)**
                                               m. Jacob Freud 29 July 1855

(B) PATERNAL LINE

Ancestors in Lithuanian Principalities (from late Middle Ages)
| |
Three Generations in Tysmenitz & Buczacz, Galicia (Poland > Austria)
18th Century
Peppi née Hoffmann m. to Schlomo Freud——————————brother
                | born in Buczacz |
                | d. 1856 Tysmenitz   Romanian branch
                |

Kallamon **Jacob Freud**——Abae——————————Josef——————sister
b. 1815 Tysmenitz   Breslau merchant   d. Vienna 1897
d. 23 October 1896 | convicted felon
    in Vienna   son and daughter |
3rd wife Sigmund's insane by 20;   one son had epilepsy;
   mother, Amalie   another son   two children normal
        | hydrocephalic;
Sigmund b. May 6, 1856   one normal daughter
Freiberg, Moravia   \
(7 younger siblings)   \ Sigmund's half-brothers, Emanuel and Philip,
                          in Manchester (former w Russian wife Maria)

1

Vaterlandslosigkeit

On account of certain events which had occurred in the city of Rome, it had become necessary to remove the children to safety, and this was done.... I was sitting on the edge of a fountain and was greatly depressed and almost in tears. A female figure—an attendant or nun— brought two boys out and handed them over to their father, who was not myself. The elder of the two was clearly my eldest son.... This dream was constructed on a tangle of thoughts provoked by a play which I had seen, called Das neue Ghetto *[The New Ghetto]. The Jewish problem, concern about the future of one's own children, to whom one cannot give a fatherland of their own, concern about educating them in such a way that they can move freely across frontiers—all of this was easily recognizable among the relevant dream-thoughts.*

—Freud (from the analysis of his dream "My Son, the Myops," published in *The Interpretation of Dreams*, as cited in Alexander Grinstein, *Sigmund Freud's Dreams*, pp. 317-331 [chap. 6(G), p. vi]. Freud attended a performance of Theodor Herzl's play "The New Ghetto" in early January 1898.)

By early modern times the paternal ancestors of Freud were living in Lithuania. He believed that persecution of the Jews had forced them to retreat eastward from the Rhineland in the fourteenth or fifteenth century. Of their subsequent route to Eastern Europe nothing is known. Freud's short "Self Portrait" published in 1925 tells us only that his forefathers began making their way back west "from Lithuania, through Galicia to German Austria, in the course of the 19th century."[1] The passing reference to Lithuania (Litau) is a key to the historical background of Freud's Russia and its personal significance for him.

Freud's chronology of the exodus from Lithuania presents his family history in a greatly condensed form. Gravestone inscriptions in the Jewish cemetery at Galician Buczacz indicate that his direct lineage had settled there by the early eighteenth century.[2] At that time Buczacz was about forty miles from the Russian border, on Polish land north of the Carpathians, which was annexed by Austria in 1772 and renamed Galicia. In compliance with Austrian law, the surname Freud was first adopted in 1787. No way has yet been found to trace the genealogy back to branches of the family left behind in Lithuania or elsewhere. Undoubtedly there were a great many such kinfolk, and some of them must have appeared in Vienna from time to time throughout Freud's life, in the vast and ever-growing emigration of Jews from the Russian Empire. These *Ostjude* play a diverse role in the psychoanalytic literature—as tragic victims, as comic stereotypes, and as revolutionaries. For Freud they also summoned up images of a dark and savage ancestral terrain. But we are getting ahead of the story.

The Lithuania of Freud's ancestors was acquired piecemeal by the Russian Empire toward the end of the eighteenth century, through the partitions of Poland. The region includes the ancient cities of Vilna and Kovno (Vilnius and Kaunas in modern Lithuania), as well as Grodno, Minsk, Pinsk, Vitebsk, and Mogilev (now administered by the Belorussian Republic). Freud's father came from a line of merchant *Wanderjude*, who in their day must have known all these commercial centers. Jews comprised only 10 percent of the general population in the Lithuanian provinces, but in the cities they were a major cultural force. For example, by the late nineteenth century Mogilev was 40 percent Jewish and Pinsk 67 percent. The Russian regime assigned the whole territory to the Pale of Jewish Settlement (in 1804). Here, in the era of pogroms (from 1881), anti-Semitic atrocities under tsarist and Bolshevik rule became notorious worldwide. Although the name "Lithuania" was suppressed by Russia after 1840, it was preserved by Lithuanian nationalists and in popular Western usage. Freud perceived the historical Lithuania of his ancestors in the light of subsequent violence and, as we shall see, with a conscious sense of "there but for the grace of God go I." In *Civilization and Its Discontents,* published in 1930, he foresaw the eventuality of genocide in Russia at the hands of the Communists. This view of human tragedy and destiny emerged from decades of personal and clinical experience, in which the problem of Russian national character played a significant role.

Two figures of importance in defining Russia for Freud were directly connected with the Lithuanian provinces. Max Eitingon, who became his righthand man in the international psychoanalytic movement, was born in 1881 in Mogilev, a city near the Russian Orthodox heartland. All his life Eitingon remained active in Russian émigré circles and served Freud as a source of Russian culture. It was he, for example, who presented Freud with the complete works of Dostoevsky in 1910. Dostoevsky himself traced his family roots to Pinsk, and his daughter Aimée in her memoir (published as *Dostojewski, geschildert von seiner Tochter* in 1920), endowed him with a mythic lineage of "Lithuanian" origin.[3] This ethnic embellishment lends a fitting symmetry to Freud's dialogue with Dostoevsky, an episode to which in due course we shall return.

Freud's mother, Amalie Nathansohn (1835-1930), had many close relatives in Russia. She was born in Brody, a notorious smuggling town then on the Russian border of Galicia, where her father's family had lived as prominent merchants and rabbinical scholars since the seventeenth century. One of Amalie's uncles (not identified) raised six children somewhere in Russia, and two of her older brothers settled permanently in Odessa: Hermann, a broker (1822-1895), and Nathan (born about 1825).[4] Amalie herself—regarded by her grandson Martin as "a typical Polish Jewess" and "certainly not what we would call a 'lady'," but quick of wit and highly intelligent—spent part of her childhood in Odessa.[5] Then she moved with her parents to Vienna—in time for her to applaud the role of Jewish students in the Revolution of 1848, which she recalled with enthusiasm. Recent research suggests that her brothers Hermann and Nathan themselves participated in the Vienna uprising, and escaped arrest only by returning to Odessa, where they evidently prospered.[6]

Sigmund Freud's cousin Simon (the son of Hermann Nathansohn) was an officer in the Austrian army who later made his home in Odessa. He appears, in uniform, with Sigmund and others in a family photo of 1876. In 1883, he had his bank remit a sum of money to Freud's sister Anna for her wedding, a gesture that Sigmund Freud privately criticized as indelicate and "really not much from a rich uncle."[7] This suggests that the source of the funds was ultimately his Uncle Hermann, the Odessa broker. Freud's reproach was an ironic jest that cut two ways (that is, what a vulgar way to give money—and so little of it!) for the amusement of his own bride-to-be. It has been suggested (from evidence in an unpublished letter written by Freud's son Oliver) that Hermann was in fact the uncle "loved and honored" who figures in *The Interpretation of Dreams*.[8] Freud's other Odessa uncle, Nathan, had a daughter who married a doctor. One of course wonders whether they somehow contributed to the early appreciation of psychoanalysis in the Odessa medical community (1909). In any event, it is evident that the Odessa family connection remained vital through most of Sigmund Freud's life. His maternal grandmother, Sara Nathansohn née Wilenz, moved back to Odessa to live with one of her sons, and there remained, it is said, to a very great age.[9] And his mother, frequently consulted by Freud on matters of intimate family history when he was writing *The Interpretation of Dreams*, was visited at least weekly by her son until her death in 1930. The exceptional closeness of his maternal bond helped keep the family ties with Russia alive in Freud's consciousness, and nourished his revolutionary idealism, which lasted (with growing reservations) into the early years of the Stalin era.[10]

Two of Freud's close relatives who lived in Rumania engaged in commercial ventures across the Russian border. One of these was Uncle Josef of Jassy, a younger brother of Freud's father, who concluded his Russian enterprises as a convicted felon in 1865. After serving four years in an Austrian prison, he lived until 1897 in Vienna. His story, which understandably made a strong impression on Freud, deserves a more leisurely telling below. The other kinsman in Rumania was Moriz Freud of Bucharest (1857-1920), a distant cousin who in 1886 married Freud's sister Marie. In a letter of 1898 Freud half-jokingly referred to Moriz as "half-Asiatic" (with manners, that is, smacking too much of the eastern hinterlands) and "suffering from pseudologica fantastica."[11] In Freud's authorized biography by Ernest Jones, we are told that his father in old age seized "a momentary hope" and traveled to Russia on some unknown business transaction. It was in July 1883 that "a Rumanian cousin got the old man to travel to Odessa." This might have been Moriz Freud, or one of Uncle Josef's sons. The enterprise promised to yield perhaps "a few hundred gulden" (says Jones), but it fell through.[12] There were indeed people in Odessa, as we have seen, on whose help Jacob Freud might have counted, such as his wealthy brother-in-law Hermann Nathanson. The nature of his business in Russia, however, remains unknown—like the nature of Jacob Freud's livelihood in general during his decades in Vienna. No matter what he hoped to accomplish in Odessa, a Jewish merchant's trip to Russia at that time, just two years after the assassination of Tsar Alexander II and the outbreak of pogroms that followed, has a certain aura of adventure about it, especially for a man of nearly sixty-eight years who had lived quietly (so far as we know) in Vienna for a quarter century. Had Freud's father, in his earlier active traveling days as a cloth merchant, made trips to Russia? In all likelihood, but the sources are silent on this point, and leave it to one's imagination to sketch in the purpose of Jacob Freud's late quixotic journey. No doubt the imagination of Sigmund Freud followed his father across the border of the Russian Empire in 1883.

Freud's earliest published dicta on the Russian state appear in a letter of 15 August 1877 to an old boyhood friend, Eduard Silberstein. Here he berated the Russian ruling class and particularly the Romanov dynasty, in the following terms:

> I have nothing against the Russians. I even loved them *a priori*. They impress me from afar, and moreover I know nothing about them. I have in mind instead only the nation, the ruling circles, and above all the Romanovs, those insane rulers, bad citizens, and untalented soldiers, those apes of the Berlin corporal who boasts of victories! I don't know enough to hate them, and only console myself with the fact that they are digging their own grave. The times call for one to become a [bomb-throwing] Petroleur.[13]

The historical context of these striking remarks can be readily reconstructed. Silberstein for several years had resided in Rumania (Braila). On 24 April 1877, Russia declared war against the Ottoman

Empire, and in June the Russian army crossed the Danube. Led by Grand Duke Nicholas and the tsar himself, they suffered major defeats and by midsummer pressed the Rumanian army to join forces with them. The war thus directly menaced Freud's relatives in Rumania, and of course his friend Silberstein. The language of Freud's outburst was perfectly apt for the political moment. His muted and prophetic death wish for the tsar caught the spirit of the times. In less than four years Alexander II was assassinated, after a dozen or more unsuccessful attempts that had begun in 1865.

War and revolution were dominant historical themes of Freud's Russia, to underscore an obvious fact. To be sure, as a schoolboy he had eagerly studied the military history of ancient civilizations (idolizing Hannibal, as he later noted), and the Austria of his day also afforded many lessons in the art and futility of war. In July 1866, when Freud was ten and lived in Vienna, the decisive battle of the Austro-Prussian War was fought at Königgrätz (Hradec Králové), the defeated Austrian army retreating some eighty miles to Olmütz (Olomouc), within forty miles of Freud's birthplace in Moravia.[14] The schoolboy followed the campaign, marking the positions on a map with flags.[15] Twenty years later, as a doctor in the reserves, Freud himself was on maneuvers at Olmütz. In a psychological and actual sense of which he was keenly aware, this region was Freud's personal homeland. Here was a beloved countryside, here remained lifelong family friends, and here thanks to his Czech nanny and her children he had been raised bilingually up to the age of three.[16] These facts and some of their long-unconscious ramifications—such as the Czech nanny who was his "instructress in sexual matters" during early childhood—are reconstructed in *The Interpretation of Dreams* and letters of that period.[17] Not long ago it came to light that Freud once planned to take a position in Prague, a city that played an imposing role in his psyche.[18] One may suggest that a certain latent empathy for Czech nationalism was part of Freud's complex political nature.[19] But in his youth he shared his father's enthusiasm for Bismarck and the ideal of German unification, and as a medical student in the 1870s he was a Pan-German activist.[20] The rise of public anti-Semitism in the 1880s redefined his world view toward its mature ambivalence. Discussing the prospect of war with Giles de la Tourette at Charcot's salon in 1886, Freud (who was fortified with cocaine) declared that he was a Jew adhering neither to Germany nor to Austria. But privately he confessed to his fiancée that this claim made him uneasy, "for I feel stirring within me something German which I long ago decided to suppress."[21]

This superficial résumé gives some idea of Freud's national identity when, at the age of thirty, he began to realize his true vocation. Having entered the University of Vienna in 1873, he pursued a diverse career in experimental physiology until he was persuaded by his financial circumstances to take a medical degree (which he obtained in 1882) and begin clinical practice in the Vienna General Hospital. Assignments to the psychiatric clinic (under the eminent brain anatomist Meynert) and to the department of nervous illnesses provided opportunities for further laboratory work in these areas. Shortly before his departure for Paris to study with Charcot on a prize travel grant in 1885, he received an appointment to the Vienna University medical faculty as an unsalaried lecturer (*Privatdocent*) in neuropathology and continued working on brain anatomy. Meanwhile he had become engaged on 17 June 1882 to Martha Bernays, his future wife, who the following year was taken by her family 500 miles north to Wandsbek, a suburb of Hamburg. The betrothal was extended for more than four years. In Freud's published letters to his fiancée, his character is more frankly and effusively revealed than in any other source, except perhaps in his correspondence with Jung.

In the passage below, from Freud's letter to Martha of 28 April 1885, his personal view of Russia is again demonstrated along lines that not only reflect the political moment but also suggest a deeper emotional response. The letter has often been quoted (for example, in the preface to the biography by Jones), but with abridgments and mistranslations that obscure the meaning of Freud's references to Russia.

This has been a bad, barren month. How glad I am it is soon coming to an end! I do nothing all day; sometimes I browse in Russian history, and now and again I torture the two rabbits which nibble away at turnips in the little room and make a mess of the floor. One intention as a matter of fact I have almost finished carrying out, an intention which a number of as yet unborn and unfortunate people will one day resent. Since you won't guess what kind of people I am referring to, I will tell you at once: they are my biographers. I have destroyed all my notes of the past fourteen years, as well as letters, scientific excerpts, and the manuscripts of my papers. As for letters, only those from the family have been spared. Yours, my darling, were never in danger. And so, all old friendships and relationships presented themselves once again and then silently received the death-blow [*den Todesstreich*] (my fantasy is still living in Russian history); all my thoughts and feelings about the world in general and about myself in particular have been found unworthy of further existence. They will now have to be thought all over again. I certainly did manage to scribble a great deal, but the stuff was engulfing me, as sand buries the Sphinx, and soon only my nostrils would be visible above the mound of paper. I couldn't have gone on, or died, while still worrying about who would get hold of those old papers. Everything, moreover, that lies beyond the great turning point in my life, beyond our love and my choice of profession, died long ago and must not be denied a decent burial. As for the biographers, let them complain, we have no desire to make it too easy for them. Let each of them suppose his concept of "The Hero's Formative Years" is right. Already I like to anticipate how they will all go wrong.[22]

Clearly, no biographer could resist this moment where, albeit in jest, Freud anticipates by a quarter century his fame ... and his biographers. His life story is here projected as a shrewd evasion of all the conventional melodramatic formulas. He casts himself in the role of a sinister underground figure who destroys his own identity and buries the past. And he identifies with the mysterious Sphinx, whose riddle and existence are threatened by the shifting sands of his own paper trail, that is, the accumulating clues to his archaic and clandestine identity. The "choice of profession" (medicine), to which Freud here concedes finality, in fact unfolded slowly over the next fifteen years—along lines unconsciously encoded in these poetic words addressed to his fiancée. Now we may enquire why at this moment Freud happened to be reading Russian history, in which his "fantasy was still living" as he wrote this emblematic letter, and more precisely how Russia contributed to the symbolism of that fantasy.

As a recurrently active military threat, Russia was a source of increasing anxiety in Austria throughout Freud's lifetime. Some aspects of his early personal response to this situation have been noted. But the history of Russia's latest internal development, particularly the rise of political opposition and terrorism since the 1860s, was not well documented in the West. Engels observed in 1882 that no Russian proletarian movement had been reported in the first edition (1847) of *The Communist Manifesto*, but in the meantime Russia had clearly become "the vanguard of revolutionary action in Europe."[23] This fact had been convincingly established by the assassination of the tsar on 1 March 1881. Two years later, as we have seen, Jacob Freud undertook a business trip to Odessa, an event that might have drawn his son's attention to modern Russian history. The decisive stimulus in this direction, however, was probably Freud's encounter and friendship with an Orthodox Russian colleague, Dr. L. O. Darkshévich (1858-1925), who was to become one of Russia's leading neuropathologists. Since 1883 he had studied brain anatomy with a number of specialists in Berlin and Vienna, and in January 1884 he met Freud in Meynert's lab. Darkshevich proposed to translate one of Freud's papers (a method for preparing specimens), and they became close friends. At one point Freud introduced Darkshevich to his father. Presumably Jacob Freud's trip to Russia figured in the conversation. In March 1885, the Russian doctor left Vienna for Leipzig, where he once exchanged letters with Freud. Toward the end of that year they met again in Paris, and during Freud's months there with Charcot, which determined the course of his professional life, Darkshevich was his closest friend. In Freud's letters from Paris, the Russian's personality and national character are described in some detail ("a quiet and profound fanatic," "his soul absorbed in the fatherland, religion, and brain anatomy"), which we will consider in the next chapter. Suffice it to say that such a friend must have motivated Freud to study Russian history more deeply than he had before, and might well have guided him to the most reliable and engaging sources.

Freud's symbolic "death blow" to all his old friendships and relationships—a scenario directly inspired by Russian history, as he explains—of course mimics certain principles of the revolutionary movement, principles that had been violently applied by terrorists in recent decades. Freud's early favorite, Ludwig Feuerbach, had first proposed the doctrine of a radical break with the past to gain the power and passion for new creativity, an idea given new currency by Bakunin.[24] The latter's short essay, "The Reaction in Germany," published in 1842, appeals to the Spirit of Destruction as the source of all new life, and ends with a famous aphorism adopted by generations of Russian radicals: "The passion for destruction is also a creative passion" (Die Lust der Zerstörung ist auch eine schaffende Lust).[25] The latest German publications on Russian history that might have stimulated Freud's fantasy along these lines in the spring of 1885 would include Alphons Thun's *Geschichte der revolutionären Bewegungen in Russland* and more likely *Das unterirdische Russland* by Stepniák, the pseudonym of Sergéi Mikháilovich Kravchínskii, who was an authentic veteran of the revolutionary movement, and whose book was well calculated to fire the imagination.

Stepniak tells the modern legend of Russian nihilism (revolution) with parallels from antiquity, a commonplace of historiography that was very much to Freud's taste. The terrorist as a type is extolled as martyr and hero, proud as Satan rebelling against God, but a terrestrial God who trembles before his opponent "unlike the old Jehovah of Moses!" Moscow, the central and symbolic field of battle, is "a half Asiatic city, immense as the antique Babylon or Nineveh." Efforts to plant bombs under railroad tracks are glorified as "Egyptian labors." Petersburg, the bureaucratic seat of the Romanov empire, is likened to ancient Rome and Byzantium—a typical, decaying despotic monarchy doomed to overthrow by the Praetorian Guard. The first revolutionary policy spelled out by Stepniak is the liberation of women, who seek to gain their natural rights through "the liberty of love." Hailed as one of the primary theorists of the movement is "the great Michael Bakunin, the genius of destruction." Stepniak closes his gallery of revolutionary sketches by appending a letter of the People's Will Executive Committee addressed to Alexander III ten days after his father's assassination in 1881, demanding civil liberties and warning that "regicide in Russia is very popular." Without immediate radical changes in government policy, Stepniak foresaw that "a terrible explosion, a bloody Revolution, a spasmodic convulsion throughout all Russia, will complete the destruction of the old order."[26] Whether or not Freud ever held Stepniak's book in his hands, this is clearly the Russian history—current history—that dominated his fantasy when he delivered a death blow to the record of his past relationships. Much of his own ego, that "dark despot," had to die too so that the creative eros of psychoanalysis might begin to flourish.[27] More than three decades later, Freud accepted the concept of a human death instinct, duly credited (in *Beyond the Pleasure Principle*) to his remarkable young colleague from Rostov-na-Donu, Sabina Spielrein. The doctrine of a destruction instinct was in great part a Russian contribution to psychoanalysis, which Freud at first resisted as an inherent feature of the Russian psychic material, rather than a genetic trait of the human species.[28]

Freud's amateur interest in history and archaeology generated a wealth of material, examples, and analogies scattered through his works and dreams, which his biographers have sifted for clues to his personality.[29] The primary model and imperative for such research is of course *The Interpretation of Dreams*, in which, for example, Freud's own dreams of Rome (superimposed on Prague) are plumbed and made to divulge the complex yearning, anxiety, and anger of a Viennese Jew struggling to overcome or escape anti-Semitic surroundings, but tormented at the same time by the emotional claims of long-lost homelands. We have noted in the introduction that this north-south (Prague-Rome) schema of Freud's psychic archaeology— first suggested by his own self-analysis—has been much elaborated, but in fact the northern quadrant is less known. Let us review and amplify some of its main features. Prague represents on the one hand the dreamy, erotic realm of childhood, the Moravian Czech village of Freiberg (Příbor), a Czech nanny, the Czech language, and Freud's adolescent first love.[30] On the other hand, Prague was a bastion of militant Czech nationalism, site of the 1898 Pan-Slav Congress (celebrating the revolutionary events of fifty years earlier), and a threat to the stability of Freud's Germanic world—facts ambivalently incorporated into his dreams, which echoed their seditious impulse. Half a dozen times between 1896 and 1898 Freud proposed a "Prague Congress" with his Berlin friend Fliess, only to cancel it because of anti-German agitation. They settled on Reichenau (Bohemia) in June 1898, at the very time of the Pan-Slav gathering in Prague. Meanwhile, during the early 1890s, Freud four times took his family to Reichenau for summer vacations, and in the summer of 1898 visited a patient near Hradec Králové (Königgrätz, eastern Bohemia). A wet nurse for Freud's daughter Mathilde had been found in 1887 at Moravian Roznau (Rožnava), near Freiberg. It seems likely that the Freuds' staff of four domestics—always gentiles—included others from the rural Czech populace.[31] Thus, the "northern" sector of Freud's psyche and dreams was by no means restricted to the experience of childhood, but was activated by day-residues from his professional and domestic life. As for Rome, the "southern" sector, it represented for Freud an ultimate threat to Jewish identity (the specter of Herod, the power of Catholicism), but also an ultimate goal of glorious conquest by the intellect. In psychoanalytic terms, as symbols of the self and destiny, Prague and Rome were two sides of one coin.

The north-south model of Freud's psyche, as we have argued, is altogether too narrow and restrictive. Let us consider a more ecumenical view of the subject, from *Civilization and Its Discontents*:

> Happiness ... is something essentially subjective. No matter how much we may shrink with horror from certain situations—of a galley-slave in antiquity, of a peasant during the Thirty Years' War, of a victim of the Holy Inquisition, of a Jew awaiting a pogrom—it is nevertheless impossible for us to empathize with such people.[32]

Freud goes on to adduce variables in these classic victims' sensibilities—innate obtuseness, methods of narcosis, fading of hopes, mental protection against suffering—which actually have nothing specifically to do with the historical situations listed. In fact, Freud's claim that he cannot empathize with these particular victims suggests that indeed he tried to do so, and the generalizations about sensibility serve to distance him emotionally from situations that were personally meaningful. His typology of victims in history is by no means random, but instead projects the "endopsychic" (private) myth of national identity cultivated by Freud all his life. The galley slaves represent ancient Rome and Egypt, objects of his archaeological fascination and recurrent metaphors of the layered psyche. The Thirty Years' War here probably stands for the oppression of Czech peasants by their Bohemian lords, and for the struggle of Czech armies to defeat the invading Swedes in the early 1630s, events that were legendary in Freud's native Freiberg and in fact inscribed there on a memorial plaque.[33] Czech suffering, rebellion, and valor are part of the myth of Freud's lost childhood homeland. Spain, the third quadrant, recalls Freud's juvenile Hispanophilia and the comic correspondence with his friend Silberstein. But more urgently the Inquisition speaks of religious persecution, the plight of the Jews, and Dostoevsky's "Grand Inquisitor" (in *The Brothers Karamazov*), which Freud had recently studied with great care.[34] Finally, completing the egocentric symmetry (south-north—west-east), the Jew awaiting a pogrom (*den Pogrom*) is of course in Russia, another mythic fatherland, where the victim's suffering is not only historical but also contemporary. Each quadrant was clearly part of Freud's own psychomythology, the "endopsychic myths" that appeared as by-products of *The Interpretation of Dreams* but whose roots can be traced back to his childhood, his family history, and the ancient ordeals of the Jews.[35] The point to be repeated is that Russia—the East Front—was an active part of Freud's psyche, a part consistently overlooked.

Freud's authorized biography charts "the ancient march of the family" from Palestine to Rome, Cologne (according to tradition), Lithuania, Galicia, Moravia, Vienna, and at last to his exile and death in London.[36] During his last decades, Freud completed the circle back to his Old Testament roots and, characteristically, beyond in his "novel" about the Egyptian Moses (*Moses and Monotheism*). His own Jewish identity, the subject of much scholarship and controversy, also served Freud as material for psychoanalysis and endopsychic myth-making. Behind the scenes he recognized that these idiosyncratic speculations might be seen as a bit cracked—*meschugge*.[37] This willful vulnerability is most evident in his self-analytic masterpiece, *The Interpretation of Dreams*, a tour de force of genius and eccentricity. One of his own dreams was to have served as the introductory "specimen," but it gave offense to his Berlin friend and confidant Wilhelm Fliess and so was dropped, thus becoming the much-debated "lost dream." In a passage only recently published, Freud wonders exactly what it was that Fliess found objectionable: the references to his anxiety, to his wife, to his poverty, or perhaps *die Vaterlandslosigkeit*. The last term means, in its neutral sense, "[my] lack of a fatherland."[38] But, anticipating reproach, it would mean "[my] lack of patriotism" and ultimately a combination of the two, as a common term of abuse directed against Jews (as well as Social Democrats) in the German and Austrian press by the turn of the century. Freud's use of the word here undoubtedly combines all three meanings, ironically suggesting his awareness of elements in the censured dream that might invite anti-Semitic attack. Whether or not the "lost dream" was in fact suppressed by Freud (or published in some form that has not been recognized), *Die Traumdeutung* throughout flaunts the author's Jewish identity both humorously and aggressively, and directly confronts the "Jewish problem." Ironic recognition of *Vaterlandslosigkeit* is central to Freud's identity. This is the tactical position from which he saw the world, including of course the eastern front.

Notes

1   Sigmund Freud, "An Autobiographical Portrait" (Selbstdarstellung) (1925), in *Standard Edition of the Complete Psychological Works of Sigmund Freud*, vol. 2, pp. 7-8.

2   Marianna Krüll, *Freud and His Father*, p. 89.

3   Aimée Dostoevsky, *Fyodor Dostoevsky*, pp. 6-8; Vladimir Seduro, "The Problem of F.M. Dostoevski's Origin.".

4   See Freud's family tree, p. 8.

5   Josef Fraenkel, ed., *The Jews of Austria*, p. 202; Martin Freud, "Who Was Freud?" in Josef Fraenkel, ed., *The Jews of Austria*, p. 200; Ernest Jones, *The Life and Work of Sigmund Freud*, vol. 1, p. 3.

6   Peter Swales, personal communication, 18 July 1990.

7   Sigmund Freud, *The Letters of Sigmund Freud*, p. 42.

8   Peter Swales, personal communication, 18 July 1990; Marianna Krüll, *Freud and His Father*, p. 139.

9   Marianna Krüll, *Freud and His Father*, p. 234.

10   See below, chapter 8.

11   Sigmund Freud, *The Complete Letters of Sigmund Freud to Wilhelm Fliess*, p. 311.

12   Ernest Jones, *The Life and Work of Sigmund Freud*, vol. 1, p. 157.

13   Sigmund Freud, *Jugendbriefe an Eduard Silberstein*, pp. 188-89.

14   Agatha Ramm, *Germany 1789-1919*, p. 299.

15   Anna Freud Bernays, "My Brother, Sigmund Freud."

16   Siegfried Bernfeld, "An Unknown Autobiographical Fragment"; Josef Sajner, "Sigmund Freuds Beziehung"; Sigmund Freud, "Jugendbriefe Sigmund Freuds" (to Emil Fluss, 1872-74); John E. Gedo & Ernest Wolf, "Die Ichthyosaurusbriefe"; Marianna Krüll, *Freud und sein Vater*; Marianna Krüll, *Freud and His Father*; Harry T. Hardin, "On the Vicissitudes of Freud's Early Mothering."

17   Sigmund Freud, *Standard Edition of the Complete Psychological Works of Sigmund Freud*, vol. 4, pp. 195-97; Sigmund Freud, *The Complete Letters of Sigmund Freud to Wilhelm Fliess*, pp. 176, 219, 220, 225, 233-34, 238-39, 253, 268-73, 284-86, 289, 299, and 347.

18   Sigmund Freud, *The Complete Letters of Sigmund Freud to Wilhelm Fliess*, p. 423; Kenneth A. Grigg, "All Roads Lead to Rome"; Carl E. Schorske, "Politics and Patricide in Freud's Interpretation of Dreams."

19   Ernest Jones, *The Life and Work of Sigmund Freud*, vol. 1, p. 12: assumption of anti-Semitism in Freiberg denied by Josef Sajner in his "Sigmund Freuds Beziehung"; Paul C. Vitz, *Sigmund Freud's Christian Unconscious.*

20   Ernest Jones, *The Life and Work of Sigmund Freud*, vol. 1, p. 192; Sigmund Freud, *The Complete Letters of Sigmund Freud to Wilhelm Fliess*, p. 322; Carl E. Schorske, "Politics and Patricide in Freud's Interpretation of Dreams."

21   Sigmund Freud, *The Letters of Sigmund Freud*, p. 203.

22   Sigmund Freud, *Briefe, 1873-1939*, pp. 144-46; Sigmund Freud, *The Letters of Sigmund Freud*, pp. 140-141; Ernest Jones, *The Life and Work of Sigmund Freud*, vol. 1, p. xii-xiii.

23   Preface to Russian edition of 1882; Karl Marx, *Communist Manifesto*, pp. 122-24.

24   Hans Kohn, *Pan-Slavism*, p. 90; for Freud's early admiration for Feuerbach, see Sigmund Freud, *Jugendbriefe an Eduard Silberstein 1871-1881*, pp. 82, 111, and 242; Hans Küng, *Freud and the Problem of God*, pp. 3-7, 43, and 75-81; Paul E. Stepansky, "Feuerbach and Jung as Religious Critics," pp. 215-239.

25   Mikhail Bakunin, *Bakunin on Anarchy*, p. 57; James L. Rice, "Russian Stereotypes in the Freud-Jung Correspondence," p. 29.

26   Stepniak, *Das unterirdische Russland.*

27   Theodor Reik, *Listening with the Third Ear*, chap. 8, "Love and the Dark Despot."

28   James L. Rice, "Russian Stereotypes in the Freud-Jung Correspondence"; and chapter 4 (below): "Russian Material."

29   Suzanne Cassirer Bernfeld, "Freud and Archaeology"; Eva M. Rosenfeld, "Dream and Vision."

30   Siegfried Bernfeld and Suzanne Cassirer Bernfeld, "Freud's Early Childhood"; Bernfeld, S. 1945; Josef Sajner, "Sigmund Freuds Beziehung"; Sigmund Freud, *The Complete Letters of Sigmund Freud to Wilhelm Fliess*, pp. 219-220 and 225; note 29, above; Sigmund Freud, *The Interpretation of Dreams*, in *Standard Edition of the*

Complete Psychological Works of Sigmund Freud, vol. 4, pp. 194-97, and 224-26. See also chapter 3, below, note 32.

31   Ernest Jones, *The Life and Work of Sigmund Freud*, vol. 1, p. 321-2, 334; Sigmund Freud, *The Letters of Sigmund Freud*, p. 225; Martin Freud in Josef Fraenkel, ed., *The Jews of Austria*, p. 204. Freud himself as an infant was taken to Roznau spa in 1857 (Marianna Krüll, *Freud and His Father*, p. 245).

32   Sigmund Freud, *Civilization and Its Discontents*, in *Standard Edition of the Complete Psychological Works of Sigmund Freud*, vol. 21, p. 89.

33   Siegfried Bernfeld and Suzanne Cassirer Bernfeld, "Freud's Early Childhood," p. 109; Ernest Jones, *The Life and Work of Sigmund Freud*, vol. 1, p. 11.

34   Max Schur, *Freud, Living and Dying*, p. 404.

35   Sigmund Freud, *The Complete Letters of Sigmund Freud to Wilhelm Fliess*, pp. 284-86 (3 and 12 December 1897).

36   Ernest Jones, *The Life and Work of Sigmund Freud*, vol. 1, pp. 12-13.

37   Sigmund Freud, *The Complete Letters of Sigmund Freud to Wilhelm Fliess*, p. 286 (12 December 1897).

38   Freud, *Briefe an Wilhelm Fliess*, p. 345; Sigmund Freud, *The Complete Letters of Sigmund Freud to Wilhelm Fliess*, p. 315 (9 June 1898).

2

Physician to the Tsar

A modest grant allowed Freud to work in Charcot's famous clinic before settling down at last to private medical practice and matrimony. His four months in Paris, from 13 October 1885 to 28 February 1886, with two weeks' holiday in Wandsbek, are documented chiefly in letters to his fiancée, Martha Bernays. Midway through his stay, at emotional ebb, he felt himself under the full impact of the city, and "waxing poetical" compared it to an overdressed Sphinx "who gobbles up every foreigner unable to solve her riddles." Paris was "one long confused dream" from which he would gladly awaken.[1] He attended the brilliant gatherings at Charcot's mansion with "a little cocaine to loosen my tongue" (or to calm his nerves, or to relieve the boredom, as the occasion demanded).[2] His expansive epistolary manner also revealed the effect of cocaine, as he himself observed, and use of the drug may have colored many episodes of Freud's Paris dream.[3]

At times, his clinical studies with Charcot and associates were deeply inspiring, and Freud now turned his attention to medical matters (hysteria, hypnosis), which later helped lead him to psychoanalysis. But these tentative explorations grew out of depression, devaluation of his own "silly things" on brain anatomy, and loss of confidence in his own genius for scientific work.[4] Freud's last letter from France, that has been published in full (10 February 1886), begins by exclaiming: "What a magic city this Paris is!"—but toward the end lurches into revelations about his family's hereditary "neuropathological taint": "These stories are very common in Jewish families. But now that's enough about medicine." This abrupt confession of family pathology (which smacks of cocaine, but also owes something to Charcot's casual theorizing about racial heredity) anticipates the Oedipal quest of psychoanalysis.[5]

By the close of his Paris campaign, Freud stands forth as hero, or anti-hero, of his own mythic world. He declares to Martha, on a crest of cocaine: "I have often felt as though I had inherited all the defiance and all the passions with which our ancestors defended their Temple and could gladly sacrifice my life for one great moment in history."[6] This bravado is characteristically tempered by irony, but we discern here one of the great egos of our age, an ego of defiance and self-sacrifice, thwarted by the Parisian Sphinx of destiny. The longing for martyrdom to achieve "one great moment in history" reminds us of Russian nihilism (a "death blow" to the past) and the heroes of Dostoevsky who also long to sacrifice all of life (or at least ten years of it) for one exalted moment.

Freud's first weeks in Paris were "lazy," his mood "melancholy," his visits to stuffy theaters plagued with migraine. In later years we have evidence that he treated his migraines with cocaine, which may well have been the case here too.[7] Freud's current research was on brain anatomy, which he had begun two years earlier in Vienna. Charcot, when at last they met, had approved his request for brains of juvenile cadavers, to be used in Freud's experimental work. Early in November 1885 at Charcot's clinic, Freud again met his Russian acquaintance from Vienna, Liberius Darkshévich, a specialist in brain anatomy now spending his last year of extensive study abroad before returning to claim a promised professorship at Kazan University. Arriving late at the clinical demonstration (because of the "lazy" and "serene" mood that possessed him), Freud noticed in the audience "a narrow, pale skull covered with thin, fair hair" (a phrenologically descriptive touch, apropos of brain anatomy), which gave him a nod of recognition and proved to be "my friend *in cerebro* Darkshevich, from Moscow." Here another little jest signalled their previous collaboration in brain anatomy, Darkshevich having kindly and voluntarily translated a paper of Freud's into Russian for publication. But *in cerebro* also suggests something austere and forbidding, an initial emotional wariness in Freud arising from the fact that after he and Darkshevich had once written to each other (following the latter's move to Leipzig), "I never got an answer to my reply." Freud was always vulnerable to such neglect. Now, after twenty months or so, they met again in Paris, where Freud had become negligent and uneasy about his scientific work. The letter that follows these ambivalent opening words dwells upon the remarkably *disciplined* character of Darkshevich, his Russian friend *in cerebro*, "a quiet and profound fanatic ..., averse to all distractions ..., his soul absorbed in the fatherland, religion, and brain anatomy."[8]

Freud's character sketch of "my Russian Darkshevich" begins by ostensibly recapitulating his first impressions in Vienna, but the depth of his observations and the phrases employed may rather reflect their friendship which they renewed in Paris at once after their chance meeting at the clinic. Walking his friend home, Freud found him "unchanged and in his own quiet way very friendly"—apparently a new discovery. Freud was touched that Darkshevich remembered his engagement, enquired after Martha's health, and hoped the wedding would soon take place. Darkshevich also asked after Freud's father, whom he had once met in Vienna. That evening they went out for dinner and continued their talk over tea in Darkshevich's room. Of course they spoke in German, an obligatory language for Russian scientists, in which Darkshevich must have become fluent during his five years abroad, if not earlier. For Freud this was a relief, for his command of spoken French was weak, which severely limited his social life in Paris. Thus, in the company of Darkshevich "I began to feel less isolated." But at the same time, this Russian friend was the very model of productive scientific ambition, and one whose fanaticism was an implicit reproach to Freud's limbo.

Freud recalls how he had first been attracted, in Vienna, by "a certain melancholy" in his colleague "typical of Ruthenians and Little Russians [Ukrainians]." This stereotype would seem to derive from the experience of Freud's parents in Galicia, Podolia, and Odessa, their anecdotes of life in proximity with the East Slavs of those regions, and perhaps Freud's own encounters with these nationalities in Vienna. In fact Darkshevich (1858-1925) was born in Jaroslavl', an ancient city of the Russian heartland some 150 miles northeast of Moscow. He had graduated from Moscow University in 1882, and thus had come to Vienna "from Moscow," though he was not literally a Muscovite. Freud had gotten to know him better when Darkshevich

translated his paper in January 1884, and then slowly the Russian
began to confide. This was when Freud first "discovered in him" a
grander stereotype of intellectual heroism, a single-minded fanatic
whose "soul was engrossed with the fatherland, religion, and brain
anatomy"—"seine Seele war ausgefüllt vom Vaterland, der Religion,
und der Hirnanatomie."[9] There is, of course, a light irony in the
anticlimax, in which one detects something defensive, since Freud's
own fanatic devotion to brain anatomy was on the wane. Irony of a
different sort applies to "soul," "fatherland," and "religion"
(particularly the patriotic Russian Orthodoxy of Darkshevich),
concepts alien to Freud. But the immediate scientific goal of
Darkshevich (revealed to Freud in Vienna) was concrete, practical,
and impressive: "His ambition was to write the first comprehensive
treatise on brain anatomy in the Russian language."

In the intervening months before Paris, Freud had read "several"
new interesting publications on brain anatomy by Darkshevich. Now
he learned of the professorship promised to his friend by "the Russian
government," which certainly reminded Freud, as a Jew, that such
recognition for himself from the Austrian authorities was a most
unlikely prospect—one which indeed he never achieved in full
measure. At their cozy reunion over tea, Darkshevich showed Freud
his most recent publications, in one of which Freud's method for slide
preparations was mentioned. Apropos, he flattered Freud by recalling
that "the method" had been admired by colleagues in Leipzig. Freud
welcomed these kind words about "my minor scientific
achievements," but to Martha he adds in the next breath: "His book is
well advanced; he works in a grand manner, with Russian diligence
[mit russischem Fleiss] and great sobriety." Freud joked with
Darkshevich about the melancholy he had observed in him. The
Russian explained that he too was in love and lived in anticipation of
letters from abroad, just as Freud. This revelation brought them closer,
Freud claims, adding that "as he is not looking for any form of social
life or pleasure [Vergnügen], he is just the right kind of company for
me." They agreed to make an excursion to Versailles on the next
Sunday—a date that Freud cancelled at the last moment because of
"migraine" after a long evening (of evident pleasure) at the theater,
where Sarah Bernhardt appeared in the "bewitchingly" erotic title role
of Sardou's Theodora.

The portrait of Darkshevich is one of the most complex character sketches in Freud's published letters. In this figure, a Russian stereotype of melancholia (a pathology) is combined with another Russian stereotype of diligence and sobriety, a fanatic soul that rejects society *and pleasure*—in the name of fatherland, religion, and medical science. Freud cringes before this apparition and tries to flee from it. In Paris he found intermittent escape from diligence, sobriety, and his own melancholia by seeking pleasure in society and cocaine. Darkshevich appeared before him like some nihilist caricature ("a skull") and an alter ego that repelled him more than it attracted, in fact not at all "the right kind of company."

Oddly enough, a second Russian now abruptly entered Freud's life as a guide to theaters and dining spots. At first he is vaguely mentioned only as "one of my Russians" who accompanies Freud to Sarah Bernhardt's spectacular performance as the Byzantine Empress Theodora. Before the Russian is identified, the entire plot of Sardou's historical drama is recapitulated in lavish detail, ending with special praise for the actress's art: "As for her caressing and pleading and embracing, the postures she assumes, the way she wraps herself around a man, the way she acts with every limb, every joint—it's incredible."[10] Again a throbbing migraine is the penalty for his pleasure, probably induced by the two hours of intermissions for beer and cigars. At last Freud introduces his companion for this escapade:

> The Russian I went with was Dr. Klikovich, Botkin's assistant, a vivacious, shrewd, and amiable young man to whom I owe several practical hints. He pointed out to me a modest eating place where one can get for thirty centimes what costs sixty in a cafe, and took me to a new restaurant where one can eat *à prix fixe* and yet choose one's dishes, get twice as much to drink and more to eat than at Duval's, and yet pay twenty centimes less per meal. I would save more if I drank wine instead of beer, would pay 1.60 francs instead of 2.00. Today, Sunday, an excursion to Versailles [with Darkshevich] had been planned, but I have decided to give my head and my pocket a rest. I hope to go to several lectures with my other Russian, the scientific one, who has invited me to tea this evening.

One has the impression that Freud had entered a struggle with the forces of good and evil, "his" Russians representing the division in his soul. This burlesque view of the situation is enhanced by the curious name of the lively and shrewd Dr. Klikóvich, which could be satirically derived from *Clicquot* (Russian: *klikó*), a brand of champagne once rhapsodized by Pushkin and popular enough in the Russia of that century to be almost synonymous with the generic beverage. In the official biography of Freud, Klikovich does not appear, but his gregarious nature (as theatergoer) is mistakenly assigned to Darkshevich.[11] Klikovich is not mentioned again in the published letters, but the tone of Freud's social life in Paris suggests that he did not lose sight of his vivacious and knowing Russian friend.

Apparently Klikovich also disappeared from the annals of medicine, quite unlike his eminent Moscow chief, Dr. Botkin. Noteworthy is Freud's first reference to Klikovich as "Botkin's assistant," indicating that the reputation of Botkin had been made known to Martha in some earlier context. Dr. Sergéi Petróvich Bótkin (1832-1889) was physician to the tsar. Russia's pioneer in modern clinical techniques, he had studied with Claude Bernard and in leading Berlin clinics, and earned an international reputation in physiology and pharmacology. He was the founder of teaching clinics and hospitals for the poor. Botkin is credited with establishing the new concept of Russian medicine that Pavlov later termed *nervízm*, emphasizing the whole organism in its environment, dominated by the nervous system. Early in his career he participated in the Crimean War, assigned to a medical brigade under the patronage of the imperial family, and in the Russo-Turkish War of 1877—when Freud predicted that the Romanovs were digging their own grave—Botkin served as a medical volunteer at the front for ten months. By then he was well known to the Russian public as medical consultant to the Ministry of Interior and as president of the Society of Russian Physicians in St. Petersburg. His name was a household word among educated Russians, so that Dostoevsky (whose chronic pulmonary illness was diagnosed by Botkin in 1867) once joked that his readers, addicted to lying about anything, and above all about their illnesses and treatment, would even lie about "the miraculous cures performed upon you by Botkin."[12] For Freud, the medical philosophy of Botkin held no special appeal. His iconic use of the Russian's name conjured the idea of dazzling professional success—as physician to the tsar. Likewise, the reference to Klikovich as "Botkin's assistant" conjures the vision of a dazzling career made easy by the patronage of a great figure.

Freud's chosen mentor was also famous as consulting physician to the tsar. Jean-Martin Charcot (1825-1893) enjoyed a public eminence and international reputation considerably greater than Botkin's by the 1880s. He had been summoned to Russia to treat members of the imperial family already in the reign of Alexander II. His letter of 8 March 1881 (a page of which has been published in facsimile) was written while visiting villages in the Russian countryside. He includes his drawings of a church, some rather substantial houses, a peasant sleigh, and a patient (or himself) bundled up in a cloak and fur hat. Addressing his family fondly as "my white wolves," he warns them against "the great enemy of a foreigner traveling in Russia"—the heat! No doubt he meant the stifling interiors of inns and dwellings that he visited. The date of this letter shows that he was in Russia at the time of Alexander's assassination, or very soon after.[13]

By the time of Freud's visit to Paris, Charcot was well known to the Russian public. In a comic tale by Chekhov titled "Psychopaths," published in the *Petersburg Gazette* in October 1885, Charcot is summoned from Paris as medical expert in a murder trial. Because the spinal cord had not been examined during the autopsy, he orders the victim to be exhumed before rendering an opinion. Chekhov himself was trained as a doctor, but here he was writing for a general readership.[14] In Europe and, of course, in Paris, Charcot's Russian connection was a sensational aspect of his public image. Freud too was inevitably struck by this spectacle of lucrative consultation in exotic Muscovy, and years later in Vienna, as we shall see, his imagination lived again in Russia, casting him (comically) in his mentor's role as physician to the tsar.

Freud's debt to Charcot was great, as much for style and inspiration (beyond the measurable limits of brain anatomy) as for specific medical ideas. The famous clinician first struck him as "a worldly priest from whom one expects a ready wit and an appreciation of good living."[15] After a month of lectures and demonstrations, Freud declared that Charcot was "simply wrecking all my aims and opinions. I sometimes come out of his lectures as from out of Notre Dame, with an entirely new idea about perfection." Conversely, "I no longer have any desire to work at my own silly things."[16] The following month he endeared himself to Charcot by arranging to become the translator of his *Clinical Lectures*, a distinction certain to win him some recognition in Germany. It would also "pave the way for my own book when that is ready for publication."[17]

He diligently worked to carry out Charcot's commission (a first volume appeared in Vienna the following year), which obviously cut into his own research time while plunging him more deeply into the seductive world of Charcot's ideas. Meanwhile he confessed to Martha that he was not happy and had decided to join her for the holidays.[18] At the close of his last published letter before departure, he says that "the Russian" (Darkshevich) has come by to visit, "and I have read my opus to him."[19] The nature of this opus is not known. Freud's plan for a book was apparently dropped.

By New Year's Freud had returned to Paris. One of his first letters was in response to Carl Koller, an ophthalmologist who had introduced the use of cocaine as a local anesthetic for eye surgery, following the lead of Freud's general studies of the drug in 1884. Freud congratulates his former colleague on his career and in passing reminds him of the small credit due him for the cocaine discovery.[20] Freud's personal use of cocaine becomes a leitmotif of his letters from Paris during the latter half of his stay. Thus it seems appropriate to say a few words about his earlier, and later, involvement with the substance.

Intrigued by medical reports that began to appear in the late 1870s, Freud experimented with the drug and published several papers on its effects. Among the latter, he noted the elimination of fatigue from long, intensive mental or physical work, reduction of the need for sleep, and an aphrodisiac quality.[21] The authorized biography suggests that Freud began using cocaine to ward off chronic depression, stress, and anxiety.[22] Perhaps the most significant effect, in the long run, was Freud's sense that cocaine "steels one to intellectual effort."[23] He supplied the drug to friends and colleagues, his sisters, and his fiancée. On 2 June 1884, he wrote to Martha that he would confront her as "a big wild man who has cocaine in his body," adding that "in my last severe depression I took coca again and a small dose lifted me to the heights in a wonderful fashion."[24] His disciple and biographer Ernest Jones admits that Freud "was rapidly becoming a public menace" as a cocaine pusher, but insists that he did not possess the "disposition" to develop a drug addiction.

Following his return to Paris, Freud used cocaine to get rid of anxiety and shyness, as he began attending Charcot's elite social gatherings. It seemed to help him speak more freely, to calm his nerves, or at times to overcome boredom. Writing of his witty performance at one party, he recognizes parenthetically that his social success had been "rather the achievements of cocaine."[25] On another occasion, the dose of cocaine taken more than three hours before he is due at Charcot's induces, as he admits, a mood of unbuttoned "silly confession" in the letter he is writing. It is here that he admits he no longer sees himself as a genius, but stands defiantly ready to sacrifice himself for one great moment in history.[26] The last of the letters from Paris published in full, evidently written at midnight after a party, very long and scrambled, contains a scene emblematic of the protracted cocaine episode. At Charcot's clinic, an eminent New York ophthalmologist, author of several papers on cocaine, greeted Freud with praise. A bystander asked Freud: "Have you also written about cocaine?" And the New Yorker exclaimed: "Of course he has, it was he who started it all."[27] It was Freud's only moment of professional glory in Paris—thanks to coca. As a footnote we may add that he continued to use it for migraines into the 1890s and learned from his friend Fliess to apply it to his nostrils for other conditions as well.[28] Earlier he had been in the habit of taking it orally. With repeated treatments, by June of 1895 he observed that "I need a lot of cocaine," and it was on 24 July 1895 that "the secret of the dream revealed itself to Dr. Sigm. Freud."[29] On 26 October of the following year, two days after the death of his father, he reported that "the cocaine brush has been completely put aside."[30] But this was no moral vow of abstinence, and in all likelihood his epic quest to discover the mysteries of his own psyche over the next three years owed something to the effects of coca. If this were found to be true, it would obviously not diminish in the slightest the historical significance of *The Interpretation of Dreams*. Finally, it would not be unreasonable to suppose that Freud resorted to cocaine in the following decades of intellectual exertion and physical pain, especially following the operations for cancer of the palate that commenced in 1923. No evidence for this speculation has come to light.

Freud's long midnight letter from Paris of 10 February 1886 includes a penultimate paragraph, quite out of the blue, about "a considerable 'neuropathological taint,' as it is called," in his father's family. This confession to his fiancée is important on the one hand as an essential key to his ethnic identity and character, and on the other hand as one more symptom of the self-devaluation evident throughout his months in Paris. His uncle (Abae) had four children, three with major mental problems (two insane, one hydrocephalic). Freud "had so completely forgotten this uncle that I have always thought of my own family as free from any hereditary taint." But the prospect of a medical appointment in Breslau had reminded him of his afflicted cousins. Now he also recalled that his other "very unhappy" uncle in Vienna (Josef) had a son who "died an epileptic." Freud's Uncle Josef was destined to be a major dream figure discussed in *The Interpretation of Dreams*, and his truly remarkable "unhappiness"—a major episode in the story of Freud's Russia—is the subject of our next chapter. Nothing more definite is known about the illness of his son, but a diagnosis of epilepsy, the ancient *morbus sacer*, would have a strong emotional impact upon the whole family. Medicine had long regarded epilepsy in an individual as a sign of probable hereditary "neuropathological taint" in the immediate family, just as Freud here seems to accept. This medical problem played a dominant role in the life and creativity of Dostoevsky, himself a victim of epilepsy; thus, Freud's family history of epilepsy, such as it was, has a certain bearing on his view of Dostoevsky, to be considered more carefully below. Five of Freud's siblings seemed free of "taint," but in himself and his sister Rosa he saw "a nicely developed tendency toward neurasthenia." He had in mind his depressions, nervous exhaustion, and perhaps the migraines.[31] Freud told Martha that as a neurologist he could take care of himself (like a sailor at sea), but she must be sure to keep her nerves in good condition for the sake of their children. With ambivalent irony he urged her not to worry: "These stories are very common in Jewish families." The allusion to Jewish families, made with an air of clinical authority, may derive from Charcot, who in several lectures during the 1880s elaborated his view that "Jewish families furnish us with the finest subjects for the study of hereditary nervous disease." (At the same time, he did not fail to point out the great role played by the Jews throughout history.)[32] Perhaps this idea was commonplace, but uttered by the charismatic Charcot it may have contributed to Freud's introspective reorientation. In this regard we note that toward the end of January 1886 he had purchased a dynamometer for the purpose of studying "my own nervous condition." In the same letter to Martha he announced that he had set aside his work on brain anatomy in order to study a disoriented patient in Charcot's clinic.[33]

During his last weeks in Paris Freud remained in close contact with Darkshevich. Once, sitting beside "my sick Russian friend," he happened to mention a small discovery he had made in Vienna but left unpublished because the ideas needed development. Darkshevich immediately produced his own notes on the same subject, adding that a colleague who knew his results would probably publish them first. "No, dear friend, we will publish it together," said Freud, and plunged into further research for the next three days, setting aside his own current work and his translation for Charcot. A collaborative neurohistological report by Freud and Darkshevich was published a few months later.[34] Our interest in this incident lies in Freud's sudden dramatic impulse to assist his Russian friend, whose major work on brain anatomy meanwhile progressed while Freud's own modest research in the field was neglected and soon abandoned altogether.

Lab research in brain anatomy gave way to clinical work when Charcot assigned Freud responsibility for a case at the Salpêtrière. Probably it was in connection with this case that Charcot suggested to Freud, shortly before his departure, that he make a comparative study of hysterical and organic paralysis (presumed to be of mental and physical origin, respectively). This was a major area of research in France and England at the time. One aspect involved the study of epilepsy, the differential diagnosis between epilepsy and hysteria (the former considered organic, the latter "mental" or "nervous"), and seemingly transitional forms of these two mysterious illnesses. Freud's approach to this problem, basically determined by Charcot, is important for our purposes because it later served to color his view of Dostoevsky's epilepsy and accordingly his analysis of the Russian writer's character and creativity.[35] Just one week before parting with Charcot, Freud outlined some ideas for the study his mentor had suggested, but worried about submitting them for criticism "since Charcot does not like people intervening with clever ideas." But he decided to hand in the project because "I don't want to be cowardly, and after all my Russian friend [Darkshevich] likes both the ideas."[36]

Charcot did not agree with the ideas, but promised to publish them once Freud had worked them out.[37] The point here is the remarkable authority that his Russian friend had acquired in Freud's eyes. This fanatic soul—"filled to overflowing with fatherland, religion, and brain anatomy"—was a major force in the long confused dream of Freud's Paris.

The encounter with Darkshevich recalls an earlier scientific episode from the very beginning of Freud's career. His first published paper (1877) reported some findings about sensory cells in a genus of fish. The next year, having looked through translated abstracts of the Russian literature, he had to admit that a certain Kuchin had announced much the same discoveries "as long ago as 1863."[38] This serves to remind one of the rapid rise of Russian science, notably in the field of physiology. Kuchin was a sign to Freud of competitive life forms beyond the Russian border. In the case of Darkshevich, the Russian competition loomed much larger on Freud's horizon. What drove Freud out of exact science was some combination of his own depression (devaluation of his worth), the magnetism of Charcot, and the forbidding example of Darkshevich. The Russian's obsessive nature seems a caricature of the Russian nihilist, indeed a caricature of Freud's own making, along lines of the historic stereotype. Society and pleasure were rejected in pursuit of a selfless goal. Such a destiny repelled Freud, who had an innate streak of hedonism, limited but stubborn. One recalls that the hero of Chernyshévsky's *What To Do?*, a classic of nihilism published in 1863, permits himself just one pleasure: the best Havana cigars.

Darkshevich occupied several distinguished posts in Russia and became a professor at Moscow University in 1917. His textbook, *A Course on Nervous Illnesses*, was a standard work in Russia until the 1930s. His long essay on hysteria (published in Russian in 1915) ends on a note of faith, declaring that the "emotive constitution" of humanity from which hysteria springs is also a sign of our spiritual perfectability. In passing, Darkshevich rejects Freud's sexual etiology of hysteria politely but categorically.[39] This was more than just token recognition of an old friend (when their countries were at war), for by that time psychoanalysis had been well publicized in Russia, sufficiently to require some response from official medicine. One of the last publications of Darkshevich is a pamphlet, *On the Question of*

Hysteria in the History of Nations: The Apostle Paul (published in Russian in Berlin in 1923). It bears out Freud's observation of the author's deeply religious nature, shows a stubborn faith in the hidden spiritual resources of mankind, and may contain an implied tribute to the late work of Charcot on faith healing.[40] There is no indication that Freud was aware of Darkshevich's last work. Yet in a way it prefigures his own psychological enquiry into biblical material.

With friends like Klikovich and Darkshevich, one might feel motivated to explore Russian national culture more deeply. A year earlier, we have seen, Freud had found time from his busy schedule to read Russian history, which captured his imagination. Although there is no evidence, two events might have prompted him to read some of the classics of Russian literature during his months in Paris. Ivan Turgenev, one of the greatest figures in European literature, died on an estate near Paris on 22 August 1883. Foul play had been suspected by the dying man, Charcot was baffled by symptoms of metastasized lung cancer that science had yet to explain, and an international incident threatened to develop. The French government ordered an autopsy, performed by the leading forensic specialist Brouardel—whom Freud met socially at Charcot's two years later and whose lectures he attended. The post mortem revealed natural causes of death, and the largest brain then known to medical science (2,012 grams, 35 percent larger than the adult British male average of 1,409 grams).[41] This fact might have alerted Freud, a brain anatomist, to the works of Turgenev, available in complete German editions since 1865. To end this line of conjecture it may be noted that Turgenev's famous novella "First Love" is a profound, precocious, and quite unforgettable study of the Oedipal complex.

The other event that called attention to Russian literature in Freud's Paris is the appearance of De Vogüé's influential, pioneering study *Le roman russe*, parts of which were serialized in *La Revue des Deux Mondes* from 1883 to 1885. The essay on Dostoevsky (who died in 1881) appeared in the issue of 15 January 1885, less than a year before Freud arrived in France. The series of articles came out as a book in June 1886, after Freud had left Paris.[42] DeVogüé, who had recently spent seven years in St. Petersburg, described Dostoevsky as "the soul of a woman in the body of a Russian peasant," a flamboyant phrase that anticipates Freud's theory of bisexual ambivalence ruling the

Russian novelist's psyche. If Freud's Russian friends and the sensational politics of their nation made him look, even superficially, into the Russian literary world, translated materials were now at hand, as well as striking critiques.

Dostoevsky, whose European vogue began a few decades later, could logically have been called to Freud's attention by his intimate friend and colleague Dr. Darkshevich. Even if the Russian novelist's idiosyncratic patriotism was perhaps discreetly overlooked in their conversations, the pathologies described in his works, above all the mental cases, were of singular interest for medical men and neuropathologists such as Freud and Darkshevich. Dr. Vladimir Chizh, a Petersburg forensic pathologist, had just published a study of *Dostoevsky as Psychopathologist*, serialized in the summer of 1884 in a Russian journal, *Russkii Vestnik*, as popular as *La Revue des Deux Mondes*. A separate edition appeared in 1885. Undoubtedly Darkshevich was aware of it. The author saw Dostoevsky as a great intuitive observer of abnormal psychic phenomena, with uncanny precision in describing minute and obscure clinical details. His argument is documented with a clinical inventory of types from the novels and stories.[43] Darkshevich may have called Freud's attention to these extraordinary medical materials. But if he did not, in due course Freud found his own clinical approach to the Russian national character and his own diagnostic view of Dostoevsky's creative genius.

Freud's retrospective view of Paris, reported in a brief memoir by a casual acquaintance who met him half a century after the fact, could have some bearing on his early awareness of Russian literature. On 8 May 1934, he was interviewed by the writer and journalist Giovanni Papini. Freud told Papini that his true vocation had always been that of the novelist or poet, not the scientist. Psychoanalysis, according to Papini's report in *Colosseum*, Freud considered "no more than the interpretation of a literary vocation in terms of psychology and pathology." Goethe's *Werther* had taught him catharsis of obsession, cure by liberation. Zola above all had made Freud sensitive to "the shameful secrets" of human behavior and the unconscious. And symbolism taught the value of dreams assimilated by poetry, and the role of symbols and allusions in art. Psychoanalysis was born not from suggestions by his senior colleague Breuer, nor from clever ideas of

Nietzsche or Schopenhauer, but "as a result of the scientific transposition of the literary schools I like best." The decisive influence of his stay in France in 1885 and 1886 came not from Charcot but from the rich and active French literary life:

> In the evenings I frequented the cafés of the Latin quarter and read the books most discussed in those years. The literary struggle was at its height. Symbolism raised its banner against Naturalism. Mallarmé and Verlaine were gaining influence over the young generation at the expense of Flaubert and Zola.

Brilliant pieces by Huysmans, Verlaine, Mallarmé, and Rimbaud appeared while he was in France, and the conflicting schools of romanticism, naturalism, and symbolism "were the inspiration of all my later work." This aesthetic life is virtually unmentioned in Freud's published letters from Paris—the Latin quarter, the avant garde writers—but his fiancée was not an intellectual and would not, perhaps, have expected or appreciated his reflections on these matters. Freud may have been reluctant to write at that time about activities seemingly at odds with medical dedication. Of course several hundred letters from the era have not been published, while only a dozen or so have. In any case, the passion for literature seems not at all out of character, and he may have been telling the embellished truth to Papini in a whimsical moment of frankness late in life, while at work on *Moses and Monotheism*—routinely referred to as "a novel." If in Paris he was attentive to the latest literature in vogue among intellectuals, as Charcot's salon encouraged him to be, then it is of course all the more likely that he read some Turgenev and Dostoevsky, out of special consideration for his Russian friends.[44]

In Paris Freud came in contact with a number of doctors whose careers had a certain fairy-tale element of success: Charcot, frequently summoned to Russia as physician to the tsar; Darkshevich, already chosen by his fatherland for a distinguished position and dedicated to his work with religious zeal; even in a sense the bon vivant Klikovich, as assistant to the great Botkin, who was in fact physician to the tsar. The quixotic fantasy of a similar success underlies Freud's jest of 1898, when he read in the papers of the peace manifesto issued by Tsar Nicholas II. According to Freud's official biography, he had been uneasy about the prospect of war with Russia for many years, at least since 1886: "The thought of war with Russia was never far away."[45] The rhetoric of peace from bellicose Russia was paradoxical, almost "revolutionary," as Freud wrote to Fliess:

> The big news of the day, the czar's manifesto, also touched me personally. Years ago I diagnosed that the young man—fortunately for us—suffers from obsessional ideas, is overly kind, and "unable to bear the sight of blood," like Koko in *The Mikado*, who at the same time is the Lord High Executioner. Two people would be helped if he and I could be brought together: I'd go to Russia for a year, cure him just enough so that he won't start a war.
>
> ...
>
> The most unforgettable thing about the manifesto is its revolutionary language. If such utterances on militarism appeared in editorials in a democratic paper, they would immediately be confiscated in Austria; and in Russia itself [the writer] would be sent to Siberia.[46]

Gilbert and Sullivan's *Mikado* was a hit in 1885, and Freud had many opportunities in subsequent years to see it performed in major cities of Europe. In Freud's comic anecdote, which originated "years ago," we see his fantasy living again (or still) in Russian history. Now it is he who is cast, with characteristic irony, in the role of physician to the tsar.

Notes

1   Sigmund Freud, *The Letters of Sigmund Freud*, p. 187-8 (3 December 1885).

2   18 January 1886; 20 January 1886; 2 February 1886.

3   2 February 1886.

4   24 November 1885; 2 February 1886.

5   Sigmund Freud, *The Letters of Sigmund Freud*, pp. 206-211; Jan Goldstein, "The Wandering Jew and the Problem of Psychiatric Anti-Semitism.".

6   2 February 1886.

7   Sigmund Freud, *The Complete Letters of Sigmund Freud to Wilhelm Fliess*, p. 49.

8   Sigmund Freud, *The Letters of Sigmund Freud*, pp. 177-78 (4 November 1885) in which *Vaterland* is mistranslated as "motherland."

9   Sigmund Freud, *Briefe, 1873-1939*, 2nd ed., p. 181.

10 Sigmund Freud, *The Letters of Sigmund Freud*, p. 181 (8 November 1885).

11 Ernest Jones, *The Life and Work of Sigmund Freud*, vol. 1, p. 177.

12 "Something About Lying," *Diary of a Writer, PSS*, 21, 118-9.

13 Henri Ellenberger, *The Discovery of the Unconscious*, illustrations following page 300, fourth side.

14 A. P. Chekhov, *Polnoe sobranie sochinenii i pisem*, vol. 4, pp. 408-411.

15 Sigmund Freud, *The Letters of Sigmund Freud*, p. 175 (21 October 1885).

16 Ibid., p. 185 (24 November 1885).

17 Ibid., p. 189 (12 December 1885).

18 Ernest Jones, *The Life and Work of Sigmund Freud*, vol. 1, p. 208, citing Freud's letter of 9 December 1885.

19 Sigmund Freud, *The Letters of Sigmund Freud*, p. 191 (18 December 1885).

20 Sigmund Freud, *Briefe, 1873-1939*, 2nd ed. (1 January 1886)

21 Sigmund Freud, *Cocaine Papers*, pp. 60 and 73.

22 Ernest Jones, *The Life and Work of Sigmund Freud*, vol. 1, p. 84.

23 Sigmund Freud, *Cocaine Papers*, p. 60.

24 Ernest Jones, *The Life and Work of Sigmund Freud*, vol. 1, p. 84.

25 Sigmund Freud, *The Letters of Sigmund Freud*, p. 196 (24 January 1886).

26 Ibid., pp. 201-202 (2 February 1886).

27 Ibid., pp. 206-11 (10 February 1886).

28 Sigmund Freud, *The Complete Letters of Sigmund Freud to Wilhelm Fliess*, p. 49 (30 May 1893).

29 Ibid., p. 417.

30 Ibid., p. 201 and index ("Cocaine: Freud's use").

31 Sigmund Freud, *The Letters of Sigmund Freud*, p. 210 (10 February 1886).

32 Jan Goldstein, "The Wandering Jew," p. 536.

33   Sigmund Freud, *The Letters of Sigmund Freud*, pp. 199-200 (27 January 1886).

34   Ibid., p. 192 (17 January 1886) and note. Ernest Jones (*The Life and Work of Sigmund Freud*, vol. 1, p. 205) was wrong to assign major credit to Freud. Sigmund Freud, *Cocaine Papers*, pp. 309n.

35   Ernest Jones, *The Life and Work of Sigmund Freud*, vol. 1, pp. 232-3; Freud worked on his paper over the next few years, and published it at last in *Archives de Neurologie* a few months before Charcot's death (1893). Of course by the time Freud wrote "Dostoevsky and Parricide" much more had been published on the differential diagnosis of hysteria and epilepsy, which will be taken into account below.

36   Ibid., vol. 1, p. 233, citing Freud's letter of 21 February, 1886.

37   Ibid., vol. 1, p. 234, citing Freud's letter of 25 February, 1886.

38   Ibid., vol. 1, p. 47.

39   L. O. Darkshevich "Moe ponimanie isterii," p. 1021.

40   J.-M. Charcot, "Le foi qui guérit."

41   S. P. Botkin, "Mnenie S. P. Botkina o khode bolezni I. S. Turgeneva,"; B. P. Aleksandrovskii, "Istoriia bolezni Ivana Sergeevicha Turgeneva," pp. 741-44; E. I. Likhtenshtein, "Istoriia bolezni I. S. Turgeneva."

42   F. W. J. Hemmings, *The Russian Novel in France*, pp. 27-28.

43   James L. Rice, *Dostoevsky and the Healing Art*, pp.200-210.

44   Giovanni Papini, "A Visit to Freud," pp. 98-102..

45   Ernest Jones, *The Life and Work of Sigmund Freud*, vol. 1, pp. 338 and note, 172, 193.

46   Sigmund Freud, *The Complete Letters of Sigmund Freud to Wilhelm Fliess*, pp. 325-26; Sigmund Freud, *The Origins of Psycho-Analysis*, pp. 263-64.

3

Counterfeit Rubles

Central to Freud's life, chronologically and strategically, is *Die Traumdeutung* (The Interpretation of Dreams), which he always regarded as his capital work. It remains a formidable challenge to biographers, because fragments of Freud's past and present, distorted and comingled in dreams, are selectively and circumspectly explicated, ostensibly to illustrate structural principles of the dream process yet with notes of confession and self-assertion at every turn. The backstage preparation of this famous book is documented in Freud's letters to his Berlin friend Dr. Wilhelm Fliess. Published at first in a carefully abridged edition in 1954 as *The Origins of Psycho-Analysis*, Freud's letters to Fliess have recently appeared in full.[1] The episodes that chiefly concern us go back to Freud's childhood in Freiberg (Moravia) and his early schooldays in Vienna. But they resurface here in the context of *Die Traumdeutung*, entangled in the fabric of dreams and the half-truth of Freud's analysis, and so figure in the creative crisis of his middle years.

To illustrate the principle of distortion in dreams, Freud analyses the first half of "the dream of my uncle with a yellow beard." The pivotal figure is identified as his Uncle Josef Freud—the same whose son was a victim of epilepsy and so contributed to Freud's concern about the family "neuropathological taint" (as he wrote from Paris in a letter we have discussed above). This aspect of Uncle Josef's story is nowhere mentioned in Freud's analysis. Here is the dream fragment; if the continuation was included elsewhere in *Die Traumdeutung*, it has yet to be identified:

My friend R. was my uncle.—I had a great deal of affection for him.... I
saw before me his face, somewhat changed. It was as though it had been
drawn out lengthwise. A yellow beard that surrounded it stood out very
clearly.[2]

Behind the dream was a rumor, in the spring of 1897, that Freud
would be recommended for a professorship, an honor promised
already to his friend R. Because they were Jews, there was little
chance that the ministry would ever act on the recommendations. The
strong feeling of "affection" was a double dream-distortion, for Freud
felt only esteem for R., and "I had naturally never had any feeling of
affection for my Uncle Josef." The dream, as Freud explains it, had
attributed certain bad personal qualities of Uncle Josef to R. in order to
deny that anti-Semitism had blocked his promotion—which left Freud
hope that his own ambition would be realized. That is, it left him hope
that his Jewish identity was not an obstacle to success. In this light the
"unhappy story" of Uncle Josef is briefly recapitulated.

When Freud wrote to Martha in 1886 about Uncle Josef's son who
"died an epileptic," he parenthetically noted that Uncle Josef himself
was in some other respect "very unhappy." Now he told the world that
more than thirty years earlier Uncle Josef "in his eagerness to make
money" was involved in "a transaction of a kind that is severely
punished by the law" and "was in fact punished for it."[3] As a result,
the hair of Freud's father turned grey "from grief" in a few days.
(Freud points out that his own hair at the time of the dream was
passing through an "unpleasing" yellowish brown stage on its way to
grey.) His father always declared afterward that Josef "was not a bad
man but only a simpleton [ein Schwachkopf]." (Thus, the dream
insinuated that Jewish colleagues who failed to become professors
were criminals or simpletons, not victims of official anti-Semitism.)
Such is the outline of Uncle Josef's criminal past, as revealed in Die
Traumdeutung.

The official biography of Freud suggests that Uncle Josef was only
fined for a misdemeanor, because Austrian police archives had no
record of imprisonment.[4] But the recent research of Renée Gicklhorn
has more carefully combed police records, diplomatic archives, and
newspapers, disclosing that Josef Freud was arrested in Vienna on 20
June 1865, in possession of counterfeit rubles (more precisely, 359

fifty-ruble notes, a face value of 17,950 rubles). Having sought a buyer for one hundred such bills, he was denounced, arrested in a sting operation, tried on 21 February 1866, and sentenced along with one accomplice to ten years in prison. Annual petitions for clemency from his wife Rebekka are on record only until 1870, suggesting that Josef may have been released then, after serving four years. At the time of his arrest, Sigmund Freud was a nine-year-old Vienna schoolboy.[5]

The affair was covered in some detail, the day after Josef's trial, by two leading newspapers,*Wiener Zeitung* and *Neue Freie Presse*, the latter boasting the largest circulation and read by everybody. Boys in gymnasium like young Sigmund Freud (the Viennese Gicklhorn assures us) all read the newspapers attentively. Josef Freud, it was reported, claimed that a certain Osias Weich, whom he met in Galacz in 1864, had obtained the counterfeit money from "a gentleman in England."[6] Weich, he said, gave him the forged rubles as security on a loan. The two of them had met frequently at the Leipzig Fair, where Russian merchants regularly circulated rubles in quantity. Weich, arrested in Leipzig, implicated a certain Mrs. Lewy in London as the source of the counterfeit rubles. A deposition from the Imperial Russian Bank stated that the forgeries were of a familiar type, copperplate engravings run off by lithograph on ordinary paper, that had flooded all European trade centers and had already led to several convictions. In attempting to shift the major guilt from himself, Weich referred to Josef Freud's "family in England" as a link to the counterfeiters. Both men were sentenced to ten years, but the case of Josef Freud was referred to a higher court for possible mitigation of sentence. Perhaps in fact a lighter sentence was imposed, which would explain his apparent liberation in 1870.

The reference in court to the Freud family in England brought the affair closer to home for Sigmund Freud, whose two elder half-brothers Emanuel and Philipp had emigrated to Manchester in 1860. They had all lived in Freiberg during Sigmund's earliest years, and he had visited Manchester in 1875, when he was struck by their advance toward prosperity as sellers of cloth and jewelry.[7] In 1878 Freud saw Emanuel in Vienna, and both of his brothers when they were in Leipzig on business some years later.[8] There is a vague family legend, told by Freud's niece Hella Freud Bernays, that Philipp and Emanuel at times traveled to Russia.[9] It is worth noting that Emanuel's wife

Maria was born in the Russian Empire—the village of "Milov" (her father was a rabbi from the likewise unlocated "Ragewilla," perhaps in the old Lithuanian Principality).[10] Following Jacob Freud's unsuccessful business trip to Odessa in 1883, Sigmund wrote to Emanuel and Philipp, urging them to help his father out of "his present predicament."[11] In later years the brothers kept in touch with Freud, visiting him in Vienna during May 1896 and June 1900—in the era of *Die Traumdeutung*.[12]

With this background information on Freud's half-brothers in Manchester, we are better prepared to understand various details in the investigation of Uncle Josef. Renée Gicklhorn has located and published a memo of 16 October 1865 from the Austrian Minister of Police (Belcredi) to the Foreign Ministry.[13] This was the third such counterfeiting case in Vienna within a few months. Josef Freud— arrested (as we have seen) on 20 June 1865, with 359 forged fifty- ruble notes—had resided in Vienna since 1861, and earlier in Jassy, Moldavia. A son-in-law in Hungary, who had married into the family just a year before the investigation, was arrested on suspicion of conspiring with Josef, but eventually was released. The legitimate business of Josef Freud was trade in English ironware, which had taken him on recent commercial trips to Galatz, Leipzig, Breslau, London, Birmingham, and Manchester. The link with England was suspicious because this was the presumed stronghold of the ruble counterfeiters.

A search of Josef's Vienna apartment turned up letters from "two sons of the brother of Josef Freud, now in England"—who could only have been Emanuel and Philipp. One of these letters (which are only paraphrased in the police report) claimed that Josef's two nephews in England had "as much money as the sand on the seashore," while another asked Josef "whether the lucky star of the House of Freud had risen for him" and whether he could "find a bank for the goods, one with larger, quicker, and more profitable outlets."[14] The police had already concluded that the forgers of fifty-ruble notes had been operating somewhere in England since late 1862 or early 1863. Polish émigrés were suspected of issuing the notes originally to support "rebellious, national causes"—that is, the Polish insurrection of January to October 1863 that had begun in Warsaw and spread east to the Lithuanian territory, home of the Freuds in centuries past. The

Austrian police surmised that "almost exclusively Israelites of Polish origin" were responsible for circulating the counterfeit rubles.[15]

Evidently Emanuel and Philipp Freud were not implicated in Uncle Josef's crime, even though the police knew he had been in Manchester. Perhaps their letters to him were not posted from Manchester, or had been carried privately. Nor apparently did the police trace the reference to "two sons of Josef Freud's brother" back to the brother himself—Sigmund Freud's father Jacob in Vienna. The apartment of Jacob Freud, it has been argued, should have routinely been searched during the investigation of his brother Josef.[16] There is no indication that this happened. If the police in Vienna were unaware of his existence, the most intriguing question that arises is that of Jacob Freud's livelihood. In Moravia as a reasonably prosperous tradesman he had been duly assessed, but after he moved from Freiberg to Vienna in 1860, the name of Jacob Freud never appeared in the Vienna trade directory nor on the roll of commercial licenses; therefore he paid no taxes. Nevertheless, he supported a family of nine, moved a number of times to more spacious apartments (including always a private room for the precocious Sigi), and could afford such luxuries as an oil lamp and a piano. Perhaps in reality it was a fairly modest level of affluence, yet it remains a mystery that no record of income has been discovered.[17]

One theory is that the Freuds survived thanks to the traffic in counterfeit rubles, for which Uncle Josef, the "simpleton," had come to grief, and in which Jacob's sons Emanuel and Philipp came close to being implicated.[18] Whether or not he was part of an international counterfeiting conspiracy, there was good reason, it would seem, for Jacob's hair to turn grey in a few days—a symbolic aging nigh unto death with which Sigmund Freud, the dreamer of 1897, strongly identified. The symbolic meaning of counterfeit rubles—the covert Uncle Josef theme—is not only Jewish identity confronting anti-Semitism, and the *Wanderjude* heritage subverting official nationalism, but the international idea and movement of political anarchism and revolution. These are concepts which underlie and permeate Freud's *Traumdeutung*.

The professorship recommended for Freud by the eminent Krafft-Ebing and Nothnagel, and the latter's remark about "difficulties" that would prevent the ministry from acting, are mentioned in a letter to

Fliess of 8 February 1897. In *Die Traumdeutung* Freud shifts this event to "the spring of 1897," and imprecisely dates his Uncle Josef dream from the night after a visit by an anonymous friend who, in the same professional limbo, made frequent obsequious visits to the ministry. Remarkably, Freud never mentions the fact that Uncle Josef died in Vienna on 3 May of that very year, shortly before or after the dream.

This death seems doubly significant. First, it lends a conscious distancing and a peculiar coldness to Freud's assertion that "I had naturally never had any feeling of affection for my Uncle Josef" (despite the dream's sense of "a great feeling of affection for him"). Incidentally, Freud's ostensible rejection of Uncle Josef also runs counter to the feelings of his own father, "who always used to say that Uncle Josef was not a bad man but only *ein Schwachkopf.*" Second, the unmentioned death of Uncle Josef is important because Freud in his dream-interpretation pointedly identifies with Josef (and with his own father, who had died half a year earlier), observing that "the name Josef plays a great part in my dreams—my own ego finds it very easy to hide itself behind people of that name, since Joseph was the name of a man famous in the Bible as an interpreter of dreams."[19] In short, the seeming coldness toward Uncle Josef is deceptive. Freud's dream is dominated by Uncle Josef's presence, and Josef's crime is publicized by Freud as a challenge—albeit muted—to authority.

* * *

The counterfeit ruble episode touches several facets of Freud's Russia. Before summing up the importance of the case, we need to consider it more carefully in the labyrinthine context of *Die Traumdeutung*. The problem of Freud's professorship and the official anti-Semitism that kept him from it became a recurrent theme in his book. He told Fliess on 9 February 1898 that a recent rumor of the ministry's good intentions had resulted in "a delightful dream which unfortunately cannot be published" because the images of his childhood nurse, his mother, and his wife were combined and treated in some unmentionable fashion, which constituted "a reproach" particularly to his wife.[20] The following month, on 15 March 1898, he hoped Fliess would not object to "the candid remarks in the dream about the professor," which would certainly make the philistines say he had done the unthinkable. One feature of this dream, Freud observed, might seem "odd": the way it represented his ambition—which was true also of the Uncle Josef dream. Freud promised to work out the explanation later, but he already knew that the psychology of Oedipus (and Hamlet) provided the key.[21] The latent content was on the one hand political (ambition = death wish against authority = parricide), and on the other hand erotic (ambition = desire for the mother). There is no erotic component in the published dream of Uncle Josef, but we recall that its concluding fragments ("a thought followed by a picture") are expressly omitted.

A few months later, on 9 June 1898, Fliess "condemned" one of Freud's dreams and "the sentence was passed" (to exclude it from the book). The dream in question was almost certainly the one which they had recently discussed. Freud admitted that he had lost "the feeling of shame required of an author," yet he regretted the loss of the dream and had "no hopes of finding a better one as a substitute." It was "a beautiful dream," and beautiful dreams did not occur without indiscretion. At this point (in a passage suppressed in the first edition of the letters to Fliess, and just lately restored) Freud moves to defend his dream and asks his friend to say exactly why he found fault with it, and precisely what it was that malicious critics might attack in it. Was it, perhaps, the discussion of his own anxiety, "or [my wife] Martha, or the *Dalles* [Yiddish: poverty], or my lack of a fatherland?"[22]This synopsis of delicate subject matter combines ambition, the erotic, and the political, culminating in the central problematic issue discussed above in chapter 1: *die Vaterlandslosigkeit*. This term conveys both Oedipal overtones (a reproach to the father) and an ironic challenge to anticipated anti-Semitic readers (who attacked Jews as *die Vaterlandslos*, or unpatriotic subversives). In conclusion, Freud called on Fliess to make his objections more specific, "so that I can omit what you designate in a substitute dream, because I can have dreams like that to order."[23] In less than two weeks, still "mourning the lost dream" and "as if out of spite" for its loss, Freud indeed did have "a substitute dream," but because of the meaning of certain symbols, he felt that it too could not be used.[24]

The fate of Freud's "lost dream" has caused some speculation in the psychoanalytic literature.[25] Our feeling is that Freud at last found a way to smuggle the sensitive material into his book. Nearing completion of the manuscript, he wrote Fliess on 1 August 1899 that "the loss of the big dream you eliminated is to be compensated for by the insertion of a small collection of dreams (harmless, absurd dreams; calculations and speeches in dreams; affects in dreams)."[26] It may also be that the "substitute dream," or in fact the "lost dream" itself, proved serviceable after all, with a certain degree of editing.

One of the richest of Freud's published dreams is one he had on the train to Aussee, west of Vienna, traveling to join his family on vacation. At the station before his departure he observed Count Thun rather pompously boarding his private train for an audience with the Emperor at Ischl (also on the western line, beyond Aussee). The count, who represented conservative factions in Bohemia and Moravia, had been appointed president of the Council of Ministers in March 1898. Hitherto, the Count Thun dream has been dated in August, when Freud began his own vacation. However, it is now clear from his correspondence that he joined his family in Aussee also briefly in June, in fact returning to Vienna the same day (20 June 1898) that he wrote to Fliess about "mourning the lost dream" and recently having "a substitute dream." Let us proceed on the assumption that the Count Thun dream is that substitute, edited to accommodate public prejudice and the feelings of Freud's family.

Even as it stands, this is avowedly a dream of "revolutionary ideas" and "megalomania" (albeit infantile) driven by ambition, a bourgeois challenge (albeit quixotic) to the Austrian state. As such, this dream belongs to the "professorship" series and may be considered as a companion piece to the Uncle Josef dream, the essence of which is likewise "pathological ambition." The Uncle dream lacks erotic content, though two final segments are omitted. Similarly, in his commentary on the Count Thun dream Freud refrains from detailed analysis of the last two segments: "What compels me to make this suppression is sexual material."[27] However, a good deal of sexual material is near the surface, thinly veiled by symbolism that Freud partially explains. The world of Freud's dreams is a wonderland in which it often seems (as Humpty-Dumpty observed) that words can mean whatever one wants them to mean. Yet Freud pondered his dream-texts for three to five years before publishing his interpretation, which lent a definite symbolic unity to the whole. Each dream circles back to certain underlying issues, and if one has has patience, the Count Thun dream circles back to the underlying problems of the Uncle Josef dream.

In Freud's preamble to the dream, Count Thun enters his private coach (with many luxurious rooms) and departs without delay, leaving Freud to haggle with a conductor for a single compartment that lacks a lavatory. While waiting for his train, Freud impotently whistles a revolutionary aria from *The Marriage of Figaro*. The whole dream, from Emperor Franz Josef's jubilee year of 1898, is imbued with the revolutionary spirit of 1848. In the dream, Count Thun's contempt for a crowd of German students makes Freud flair up with anger—to his waking amazement, because his own Pan-German nationalism had been by 1898 long since rejected.

In the dream's second scene (less distinct), the dreamer has to escape from the university, its main entrance blocked, through a series of splendid rooms (*Zimmern*), public reception rooms (*offenbar Regierungszimmern*), to a corridor guarded by a housekeeper, a stout old wench (*Frauenzimmer*). Rejecting her offer to light the way down the staircase, he feels clever at avoiding inspection, and escapes to "a steep ascending path."

In the third scene, the problem of escape from a building (*Haus*) escalates to escape from the city (*Stadt*). Now the stations (*Banhöfe*) are all cordoned off, prohibiting access to the lines to Krems, Znaim, and Graz (= northwest and north to Bohemia and Moravia, and south en route to Rome). The train to Znaim is specifically ruled out by the dreamer because he believes the Imperial Court (*Hof*) will be in session there. In reality, the Austrian Court never met there, but Znaim was a stop en route to Count Thun's imposing castle at Tetschen, which Freud knew well, and to connecting trains for the region of Freud's earliest childhood.[28] The dreamer opts for Graz, which Freud links with a sense of unfettered well-being (and the popular phrase "Was kostet Graz ?" [Hang the expense!]). But instead he finds himself seated in a coach on a commuter line (*Stadtbahn*).

In the last scene, the dreamer, in the role of a sicknurse, stands in front of a train station, holding a urinal for a blind old man (identified as his father, who had been incontinent in his terminal illness). Absurdly, the dreamer sees his position as a strategy to avoid being noticed by the ticket collector, but at the same time (in Freud's obscure analysis) he mocks his father and proudly revels in his psychoanalytic discoveries, symbolized in the most humble of clinical implements. Freud traces this scene back to a childhood incident, when he urinated in his parents' bedroom and his father exclaimed: "The boy will come to nothing" (Aus dem Buben wird nichts werden), echoed in a popular political joke that Count Thun was really Count *Nichtsthun* (Do-Nothing). Freud notes that in fact he himself was the *"Nichtsthun"* on a holiday, who had yet to prove himself, while the count was on serious business. Thus the central theme of the Count Thun dream is Freud's ambition (as he notes), which paradoxically hinged upon serious treatment of the most trivial and unspeakable things. As an analogy (in connection with the Thun dream) he suggests a Viennese party game that comically replicated art treasures out of worthless materials; for example, a poisoned chalice of Lucreczia Borgia fashioned from a hospital urinal.[29]

While the old man of Freud's dream is clearly identified as his father, the old woman (housekeeper) symbolically represents his mother (nurse, wife), identified as "a witty old lady" to whom he shows ingratitude in the dream, "ill repaying her hospitality and the many good stories I heard while staying at her house." The "public rooms" (*offenbar Regierungszimmern*) of her house symbolize "public women" (*ärarische Frauenzimmern*), a play on the vernacular term for "woman/wench," the roots of which literally mean "woman-room." It is remarkable that in his analysis of this point Freud shifts from the standard German for "public" (*offenbar*) to an approximate synonym in Austrian dialect (*ärarische*), which connotes "belonging to the state or public exchequer." Introduced in parentheses, the dialect term has the stylistic effect of a wink, an in-group joke, suggesting that these women served Count Thun at the public's expense. The subversive dreamer Freud has "entered" them all on his escapade. A psycholinguistic factor, which does not figure in Freud's analysis yet is consistent with the ambivalence and sexual rebellion of his dream, is that *ärarische* by a reduplicated syllable conceals *arische* (Aryan), with the ethnic overtones popularized by Theodor Poesche and others.[30] Finally, it is worth noting that the Austrian dialect form *ärarische* has a Czech equivalent in common usage (*erární*), recalling the fact of Freud's Czech fluency in childhood, and associated here with the Bohemian interests of Count Thun. At this point it is necessary to say a word about Freud's Czech Catholic nanny in Moravian Freiberg (Příbor) who contributed to his bilingualism and who served as "my teacher in sexual matters."[31]

A book about Freud's Russia cannot overlook the "Czech theme" in his life, which rose insistently to consciousness during the years when *Die Traumdeutung* was produced. The Moravian landscape of his native Freiberg (97 percent Czech), revisited by Freud when he was seventeen and later on many family summer vacations, returned regularly to his dreams as a realm of idyllic perfection.[32] It was the scene of his first love, superimposed upon the more profound first love of his mother—and his Czech nanny. In *Die Traumdeutung*, concluding his comments on the series of four dreams about Rome (dreamt just before and after the Uncle Josef dream, and discussed immediately after it), Freud recalls dreaming of German signs in Prague, where German signs were opposed by Czech nationalists. This signalled his anxiety about anti-German demonstrations by the Czechs on the eve of the planned visit to Prague (which his dream therefore transformed into Rome), and a desire, dating from his days as a student Pan-Germanist, "that the German language might be better tolerated in Prague." Then he added:

> Incidentally, I must have understood Czech in my earliest childhood, for I was born in a small town in Moravia which has a Slav population. A Czech nursery rhyme [*Kindervers*] which I heard in my seventeenth year printed itself on my memory so easily that I can repeat it to this day, though I have no notion what it means. Thus there was no lack of connections with my early childhood in these dreams either.[33]

One may suppose that Freud's Jewish friends who remained in the vicinity of Freiberg (and some who moved south to Brünn [Brno]) grew up with an active command of Czech, among them the girlfriend of his youth, who was of course the most likely source of the nursery rhyme which he learned so readily and so late, at seventeen. In the course of researching his Czech nanny, "prime originator" of his psychic being, who provided him with "the means for living and going on living," Freud consulted his mother.[34] It is, by the way, always rather astonishing to recall that his mother was his confidante, and reader. She told him that the nurse "was always carrying you off to some church; when you returned home you preached and told us all about God Almighty."[35] When Freud was barely three years old, the nanny was caught stealing cash (and little Sigi's toys!), and was jailed for ten months. Young Sigmund had been her accomplice, stealing coins and giving them to her.[36] When Freud wrote to Fliess about the 3 December 1897 dream of Prague as Rome (with German signs), he proposed that they meet in Breslau instead of Prague. Apropos, he recalled passing through the Breslau railroad station at the age of three, en route from Freiberg to Leipzig and eventually to Vienna— leaving behind his jailed nanny. In Breslau he first saw gas streetlights, which made him think of "spirits burning in hell"—clearly another memento of his Catholic nurse.

When Freud called his nanny "my teacher in sexual matters," he had in mind primarily his toilet training. She also bathed him once in "reddish water" which she had just used herself.[37] Memories of these intimacies lived on, mingled with images of the Christian God, the Catholic mass, petty theft, jail, and souls burning in hell. These were among the dominant impressions of Freud's infantile sexuality, in his mature understanding. Dream logic linked the Czech nanny's subversive eroticism with Count Thun (pillar of the Bohemian landed gentry, whose authority and women the dreaming Freud covertly takes), and with the city of Prague (as Rome, symbol of the mother and thus of unattainable ambition).

In the latter half of the second edition of *Die Traumdeutung*, published in 1909, among "Some Further Typical Dreams," Freud introduces "a strikingly innocent dream" that embodies "a crudely erotic wish," as an example of its type.[38] The anonymous dreamer, mentioned only in passing, was arguably Freud himself.[39] The manifest dream content, the symbolism and interpretation, all support this thesis. The details lead us to believe that this could be Freud's "lost dream," or more precisely the portion of its "substitute" that made the whole unpublishable. The solution, as Freud had written Fliess, was to introduce a serious of "innocent" fragments. Prudence dictated that this particular fragment be suppressed, kept anonymous, and published at last in the second edition two hundred pages removed from its original context—the dream of Count Thun. The fragment belatedly supplied begins:

Set back somewhat between two stately [*stattlichen*] palaces is a little house [*Häuschen*] with closed doors. My wife leads me along a short stretch of street up to the little house, pushes the door open, and I slip quickly and easily into the interior of a steeply rising courtyard [*eines schräg aufsteigenden Hofes*].[40]

Freud unequivocally identifies this symbolic action as "an attempt at coitus from behind [*von rückwärts*]" ("the two stately [*stattlichen*] buttocks of the female body"). The ascending "narrow passage" (as the courtyard is reshaped in Freud's analysis) represents the vagina. The wife's assistance "forces us to conclude" that in waking reality the dreamer refrained from making "attempts of this kind" out of "consideration" for her. Thus in the dream the "consideration" (*Rücksicht*—literally "behind-sight") is reversed, and the dreamer's erotic wish is fulfilled, but not by his wife. According to the unidentified dreamer, on the day before the dream a young girl had joined his household (*Haushalt*), apparently a servant. She aroused his pleasure and gave him the impression that she would not resist "such an approach," that is, from behind. "The little house between two palaces" is a memory from the dreamer's visit to Prague Castle (a vast complex of buildings), and was thus a reference to the girl, who was a native of Prague.

A number of features link this dream with Freud's own life and fantasy world. Freud's "substitute dream" (the one he dreamt as if "in spite" while "mourning the lost dream") was rejected specifically because of its symbolic "house constructed of building blocks" which collapses—evoking for Freud a line from an old student song: "We had built a stately political [*staatliches*] house." Freud here emphasized (in his letter to Fliess of 7 July 1898) the song's symbolic play on words (political:stately/*staatliches:stattliches*).[41] This led Freud's doctor and biographer Max Schur to conclude that the "lost dream" had been suppressed for some political reason, probably connected with Freud's allusion (in his previous letter to Fliess) to "being without a fatherland"—the issue of Jewish identity and anti-Semitism, as we have explained above.[42] The Prague dream also hinges on a pun about "stately" buildings, but with a symbolic meaning that is erotic rather than political. The Count Thun dream (with its theme of entering rooms [women] of the state) combines both symbolic meanings of the *stattlich/staatlich* pun. The *"Haus"* episode of the Thun dream also concludes with the dreamer's escape, assisted by the old housekeeper, to "a narrow, steep ascending path ..." and out of town in the desired direction northward to Znaim (and Prague). This route is blocked by the dreamer's irrational fear of the Imperial Court (*Hof*). The Prague dream-fragment transforms this blocked situation into wish-fulfillment, as the dreamer is assisted by his wife to a little house between two stately (plump) palaces, and into "a steep ascending courtyard (*Hof*)." We recall that one of Freud's dreams of this period (early 1898) was considered unpublishable because "its second meaning shifts back and forth between my nurse (my mother) and my wife, and one cannot really publicly subject one's wife to reproaches of this sort in repayment for all her labor and toil."[43] In the dream "condemned" by Fliess, the role of Freud's wife was again singled out as unpublishable (along with his depression, his poverty, and his being "without a fatherland").[44] The Prague dream's "Czech theme" (nanny), the dreamer's unapproachable wife and alluring servant, match these criteria.

For more than two years preceding the Count Thun dream, which occurred in early 1898, Prague had been on Freud's mind as the proposed site for a meeting with Fliess, a meeting repeatedly put off and finally cancelled out of concern (chiefly Fliess's) for political violence. As early as 1891 a bomb had exploded on the Prague-Reichenau railway. Nevertheless, Freud repeatedly urged a meeting in the Bohemian capital. On 7 March 1896, he wrote that "neither of us, I presume, knows [Prague]."[45] But this does not mean that he had never been there. In a recently published letter dated 14 September 1900, Freud reports running into Professor Sigmund Mayer "from Prague— whose assistant I was to have been."[46] Mayer (1842-1910), author of a general study of the sympathetic nervous system, was a historian of science expert in talmudic medicine, and the editor of *Lotos*, a Prague journal of natural science. When Freud planned to collaborate with him, probably in the late 1870s, he may have visited Mayer in Prague. Once, in July 1882, as a joke, Freud pretended that he was a resident of Prague, which he probably would not have done without some knowledge of the city.[47]

In any event, by 3 January 1897 the Prague "congress" with Fliess was again proposed and planned for Easter.[48] On 29 March Freud wrote: "I thirst [long] for the days in Prague" (Ich lechze nach den Tagen von Prag).[49] Yet in April, out of deference to Fliess, their meeting place was again changed, to Nuremburg—which Freud reached by rail via Prague.[50] On 3 December 1897, Freud reported his dream of Prague as Rome, and recalled that in their (aborted?) plan to meet in Prague "dreams played a big part," and that the Prague-Rome dream "fulfilled my longing to meet you in Rome rather than Prague."[51] For all the planning, it remains unclear whether the desired Prague meeting ever took place.

Let us add that Freud's frequent professional and recreational travels in Bohemia almost certainly had taken him through Prague, where the Castle (*Hrad*) is a most compelling and visible attraction for any visitor. The anonymous Prague Dream fragment may, therefore, be attributed to Freud himself, and central in the dream is the theme of his multifarious Czech nanny, a theme that life repeated. In 1887, a wet nurse for his infant daughter Mathilde came to Vienna from Roznau, a Moravian health resort about fifteen miles southeast of Freiberg.[52] The same resort, incidentally, had been visited by Freud as an infant, with his mother and nanny.[53] This may point to a certain continuity and the family's reliance on the Roznau staff and acquaintances in the area to help them hire female domestics for service in Vienna. The conjecture gains credibility from recollections of Freud's son Martin (1889-1967):

> It took quite a long time before I, as a young boy, understood my position as a Jew. I knew that the servants—we had more than a middle-class family can afford today: cook, chambermaid, nanny and charwoman, poor and uneducated people—were Christians, and that our friends and visitors, well dressed, and in my eyes wealthy and important, were Jewish, so I got the wrong impression: that the Jews were the leading class in Vienna—which was my world—and the Christians second best.[54]

Thus Freud's household during the 1890s met all the conditions of the Prague dream fragment and its analysis. Given the number of servants and a reasonable turnover, it is likely that some of the women referred by family connections in Moravia were natives of Prague or resided there.

There is no need to suggest any actual impropriety, whether of Freud's anonymous dreamer or of Freud himself, nor even any seductive behavior by the woman, because the whole episode hinges on fantasy and the symbolic eroticism of Prague. The symbolism of course is here essentially Freud's, an integral part of his dream world's "Bohemian," subversive tendency. The fantasy of intercourse *a tergo more ferarum* is also Freud's, an enthusiasm perhaps thwarted by marital circumstance, as he suggests of his dreamer, though in this regard too the obstacle may have been imposed not by his partner but by his own puritanical reserve ("only consideration for her restrained the dreamer from making attempts of this kind"). But when the dream fulfills the wish with another woman through the wife's assistance, the result might be seen as a reproach to the spouse. By publishing this material in 1909 (buried, to be sure, in the back pages of the edition), Freud made his reproach dimly manifest. By that time, as he wrote to Emma Jung two years later, Freud felt that his "marriage had long been 'amortized'."[55] The lingering fantasy of *coitus more ferarum* retained its symbolic potency and assumed central importance in Freud's analysis of the Wolf-Man, his famous Russian patient who entered treatment in 1910. The story of the Wolf-Man is told in a subsequent chapter. Here suffice it to say that the elaborately "archaic" psyche attributed to the Orthodox Russian from Odessa owes much to the projected fantasy of his analyst, "born in a small town in Moravia which has a Slavic population."[56]

* * *

Freud's *Traumdeutung*, as its very title suggests, is a pastiche of deception and revelation. The dreams themselves distort the dreamer's true wishes in order to make them acceptable, much as the political writer with truths disagreeable to the authorities must circumvent the censorship with allusions.[57] This political analogy, apropos of the Uncle Josef dream, is elaborated in a letter of 22 December 1897:

> Have you ever seen a foreign newspaper which passed Russian censorship at the frontier? Words, whole clauses and sentences are blacked out so that the rest becomes unintelligible. A Russian censorship of this sort comes about in psychoses and produces the apparently meaningless deliria.[58]

The political psychology of dreams cuts two ways. A slander—as in the Uncle Josef dream—is concealed by a feeling of affection. And Freud when he interprets his own dreams for his readers employs "similar distortions." His everyday politeness is "to a large extent dissimulation of this kind."[59] His interpretation of the Uncle dream clearly equates the dreamer (and his father) with Uncle Josef, a symbol of Jewish identity, vulnerability, and mortality, but just as clearly states that "I had naturally never had any feeling of affection for my Uncle Josef"—because (it is implied) of his arrest and conviction as a dealer in counterfeit rubles. This slander, one feels certain, conceals a feeling of admiration and affection for the genuinely subversive figure of Uncle Josef, whose crime had an international scope implicating family members from England to Hungary and challenging the authority of the Imperial Russian Bank. Perhaps Uncle Josef was after all a crook and a simpleton, yet his crime had a certain undeniable chutzpah. A similar achievement can be claimed for *Die Traumdeutung*, a public double-dealing in the human psyche. Freud of necessity traded in counterfeit rubles of the dream world, forging them to pass frontiers of his own fantasy and foist them onto the world. Apropos of the Uncle Josef dream, Freud says that the obligation to distort his interpretation for the reader resembles the exercise of social power through dissimulation, or poetic license, because (quoting a favorite passage from Faust): "Das besten, was du wissen kannst,/Darfst du den Buben doch nicht sagen" (After all, the best of what you know /may not be told to boys).[60]

In 1900, Freud reflected that "the secret of the dream" had revealed itself to him on 24 July 1895, following the dream of "Irma's injection." The essence of this dream, it is now known, was guilt and self-justification for an act of horrendous surgical malpractice performed by his friend Fliess upon a patient of Freud's in March of that year.[61] Their complicity in this professional misdeed seems to underlie Freud's obsessive self-analysis and his choice of Fliess as sole confidant and critic for his work in progress. After it had been published, their friendship soon dissolved. Meanwhile the work acquired a private life of its own, beginning with the death of Freud's father on 25 October 1896. In Freud's "inner self," he wrote, "the whole past has been awakened"—by the death of his father.[62] *Die*

Traumdeutung is remarkable not only for its insight into the structure and function of dreams, but also for the manner in which the mundane, private, and frequently comic material of Freud's past and present, dreaming and waking, are made public and politicized. This creative act consumed and redefined the author, a truism of any great book's making, but more literally so for Freud than for anybody else.

The political, historical, and moral dimensions of Freud and his dream book have inspired a good deal of significant scholarship.[63] Carl Schorske, a major inspiration in the early stages of my work, noted in passing the role of the Uncle Josef dream as a political fantasy.[64] Freud in fact elaborated the political theme with references to the Uncle dream scattered through his book, beginning with his comparison of the dream to circumvention of political censorship. The Uncle dream (with dream "wit") suggested that Jewish colleagues had been denied promotion not because of prejudice, but for minor brushes with the law (hitting a pedestrian with a bicycle, being blackmailed by a woman). Freud the dreamer, with "unblemished character," could therefore rest easy about his promotion, since ethnicity was wished away. But the other side of the coin was his identity with Uncle Josef (still alive in Vienna at the time of the dream), a convicted felon whose traffic in counterfeit rubles was more than a symbolic gesture of *Vaterlandslosigkeit*, in the sense of "unpatriotic" (hence subversive) action. Identity with such an uncle, if revealed, might indeed block Freud's chance for a professorship, because the crime was not only a major one, it had also been attributed by the police primarily to Jews. Better, surely, not to have such skeletons in the closet! Nevertheless, Freud positively flaunted Uncle Josef's criminal record in print. He suppressed the exact nature of the crime, but the records were readily available to the ministry on which his promotion depended. The symbolic role of Uncle Josef in *Die Traumdeutung* is both self-destructive and self-assertive, and defiant of authority.

The wish for a professorship, as it grotesquely bodied forth in the Uncle Josef dream, was a "pathological ambition" and "craving" that Freud had not recognized in himself.[65] In the dream's emotional fabric, he detected childhood material: a peasant woman's prediction that he would be a great man, and a poet-improvisator's forecast (when he was eleven) that he would become a cabinet minister. Accordingly, his first ambition was to be a lawyer. But as a medical man the path to a ministerial career was closed to him. The Uncle dream sought to escape from "the dreary present"—the present of mediocre, pathological, and probably futile medical ambition—back to the past of grandiose political ambition for ministerial power. (The moment when greatness was predicted for the boy Freud, incidentally, was in 1866, just when Uncle Josef came to grief "in his eagerness to make money.")[66] The dream achieved its end by "mistreatment" of Jewish colleagues, that is, the dreamer had sat in judgment of them and secretly slandered them "as though I myself were the minister." Freud had thus "turned the tables on His Excellency with a vengeance!" If the minister refused to promote Freud, then Freud would "step into his shoes!"[67] The wish for promotion became a death wish directed at the authorities.[68] Finally, Freud reasserts his identity with Uncle Josef and other dream figures bearing that name. His ego, he says, found it very easy to hide behind anyone with that name because it belonged to a man famous in the Bible as an interpreter of dreams.[69] Freud's identification with Joseph of Egypt has been ingeniously and elaborately argued in the psychoanalytic literature.[70] But Freud's allusion to the biblical Joseph, buried in a footnote more than five hundred pages into his book, may also be a mere conceit: behind one dream interpreter is the ego of another dream interpreter! We hold a brief instead for Uncle Josef the convicted felon, Freud's unhappy paternal kinsman, "not a bad man but a simpleton," dealer in thousands of counterfeit rubles, whose son had epilepsy—the ancient *morbus sacer.* Here was a figure preeminently worthy to serve as alter-ego of Sigmund Freud. International criminal conspiracy was, after all, a more progressive ambition than soothsaying for the pharaohs, though in fact Freud saw psychoanalysis in the light of both callings. Here one recalls the line from Virgil chosen as epigraph to *The Interpretation of Dreams*, a line suggested no doubt by Georg Brandes's identical use of the quotation for his biography of Freud's hero Lassalle: "Flectere si nequeo superos, Acheronta movebo" (If I cannot persuade anyone above, then I will shake the underworld).[71]

Notes

1   Sigmund Freud, *The Origins of Psycho-Analysis*; Sigmund Freud, *The Complete Letters of Sigmund Freud to Wilhelm Fliess*.

2   Sigmund Freud, *Standard Edition of the Complete Psychological Works of Sigmund Freud*, vol. 4, pp. 137-38.

3   Ibid., vol. 4, p. 138.

4   Ernest Jones, *The Life and Work of Sigmund Freud*, vol. 1, p. 4n.

5   René Gicklhorn, *Sigmund Freud und der Onkeltraum*.

6   Marianna Krüll, *Freud and His Father*, p. 271.

7   Ibid., p. 173.

8   Ernest Jones, *The Life and Work of Sigmund Freud*, vol. 1, p. 157.

9   Personal communication, 9 November 1984.

10   Marianna Krüll, *Freud and His Father*, p. 235.

11   Sigmund Freud, *The Letters of Sigmund Freud*, p. 86 (10 January 1884).

12   Sigmund Freud, *The Complete Letters of Sigmund Freud to Wilhelm Fliess*.

13   René Gicklhorn, *Sigmund Freud und der Onkeltraum*, pp. 39-41.

14   Ibid., p. 40.

15   Marianna Krüll, *Freud and His Father*, p. 165.

16   René Gicklhorn, *Sigmund Freud und der Onkeltraum*, p. 17.

17   Marianna Krüll, *Freud and His Father*, p. 147-151.

18   Ibid., p. 149-51.

19   Sigmund Freud, *Standard Edition of the Complete Psychological Works of Sigmund Freud*, vol. 5, p. 484n.

20   Sigmund Freud, *The Complete Letters of Sigmund Freud to Wilhelm Fliess*, p. 299.

21   Ibid., p. 304.

22   Ibid., p. 315.

23   Ibid., p. 315 (9 June 1898).

24   Ibid., p. 317 (20 June 1898).

25   Ibid., pp. 10 and 316n; Max Schur, "Some Additional 'Day Residues' of the Specimen Dream of Psychoanalysis," p. 75.

26 Sigmund Freud, *The Complete Letters of Sigmund Freud to Wilhelm Fliess*, p. 363.

27 Sigmund Freud. *Standard Edition of the Complete Psychological Works of Sigmund Freud*, vol. 4, pp. 214-15.

28 Sigmund Freud, *The Letters of Sigmund Freud*, pp. 15-17 16 (July 1882).

29 Sigmund Freud, *Standard Edition of the Complete Psychological Works of Sigmund Freud*, vol. 4, pp. 216-17.

30 J. P. Mallory, *In Search of the Indo-Europeans*, pp. 266-270.

31 Sigmund Freud, *The Complete Letters of Sigmund Freud to Wilhelm Fliess*, p. 269 (4 October 1897).

32 Siegfried Bernfeld and Suzanne Cassirer Bernfeld, "Freud's Early Childhood"; Siegfried Bernfeld, "An Unknown Autobiographical Fragment"; Sigmund Freud, "*Jugend*briefe Sigmund Freuds" (to Emil Fluss, 1872-74); Sigmund Freud, *Jugendbriefe an Eduard Silberstein 1871-1881*; John E. Gedo & Ernest Wolf, "Die Ichthyosaurusbrief"; Josef Sajner, "Sigmund Freuds Beziehung zu seinem Geburtsort Freiberg"; Heinz Stanescu, "Unbekannte *Briefe* des jungen Sigmund Freud"; Heinz Stanescu, "Young Freud's Letters to His Rumanian Friend Silberstein."

33 Sigmund Freud, *Standard Edition of the Complete Psychological Works of Sigmund Freud*, vol. 4, pp. 195-96 and 323.

34 Sigmund Freud, *The Complete Letters of Sigmund Freud to Wilhelm Fliess*, pp. 268-9 (3 October 1897).

35 Ibid., p. 271 (15 October 1897).

36 Ibid., p. 269 (4 October 1897).

37 Ibid., p. 269 (3 October 1897).

38 Freud, *Standard Edition of the Complete Psychological Works of Sigmund Freud*, vol. 5, chap. 6, sec. E, p. 397.

39 Kanzer, personal communication, 7 September 1985.

40 Sigmund Freud, *Gesammelte Werke*, vol. 2/3, p. 402.

41 Sigmund Freud, *The Complete Letters of Sigmund Freud to Wilhelm Fliess*, p. 318n.

42 Max Schur, "Some Additional 'Day Residues' of the Specimen Dream of Psychoanalysis," p. 75.

43 Sigmund Freud, *The Complete Letters of Sigmund Freud to Wilhelm Fliess*, p. 299.

44 Ibid., p. 315.

45 Ibid., p. 176.

46 Ibid., p. 423.

47 Sigmund Freud, *The Letters of Sigmund Freud*, p. 17.

48 Sigmund Freud, *The Complete Letters of Sigmund Freud to Wilhelm Fliess*, pp. 220 and 225.

49 Ibid., p. 233.

50 Ibid., pp. 234, 238-39 and 253.

51 Ibid., pp. 284-85.

52 Sigmund Freud, *The Letters of Sigmund Freud*, p. 225.

53 Marianna Krüll, *Freud and His Father*, p. 245.

54 Josef Fraenkel, ed., *The Jews of Austria*, p. 204.

55 Sigmund Freud and C. G. Jung, *Briefwechsel*, p. 456.

56 Sigmund Freud, *Standard Edition of the Complete Psychological Works of Sigmund Freud*, vol. 4, pp. 195-96.

57 Ibid., vol. 4, pp. 140-42.

58 Sigmund Freud, *The Complete Letters of Sigmund Freud to Wilhelm Fliess*, p. 289.

59 Sigmund Freud, *Standard Edition of the Complete Psychological Works of Sigmund Freud*, vol. 4, 142.

60 Sigmund Freud, *Standard Edition of the Complete Psychological Works of Sigmund Freud*, vol. 4, p. 142; Cf. Sigmund Freud, *The Complete Letters of Sigmund Freud to Wilhelm Fliess*(3 December 1897, 9 February 1898, 9 June 1898).

61 Alexander Grinstein et al., eds., *Sigmund Freud's Dreams*, p. 56; Sigmund Freud, *The Complete Letters of Sigmund Freud to Wilhelm Fliess*, pp. 116-18 and 417; Jeffrey Moussaieff Masson, *The Assault on Truth*, pp. 55-106.

62 Sigmund Freud, *The Complete Letters of Sigmund Freud to Wilhelm Fliess*, p. 201-202.

63 Siegfried Bernfeld, "Sigmund Freud, M.D."; Philip Rieff, *Freud: The Mind of a Moralist*; Paul Roazen, *Freud: Political and Social Thought*; Carl E. Schorske, "Politics and Patricide in Freud's Interpretation of Dreams"; Kenneth A. Grigg, "All Roads Lead to Rome"; William J. McGrath, "Freud as Hannibal"; Stanley Rothman and Phillip Isenberg, "Sigmund Freud and the Politics of Marginality"; Edwin R. Wallace IV, "The Primal Parricide"; William J. McGrath, *Freud's Discovery of Psychoanalysis*.

64   Carl E. Schorske, "Politics and Patricide in Freud's Interpretation of Dreams," in *Fin-de-siècle Vienna*, p. 187.

65   Sigmund Freud, *Standard Edition of the Complete Psychological Works of Sigmund Freud*, vol. 4, pp. 192-93.

66   Ibid., vol. 4, pp. 193-94.

67   Ibid.

68   Ibid., vol. 4, pp. 196-98.

69   Ibid., vol. 5, p. 484 n2.

70   William J. McGrath, *Freud's Discovery of Psychoanalysis*.

71   Georg Brandes, *Ferdinand Lassalle*; Carl E. Schorske, "Politics and Patricide in Freud's Interpretation of Dreams," in *Fin-de-siècle Vienna*, p. 200; Sigmund Freud, *The Complete Letters of Sigmund Freud to Wilhelm Fliess*, p. 361.

4

Russian Material

This Dr. Asatiani from the Moscow Clinic complains about the lack of therapeutic results. Aside from the imperfection of his art, I think the trouble lies with the Russian material, wherein the individual is as ill-differentiated as a fish in a shoal.
—Jung to Freud, 2 June 1909

Your Russian (and I must tell you again how I admire your patience, or rather your resignation) probably has some utopian dream of a world-benefiting therapy, and feels the work is not getting on fast enough. I believe their race more than any other lacks the knack for self-inflicted drudgery.
—Freud to Jung, 3 June 1909

Remember Lassalle's fine sentence about the chemist whose test tube had cracked: "With a slight frown over the resistance of matter, he gets on with his work." In view of the kind of material we work with, it will never be possible to avoid little laboratory explosions.
—Freud to Jung, 18 June 1909

During the first decade of the twentieth century, Freud's reputation as analyst of the psyche spread at first slowly in Vienna, then to England, Switzerland, the United States, and Russia. The Russian psychoanalytic movement had its beginnings in 1908-9 in Moscow and Odessa independently.[1] Prior to this acclaim, Freud's professional contacts with Russia are obscure. One of his early cases of hysteria was Fanny Moser, represented in the history published in 1893 as "Frau Emmy von N., age 40, from Livonia."[2] Treatment of this wealthy patient, which included hypnosis and massage, involved a visit to one of her estates "in the Baltic Provinces of Russia," that is, north of Lithuania, the home of Freud's ancestors. Freud's editors question both the chronology and the location of this case, but for our purposes it would be equally or more significant if Freud's medical mission beyond the Russian border were purely imaginary, like his joke about healing the tsar. In a recently published letter of 18 June 1900, Freud mentions routinely and in passing a patient (male) "from Zhitómir in Russia," and another patient (female) who had come to him from the same city two years earlier.[3] Zhitomir, eighty miles west of Kiev, lies along the trade route traveled by Freud's father and cousins in the 1880s and earlier: Odessa—Zhitomir—Brody—Vienna. Freud's early medical contacts with Russia may have included other private cases like his anonymous patients from Zhitomir, in all likelihood referred through family connections. One of his Odessa cousins, it will be recalled, was married to a doctor.

Russia of course imposed itself on Freud's Vienna through current events sensationally reported by the press: renewed pogroms in 1904, the First Revolution in 1905, emigration, terrorist acts at home and abroad, the constant threat of war, and war itself. Some record of Freud's attention to these imposing developments is provided in the published minutes of the Vienna Psychological Wednesday Society, formed in the autumn of 1902 and reconstituted on 15 April 1908 as the Vienna Psychoanalytic Society.[4] An active member from the beginning was Alfred Adler, whose wife Raisa (Epstein) came from a wealthy Moscow family of merchants and railroad tycoons, though her own political views were far to the left.[5] Her marriage to Adler in 1897 was celebrated in the Jewish community of Smolensk, a major city of the ancient Lithuanian territory, Freud's ancestral homeland. As of 1897, Raisa, who had received a good liberal education, moved in Vienna University circles. The Adler household had frequent Russian guests, including active revolutionaries—among them Leon Trotsky, whose wife became Raisa's close friend. Some of the Russian emigrés became Alfred Adler's patients, one of whom was Trotsky's right hand man Adolf Joffe, later himself a contributor to the

Russian psychoanalytic literature (on the unconscious).[6] It was through Joffe that Trotsky became acquainted with psychoanalysis, which fascinated him despite its "vague and unstable" aspects and susceptibility to "fanciful and arbitrary ideas," as he later recalled.[7] Though Trotsky was in Vienna from 1907 to 1914, Freud never met him, even though he later reported being keenly aware of him, holding forth in the Café Central.[8] It is interesting that Trotsky first visited Vienna in the early autumn of 1902 en route to his meeting with Lenin in London. He had traveled from Odessa along the way familiar to Freud's father and kinsmen, via Zhitomir to Brody, where he entered Austria with the help of Ukrainian and Jewish smugglers.[9] Arriving in Vienna, he was assisted on that occasion by the leader of the Austrian Social Democrats, Victor Adler (no kin to Alfred), with whom Freud as a student once nearly fought a duel.[10] In extending hospitality to Trotsky, Victor Adler was assisted by his Russian daughter-in-law, Katya.[11] These coincidental facts remind us that Freud's Viennese community was on the one hand very compact and on the other hand closely and intricately linked with Russia.

The recorded minutes of the Vienna Psychoanalytic Society begin with the year 1906 and continue with full entries until 1915, when the secretary (Otto Rank) was called up for active military duty.[12] Thereafter the record is fragmentary. Here we propose to survey the Russian topics discussed in Society meetings down to 1910, when Freud's international reputation was well established and other sources appear to command our attention. Omitted from this discussion are a number of papers on Dostoevsky, to be considered in another context.[13]

On 23 January 1907, the Society was first visited by Max Eitingon, a medical student at the Burghölzli in Switzerland writing his dissertation on psychological testing of epileptics.[14] Soon he underwent a didactic psychoanalysis with Freud and became one of his closest colleagues in the international movement. Eitingon was a Jewish native of Mogilev, the easternmost commercial center of the Lithuanian territory. When he was twelve, he had moved for a time to Buczacz in Galicia (where four generations of Freud's ancestors are buried) and settled with his parents in Leipzig. He studied philosophy at Marburg before entering the medical field. As a man of significant wealth he was unique among the psychoanalytic pioneers and generous to the movement.[15] No doubt it is partly for this reason and partly because of his family roots in precisely the localities of Freud's own East European background that Eitingon soon became and remained a close and trusted associate.

Born to privilege in the Russian Empire, Eitingon was a lifelong Russophile. Jung, who supervised Eitingon's psychiatric residency, joked to Freud in a letter dated 25 September 1907 about the bachelor Eitingon's "uninhibited polygamous instinct," adding that "he will certainly never amount to anything; one day he may become a member of the Duma."[16] This jest about the Duma (the Third Duma had just been convened) weaves a stereotype of Russian democratic impotence into Jung's thumbnail portrait of Eitingon ("a totally impotent gasbag"). At the same time, the joke contrasts Russian parliamentary weakness with Eitingon's unfettered sexuality. Having expressed his envy of Eitingon and having eased the envy with ethnic condescension, Jung continued ambivalently by alluding to the new "vogue for sexual short-circuit" in therapeutic treatment. He concludes sternly, but with a major loophole: "Sexual repression is a very important and indispensable civilizing factor, even if pathogenic for many inferior people [*Minderwertige*]." This comes back full circle to an unspoken final judgment of Eitingon, nationally typed by his supposed sexual license, by an erotic potency that offset (and possibly accounted for) the political and intellectual impotence. Behind this stereotype lies a more complicated episode, which will be examined in due course: Jung's own growing erotic involvement with one of his patients, another Russian Jewish medical student—Sabina Spielrein.

Max Eitingon soon became one of Freud's primary sources of Russian culture and a permanent link with the Russian world. In 1910 he presented Freud with the Munich edition of Dostoevsky (in twenty-two volumes, several at that time yet to appear), and through friends in Geneva negotiated the first Russian translation of *Psychopathology of Everyday Life*.[17] During his first visit to the Vienna Psychoanalytic Society in January 1907, Eitingon initiated a discussion of racial purity, rejecting the idea where Jews were concerned because "after all, there are only limited possibilities of selection."[18] At the next meeting, he asked whether the frequency of neuroses is greater among Jews, to which most present answered in the affirmative. One of the discussants (Sadger) noted particularly numerous cases of obsessive neurosis among Polish Jews, and another (Stekel) stated that the exceptionally neurotic character of the Russian Jews demonstrated the importance of social factors (specifically "the amount of inhibitions") in determining "what sort of people become neurotic."[19] However, when Adler reviewed a case history involving a wealthy Russian Jewish student, both his presentation and the discussion that followed made no issue whatsoever of the patient's Russian background. The "Russian" factor in Russian Jewish patients was clearly a variable that came into play only in special cases.[20] The limited discussion of the issue reveals only that it was seen as a problem, while reminding us that many of Freud's colleagues treated a number of patients from Russia at this time, as he did himself.

At the meeting of 10 April 1907, Dr. Fritz Wittels discussed the case of Tatiana Leontieva, a Russian revolutionary who had murdered an innocent man while attempting to assassinate a tsarist official in Switzerland.[21] He regarded Leontieva as a hysteric, comparing her with various female assassins in history (the biblical Jael and Judith, Charlotte Corday) and commenting on the symbolism of their choice of weapons. Adler dismissed these observations, offering instead his own views of the Russian revolutionary character:

> Alienation from the mother frequently occurs in Russian women.... Above all, one must note the ascetic attitude toward life which most revolutionaries (men and women) have. Leontieva belonged to a sect which despised and suppressed all free sexual activity. In Russia the suppression from above has led to a release of sadism. As a rule, all revolutionaries are benevolent, charitable, and unassuming; but from time to time their sadism breaks through. In the final analysis, this release is basically provoked by the sexual repression.

This view of Russian character (a volatile, self-imposed repression of eros and destruction, politically reinforced from above, with intermittent sadistic explosions) became a popular stereotype in prewar Central Europe, with the sexual element muted except in psychoanalytic circles. Aspects of the stereotype are evident in Freud's analysis of the Wolf-Man and in his view of Dostoevsky.

A more marginally "Russian" contribution to the Society was Adler's lecture "On the Psychology of Marxism."[22] Marx's great achievement, he said, was to make unconscious social repressions conscious. Conditions of production were shown to be determined by the deflection of instinctive aggression. On a higher level of civilization appeared altruistic sublimations (sympathy, charity), "which are to rule the world from now on." Psychoanalysis, on the other hand, argued that the altruistic "ideas" were "neither innate nor derivatives of a moral sense," but affective states arising from sensitivity to degradation and rejection of it. Because the affective state must always fight degradation, it is impossible for a class-conscious proletariat to accept an attitude of "fatalistic resignation." (According to the editors of the *Minutes*, this remark about the proletariat shows the influence of Trotsky, Adler's personal friend.)[23] Freud observed that progress and culture required more and more repression of the instincts, while at the same time the consciousness of mankind was expanding and including awareness of instincts and forces hitherto repressed in the unconscious. There are beautiful examples of repressed instinct in poetic works, he added, citing Rank's unpublished study of "The Incest-Motif."[24] At first these two historical processes seem to contradict each other, for increased repression should drive more into the unconscious instead of releasing it. But in fact the processes are complementary: "The enlargement of consciousness is what enables mankind to cope with life in the face of the steady progress of repression." Again Freud cited Rank, *The Artist: The Beginnings of a Sexual Psychology.*[25] Adler had overlooked the true analogues of social repression in sexual repression (shame, disgust, and the incest barrier), but Freud agreed with him, that the way was now clear to introduce psychology into historical studies. The editors of the *Minutes* here cite Freud's *Totem and Taboo*, *Civilization and Its Discontents*, and *Moses and Monotheism*, and the list could be extended. On the other hand, the impulse to introduce psychology into history underlies the earliest stages of psychoanalysis in Freud's private imagination, for instance in the concept of an "endopsychic mythology"—myth projected from the psyche.[26]

Meanwhile, Freud had made the acquaintance of C. G. Jung, the great Swiss psychiatrist who achieved his intellectual maturity through a trying apprenticeship in the psychoanalytic movement. From 1906 to 1914 Jung and Freud exchanged 360 personal letters, most of them mailed between Zürich and Vienna. These years saw the consolidation of an international Freudian school by 1909 and multiple schisms within the movement, from the defection of Adler in 1911 to the final alienation of Jung himself. Publication of the Freud-Jung correspondence in 1974 caused some chagrin and grief among orthodox analysts because of indecorously ironic remarks about patients and waspish backbiting aimed at colleagues by the masters, off the record. But for the biographer these letters are most welcome, revealing Freud (and Jung) as normal humans, more or less at ease, frank, and even playful, as in no other sources that have come to light.

Given the era and the specific localities—Lenin's Zürich and Trotsky's Vienna—it is not surprising to find that remarkable Russians and Russian political issues now and then figure, oddly and elliptically, among the welter of topics raised in the Freud-Jung *Briefwechsel*. Out of the fragmented data an incident of sorts emerges, with a Russian cast in the role of seductress (later heroine), Jung as victim (unmasked as villain), and Freud himself intervening "Sherlock Holmes-like" (as he put it) to help solve the case. Beyond its intrinsic and eccentric appeal, this material holds a threefold significance. The focal episode concludes on the eve of Freud's most celebrated case, his analysis of the Wolf-Man, a Russian millionaire from Odessa. Second, the Freud-Jung letters provide interesting information about the beginnings of Russia's own abortive psychoanalytic movement. Finally, the Russian stereotypes considered here provide a context for the emergent idea of a human destruction instinct, which can now be seen as a distinctively Russian contribution to psychoanalytic theory.

Jung's Zürich had long been a preferred base for Russian students, many of them dissidents or sometime revolutionaries. In the immediate period that concerns us, at least five medical students from Russia participated in Jung's psychoanalytic discussion group, each of whom later made professional contributions to the movement. These included Fanny Chalewsky from Rostov-on-the-Don, who earned her M.D. in Zürich in 1907; Esther Aptekmann, who earned her M.D. in 1911; Tatiana Rosenthal, who was a student from 1901 to 1905 and from 1906 to 1911 and who earned her M.D. in 1911; Sabina Spielrein, also of Rostov-on-the-Don, who was a student from 1905 to 1911 and earned her M.D. in 1911; and Max Eitingon, who earned his M.D. in 1909. All were Jewish, an ethnic identity that played an important part in Jung's personal relationships with them and with Freud. Of their political orientations during these student years little can be said with certainty, though it is significant that Rosenthal interrupted her studies to participate in the 1905 Revolution and returned permanently to Russia in 1911. Aptekmann and Spielrein returned in 1923. Rosenthal committed suicide in 1921, and the following year a detailed account of her life was published in the *International Journal of Psycho-Analysis*. The profile of her youthful radical idealism is no doubt typical of many young revolutionaries:

> ... full of enthusiasm for social amelioration ... joined the social democratic party ... studies interrupted several times by her zeal for the revolutionary agitation in Russia ... in 1906 returned to Zürich weary and dispirited, wavering between medicine and law ... by accident came across Freud's *Interpretation of Dreams* and was full of enthusiasm, foreseeing a new horizon for psychology along the path of self-revelation to which Freud points the way ... She exclaimed: "What a harmony we might have with the combination of Freud and Marx!"[27]

Such views, though not universal among Jung's Russian students, certainly had a prominent currency and contributed to the national stereotype, notably the combined enthusiasm for revolution and utopian idealism, and the ideological counterpoise of destruction and renewal. It may be added that Tatiana Rosenthal's discovery of psychoanalysis was probably not by accident, because Jung's contact with Freud also dates from early 1906.

When they first exchanged offprints and salutations, Freud was fifty, Jung thirty. Jung's appointment at Zürich University and his residency in the prestigious Burghölzli Hospital gave him a distinct professional advantage over Freud, whose adjunct professorship in Vienna was awarded after an unseemly seventeen-year wait.[28] Surprisingly soon, the recently wed Jung revealed that "my wife is rich"; only much later Freud described the economic hardship of his own family life.[29] Their ethnic differences rarely surface in the letters, though they are often discernible enough between the lines. Freud makes the point with outspoken humor in letters to Karl Abraham, a German Jew who had served under Jung for seven years before moving back to Berlin in 1907. Wryly teasing Abraham, Freud suggested that "it was only by [Jung's] appearance on the scene that psychoanalysis escaped the danger of becoming a Jewish national affair." This in part determined Freud's patient diplomacy in courting

Jung as his chosen successor. Nevertheless, Freud professed "a personal liking between us on which I count."[30] The courtship extended both ways, entailing a component of love that is common enough in enthusiastically shared intellectual business, but with this difference: in psychoanalysis, according to Freud, the business *itself* is love (sexuality, Eros).[31] From the first, Jung felt not only the outward public and professional resistance to Freud's sexual theory, but also the inward pressure of an all too genuine erotic transference in psychoanalytic therapy sessions, further complicated by the attractive power of Freud's own personality. After their first meeting in Vienna in March 1907, Jung experienced a lingering "amiable complex," a compulsive attraction to Jewish women, and at last "the Jewess popped up in another form in the shape of my patient." This patient was in fact one of his Russian students, who moreover served as his "psychoanalytic test case."[32] These professional, ethnic, and erotic pressures underlie the Russian stereotypes employed in the correspondence with Freud.

The Russian student with whom Jung became sexually involved was Sabina Spielrein. She enters the correspondence first anonymously in Jung's second letter, dated 20 October 1906, which he closes by seeking advice on a "difficult case, a 20-year-old Russian girl student, ill for six years." Jung's capsule case history focuses upon certain luridly sensational symptoms from the girl's childhood, perfectly illustrating Freud's theory of anal eroticism. Jung may have reported these symptoms as a conciliatory offering to his correspondent, for in the same letter he expresses apologetic concern that "the 'sexual' standpoint I have adopted is too reserved."[33] Freud reassured him on this point, offered a long diagnostic commentary on "your Russian girl," and declared himself "delighted."[34] The same, unmistakably distinctive case materials were later used by Jung (but without identifying his patient as Russian) when he tried to defend Freud's views at the Amsterdam congress of 2-7 September 1907. Jung took so much criticism on this occasion that Abraham alluded to it as "Jung's defeat in Amsterdam."[35] Jung's chagrin was no doubt an immediate factor in his outburst against Eitingon (out of envy of his sexual freedom, as discusssed above). This tallies with Abraham's report to Freud that Jung had in fact greatly played down Freudian sexual theory in his Amsterdam presentation.[36] Jung was doubly

guilty of making a public issue of Freudian theory and of failing to
follow through. His personal relationship with Freud by now made
escape from this dilemma difficult.

In only one letter does Jung deal specifically with Russian content
from Spielrein's analysis. He discusses her compulsive recall of a
poem, mistakenly attributed by Jung to Lermontov, actually Pushkin's
short lyric *Ptichka* (The Bird).[37] Its two stanzas tell how an exile finds
consolation by liberating a captive bird, giving the gift of freedom.
Jung interpreted Spielrein's obsession with the poem's imagery as a
symbolic seduction of him, an exhortation to let himself go, to "let the
birdie out." The patient, he said, admitted that her greatest wish was
"to have a child by me, who would fulfill all her unfulfillable wishes."
But equally she desired "to help someone to perfect freedom through
psychoanalysis" (perhaps much the same thing, if that "someone"
were her analyst). The latter wish, professionally sublime at least at
face value, has the Russian ring of revolutionary idealism.[38] With
increasing alarm, on 10 October 1907, Jung mentioned his partially
cured patient "making me the object of sexual fantasies."[39] This
complaint, just a few weeks after the disastrous Amsterdam congress,
was probably occasioned by his difficult Russian patient. But the
worst was yet to come.

Over the next two years things became so tense between Jung and
Spielrein that it seemed "the relationship could be rounded out only by
sexual acts." But at first Jung "imputed all the wishes and hopes
entirely to my patient without seeing the same thing in myself."[40] On 7
March 1909, Jung wrote that his former patient (whom he had
dismissed) had "kicked up a vile scandal solely because I denied
myself the pleasure of giving her a child." He claimed always to have
acted the gentleman, yet complained that he did not feel "clean" when
faced by the woman's "fabrication of filth [*Schmutzfabrikation*]."[41]
Freud met Jung's anxiety with a rather slighting good humor. He
reported that some woman had recently introduced herself to a
colleague as Jung's mistress, a rumor Freud claimed to have lightly
dismissed. Quite cheerfully Freud pronounced: "To be slandered and
scorched by the love with which we operate—such are the perils of
our trade."[42] He then quotes Lessing's *Nathan the Wise* ("One way or
another, the Jew will be burned") and Goethe—Jung's reputed
grandfather, as Freud here slyly recalls ("In league with the devil and

yet you fear fire" [*Faust*]). Freud also chides Jung for lapsing into a "theological style," thus lightly alluding to their ethnic difference and challenging Jung to pursue psychoanalysis boldly, at his peril. But Jung was not up to such zestfully masochistic professionalism, and confessed that the story about his supposed mistress "gives me the horrors."[43] The atmosphere of rumors thickened and soon produced a crisis.

Early in June 1909, Jung was convinced that his former patient Spielrein was spreading the story "that I shall soon divorce my wife and marry a certain student." Panic drove him to request Freud's assistance in a detailed telegram (not extant), despite the fact that ordinary mail took only one day. In his follow-up letter of 4 June 1909, Jung repeated his request that Freud act as go-between, and so it is that his Russian patient is at last named in the correspondence:

> Spielrein is the person I wrote you about. Her case was published in abbreviated form in my Amsterdam lecture of blessed memory. She was, so to speak, my psychoanalytic test case, for which I remembered her with special gratitude.... She was, of course, systematically planning my seduction, which I considered inopportune. Now she is seeking revenge.[44]

In the same letter, Jung alluded to his recurrent attraction to Jewish women (the "amiable complex" precipitated by his visit to Vienna), adding that "the Jewess has popped up in the form of my patient." Thus Jung's "psychoanalytic test case" seemed to explode in scandal, ludicrously compounded by his complaint of a Semitophilic neurosis. It was as though the Viennese sexual theory he accepted with such misgivings and reservations had forced itself upon him, bodily and psychically, in the alluring and intense person of Sabina Spielrein. Let it be noted that her diaries and letters (discovered in Geneva in 1974) tell the story of her affair with Jung maturely and compassionately, but cast him in the role of seducer, as she wrote to Freud on 11 June 1909, just a week after Jung's letter quoted above.[45] This unnerving fiasco, which Jung at first understood so dimly, underlies and colors his judgment of other Russians, including the uninhibited and independent Max Eitingon and others yet to be considered.

Freud clearly enjoyed witnessing these contretemps and responded to them with merriment. He wrote that he too had once had *a narrow escape* from a female patient (English in the original—a stock phrase from his favorite author, Arthur Conan Doyle), and he agreed to come in on the case himself, but without revealing to Spielrein what Jung had told him, "as though the most tenuous of clues had enabled me Sherlock Holmes-like to guess the situation."[46] It is amusing that by this time (18 June 1909) Freud had already learned Spielrein's side of the story from the lady herself, and thus he was playing his Sherlock Holmes game with both of the troubled lovers. In the context of the still unresolved crisis, Freud quoted a favorite quip from Lassalle about the chemist whose test-tube has cracked: "With a slight frown over the resistance of matter, he gets on with his work." Freud added that "it will never be possible to avoid such little laboratory explosions." By such experimental accidents, he concluded, one learns "what part of the danger lies in the material, and what part in our way of handling it." It is important to recall that the particularly resistant, explosively dangerous "material" was in this case Russian—although for the moment Freud remained ignorant (or feigned ignorance) of this fact: writing to Jung, he seemed only aware that "Fräulein Spielrein" was Jewish. Not until the whole affair was cleared up did Freud inquire about Spielrein's somewhat imperfect command of German, whereupon Jung explained that she was "a Russian."[47] Apparently, Freud played his Holmesian role well. Within a few weeks Spielrein went to Jung and convinced him she was not responsible for the rumors; a tearful reconciliation followed.[48] Two years later Spielrein finished her medical studies, moved to Vienna, and became an active and important contributor to the psychoanalytic movement.[49]

Just before the climax of the Spielrein affair, Jung was visited by a psychiatrist from Moscow, inquiring about the latest psychoanalytic concepts and techniques.

A man from the Moscow Clinic is with me now for instruction (tiring enough with the help of a female interpreter) on, of all things, the latest development, namely "resistance analysis" (I think that is what you call it). This Dr. Asatiania (such is his name) complains about the lack of therapeutic results. Aside from the imperfection of his art, I think the trouble lies with the Russian material, where the individual is as ill-differentiated as a fish in a shoal. The problems of the masses are the first things that need solving there.[50]

M. M. Asatiani (by birth a Georgian) was a staff member of the Moscow University Outpatient Clinic, then headed by Professor V. P. Serbsky, who was well abreast of Freudian theory. Freud was in fact already in touch with Asatiani's immediate supervisor, Nikolai Evgrafovich Osipov (1877-1934), a key promoter of psychoanalysis in Russia and, after the Revolution, in Prague.[51] In 1910 Asatiani collaborated with Osipov and others in establishing a Russian journal devoted chiefly to reporting and developing psychoanalytic theories and applications. *Psikhoterapiia* was edited in Moscow for five years (1910-1914) by N. A. Vyrubov.[52] Asatiani's visit to Jung thus heralded a genuinely professional first wave of psychanalytic ferment in Russia. In time, feedback from this movement, and its fate, became another important dimension of Freud's Russia.

But what of Jung's condescending characterization of the Russian psychic material, wherein individuals seemed "as ill-differentiated as fish in a shoal"? The simile was well suited to Jung's immediate experience of self-doubt, professional ineptitude, and failure to differentiate in the Spielrein affair, which had forced him to admit to Freud the imperfection of his own therapeutic art. One recalls also his regular intellectual contact with five Russian Jews in his psychoanalytic discussion group, including not only Eitingon (who had studied with the neo-Kantians at Marburg), but also at least one active revolutionary (Tatiana Rosenthal), not to mention the highly gifted Spielrein herself. It was convenient for Jung to shift attention (his own and Freud's) to a Russian stereotype of biological and social inferiority. The fish image that figures in the stereotype also signals Jung's wish to escape "the oppressive sense of your paternal authority," as he had recently expressed it to Freud, to escape the sexual anxiety imposed by psychoanalysis into what he termed "psychosynthesis," lower phylogenetic depths, obscurities of myth and the occult, a universal phenomenology of the spirit. More frankly and immediately, he desired a way out: a profession that dealt with something more aesthetically manageable and less socially volatile than human sexuality. This soon led to his break with Freud and what we know now as Jungian psychology. In Jung's later (1934) racial stereotyping and statements about "the Aryan unconscious," one finds reference to Freud's "great mistake" in "applying Jewish categories, which are not even binding for all Jews, indiscriminately to Christians,

Germans or Slavs."[53] Freud's own ventures into "endopsychic myth" were published as frankly speculative essays, not to be confused with clinical psychoanalysis, with one major exception: his case history of the Wolf-Man—an "archaic" Russian personality—conceived as a polemic against Jung and so confronting him (to some degree unconsciously) on his own ground. The Wolf-Man's story is told in the following chapter.

Jung's Russian stereotype is embellished with a political corollary: in Russia, he observed, problems of the masses were the first that needed solving; problems of individuals could not be clinically isolated in the formless mass. This occult image of the Russian psyche might have been transmitted to Jung by one of his Zurich Russian contacts, possibly derived from M. O. Gershenzon's article "Creative Self-Consciousness," published six months earlier and widely discussed in the Russian press:

> Personalities there were none—there was a uniform mass.... The mass of the intelligentsia was faceless, with all the characteristics of the herd: in the sluggish inertness of its radicalism and in its fanatical intolerance.[54]

Wherever Jung may have received his stereotype of Russian national character, certainly it was not made up out of whole cloth. The partial convergence of his formula with Gershenzon's may stem from a commonplace of the Western press.

Freud's responses to Jung's remarks about his Russian (in fact, Georgian) visitor are quoted above as epigraphs to this chapter. Freud's Russian stereotypes, unlike Jung's (which are carping), are more clearly meant as jokes. Characteristically Freudian, the jokes work subtly at the joker's own expense in a classic tradition of Jewish humor.[55] When Freud refers to the Russian race's lack of "the knack [or art] of self-inflicted drudgery" (*die Kunst sich zu plagen*), the drollness of anticlimax requires that we read between the lines "the knack which *we* poor drudges have in spades." Incidentally, the word "race" is omitted from this passage in the English edition.

Just a few lines above this jest, Freud mentions Spielrein's first baffling message to him, which he forwards to Jung, asking him to explain it if he can, but "certainly not to go to any trouble" (*gewiss nicht zu plagen*). The double use of the verb *plagen* should not be overlooked. It hints that in fact Jung's own "knack for drudgery," like that of the Russians, was being brought into question. Even at their first meeting Jung had revealed a strong inclination toward the fishy depths of occultism, and now he was threatening to defect from the self-punishing discipline of psychoanalysis. The very style of Freud's joke, its ironically flaunted masochism, represents an exclusive humorous idiom which Jung could not have found congenial. Its attitude was quintessentially that of Freud toward Jung, as expressed a year earlier to Karl Abraham. Admitting his certainty of "suppressed Swiss anti-Semitism," Freud also teased the long-suffering Abraham (who had served as Jung's subordinate) by suggesting that "we as Jews, if we wish to join in, must develop a bit of masochism, be ready to suffer some wrong."[56]

Another element in Freud's Russian stereotype quoted above (in our epigraphs) alludes humorously to a "utopian dream of world-benefiting therapy." The separate components of this phrase are grouped differently in the German original (*utopische, weltbeglückende Therepieträume*), and the compound keyword "therapy-dream" (a frivolous, hasty, utopian pursuit) evokes the reverse image of "dream therapy" (the slow, painstaking, Freudian discipline). Indeed, the whole psychoanalytic movement grew literally out of Freud's dreams during the 1890s and out of his unrelenting, unsparing, but often joking self-analysis. In this regard we recall his joke of 1898, of traveling to Russia to heal the tsar, leaving just enough obsessive fear of blood to prevent him from waging war. Here Freud indulged in a humorous "utopian therapy-dream" of his own. His comic fantasy of a world-saving, utopian therapy underlies his own stereotype, generated a decade later, which can be understood in this respect too as typically Freudian, subtly sardonic wit. By joking at the expense of himself and his subject or his audience, he mitigates and diffuses the abrasiveness of his humor.

Behind this private banter, events were unfolding which supply another context. Austria had annexed Bosnia and Herzegovina on 6 October 1908. Pan-Slavic agitation was again on the rise in Bohemia. "The Slavic Threat" was front-page news in Vienna (*Ostdeutsche Rundschau*, 22 May 1909). Utopian proposals for peace had faded from the scene. In this light we perceive a final, ominous element in Freud's stereotype: the Russian feels that "the work is not getting on fast enough" and seeks a swifter cure. The implication is that any hasty cure emanating from Russia might prove worse than whatever ails the world.

During the prewar era, Europe at large was well acquainted with an essential and underlying Russian stereotype, derived from Russian cultural and political history. This was summed up in 1906 by *Die Fackel,* one of Vienna's most popular magazines.[57] An article on decadent personality by Erich Mühsam defines decadence as "radical skepticism in world view, basic negation of all conventional values, a nihilistic temperament as expressed in Turgenev's *Fathers and Sons* and as Peter Kropotkin pictures the Russian nihilists in *Memoirs of a Revolutionist.*"[58] The specific nihilist models cited here exemplify both self-destructive and aggressive factors. The romantic capstone to these clichés of national character might again be found in the famous phrase coined by Bakunin in 1842 that still enjoyed free-floating currency as an ultimate Russian aphorism: "Die Lust der Zerstörung is auch eine schaffende Lust" (the passion for destruction is also a creative passion). This statement from Bakunin's essay on "The Reaction in Germany" was quoted once more by S. L. Frank in his essay "The Ethics of Nihilism," published in *Vekhi* (Milestones), the famous anthology of 1909 that also contained Gershenzon's article cited above, with the ironic remark that the word "also" (*auch*) had long since vanished from Bakunin's formula.[59] We have seen that at an earlier stage Freud studied the history of the rising Russian revolutionary movement, with its philosophy of nihilism and terror. Given the Vienna intellectual's obligatory attention to the press, one cannot doubt that Freud was fully alert to the acceleration of Russian radical politics in the prewar decades. One further indication of the political climate may be noted in a *Fackel* editorial preceding the piece on Russian nihilism and ironically deploring Austria's backing of a Russian loan ("true to our established principle of binding ourselves to bankrupt powers so as to offend the power of the future"). By supporting tsarism, it was feared, Austria earned the enmity of "rising young Russia."[60]

Soon after Sabina Spielrein received her medical degree, she moved to Vienna. On 11 October 1911, the very day of Adler's exit, she joined the Psychoanalytic Society. Her major theoretical contribution of this era fulfilled stereotypical expectations of the Russian nature with wonderful precision. It was a compact treatise imposingly titled "Destruction as the Origin of Being."[61] Her evidence was taken from psychoanalytic literature and clinical experience, dreams, myth, fairy tales, and sagas (including a symbolic interpretation of the death of Oleg in the Russian *Primary Chronicle*); from artistic literature and opera (Shakespeare, Gogol', Wagner, and, above all, Nietzsche); and from the behavior of lower life forms (the fatal mating of mayflies). In conclusion, she declares that the human reproductive instinct should be understood to combine both a creative life instinct and a destruction instinct *(Werden- und Zerstörungstrieb)*. This was, indeed, a distinctively "Russian" contribution to the history of psychoanalysis.

Freud first encountered Spielrein in person on 12 October 1911. "She said I didn't look malicious, as she had imagined I would."[62] In formal discussions at Society meetings, he found her "very intelligent and methodical," and he slyly taunted Jung by writing him that "I must say she is rather nice and I am beginning to understand."[63] He also told Jung that he found Spielrein "bright … [with] meaning in everything she says," but that "her destructive instinct [theory] is not to my liking, because I believe it is personally conditioned." And he concluded that "she seems abnormally ambivalent," a feature which in time he came to regard as the essential Russian national character trait, ambivalence dominant both in the Wolf-Man and in Dostoevsky.[64]

Humanity's ordeal in the First World War would at last force Freud to accept, in general, Spielrein's theory of a destruction instinct and to give her his recognition in print. A note in chapter 6 of the 1920 edition of *Beyond the Pleasure Principle* admits his mistake in resisting the destruction theory and cites Spielrein's essay as "full of valuable matter and ideas … but unfortunately not entirely clear to me."[65] Jung agreed in 1912 with Freud's first estimate of Spielrein's thesis: "Her paper is heavily overweighted with her own complexes."[66] He also applied to her article a bawdy Horatian commonplace for artistic composition that fails: "Desinat in piscem mulier formosa superne" (what has a woman's shape above ends in a fish below). This was a fittingly spiteful last word. She had been his "psychoanalytic test case"—an all too destructively seductive test that Jung had failed. Spielrein was the one that got away.[67]

Less than a month before Spielrein appeared in Vienna, Freud met Lou Andreas-Salomé on 21 September 1911 at the International

Psychoanalytic Congress in Weimar. She was introduced to Freud by her latest lover, Dr. Poul Bjerre, a psychotherapist whom she soon discarded as he dropped out of Freud's movement and she became a disciple. Frau Lou (1861-1937) had grown up in St. Petersburg as the cherished only daughter of a senior officer in the tsarist army. During the Russo-Turkish War of 1877, which had caused young Freud to rail against the Romanov "apes," Lou at seventeen had helped prepare packages for the front and felt a surge of Russian patriotism.[68] Her Lutheran family was of French and Baltic German-Danish background but spoke the usual languages of upper-class society in the Russian capital: Russian, French, and German. Lou also had the obligatory Russian nanny and grew up reading Russian classics and early Russian Decadent poets. "We felt that we were not just in the Russian 'service', but also that we were Russians." Tatars were employed as coachmen and servants because of their religious sobriety. Thus, when Lou arrived in Zurich with her widowed mother in September 1880, one might suppose that she was to some extent acquainted with Russia's cultural diversity and political turmoil.[69] However, the five articles on Russian literature and culture that she published from 1897 to 1909 seem romantically vapid.[70] Some measure of her early (pre-Freudian) view of "the motherland" is reflected in the great poems of Rilke inspired by his affair with Lou and their travels together in Russia from April to June 1899 and May to August 1900. These lyrics dwell upon, and fantasize, the devoutly submissive poor and the "ancient, brooding, and religious aspects" of the country, as one scholar has described them.[71] A recent biographer of Rilke observes that the poet "shut his eyes to the less engaging qualities of the Russian peasantry" and created a personal Russia partly "out of love for Lou."[72] Lou, as Nietzsche and Freud also attest, was a creature compellingly easy to love. Love was also a subject that interested her intuitively and intellectually. One of her lovers reminisced ("a learned and chivalrous old gentleman") that "there was something terrifying about her embrace, elemental, archaic. Looking at you with her radiantly blue eyes she would say, 'The reception of the semen is for me the height of ecstasy.' And she had an insatiable appetite for it."[73] Here was a woman in a sense made to order for psychoanalysis: an erotic phenomenon from Freud's lost fatherland, a rich and worldly gentile, an articulately devoted disciple, a beautiful woman whose embrace—one might well imagine—was terrifyingly "elemental and archaic." If Frau Lou had not existed, it would have been necessary to invent her.

When Lou first met Freud at the Weimar Congress of 1911, her naively optimistic eagerness to learn about psychoanalysis amused Freud, and he asked whether she had perhaps mistaken him for Santa Claus.[74] The official photo of the Weimar group displays Lou, resplendent in furs, in the front row center, no doubt at the insistence of chivalrous admirers. Her entrance into Freud's circle had been achieved. In January 1912, she proposed an article (on sublimation) to Jung as editor of the psychoanalytic *Jahrbuch*, and he wrote to Freud:

> This, if it amounts to anything, would be a great step towards the "secularization" of the *Jahrbuch*, a step to be taken with great caution but one which would widen the readership and mobilize the intellectual forces in Germany, where Frau Lou enjoys a considerable literary reputation because of her relations with Nietzsche.[75]

Freud agreed, noting that Lou had used a term from chemistry (*Sublimation*) instead of the term appropriate for psychology (*Sublimierung*), and ironically hoped that she intended "to content herself with sublimation and leave sublimates to the chemists."[76] By this time Freud had probably acquainted himself with Lou's short treatise, *Die Erotik*, published in Frankfurt in 1910. Having met her in the flesh, who could resist it?—to say nothing of the fact that love was the very business of psychoanalysis. Lou's essay is dismayingly abstract, though here and there one finds some startling personal observation. For example, the act of love has an element of humor, but also a deeply instinctive shame, "which even quite young and innocent men can feel toward sexual coupling."[77] Inevitably one conjures up a large group of the "young and innocent" in the author's private clinical experience. But for the most part *Die Erotik* resembles its prototype, Lou's brief article "Physische Liebe" (Physical Love), a review of Wilhelm Völsche's study *Das Liebesleben in der Natur* (Love Life in Nature).[78] The images and analogies are drawn from natural history and traditional German philosophy of nature. It may be that Freud's little joke about "chemistry" expressed the earnest hope that Lou would not submit anything more in that bloodless and depersonalized vein. It is important to note that *Die Erotik* contains not a single reference to Freud or psychoanalysis. Furthermore, Lou there enthusiastically cites *Die sexuelle Frage* (The Question of Sex) by Auguste Forel, a Swiss neurologist and hypnotist who had rejected psychoanalysis and had been a thorn in Freud's side for several years.[79] Thus, when Lou entered Freud's circle, she came indeed as a novice in his medical art, though by no means in the science of physical love.

In the fall of 1912, when Lou moved to Vienna, Freud welcomed her at Society meetings, which against some resistance had been opened to women a few years before.[80] Sabina Spielrein had been a member for a year, until moving on to Berlin in 1912.[81] In short order Lou embarked upon a career as a psychoanalyst, practicing in Göttingen until her death in 1937. Her correspondence with Freud, over a period of twenty-five years, was an exchange of deep friendship and mutual support, not of psychoanalytic theories. Lou came to regard Freud as "the father-image which has presided over my life," while he saw her as "the poet of psychoanalysis."[82]

In her letters to Freud, Lou does not appear as an embodiment of Mother Russia, but in her memoirs she claims Russia as a determining factor in her affinity with Freud's depth psychology. The Russians and Russian literature, she declares, have strata of repression that are thinner and easier to penetrate, that are more "analyzable" than the psyche of the West. In the Russian "material" (her expression) there is a simplicity of structure, a capacity (*Befähigung*), that helps one discover the psychic problems and the expression of spiritual phenomena. No doubt she herself, as a Russian, seemed at first to offer Freud the same access to Russia's "primitive soul" (if not the "archaic embrace"), and they had many occasions to speak of these things in the prewar years when they first became friends and colleagues. Indeed, Lou's elaborate stereotype of the Russian psyche (as expressed more than two decades later) closely resembles Freud's own Russian stereotype, as consolidated in his first treatment and case history of the Wolf-Man during the turbulent years from 1910 to 1918. Her formula of the Russian psyche may have been largely influenced by his; but, on the other hand, his certainly owed something to Lou— her vital presence, her spiritual and erotic being, and the idea of her Russian past. Before she met Freud, Lou's writings gave only a dim suggestion of the Russian psychological type—in particular, toward the end of a short article on the Moscow Art Theater and Russian art published in a popular Berlin theatrical magazine in September 1909.[83] There she spoke of a Russian capacity for expansive, articulate melancholy, expressed directly in musical sounds and words and frankly in gestures, derived from "the typical fate of their nation." These images derived from Russian literary classics (Turgenev and Tolstoy) bear only a slight resemblance to the emergent psychoanalytic stereotype of Russian character, and in fact they had become commonplace in German criticism decades earlier.[84] Nevertheless, embodied in Lou such concepts easily qualified as "Russian material" for Freud. Looking back on that era in 1925, he told another friend and disciple, Princess Marie Bonaparte: "Before the war, the Russians came. I loved the Russians! The Russian women are beyond compare."[85]

Notes

1   Jeanne Neiditsch, "Über den gegenwärtigen Stand"; *Psikhoterapiia*; Sabina Spielrein, "Russische Literatur"; Jean Marti, "La Psychanalyse en Russie"; Pollock 1982; James L. Rice, "Russian Stereotypes in the Freud-Jung Correspondence"; Martin Miller, "Freudian Theory Under Bolshevik Rule"; Martin Miller, "The Theory and Practice of Psychiatry in the Soviet Union"; Martin Miller, "The Origins and Development of Russian Psychoanalysis"; Magnus Ljunggren, "The psychoanalytic breakthrough in Russia."

2   Freud, *Standard Edition of the Complete Psychological Works of Sigmund Freud*, vol. 2, pp. 48-105 and 307-309.

3   Sigmund Freud, *The Complete Letters of Sigmund Freud to Wilhelm Fliess*, p. 419.

4   Herman Nunberg and Ernst Federn, eds., *Minutes of the Vienna Psychoanalytic Society*.

5   Henri Ellenberger, *The Discovery of the Unconscious*, pp. 583-86, 590, and 594-95.

6   A. A. Ioffe, "Po povodu 'bezsoznatel'nogo' v zhizni."

7   Leon Trotsky, *My Life*, p. 220.

8   Joseph Wortis, *Fragments of an Analysis with Freud*, p. 161.

9   Leon Trotsky, *My Life*, p. 138.

10   Ernest Jones, *The Life and Work of Sigmund Freud*, vol. 1, p. 43.

11   Leon Trotsky, *My Life*, p. 141.

12   Herman Nunberg and Ernst Federn, eds., *Minutes of the Vienna Psychoanalytic Society*, vol. 1, p. xvii.

13   See below, chap. 6.

14   Max Eitingon, *Über die Wirkung des Anfalls.*

15   Sidney L. Pomer, "Max Eitingon, 1881-1943," pp. 51-62.

16   Sigmund Freud and C. G. Jung, *Briefwechsel*, pp. 89 and 90.

17   Ibid., p. 244n.

18   Herman Nunberg and Ernst Federn, eds., *Minutes of the Vienna Psychoanalytic Society*, vol. 1, p. 85.

19   Ibid., vol. 1, pp. 94-97.

20   Ibid., vol. 1, pp. 138-45. The meeting occurred 6 March 1907.

21   Ibid., vol. 1, pp. 160-65.

22   Ibid., vol. 2, pp. 172-78. The meeting occurred 10 March 1909.

23   Ibid., vol. 2, p. 173n.

24   See E. James Lieberman, *Acts of Will*, pp. 70-77.

25   Herman Nunberg and Ernst Federn, eds., *Minutes of the Vienna Psychoanalytic Society*, vol. 2, p. 174; see E. James Lieberman, *Acts of Will*, pp. 80-82.

26   Sigmund Freud, *The Complete Letters of Sigmund Freud to Wilhelm Fliess*, p. 286; Sigmund Freud, *The Concordance to the Standard Edition*: "endopsychic."

27   Sara Neiditsch and N. E. Osipov, "Psycho-Analysis in Russia," pp. 514-18.

28   Carl E. Schorske, "Politics and Patricide in Freud's Interpretation of Dreams," in *Fin-de-siècle Vienna*, pp. 181-207.

29   Sigmund Freud and C. G. Jung, *Briefwechsel*, pp. 14 and 210.

30   Sigmund Freud and Karl Abraham, *A Psycho-Analytic Dialogue*, pp. 34, 47; James L. Rice, "Russian Stereotypes in the Freud-Jung Correspondence," p. 20, note 6.

31   Sigmund Freud and C. G. Jung, *Briefwechsel*, pp. 12-13.

32   Ibid., pp. 228 and 229.

33   Ibid., p. 7.

34   Ibid., pp. 8-9.

35   C. G. Jung, "The Freudian Theory of Hysteria," in *Freud and Psychoanalysis* (New York: Pantheon, 1961), pp. 20-22; Sigmund Freud and Karl Abraham, *A Psycho-Analytic Dialogue*, p. 47.

36   Sigmund Freud and Karl Abraham, *A Psycho-Analytic Dialogue*, p. 48.

37   James L. Rice, "Russian Stereotypes in the Freud-Jung Correspondence," p. 23, note 18.

38   Sigmund Freud and C. G. Jung, *Briefwechsel*, p. 72.

39   Ibid., p. 93.

40   Ibid., p. 236.

41   Ibid., p. 207.

42   Ibid., p. 210.

43   Ibid., p. 212.

44   Ibid., pp. 228-29 and 252. The word "psychoanalytic" has been omitted from this passage in the English edition.

45   Aldo Carotenuto, ed., *A Secret Symmetry*, p. xxviii.

46   Sigmund Freud and C. G. Jung, *Briefwechsel*, pp. 234-35.

47   Ibid., pp. 238 and 240.

48   Ibid., p. 236.

49   Alexander Grinstein et al., *The Index of Psychoanalytic Writing*, vol. 4, pp. 1861-62; James L. Rice, "Russian Stereotypes in the Freud-Jung Correspondence," p. 30, note 45.

50   Sigmund Freud and C. G. Jung, *Briefwechsel*, p. 225 (2 June 1909).

51   Jeanne Neiditsch, "Über den gegenwärtigen Stand"; M. Ossipow, "Zur psychoanalytischen Bewegung"; Sigmund Freud and C. G. Jung, *Briefwechsel*, p. 138n. Freud's letters to Osipov from the mid-1920s have been published in fragments in George H. Pollock, "Psychoanalysis in Russia and the U.S.S.R.," p. 274. Copies privately circulated indicate a lively exchange of professional and political views.

52   *Psikhoterapiia*; Magnus Ljunggren, "The psychoanalytic breakthrough in Russia," pp. 174-76.

53   Vincent Brome, *Freud and His Early Circle*, p. 143.

54   M. O. Gershenzon, "Tvorcheskoe samosoznanie," p. 84.

55   Sigmund Freud, *Jokes*; Theodor Reik, *From Thirty Years with Freud*; Theodor Reik, "Freud and Jewish Wit"; Elliott Oring, personal communication.

56   Sigmund Freud and Karl Abraham, *A Psycho-Analytic Dialogue*, p. 46 (23 July 1908).

57   See Wittels, on *Die Fackel* (meeting of 1 January 1910), in Herman Nunberg and Ernst Federn, eds., *Minutes of the Vienna Psychoanalytic Society*, vol. 2, pp. 382-93; Allan Janik and Stephen Toulmin, *Wittgenstein's Vienna*, pp. 75-77.

58   Erich Mühsam, "Bohême," p. 9.

59   *Vekhi*, p. 194.

60   "Ein Vorschlag," *Die Fackel* 202 (30 April 1906), p. 3.

61   Sabina Spielrein, "Die Destruktion als Ursache des Werdens."

62   Sigmund Freud and C. G. Jung, *Briefwechsel*, p. 447.

63   Ibid., pp. 458 and 469.

64   Ibid., p. 494 (21 March 1912).

65   Sigmund Freud, *Beyond the Pleasure Principle*, p. 70n. Spielrein's contribution is solidly secure in the literature; see James L. Rice, "Russian Stereotypes in the Freud-Jung Correspondence," pp. 30-31, notes 45 and 48.

66   Sigmund Freud and C. G. Jung, *Briefwechsel*, p. 498.

67   Aldo Carotenuto, ed., *Diario di una segreta simmetria*; Aldo Carotenuto, ed., *A Secret Symmetry*, pp. x-xi (Postscript, with Magnus Ljunggren's report of Spielrein's last years in Rostov and probable death at the hands of the German occupying army).

68   H. F. Peters, *My Sister, My Spouse*, p. 49.

69   Lou Andreas-Salomé, *Lebensrückblick*, pp. 59-73: "Das Erlebnis Russland."

70   Lou Andreas-Salomé, "Russische Dichtung und Kultur," "Physische Liebe," "Russische Geschichten," and "Die Russen."

71   Patricia Pollock Brodsky, *Russia in the Works of Rainer Maria Rilke*, pp. 82-83 and 95.

72   Wolfgang Leppmann, *Rilke*, pp. 106 and 112.

73   H. F. Peters, *My Sister, My Spouse*, p. 263.

74   Ibid., p. 273.

75   Sigmund Freud and C. G. Jung, *Briefwechsel*, pp. 477-78.

76   Ibid., p. 480.

77   Lou Andreas-Salomé, *Die Erotik*, p. 18.

78   The title by Völsche, cited by Lou Andreas-Salomé in "Physische Liebe," has not been located.

79   Sigmund Freud and C. G. Jung, *Briefwechsel*, p. 27 and index: Forel, Auguste Henri (1848-1931).

80   Sigmund Freud and Lou Andreas-Salomé, *Letters*, p. 7; Lucy Freeman and Herbert S. Strean, *Freud and Women*, pp. 99-100.

81   Sigmund Freud and C. G. Jung, *Briefwechsel*, p. 228n.

82   Lucy Freeman and Herbert S. Strean, *Freud and Women*, pp. 101-102.

83   Lou Andreas-Salomé, "Die Russen."

84   Robert Byr, "Kleinere Erzählungen von Turgenjew."

85   Marie Bonaparte, unpublished notebook.

5

The Wolf-Man —
Analysis Interminable

*Personal peculiarities in the patient, a national character foreign to ours,
made empathy difficult.*

> *. . .*

My presentation has made it easy to guess that the patient was a Russian.

—Freud, "From the History of Infantile Neurosis"

*What you, avoiding the technical word, call "dualism," we call
"ambivalence." This feeling of ambivalence is a legacy from the psychic
life of primitive races; with the Russian people, however, it is better
preserved and has remained more accessible to consciousness than
elsewhere, as I was able to point out only a few years ago in the detailed
case history of a typical Russian.*

—Freud to Stefan Zweig, 19 October 1920

*I have found the history of this man's recovery scarcely less
interesting than that of his illness.*

—Sigmund Freud, "Analysis Terminable and Interminable"

Sergéi Konstantínovich Pankéev (24 December 1886-7 May 1979),
a Russian Orthodox millionaire from Odessa, was brought by his
physician to Vienna for consultation with Freud in late January or
early February 1910. Not only wealthy but intelligent, educated,
articulate, obliging, and fluent in German from childhood, he was a
psychoanalyst's dream patient. He was also the first fruit, so to speak,
of Freud's international fame, and he bore the mystique of Freud's
ancestral Russian past. Indeed, he hailed from the childhood home of
Freud's mother. Unquestionably, these personal links and their
cultural background figured profoundly in Freud's handling of
Pankeev's case. The first period of daily analysis lasted, with time out
for summer vacations, until a few days after the assassination of the
Austrian Crown Prince and his wife on 28 June 1914. Pankeev (in
German, Pankejeff) returned to Russia, and during the war (in the
winter of 1914-15) Freud drafted his famous study, "On a Case of
Infantile Neurosis," which was published in 1918.[1] From this case
history, the most influential in the psychoanalytic literature, came
Pankeev's nickname (der Wolfsmann), derived from a recurrent
childhood dream of wolves that figured significantly in Freud's
analysis.

   Having played a minor role in Kerensky's government, Pankeev
fled Russia after the Bolshevik Revolution and was again briefly in
analysis with Freud when the Red Army took Odessa on 7 February
1920. His family fortune lost, Pankeev lived thereafter in Vienna,
supporting his wife and mother with a modest job in an insurance
company. For several years Freud contributed to his support, with the
help of colleagues, and remained intermittently in correspondence
with his former patient. Following another relapse, Pankeev was
treated by Freud's American student and patient, Dr. Ruth Mack
Brunswick, supervised by Freud himself, from October 1926 to
February 1927. An account of this analysis was soon published by
Mack Brunswick.

   More than four decades later Pankeev published his memoirs and a
brief reminiscence of Freud. Another analyst and friend, the late
Muriel Gardiner, added her reminiscences of Pankeev, including a
number of his letters, from the years 1938-69.[2] A young Viennese
journalist, Karin Obholzer, has published a book of her conversations
with Pankeev from 1973, when he was eighty-six, until his death in

1979. Various researchers and commentators have compiled an extensive psychoanalytic literature on the Wolf-Man, chiefly concerning Freud's first case history, and a certain amount of "deconstructionist" literary theory.[3] Finally, there are some thirty sealed containers of correspondence between Pankeev and Freud, and others, as well as interviews and memoirs, in the Library of Congress, all closed to researchers until the years 2000 to 2014.[4] In short, instead of eking out our story from fragments, we now confront "Russian material" galore, almost an embarrassment of riches, with forbidden archival sources to entice the imagination.

The Pankeevs were wealthy landowners. Sergei's father, Konstantín (1858-1908), owned at least two large estates, one a few days' journey from Odessa and the other near Petersburg. Expelled from the St. Petersburg University law school and politically active during the populist era, Konstantin had become depressive by the time of his son's birth in 1886. Later he was diagnosed as manic-depressive, but his "manic" episodes seemed to center on explosive political events, above all the 1905 Revolution. He was involved in the founding of the Union of Liberation in 1903, and a few months later became editor of *Notes of the South* (*Iuzhnye zapiski*), a liberal Odessa monthly. His politics became more radical, he helped finance the Kadet party, and the Pankeev household was swept up in a frenzy of political action.[5]

Meanwhile, young Sergei Pankeev (who became the Wolf-Man) was raised with the traditional Russian peasant nanny, and tutors in French and German. After gymnasium, and during the Revolution of 1905, he traveled in Italy and Germany, and in the period of reaction that followed he entered the Odessa University law school, transferring the next year to St. Petersburg. In 1906, his older sister, Anna, committed suicide (by taking poison) while traveling in the Caucasus to visit the site of the poet Lermontov's fatal duel. The suicide led to Sergei's being subject to depressions, and in 1907 he confided to his father "the abnormal, pathological character of my mental condition."[6] Professor V. M. Békhterev, an eminent Petersburg clinician who had already approached the Pankeevs for a donation to his neurological institute, was consulted. He diagnosed "neurasthenia" and attempted a cure by hypnosis, including in his posthypnotic suggestion another request for funds! The family then turned to Dr. Emil Kraepelin, a leading European authority on manic-depressive illness, who had successfully treated the senior Pankeev for depression several times. Boarding the train for Munich, Sergei Pankeev recalls in his memoirs:

> Only now I became aware of a peculiar change that had come over me in the short time since I had boarded the train. It was as though a good fairy with her magic wand had dispelled my depression and everything connected with it. I was reconciled to life again and I felt in complete agreement and perfect harmony with the world and with myself. The past moved back into the remote distance and the future seemed beautiful and full of promise.[7]

His father briefly boarded the train with him, sat for a moment in the Russian traditional parting, then left. It was their last encounter. A few months later, the elder Pankeev, at the age of forty-nine and in seemingly excellent health, suddenly died in a Moscow hotel room while Sergei and his mother awaited his arrival in the country. A suicide note succinctly gave the cause of death as sleeping pills.[8]

From March 1908 until beginning treatment with Freud in February 1910, Sergei Pankeev was under the care of several doctors and voluntarily resided in various elite sanatoria. He and his family were convinced that his depressive spells were hereditary and required medical attention. Indeed, his father's will withheld his inheritance until he was twenty-eight out of concern for his mental fitness. However, the death of his Uncle Peter in 1909 gave Sergei a large income without restriction. His stays in institutions were only brief and intermittent. For about four months he lived in a sanatorium near Munich recommended by Kraepelin. In the winter and spring of 1908-9, he stayed for a few months first in a more regimented institution at Frankfurt am Main (on the advice of his Petersburg physician) and then in a sanatorium suggested by Professor Ziehen of Berlin in nearby Schlachtensee. Summers he always returned to Russia, and in the intervals he traveled about Europe with a doctor or family friend.

Despite the background of malady and the therapeutic settings, as Pankeev reminisces about these years just before his psychoanalysis, one is struck above all by his freedom of movement, judgment, and will. One also notes his alert curiosity, his artistic activity, and his social behavior as a resident in the several institutions. Paramount in this regard is his immediate attraction to the beautiful nurse, Sister Therese, who attended a fancy dress ball at the Munich sanatorium, in Turkish costume, on the very evening of Pankeev's arrival. Learning her name from another resident (a Russian lady from Odessa), he pursues Therese passionately, she resists flirtatiously, he rents a room in the city, and in fairly short order she joins him there for "a happy hour of love."[9] Their love proved permanent, enduring separations, his family's reasoned objections, the lady's justifiable outbursts of rage which he mistook for "hysteria," his Uncle Boris's efforts to divert him with Parisian prostitutes, his chronic illness, and her humble status as a nurse—divorced, with a young daughter, Else. When Pankeev found his way to Freud (the circuitous road led again through Odessa), he asked whether the doctor would permit him to be reunited with Therese, and Freud said "yes," but at first prolonged the separation for the initial months of analysis, and then extended it more than a year.[10] Unbeknownst to Freud, had he said "no" his patient would have defected forthwith to Dr. Dubois in Geneva! When the lovers were allowed to see each other again, in March 1911, Pankeev had lost track of the despairing Therese and a detective was hired to find her. She was located in Munich and soon moved to Vienna, where she and Pankeev lived together for the rest of his psychoanalysis. Only when the treatment was over in 1914 did Freud meet Therese. He declared that she "looked like a tsarina."[11] After a few weeks, Therese followed Pankeev to Odessa, where, after some struggle with his mother, they were married.[12]

The openly erotic, tumultuous, and successful romance of Pankeev and Therese seems somewhat out of step with Freud's case study (focused upon early childhood and the "archaic" psyche). Freud says that his patient "was entirely incapacitated and completely dependent upon other people when he began his psychoanalytic treatment."[13] Indeed at several earlier points in his memoirs Pankeev himself recalls his condition as "hopeless," and once he attempted suicide, as his father had succeeded in doing, with sleeping pills.[14] But more than half a century later Pankeev wrote to another former analyst: "When I came to Professor Freud at the beginning of 1910, my emotional state was already much improved.... Actually Freud never saw me in a state of really deep depression."[15] Of course, their views of the matter were relative. Moreover, it is often the understandable strategy of former mental patients to portray their symptoms with cosmetic retouching.

Freud's official biography paraphrases the analyst's letter to his colleague Ferenczi of 10 February 1910 to the effect that his Russian patient "from the age of six had suffered from obsessive blasphemies against the Almighty, and he initiated the first hour of treatment with the offer to have rectal intercourse with Freud and then to defecate on his head!"[16] This garbled account has done a fair amount of mischief.[17] Recently, the actual text of Freud's letter has been published, revealing that only upon the conclusion of the first session did Pankeev "confess" (apparently with prompting) his secret anxiety and antagonism toward Freud: "A rich young Russian whom I have taken on because of compulsive falling in love, confessed to me, after the first session, the following transference: Jewish swindler, he would like to use me from behind and shit on my head."[18] In fact, Freud's report of Pankeev's "transference" is grammatically ambiguous. Had Pankeev merely elaborated (metaphorically, of course) what he anticipated from this "swindler"? Or did Freud, by tacitly shifting the antecedent of "he," wish to convey Pankeev's hostile expressions toward himself? If the latter, the patient's outburst was in all likelihood commonplace obscenity, a defensive verbal aggression, not an expression of perverse wishes, and certainly not an "offer." This is confirmed in Pankeev's last interviews, where he recalls: "During my childhood, I had blasphemous thoughts, insulted God, and so on. And with Freud, it was the same thing. I thought, Freud is a scoundrel— that's the sort of thing that came into my mind. And I expressed that. He put up with it stoically."[19] Nevertheless, Pankeev felt at the outset that he had met "a great personality" in Freud, who proved to be a strong father figure and a wise healer.[20] In 1914, with war looming on the horizon, they seemed to part with mutual affection.

Certain factors of rapport underlie Freud's protracted analysis of Pankeev. These include painting, the Hispanic theme, and of course the Odessa connection. Pankeev as a child had expert instruction in drawing and painting, and excelled at conventional landscapes. After his father's death in 1908, he devoted himself to this art and felt that he had found his own style. That fall, paintings he exhibited were praised by the Union of South Russian Artists, though of course the establishment's opinion of a wealthy amateur is suspect.[21] He had always admired Leonardo da Vinci's portrait of a dark-haired woman, "La Belle Ferronnière," in which he now found a resemblance to Therese. This contributed to the sublimation of his love for her, and her association with a remote era and setting.[22] Her grandmother was a Spanish singer, and this romantic "Southern" background fused with Therese's Turkish masquerade persona. Pankeev's Polish Aunt Aleksandra (who shared his mother's name) had also been a professional singer. She had spent several seasons with the Madrid Opera, enchanted her young nephew with stories of Spain, and was fixed in his memory as Rosina, heroine of *The Barber of Seville.*[23] Freud—who in his youth had invented an elaborate Spanish cult with his friend Silberstein—saw the Oedipus complex veiled in Pankeev's fantasy of Spain (Therese = aunt and mother, both named Aleksandra). The exotic national complexity may be compared with Freud's own case: the essential *Vaterlandslosigkeit* of East European Jewry, his lost Russian fatherland (now confronting him in the person of his patient), and his still vigorous mother, who remained (in the eyes of her grandson Martin Freud) "a typical Polish Jewess, with all the shortcomings which that implies ... certainly not what we would call a 'lady'."[24] The obscurely "Polish" and "Spanish" elements in Pankeev's story might conceal Jewish connections. In Odessa, after all, this was likely enough.

Freud's own personal interest in the visual arts blossomed just at this time in his well-known studies *Leonardo da Vinci and a Memory of His Childhood* and "The Moses of Michelangelo." The first had been in gestation for twelve years or more, and perhaps borrowed some material from a patient seen in 1909, but received its major impetus from Dmitry Merezhkovsky's popular Russian novel *The Romance of Leonardo da Vinci,* published in 1902. Freud had read the German translation, which appeared in 1903, no later than 1907, when he listed it as one of his favorite books.[25] Merezhkovsky was indeed one of Freud's favorite authors, and Freud discussed with Pankeev, in an analytic session, another historical novel, *Peter and Alexis,* published in 1905 and translated the same year. Here, Merezhkovsky stressed the central emotional ambivalence between generations, resolved in the murder of the son.[26] The subject is reminiscent of Dostoevsky, whose foremost promoter in the West was

Merezhkovsky, coeditor of the complete works acquired by Freud in 1910 and author of numerous critical studies translated into German. (The broader impact of Dostoevsky on Freud's world is considered in the following chapter.)

Freud's "Moses of Michelangelo," a detective work that follows minor clues, pays tribute to an inspiration decades earlier by the revolutionary art critic Ivan Lermolieff, who in 1874 began to expose forged paintings in great European galleries by close attention to seemingly insignificant features such as fingernails and earlobes. His method, Freud suggests, anticipated psychoanalysis, "divining secret things ... from the rubbish-heap, as it were, of our observations."[27] Freud had been "greatly interested" to learn that the Russian pseudonym Lermolieff (apparently suggested by Lermontov, the great poet) anagramatically concealed the identity of Giovanni Morelli (1816-91), an Italian physician. Freud no doubt was charmed not only by the Conan Doyle approach to art history, but also the mystifying double identity and the romantic Russian pseudonym. Morelli had even claimed a nonexistent Russian birthplace, Gorlaw, derived from Gorli—his small estate in the Brianza.[28] Freud's critical delight in art complemented the experience of his talented Russian patient, Pankeev. Artistic creativity may lead to erotic sublimation or catharsis for the audience, and implies a double identity for the artist—an ambivalent posture on either side and thus a model of the psychoanalytic situation.

Freud's boyhood preoccupation with Spain, often whimsically comical, gave way to (and perhaps always concealed) historical interest in the assimilation and power of the Sephardim, the era of the Spanish Inquisition, the expulsion of Jews from Spain, and their resettlement throughout Europe. Freud's own family traced its history only as far as Cologne in the late Middle Ages. Therefore, Spain might well have been another homeland along the way back to Egypt. Once, Theodor Reik told Freud a joke about two Spanish nobles in Vienna who introduce themselves at the Spanish Embassy in perfect Yiddish, imagining that it is German. It turns out that they were duped by a Polish Jew on the train from Madrid. Freud insisted the hidden point was that the Spanish noblemen themselves could have been Jewish.[29] Ill-concealed in this traditional humor, needless to say, was the tragic reality. Late in life, Pankeev admitted that Therese had possibly known or suspected that her Spanish grandmother was Jewish, and perhaps this had driven her to commit suicide in 1938.[30] But there is no evidence that the Spanish or Jewish background of Therese played a role in Pankeev's psychoanalytic sessions with Freud.

During the elder Pankeev's years of work with the Constitutional Democrat Party in Odessa, many of his close political associates were of course Jewish.[31] Sergei Pankeev recalls not a trace of anti-Semitism in his father, who was in fact an active defender of the Jewish cause.[32] The Pankeev family lawyers and doctors were Jews.[33] And the Odessa physician who introduced Sergei Pankeev to psychoanalysis and personally conducted him to Freud, Dr. Leonid Drosnés, was a baptized Russian Orthodox, "but his Jewish ancestors had come from Spain."[34] When he traveled with Pankeev to Lisbon and Madrid during Freud's summer vacation in 1910, he became nervous and cut the trip short. Pankeev speculates in his memoirs that unconsciously Drosnés fled the spectre of the Inquisition.[35] Drosnés, as the companion and attending physician of Pankeev, had occasion to consult Freud, and for most of 1911 he was a member of the Vienna Society, until he moved to St. Petersburg to practice psychoanalysis.[36] Before leaving Vienna, Drosnés called on Freud on 2 May 1911 to announce that in collaboration with Osipov and Vyrubov he had founded the Russian Psychoanalytic Society.[37] We believe that Freud probably learned of the Drosnés family history and must have thought it ironically fitting that the Wolf-Man was referred to him by a converted Spanish Jew from Odessa. It was a small world, after all, and the Inquisition still loomed on everyone's horizon.

The Odessa connection that linked Freud and the Wolf-Man was further strengthened by the latter's mother, who traveled to be near her son and to consult his therapist, as she had done before in Munich, Frankfurt, and Berlin. At the end of May 1910, Freud awaited her first visit.[38] This produced a certain symmetry because just a few blocks away lived Freud's own mother (raised in Odessa), whom he regularly visited each week.

Incidentally, by this time Freud regarded Pankeev as "trustworthy." No doubt a contributing factor to the patient's stability was his regular patronage of an exclusive brothel, staffed by women from good families leading double lives, a taste he had acquired in Paris and Odessa.[39] This should be kept in mind lest we pity the poor neurotic invalid too much during his trying months of analysis and separation from Therese. To his credit, he had friends send him the required law books and kept up his work to prepare for readmission.

Pankeev says in his memoirs that Dr. Drosnés, when they first met, was probably the only person in Odessa who knew of Freud's existence and of his practice of psychoanalysis.[40] Clearly, Drosnés remained unaware of Freud's family ties with the city. But oddly enough, somebody else in Odessa who had known of Freud was Pankeev's own family doctor, Moshe Wulff (1878-1971), who had treated his late father, his mother, and Sergei himself.[41] Sometime before 1908, Dr. Wulff had gone to Berlin and met Freud's dedicated follower Karl Abraham. On 10 November 1909, Abraham wrote Freud that the Russian doctor Wulff, "hard-working and reliable," had gone back to settle in Odessa, having lost his first job in Berlin in just a few weeks because of his interest in psychoanalysis. Perhaps, he suggested, Freud might send Wulff some patients.[42] By August 1911, Wulff had moved to Vienna and had become (just half a year after Drosnés) a member of the Psychoanalytic Society.[43] Thus, two Odessa psychiatrists who had treated Pankeev and knew his family well were close colleagues of Freud, in regular collaboration, and available for consultation through the first two years of Pankeev's first analysis, down to the summer of 1912.[44] Furthermore, on 21 March 1912, Freud wrote to Jung: "In Russia (Odessa) there seems to be a local epidemic of PsA."[45] By then, Drosnés had moved on to Petersburg, and Wulff to Moscow, so we do not know anything specific about the Freudian "epidemic" in Odessa. But we can say for sure that Jung did not give a damn about psychoanalysis in Odessa, nor Freud's medical quip about it. This was strictly Freud's private merriment, an in-group joke for the *Ostjude*: "Look what my therapy has wrought in the motherland—a regular epidemic!" In short, Freud's jest puts the Russian material—the Wolf-Man from Odessa—in a less exotic light.

The case of Sergei Pankeev was written up by Freud for publication during the first winter of World War I (1914-15), after Pankeev's return to Odessa, and was published in 1918 as "From the History of an Infantile Neurosis". Four years of analysis (perhaps some 700 hours) are dealt with in 130 pages. Freud's objective here was almost exclusively to excavate "the deepest strata" of his patient's psyche.[46] This meant primarily a focus on childhood neurosis and, secondarily, speculation about the "archaic constitution" and national character that were "predisposed to an obsessional neurosis" of this type.[47] At the core of Freud's analysis is a dream that occurred just before Pankeev's fourth birthday, on 23 December 1890. It came to light very early in the treatment and was repeatedly discussed, down to the last days. The patient recalled lying in his bed, its foot toward the window, which opened by itself upon a winter scene in which six or seven white wolves (more like sheep-dogs, but with bushy foxlike tails) sat motionless but alert in an old walnut tree, looking at him. The boy screamed in terror, afraid of being eaten, and awoke. His old nanny hurried to him, and at last convinced him it had only been a dream. It was from this dream, of course, that Pankeev acquired his nickname in Freud's circle—the Wolf-Man (*der Wolfsmann*).

Freud's theory (with important reservations) was that the dream represented a primal scene of the boy's parents, copulating *a tergo more ferarum*, witnessed by the patient when he was eighteen months old.[48] Essential features of the dream symbolism concealed the erotic event. The motionless posture of the wolves encoded violent activity. Their frightening fixed gaze at him reflected the child's terrified stare at them. Winter meant summer, when the young parents enjoyed a siesta half undressed (white clothing), oblivious to the sick child resting in their room. The observed position for coitus proved to be the Wolf-Man's own preference and (through his youth) his obsession, so that housemaids seen on hands and knees were instantly pursued by him. This trait led Freud to attribute a "completely unbridled instinctual life" to his patient, contrasting sharply with Pankeev's "agreeable and affable personality, his acute intelligence and his nice-mindedness."[49] The preference for intercourse from the rear "may, after all, be regarded as phylogenetically the older form," Freud observed.[50] The fact that it was so thinly veiled by civilized decorum made Freud conclude that ambivalence was a dominant trait in his patient, manifest also in sadomasochism, intellectual hostility toward God and religion (with a veneer of piety), and the capacity for "maintaining simultaneously the most various and contradictory libidinal cathexes."[51] This "extraordinary propensity to ambivalence" was the dominant feature of a constitution that, Freud concluded, "deserves the name of archaic."[52]

Careless readers generally regard Freud as doctrinaire, but his rhetoric is hedged with classic *refutatio* (anticipation of criticism), a retreat into the hypothetical mood, however brief, which then frees him to advance his case boldly. The Wolf-Man's psychic being is repeatedly described as "prehistoric" or "archaic," thus requiring the analyst to embark upon an archaeological quest, to behave "as 'timelessly' as the unconscious itself."[53] But Freud recognizes that the traumatic force of "primal scenes" (such as observing parental intercourse, being seduced in childhood, or threatened with castration), although "unquestionably a phylogenetic heritage," may also "just as easily be imposed by personal experience."[54] Like Jung, Freud thought that psychoanalysis must redirect the science of mythology, and in turn learn from it.[55] In the study of the Wolf-Man, Freud states his full agreement with Jung "in recognizing the existence of a phylogenetic heritage." But he thought it a methodological error to accept a phylogenetic explanation for any phenomenon before the ontogenetic possibilities of infantile prehistory had been exhausted. Nevertheless, with that disclaimer made, Freud was strongly inclined to emphasize the (Russian) "ancestral prehistory" of the Wolf-Man's case.[56]

At the very outset of Pankeev's analysis on 2 February 1910, Freud had expressed his sympathy with Jung's study of mythic symbols and revealed that he too was searching in that direction, "namely, *archaic regression*, which I hope to master through mythology and the *development of language*."[57] Freud's professional interest in myth (for example, the prehistoric mythology of the "Semitic East," and the projective "endopsychic" myths of individuals) went back to the earliest conception of psychoanalysis.[58] Now, Jung's obsessive study of myth stimulated Freud to write *Totem and Taboo*, which first appeared anonymously in *Imago* in 1912-13 under the title "Some Points of Agreement between the Mental Lives of Savages and Neurotics." The first two essays are entitled "The Horror of Incest" and "Taboo and Emotional Ambivalence," and the last: "The Infantile Recurrence of Totemism." The pattern and content of this study are closely intertwined with the Wolf-Man's case history. The objective of *Totem and Taboo*, expressed in Freud's preface, was to apply psychoanalysis to "unexplained problems of national psychology (*Völkerpsychologie*)."[59]

When the first segment of *Totem and Taboo* was in press, Freud was struck by Sabina Spielrein's paper on the destruction instinct (elaborately buttressed with mythic material), but he rejected her conclusion, for the time being, because he thought that Spielrein herself seemed "abnormally ambivalent."[60] Ambivalence to a degree abnormal in the West was the dominant problem of the Russian national psyche. Such was the opinion that Freud was soon to form of Dostoevsky, an opinion first based on analysis of Pankeev, on encounters with Spielrein, and no doubt on "archaic" patterns in Freud's own psyche. Freud indeed anticipated that critics would charge him with advancing his own fantasies as Pankeev's. He could only insist that one must have the actual experience of psychoanalysis in order to grasp that the neurotic patient alone possessed the ingenuity to present primal scenes (whether archaic or infantile in origin) that fulfill all the requirements of analysis.[61] Nevertheless, a leading psychoanalyst and historian of the movement has recently emphasized the possibility that "through the Wolf Man, Freud was in quest of his own primal scene."[62] We concur, and suggest that the following passage from the case history leads directly back to the analyst's own phantasy and self-analysis:

> As often as I have been able by means of analysis to bring out a scene of this sort, [the Wolf-Man's primal scene,] it has shown the same peculiarity which startled us with our present patient too: it has related to *coitus a tergo*, which alone offers the spectator a possibility of inspecting the genitals. There is surely no need any longer to doubt that what we are dealing with is only a phantasy, which is invariably aroused, perhaps, by an observation of the sexual intercourse of animals.[63]

We have suggested above that Freud's own private phantasy of *coitus a tergo* with a Czech housemaid is expressed in his analysis of a dream about the Prague Castle, attributed to an anonymous patient whose wife could not be approached for sex in that "shocking" position. No further history of that case is reported. This "Czech material" would necessarily be linked to Freud's early childhood in Moravia, the "lost dream" landscape of his youth, and the aged Czech Catholic nanny who was his "first instructor in sexual matters." The concept of serial "first loves" with the servant class, which figures so importantly in the case of the Wolf-Man, is implied in Freud's analysis of the Prague Castle dream. This dream, perhaps omitted from the first edition of *Die Traumdeutung* out of discretion, was included in the second edition, published in 1909, shortly before Pankeev's analysis commenced. We suggest that *coitus a tergo more ferarum* was an "archaic" element of Freud's own phantasy life, indeed part of the quest for his own primal scene, a distinctly "Slavic" part, which he shared with the Wolf-Man. In this way it became a distinctive erotic feature of Freud's Russia.

In the last section of *Totem and Taboo*, on "Infantile Recurrence to Totemism," Freud pays a nice compliment to Moshe Wulff, by then returned to Odessa, who in 1912 had published a short contribution on a dog phobia in a four-year-old boy.[64] At the sight of a dog in the street, the boy would weep and promise the dog to be good (specifically: not to masturbate). Thus, he had displaced his fear of his father onto dogs, which became in effect a totemic animal.[65] It is interesting that Freud received this material, overlapping with the Wolf-Man's wolf/dog totem, from his Odessa colleague. The Russian material was reinforced by a Russian Jewish consultant, who as former physician to the Pankeev family no doubt proved useful to Freud (as he later would for Dr. Ruth Mack Brunswick when she treated the Wolf-Man in 1927). Freud's personal friendship with Wulff and high regard for him are evident in "On the History of the Psychoanalytic Movement," where he is the only trained analyst recognized in Russia.

Apropos of the further clustering of "Russian material" around the Wolf-Man, it is of some interest that an anonymous woman from Moscow was referred to Freud for treatment in August 1909 by Dr. Nikolai Nikolaevich Bazhenov (1857-1923), chief of the Preobrazhénskaia Psychiatric Hospital.[66] The fact that Bazhenov respected Freud early on was undoubtedly conveyed to the medical community in Vienna, to Drosnés and Wulff, to Pankeev, and to Pankeev's mother, thus enhancing Freud's authority. In Russia, as it has been suggested, psychoanalysis greatly rose in stature during the years before the war. Its general acceptance is reflected in the fact that from May to June 1914 one of Russia's eminent young philosophers, Ivan Il'in, came to Freud at the age of thirty-one for treatment of depression.[67] In short, the Wolf-Man did not come to Freud as some "half-Asiatic" from an altogether outlandish and unknown race of beings. Freud's characterization of Pankeev's psyche as "archaic" (a "timeless" and "phylogenetic" heritage) may be seen after all as a purely metaphoric descent into the world of myth, to meet the

challenge of Jung. Like *Totem and Taboo*, the simultaneous study of
the Wolf-Man strove in part to apply psychoanalysis to problems of
"national psychology." Whatever Russian material could be
discovered in Pankeev was therefore vividly psychodramatized. If the
material of Freud's own psyche was drawn and projected into the
process, it is hardly surprising, not only because psychoanalysis
required it, but also because Russia was part of the myth and reality of
his own family background and loomed large on the Viennese horizon.

The Russian material presented by Pankeev, colored as it was by
Freud's archaizing quest for totem, taboo, and his own primal scene,
did not remain "timeless" in the face of history. The patient withdrew
to the Russian hinterlands, war broke out, and Freud's sons were
stationed on the eastern front, frequently under fire. News of their
death, as Freud later wrote, was expected daily.[68] In July 1915, his
eldest son was grazed in the arm by one bullet, and another went
through his cap.[69] As this age of imminent death unfolded, Freud
drafted the Wolf-Man's case history. His telltale military imagery
reminds us of the circumstances. Only by submitting to the
timelessness of the unconscious can the physician hope to vanquish it
in the end. The patient remains long unassailably entrenched behind an
attitude of obliging apathy (or "respectful indifference"). His
unimpeachable intelligence is, so to speak, cut off from the instinctual
forces that governed his behavior. The distance to be covered is
immaterial: All depends on the resistance, just as an enemy army
needs months to cross a stretch of country traversed by an express
train in a few hours during peace time and which just recently was
covered by the defending army in a few days.[70] Freud extended this
Russian military metaphor in his study "The Psychogenesis of a Case
of Homosexuality in a Woman":

> The resistance has withdrawn to a certain limit, beyond which it then
> proves to be unconquerable. The resistance very often pursues similar
> tactics—Russian tactics, as they might be called—in cases of obsessional
> neurosis.... One begins to wonder how it is that such marked progress in
> analytic understanding can be unaccompanied by even the slightest change
> in the patient's compulsions and inhibitions, until at last one perceives that
> everything accomplished had been admitted only under the mental
> reservation of doubt, and behind this protective barrier the neurosis may
> feel secure.[71]

These Russian tactics (the tactics of retreat to the hinterlands) Freud clearly associated with the Wolf-Man, his most famous case of obsessional neurosis, who by this time (1920) had returned to Vienna and was again in therapy with Freud.

In Odessa, Pankeev had married Therese and completed his law studies, which had not been completely neglected during his first psychoanalysis with Freud. Eventually he was to earn a doctorate in jurisprudence. After the February Revolution of 1917 he was immediately accepted into his late father's Cadet (Constitutional Democratic) Party and appointed to the executive committee. There were weekly social gatherings, with music and dancing. No doubt Pankeev made significant financial contributions to the Kerensky government. He also mustered brief enthusiasm for lecturing on aspects of the economy. His first talk before a large elite audience was very well received, but thereafter his assignment to give public lectures in the provinces was apathetically carried out.[72] In retrospect, he believed it had been suicidal to press for victory in the war "as everything collapses around you."[73] After the Bolshevik Revolution in October, he retreated to Odessa. Theresa emigrated in September 1918, and Pankeev joined her the following spring in Vienna. Freud now presented him with a signed copy of his case history.[74] Although Pankeev (as he later recalled) felt thoroughly satisfied with his mental health and had no thought of further treatment, Freud convinced him "that there was still a small residue of unanalyzed material," which they agreed to look into the next fall. Pankeev and Therese spent the summer of 1919 on the Boden See near the village of Lindau.[75]

Although for the moment the family fortune remained secure with his mother in Odessa, Pankeev reappeared in Vienna ostensibly without any financial resources. Freud gave him a few English pounds and later took up collections from colleagues to support his Russian patient with annual donations every spring from 1920 to 1926. Meanwhile, the Wolf-Man's second analysis began in November 1919 and lasted four months, until February 1920.[76] In Pankeev's memoirs, the duration of this treatment is about twice as long, from September 1919 to Easter 1920.[77] Apart from the patient's constipation (an "hysterical" complaint that had not recurred since 1914), the content of this analysis is unknown.[78] A major emotional crisis, however, was imposed by Russian political events. On 7 February 1920, Odessa fell to the Red Army, and soon the Pankeev property was confiscated by the Bolsheviks. The Wolf-Man forever blamed Freud for dissuading him from returning to Odessa in time to save his fortune. "It's much more important for you to stay and that we treat the residual matters," Pankeev recalls Freud telling him.[79] This was an irrational grudge to nurse, first because Pankeev's mother, uncles, and lawyers in Odessa were capable of doing whatever was possible, and second because a friend managed to bring out the family jewels when he left Russia in 1922. The story of the jewels, as variously told by Pankeev, is the stuff of melodrama. At first they were assumed to be worth "thousands of dollars," and he concealed their existence from Freud for fear his charity payments would be cut off! Later (as he told Dr. Ruth Mack Brunswick in 1927) they proved to be of little value, but still he kept the secret.[80] Finally, in an interview toward the end of his life, he insisted that the jewels had not been kept secret, and that their sale had enabled him to buy a house![81] In short, wherever the truth may lie, the economy of Freud's relationship with the Wolf-Man had been forever altered by the Russian Revolution.

During the second analysis of the Wolf-Man, Freud's favorite married daughter, Sophie, suddenly died in an influenza epidemic. It seemed that the war's long threat of death had belatedly struck: "For years I was prepared for the loss of our sons, now it is our daughter."[82] At this very time (February 1920), Freud was revising the manuscript of *Beyond the Pleasure Principle*, in which he finally accepts the theory of a "death instinct" first advanced by Sabina Spielrein in her treatise on "Die Destruktion als Ursache des Werdens."[83] One recalls the private moment thirty-five years earlier, when Freud metaphorically applied to his own life Bakunin's romantic axiom: "Destruction is also a creative passion," a distinctively Russian contribution to world history. In Freud's experience it was unquestionably the war with Russia that made this Russian theory (*pace Feuerbach*) plausible. Now confronted with the Russian Revolution, and questioned by Pankeev about the meaning of mass slaughter in modern times, Freud (in 1919) could only reply that "we have 'a wrong attitude' toward death." It was a stoic, evasive view that exasperated his Russian patient.[84] As for the great political events of the world following the war, "Freud took a wait-and-see position," the Wolf-Man recalls.[85] Concerning the Russian political condition in

1920, according to Pankeev, "Freud knew absolutely nothing."[86] About the Russian psyche in general, and the Wolf-Man in particular, Freud also had much to learn. But the deficiencies in his art were not for lack of Russian material. In 1920 he could only take a wait-and-see position, like everyone else.

The Wolf-Man's third and last psychoanalysis to concern us here began in October 1926 and lasted five months, until February 1927. It was conducted by Dr. Ruth Mack Brunswick under Freud's supervision. Brunswick was an American student of Freud's, also his analysand. Upon the conclusion of Pankeev's treatment by Brunswick, she published a valuable supplement to Freud's case history. Here we are given at last some insight into the contemporary symptomatology ("a hypochondriacal *idée fixe*"), partially linked with the ambivalent personality theorized by Freud. The immediate physical problem was nothing but a recurrent pimple on the Wolf-Man's nose, which appeared in November 1923 shortly after his mother arrived from Russia with a black wart on her nose. Earlier that year, Pankeev had also been shocked by the weak appearance of Freud just after his first operation for cancer of the palate on 20 April 1923.[87] There followed a long series of visits by Pankeev to dermatologists (one of whom disarmed his hostility by suddenly dying) as well as to dentists (one of whom pulled the wrong tooth, while another was a Dr. Wolf). Appropriately enough, the symbolic castrations (deterioration of nose and teeth) recurred around Easter, when Pankeev went to pick up his annual dole from Freud.[88]

By the time Pankeev was referred by Freud to Brunswick in October 1926, the patient was carrying a pocket mirror in order to examine and obsessively repowder his nose on the street, in the doctor's waiting room, and wherever he went.[89] Brunswick's report includes a telling observation by Moshe Wulff, who had been the Pankeevs' family doctor prior to the Wolf-Man's first analysis. (Wulff, having served for several years as president of the Russian Psychoanalytic Society, emigrated to the West in October 1927 in anticipation of the Society's imminent suppression and just in time to be consulted for Brunswick's case history.)[90] The Wolf-Man, declared Wulff, "no longer plays the mother, he *is* the mother, down to the least detail."[91] Pankeev's wounded vanity seemed to activate the latent homosexuality noted by Freud as a factor in the patient's dominant ambivalence. Freud's own repeated bouts of oral surgery for cancer (clearly signaling the mortality of the healing father-figure) were symbolically identified by the Wolf-Man with his own dental agonies and with surgery performed on his nose, to which he learned to submit with masochistic ecstasy![92]

Brunswick relentlessly undermined her patient's identity as "favorite son" of Freud, pointing out that he had never been invited to visit him socially.[93] The patient himself clearly saw the advantage of being in analysis with a woman, because "he thus avoided the homosexual transference."[94] The analysis advanced from the patient's "odd, indulgent little laugh" whenever Freud's name was mentioned, to open rage against Freud, to the recollection that in Odessa his father was once called a "dirty Jew" (probably because of his politics and political associates), and at last to Pankeev's open death wish against Freud.[95] The dream of wolves recurred, which the analyst saw as the patient's conviction that "the wolves—all the fathers, or doctors!—are trying to get at him to destroy him."[96]

The report of his dentist's sudden death (read to him by Brunswick from a newspaper) made him jump up and shout, "clenching his fists and raising his arms with a truly Russian air of melodrama: 'My God, now I can't kill him any more!'"[97] Having been denied this target of wrath, Pankeev threatened to shoot Freud—and Brunswick too! And "somehow these threats sounded less empty than those which one is accustomed to hear."[98] One recalls Freud's warning to Jung that love is the material of psychoanalysis, hence "little laboratory explosions" are only to be expected. By 1927 it was apparent that hate, destruction, and death were also elements of human chemistry, sufficiently volatile even in the analytic lab.

Brunswick's reference to Pankeev's "truly Russian air of melodrama" (clenched fists raised) may serve to remind us that Freud at times also encountered in the Wolf-Man traits of character sufficiently foreign to make empathy difficult for him. But such aspects of Russian resistance are almost never specified in Freud's case history. Only at one point, where Pankeev reduces the erotically frightening image of *Wespe* (wasp) to *Espe* (aspen tree—a gentle part of the landscape, without wolves! Also. S.P. = Sergei Pankeev), does Freud remark that "like so many other people, he used his difficulties with a foreign language as a screen for symptomatic acts."[99] For

Freud, the *Espe* was nothing but noise, the meaningless phonological by-product of mutilating *Wespe*. Only the symbolic mutilation was important. He saw nothing specifically Russian in Pankeev's German slips, though clearly such psycholinguistic material invites bilingual analysis.[100] Without knowledge of Russian, this approach to the Russian material was of course closed to Freud.

Brunswick touches upon a more imposing role of Russian language in Pankeev's analysis: "I was never able to understand a single word of the Russian phrases which he occasionally interjected into his German sentences." When her patient reported a dream in which a woman masterfully drives a sleigh "declaiming verse in excellent Russian," both dreamer and therapist recognized the Russian verbal artistry as "the height of mockery" directed against a would-be analyst ignorant of Russian. Pankeev's consciously interjected Russian phrases had of course the same effect. They were an unassailable defense, a challenge to the analytic process—in a word, Russian tactics! It seems unlikely that Freud was spared this humiliation altogether.

Freud introduces the Wolf-Man as a person "of unimpeachable intelligence," and notes that his acuteness had been precociously capable of "searching out with remorseless severity the weak points of holy writ." This was a trait particularly endearing to Freud, as we shall demonstrate in his handling of Dostoevsky. Acuteness at the expense of religion may often be expressed in humor. The young Pankeev, for example, had determined that "since Christ had made wine *out of* nothing, he could also have made food *into* nothing, and in this way have avoided defecating."[101] When Brunswick naively expressed her surprise that a person of his "violent nature ... had never indulged excessively in masturbation," Pankeev replied: "Oh no, of course I only masturbated on the high holidays."[102]

When Pankeev had parted with Freud in 1914, Serbian belligerence dominated the news. Apropos, Pankeev asserted that it was a mistake to condemn a whole nation, "ascribing certain bad qualities to one and all." Anticipating war, Freud disagreed, and told his patient that "there are indeed nations in which certain bad qualities are more marked than in others"—as though reserving judgment about the Wolf-Man and the Russians.[103] But counterbalancing this view is Freud's genuinely good-humored reflection of late 1925: "Before the war, the Russians came. I loved the Russians!" That, of course, was before Pankeev threatened to shoot him. Brunswick regarded Pankeev as essentially healthy again, after therapy. She saw in him the same "keen, scrupulous, and attractive personality" that she had discerned in Freud's case study.[104] Since 1920 he had been employed by an insurance agency, a job he was to hold for thirty years. Brunswick marveled at his accommodation to loss of fortune, and attributed his resilience to his nationality: "Those who have come in contact with Russian refugees have been amazed at the rapidity of their adjustment. No one, seeing them in their new life, could guess how different the old had been."[105]

One last aspect of the Wolf-Man to be considered here is his influence on Freud's view of Dostoevsky. Freud had a strong personal incentive to begin reading Dostoevsky in 1885 with his Russian friends in Paris. Shortly thereafter, one of Freud's favorite literary critics, Georg Brandes, published a brilliant essay on Dostoevsky (conceived in correspondence with Nietzsche in 1889). It appeared in a collection of his essays, *Menschen und Werke,* published in 1894.[106] Not until 1906 did the great Germanic vogue of Dostoevsky get under way, with the publication of his works in twenty-two volumes by R. Piper & Co. of Munich. Some of the major fictions (*House of the Dead, Crime and Punishment, The Possessed, The Brothers Karamazov,* and others) had appeared in separate German and French editions during the 1880s, but were not widely known or available by 1900. Stefan Zweig, whose long essay on Dostoevsky was a major stimulus to Freud's thinking in 1920, recalled that during his university days at Berlin in 1902 he was not aware of *The Brothers Karamazov* in print, but learned of it by hearsay and borrowed a friend's manuscript copy.[107] In Vienna, by 1904, Hanns Sachs was converted by "my boundless admiration of Dostoevsky" from a philologist to an epileptologist, psychopathologist, and disciple of Freud.[108] In the fall of 1906, Adolf Häutler lectured at the Vienna Psychoanalytic Society on *The Possessed*, Dostoevsky's novel of terrorist psychology. Although this work comprises volumes 5 and 6 of the Munich edition, it had been issued first in order to create a sensation following the 1905 Revolution.[109] Other sessions on Dostoevsky were to follow in recorded Society meetings. Meanwhile, let it be recalled, early in 1910 the Wolf-Man's analysis had commenced, and at precisely that moment (February 1910) the Russophile Max Eitingon presented Freud with the complete Munich edition of Dostoevsky, with a few of the volumes still to appear on subscription.[110]

The first, oblique evidence that Freud read Dostoevsky comes from the Wolf-Man's *Memoirs* (1938) and his short *Recollections of Sigmund Freud*. Pankeev recalls that once, in an analytic session, Freud "made a psychoanalytic interpretation of a dream of Raskolnikov's" (the hero of *Crime and Punishment*).[111] Pankeev's brief account of "Dostoevsky's weakness as a political thinker" is drawn directly from Freud's essay, "Dostoevsky and Parricide" (the subject of a later chapter, below), and has no evident bearing on the dreams of Raskolnikov. However, a passage in Freud's case history of the Wolf-Man deals with the patient's ambivalent attitude toward the beating of horses: sometimes he had enjoyed doing it, but he screamed when he witnessed it. Here too he mentions the boy's attraction to butterflies and sudden fear of them, his fear of beetles and caterpillars and pleasure in torturing and killing them. These ambivalent peculiarities invite comparison with Raskolnikov, and with Dostoevsky himself in the ostensibly autobiographical "Peasant Marie."[112] The central "animal phobia" of the Wolf-Man, which "changed into an obsessional neurosis with religious content" and strong bisexual ambivalence (in Freud's analysis) closely parallels the central episode in "Peasant Marie" wherein the boy hero hysterically flees from a hallucinated cry of "Wolf!" to the comforting caresses of a "motherly" peasant ploughman. One senses that this famous story could be the paradigm of the Wolf-Man's analysis.

Pankeev tells us that Freud was "enthusiastic about Dostoevsky" because of the great novelist's understanding of the unconscious and his exploration of the Oedipal complex and parricide in *The Brothers Karamazov*.[113] However, anyone could draw this conclusion from Freud's essay "Dostojewski und die Vatertötung" (Dostoevsky and Parricide), which was published in 1928, so these comments do not necessarily take us back to the prewar analysis. Pankeev's own first reading of Dostoevsky (also Turgenev, Tolstoy, Pushkin, and above all Lermontov) dated from 1899, when he was thirteen.[114] It was a standing joke in his family that his maternal grandfather was like old Karamazov because he disinherited one of his four sons for winning a bride he had wanted for himself.[115] One imagines that this legend must have come out in Freud's first analysis and so provided an incentive to read or reread *The Brothers Karamazov*. Coincidentally, the Wolf-Man's secondary Oedipal object was a nanny named Grusha (also the generic word for "pear," recalled as a particularly luscious variety), evocative of Grushenka, Oedipal object of the Karamazovs.[116]

In his short reminiscence of Freud, Pankeev notes the analyst's high praise for Merezhkovsky's historical novel *Peter and Alexis* about the emotional ambivalence between tsar and tsarevich, resolved in murder of the son. This historical theme figures in Ruth Mack Brunswick's case study.[117] Of course, as we have already pointed out, Freud's high regard for Merezhkovsky in the years of the first analysis is made apparent in his essay on Leonardo, based directly on Merezhkovsky's biographical fiction. It should also again be recalled that Merezhkovsky was coeditor of the great Munich edition of Dostoevsky's works, acquired by Freud in 1910, and provided prefaces to four of the volumes, including *The Brothers Karamazov*. Finally, Merezhkovsky's authority as biographer of Dostoevsky had been firmly established by his study, *Tolstoy and Dostoevsky*. In this book, one of the most important in establishing Dostoevsky's reputation in the West, it can be said that ambivalence predominates as a Russian national trait. These issues will be taken up again in the following chapter, which concerns the belated but timely vogue of Dostoevsky in the world of Freud.

Some of the central ideas of "Dostoevsky and Parricide" were first outlined by Freud in his letter to Stefan Zweig of 19 October 1920, written in response to Zweig's gift copy of *Drei Meister* (essays on Balzac, Dickens, and Dostoevsky). This letter, which will be examined more carefully in connection with the essay it foreshadows, has been quoted above in an epigraph to the present chapter to suggest Freud's general view of the "Russian material." There he cites his published case history of "a typical Russian" (the Wolf-Man), specifically with reference to Dostoevsky. Precisely when he first developed and articulated these thoughts on Dostoevsky we cannot say. But it is evident that his Russian stereotypes were reshaped during his analytic sessions with Pankeev, whose character was systematically cross-referenced with what Freud knew about Dostoevsky. It is therefore important to keep in mind that the letter to Stefan Zweig of 1920 was written less than a year after the Wolf-Man's second analysis, when the Russian patient in effect challenged the authority of Freud's healing art and began to show signs of "interminable resistance" (a phrase coined by Ruth Mack Brunswick in 1928), hence "analysis interminable" (as Freud acknowledged in 1938).[118]

Further anticipating our discussion of "Dostoevsky and Parricide," it seems more than coincidence that, in the very month (May of 1926) when he began to draft his Dostoevsky article, Freud wrote to Pankeev asking him to verify the "correctness" of certain details in the wolf dream, a dream they had spent four years analyzing together.[119] Thirty years later, Pankeev would suggest that this belated enquiry by Freud had driven him into the paranoid state treated by Brunswick![120] In any event, the peak of his hostility came with his threat to shoot Freud in 1927, while Freud was still writing "Dostoevsky and Parricide." Thus, the complex personal relationship of Freud and the Wolf-Man— transference and classical countertransference—was closely intertwined with the work on "Dostoevsky and Parricide." Toward the end of his letter to Zweig, Freud wrote as follows:

> This strong tendency toward ambivalence [demonstrated a few years ago in my case history of a typical Russian], combined with the childhood trauma, may have partly determined the unusual violence of Dostoevsky's case of hysteria. Even Russians who are not neurotic are also very noticeably ambivalent, as are all the characters in almost all of Dostoevsky's novels. Nearly all the peculiarities of his production, hardly one of which has eluded you, can be traced back to his—for us abnormal, for the Russians fairly common—psychic constitution, or more correctly, sexual constitution, which could be illustrated very well in detail. Above all, everything that is alien and tormenting. He cannot be understood without psychoanalysis—i.e., he isn't in need of it because he illustrates it himself in every character and every sentence.... With you I do not have to fear the misunderstanding that this emphasis on the so-called pathological is intended to belittle or explain away the splendor of Dostoevsky's creative power.[121]

For Freud, the dominant Russian national trait was ambivalence. The Wolf-Man remarked, toward the end of his life, that the word ambivalence was too "harmless," "watered down." He preferred the term love-hate. Dostoevsky, for example, wrote a great deal about love-hate, but "psychoanalysis really has nothing to say about it."[122]

Notes

1 Sigmund Freud, *Gesammelte Werke*, vol. 12, pp. 27-157.

2 S. K. Pankeev, *The Wolf-Man by the Wolf-Man.*

3 Patrick Mahony, *Cries of the Wolf Man*, with extensive bibliography.

4 Sigmund Freud, *Finding Guide.*

5 Magnus Ljunggren, "The psychoanalytic breakthrough in Russia," p. 177.

6 S. K. Pankeev, *The Wolf-Man by the Wolf-Man*, p. 43.

7 Ibid., pp. 46-47.

8 Ibid., p. 64; Karin Obholzer, The Wolf-Man Sixty Years Later, p. 179.

9 S. K. Pankeev, *The Wolf-Man by the Wolf-Man*, pp. 49-59.

10 Ibid., p. 83.

11 Ibid., p. 90.

12 Ibid., pp. 95-96.

13 Ibid., p. 154.

14 Ibid., pp. 58, 68, and 79.

15 Pankeev to Muriel Gardner, 23 October 1970, in S. K. Pankeev, *The Wolf-Man by the Wolf-Man*, p. 89n.

16 Ernest Jones, *The Life and Work of Sigmund Freud*, vol. 2, p. 274.

17 Stanley Fish, "Withholding the missing portion."

18 Jeffrey Moussaieff Masson, Review of *Gespräche mit dem Wolfsmann*, p. 117.

19 Karin Obholzer, *The Wolf-Man Sixty Years Later*, p. 82.

20 S. K. Pankeev, *The Wolf-Man by the Wolf-Man*, p. 137.

21 Ibid., pp. 66-68.

22 Ibid., p. 56.

23 Ibid., pp. 55-56.

24 Josef Fraenkel, ed., *The Jews of Austria*, p. 202.

25   Sigmund Freud, *Standard Edition of the Complete Psychological Works of Sigmund Freud*, vol. 11, pp. 59n-60; Sigmund Freud, *The Letters of Sigmund Freud*, p. 269.

26   S. K. Pankeev, *The Wolf-Man by the Wolf-Man*, p. 146.

27   Sigmund Freud, "The Moses of Michelangelo," in *Standard Edition of the Complete Psychological Works of Sigmund Freud*, vol. 13, p. 222.

28   Giovanni Morelli, *Italian Painters*, p. 19.

29   Theodor Reik, "Freud and Jewish Wit," p. 20; Elliott Oring, *The Jokes of Sigmund Freud*, p. 50. Russian Jewish émigrés in Los Angeles tell the same joke about a Chinese waiter in a Jewish restaurant, who has been taught to speak perfect Yiddish, assuming it is English. No doubt there are many variants.

30   Karin Obholzer, *The Wolf-Man Sixty Years Later*, pp. 102-103.

31   Ibid., pp. 67 and 83.

32   Ibid., p. 83; Magnus Ljunggren, "The psychoanalytic breakthrough in Russia," p. 178.

33   Karin Obholzer, *The Wolf-Man Sixty Years Later*, p. 101.

34   S. K. Pankeev, *The Wolf-Man by the Wolf-Man*, p. 85.

35   Ibid.

36   Sigmund Freud and C. G. Jung, *Briefwechsel*, p. 495n.

37   Ernest Jones, *The Life and Work of Sigmund Freud*, vol. 2, p. 86.

38   Sigmund Freud and C. G. Jung, *Briefwechsel*, p. 324.

39   Karin Obholzer, *The Wolf-Man Sixty Years Later*, pp. 94-95.

40   S. K. Pankeev, *The Wolf-Man by the Wolf-Man*, p. 79.

41   Sigmund Freud and C. G. Jung, *Briefwechsel*, p. 495n; S. K. Pankeev, *The Wolf-Man by the Wolf-Man*, p. 301.

42   Sigmund Freud and Karl Abraham, *A Psycho-Analytic Dialogue*, p. 82.

43   Sigmund Freud and C. G. Jung, *Briefwechsel*, p. 495n.

44   Sigmund Freud, "On the History of Psychoanalysis," in *Standard Edition of the Complete Psychological Works of Sigmund Freud*, vol. 14, p. 33.

45   Sigmund Freud and C. G. Jung, *Briefwechsel*, p. 495.

46   S. K. Pankeev, *The Wolf-Man by the Wolf-Man*, p. 155.

47   Ibid., p. 200.

48   Ibid., pp. 181-82.

49   Ibid., p. 245.

50 Ibid., p. 185.

51 Ibid., pp. 171, 208, 213, and 259.

52 Ibid., p. 259.

53 Ibid., pp. 155-56.

54 Ibid., p. 238.

55 Sigmund Freud and C. G. Jung, *Briefwechsel*, p. 255.

56 S. K. Pankeev, *The Wolf-Man by the Wolf-Man*, p. 239.

57 Sigmund Freud and C. G. Jung, *Briefwechsel*, p. 291.

58 Sigmund Freud, *The Complete Letters of Sigmund Freud to Wilhelm Fliess*, pp. 227 and 286. There are eighteen references to "endopsychic(al)" in publications from 1900 to 1926 (Sigmund Freud, *The Concordance to the Standard Edition*).

59 Sigmund Freud, *Standard Edition of the Complete Psychological Works of Sigmund Freud*, vol. 13, p. xiii.

60 Sigmund Freud and C. G. Jung, *Briefwechsel*, p. 495.

61 S. K. Pankeev, *The Wolf-Man by the Wolf-Man*, p. 196.

62 Mark Kanzer, in Mark Kanzer and Jules Glenn, eds., *Freud and His Patients*, pp. 363-65 and 404.

63 S. K. Pankeev, *The Wolf-Man by the Wolf-Man*, p. 203.

64 *Zentralblatt für Psychoanalyse* 2 (1) (1912): 15.

65 Freud, *Totem and Taboo*, 166.

66 Sigmund Freud and C. G. Jung, *Briefwechsel*, pp. 245 and 245n.

67 Magnus Ljunggren, "The psychoanalytic breakthrough in Russia," pp. 179-80.

68 Freud to Ferenczi, 4 February 1920, in Sigmund Freud, *The Letters of Sigmund Freud*, p. 328.

69 Freud to Andreas-Salomé, 30 July 1915, in Sigmund Freud, *The Letters of Sigmund Freud*, pp. 309-10.

70 S. K. Pankeev, *The Wolf-Man by the Wolf-Man*, pp. 157-58 and 218.

71 Sigmund Freud, "Psychogenesis of a Case of Homosexuality in a Woman" (1920), in *Standard Edition of the Complete Psychological Works of Sigmund Freud*, vol. 18, p. 163.

72 Karin Obholzer, *The Wolf-Man Sixty Years Later*, p. 98.

73 Ibid., p. 100.

74 Patrick Mahony, *Cries of the Wolf Man*, p. 145.

75 S. K. Pankeev, *The Wolf-Man by the Wolf-Man*, p. 111.

76   Patrick Mahony, *Cries of the Wolf Man*, p. 145; S. K. Pankeev, *The Wolf-Man by the Wolf-Man*, p. 260.

77   S. K. Pankeev, *The Wolf-Man by the Wolf-Man*, p. 111.

78   Ibid., p. 270.

79   Karin Obholzer, *The Wolf-Man Sixty Years Later*, pp. 47-50, 174; S. K. Pankeev, *The Wolf-Man by the Wolf-Man*, pp. 282-83.

80   S. K. Pankeev, *The Wolf-Man by the Wolf-Man*, p. 267.

81   Karin Obholzer, *The Wolf-Man Sixty Years Later*, p. 84.

82   Freud to Ferenczi 4 February 1920; Sigmund Freud, *The Letters of Sigmund Freud*, p. 328.

83   Sigmund Freud, *Beyond the Pleasure Principle*, 49n.

84   S. K. Pankeev, *The Wolf-Man by the Wolf-Man*, p. 151; Karin Obholzer, *The Wolf-Man Sixty Years Later*, p. 50.

85   S. K. Pankeev, *The Wolf-Man by the Wolf-Man*, p. 151.

86   Karin Obholzer, *The Wolf-Man Sixty Years Later*, p. 50.

87   Max Schur, *Freud, Living and Dying*, p. 348.

88   S. K. Pankeev, *The Wolf-Man by the Wolf-Man*, pp. 268 and 283.

89   Ibid., p. 265.

90   *International Journal of Psycho-Analysis* (London) 9 (1928): 398.

91   S. K. Pankeev, *The Wolf-Man by the Wolf-Man*, p. 301.

92   Ibid., p. 302.

93   Ibid., p. 284.

94   Ibid., p. 280.

95   Ibid., pp. 280 and 285-86.

96   Ibid., p. 290.

97   Ibid., p. 283.

98   Ibid., p. 290.

99   Ibid., pp. 235-36.

100   Or trilingual: German-English-Russian; Nicolas and Maria Abraham-Torok, "Le mot magique de l'Homme aux loups"; Patrick Mahony, *Cries of the Wolf Man*, pp. 35-36.

101   S. K. Pankeev, *The Wolf-Man by the Wolf-Man*, p. 206.

102   Ibid., p. 270.

103   Ibid., p. 150.

104   Ibid., p. 296.

105   Ibid., p. 303.

106   Friedrich Nietzsche, *Briefwechsel mit Fr. Nitschl*, pp. 272, 278, 293-95, 297-302, 313, 322 (Nietzsche: "I treasure [Dostoevsky] as the most valuable psychological material that I know"), and 323-26 (Brandes to Nietzsche, 23 November 1888, with psychological profile of Dostoevsky); Georg Brandes, "Fjodor Dostojewski."

107   Stefan Zweig, *The World of Yesterday*, p. 117.

108   Hanns Sachs, *Freud*, pp. 39-40.

109   Herman Nunberg and Ernst Federn, eds., *Minutes of the Vienna Psychoanalytic Society*, vol. 1, p. 15.

110   Harry Trosman and Roger Dennis Simmons, "The Freud Library," p. 680.

111   S. K. Pankeev, *The Wolf-Man by the Wolf-Man*, p. 145.

112   Ibid., p. 161; James L. Rice, "Psychoanalysis of 'Peasant Marei'."

113   S. K. Pankeev, *The Wolf-Man by the Wolf-Man*, p. 145.

114   Ibid., p. 20.

115   Ibid., p. 14.

116   Ibid., p. 232.

117   Ibid., pp. 146 and 289.

118   Ibid., p. 283; Sigmund Freud, "Analysis Terminable and Interminable," in *Standard Edition of the Complete Psychological Works of Sigmund Freud*, vol. 23, pp. 209-253.

119   Freud to Pankeev, in S. K. Pankejeff, "Letters Pertaining to Freud's 'History of an Infantile Neurosis'."

120   William W. Meissner, "The Wolf-Man and the Paranoid Process," 1977 and 1979.

121   Sigmund Freud, *The Letters of Sigmund Freud*, p. 333.

122   Karin Obholzer, *The Wolf-Man Sixty Years Later*, pp. 137 and 175; Hanns Sachs's lecture on love-hate in Dostoevsky's "Eternal Husband," in Federn and Nunberg, *Minutes of the Vienna Psychoanalytic Society*, vol. 4, p. 225 (meeting of 14 January 1914); Dostoevsky, "The Eternal Husband" (1870), chap. 16: "Analysis," in *Polnoe sobranie sochinenii*, vol. 9 (1974), pp. 100-106.

6

Dostoevsky in Freud's World

During Freud's lifetime and before 1930, more than 700 titles by or about Dostoevsky had appeared in German editions.[1] Certain landmarks can be indicated in Freud's awareness of the author. Before 1900 there is no evidence of Freud's interest in Dostoevsky, but a critic he admired, Georg Brandes, published an influential essay in 1889 (anthologized in 1894). Anticipated in part by DeVogüé and Nietzsche, it presents a cumulative, far-sighted view of Dostoevsky that may have helped to shape Freud's understanding. At the turn of the century, Dostoevsky was not yet on the agenda in Freud's world, but *The Brothers Karamazov* became a student underground classic in Stefan Zweig's Berlin (circulating, as we have seen, in a handwritten copy) and in the Vienna of Hanns Sachs, soon to become a follower of Freud. After the Revolution of 1905, the Germanic vogue of Dostoevsky began, as R. Piper & Co. of Munich began to publish the collected works in twenty-two volumes, coedited by Dmitri Merezhkovsky. Freud acquired this edition in 1910, and his library contained many books by Merezhkovsky as well, including his novels, his famous study *Tolstoi und Dostojewski*, and his treatise on ancient Egypt and Babylon, *Die Geheimnisse des Ostens* (1924), laced with aphorisms from Dostoevsky. Finally, by chance, it was Stefan Zweig's essay on Dostoevsky (1920), presented by the author, that served as a direct stimulus of Freud's own work on Dostoevsky. Like Brandes, Zweig eloquently and comprehensively portrayed the European Dostoevsky of his era. The major contributions of Brandes,

Merezhkovsky, and S. Zweig—preeminently and creatively representative of their periods and schools—vividly delineated the Dostoevsky of Freud's world.

In a narrower sense, "Freud's world" embraced the medical and psychoanalytic literature on Dostoevsky, unpublished papers presented at the Vienna Psychoanalytic Society between 1906 and 1918, articles in Freud's *Imago* and his other journals, and occasional pieces in periodicals that he read—especially those by authors close to him (such as J. J. David, who had reviewed the first edition of *Die Traumdeutung*) or who were compelling for a variety of reasons (e.g., Hesse, Otto Kaus, Lunacharsky, and Paul Natorp). Also of note are several books about Dostoevsky (memoirs, scholarship) issued by the publisher of Freud's own work on Dostoevsky: R. Piper of Munich. Many titles of the Dostoevsky literature were catalogued in Freud's London library, and other volumes no doubt were left behind in Vienna when Freud emigrated. Also to be considered are, of course, works cited in Freud's essay "Dostojewski und die Vatertötung" (1928). Thus, the circles of Dostoevsky in Freud's world narrow at last to his own complex view of the case. The bibliographical imperatives are fairly numerous, but not insurmountable.

Although many specific sources consulted by Freud are readily identified or conjectured, one is after all confronted with the imposing mass of seven hundred titles listed in Kampmann's 1930 dissertation *Dostojewski in Deutschland*. Freud did, after all, read widely. But he was not obliged to deal with Dostoevsky in any systematic way until he accepted the invitation to write about him in May 1926. Even if it had been Freud's method (and it was not), at that time it was not possible to recapitulate the secondary literary on Dostoevsky in any efficient way. Kampmann's thesis came four years later! We may excuse ourselves from attempting a comprehensive survey of the Dostoevsky literature in German.[2] Our chief concern here will be Dostoevsky in Freud's world, more narrowly construed. Resting as it did on three whales (Brandes, Merezhkovsky, S. Zweig), Freud's world was grandly positioned for psychoanalytic speculation about Dostoevsky.

Freud read and reread Brandes's life of Lassalle, the Jewish Social Democrat leader, a hero with "chutspo"—a quality (spelled thus) to which the biographer devotes a chapter. The book's epigraph, from

Virgil ("Flectere si nequeo Superos, Acheronta movebo" [If I cannot bend the will of Heaven, I shall cause turmoil in Hell]), was adopted by Freud for *Die Traumdeutung*, as noted above.[3] In November 1883, Freud sent his fiancée a book of biographical essays by Brandes.[4] In a sequel collection, *Menschen und Werke*, Brandes reprinted his essay on Dostoevsky, first published in 1889. Freud's regard for Brandes, one feels sure, led him to this portrait of Dostoevsky without delay.

The Dostoevsky of Brandes took shape in his correspondence with Nietzsche between 1888 and 1890. Nietzsche ambiguously hailed Dostoevsky as "among my greatest sources of relief" and "the most valuable psychological material I know," for which he was grateful "however antagonistic he may be to my deepest instincts."[5] Brandes rose to meet Nietzsche's fervor (and in retrospect one may say, his incipient madness), recognizing Dostoevsky as "a great poet but an abominable creature, quite Christian in his sensual life and at the same time thoroughly sadistic. His whole morality is what you have christened 'slave-morality'."[6] At this time, incidentally, Brandes was trying to arrange a Russian lecture tour, feared that the Russian police were opening his letters, and anticipated rejection on grounds that his works were immoral. The tour took place, and he soon published a book about Russia (*Aus dem Reich des Absolutismus*, published in 1896).[7] Meanwhile, in the correspondence with Nietzsche blossomed forth the opening passage of his Dostoevsky profile: "Look at the face of Dostoevsky: half Russian peasant, half criminal physiognomie...."[8]

In this naturalistic or "phrenological" vein (*à la Lombroso*), the essay proceeds:

> Dostoevsky is the autochthonic poet, the essential barbarian without a drop of Classical blood in his veins. One notes the face! Half Russian peasant, half criminal physiognomie, flat nose, little piercing eyes with lashes trembling from nerves, a long thick disorderly beard and light hair; besides the brow of a thinker and writer, large and well-formed, the mouth full of expression, seeming to speak of countless torments, of abysmal melancholy, of pathological desires, infinite compassion, passionate jealousy, anxiety, and obstinacy! One notes this body which is all nerve, small and weak, crooked, and stubborn, afflicted since childhood with fits and hallucinations! This exterior—at first glance insignificant and common, upon closer inspection uncannily ingenious, definitely morbid and definitely extraordinary—speaks of Dostoevsky's epileptic genius, of

a spring of kindness that fills his soul, of the waves of an almost insane
sagacity that often rise to his head, finally of ambition, of quantities of
aspiration, and of jealousy that pettiness creates in his soul.[9]

Then Brandes paraphrases Dostoevsky's account of depression
following epileptic seizures, reported by Strakhov in the official
biography published in 1883: "I feel that I am a great criminal. It
seems to me that I experience an unknown guilt, a criminal deed
oppresses my conscience."[10] And, the last point to be noted here,
Brandes calls attention to the importance of "clairvoyance and
epileptic character" in all of Dostoevsky's major works.[11] Among the
dominant features that would catch Freud's clinical eye are the
challenging mix of symptoms ("nervous" and "epileptic"), the
"epileptic" traits lifted from medical textbooks (intermittent kindness,
insane sagacity, ambition, jealousy, pettiness), the "barbaric" racial
typology, and the creative genius.

Of greater complexity and more compelling for Freud were
Merezhkovsky's views of Dostoevsky because of the author's deep
rapport with his subject, his profound feeling for specific textual
epiphanies, his dynamic symbolist perspective that placed Dostoevsky
in mythic scenarios of world civilization, and his sense of
"acceleration" in Dostoevsky's fictional world, prophesying the
twentieth-century crisis of morality and politics. Seven volumes by
Merezhkovsky were catalogued in Freud's London library.[12] The great
trilogy of historical novels published in 1902 he acquired in separate
German printings: *Julian Apostata, Peter der Grosse und sein Sohn
Alexei* (which soon figured in the Wolf-Man case), and *Leonardo da
Vinci*. In 1907, Freud listed *Leonardo* among ten books not great but
"good," that is, to his taste.[13] It served as an acknowledged source for
his own study, *Eine Kindheitserinnerung des Leonardo da Vinci*
(1910). Freud's taste for Merezhkovsky's imaginatively detailed
historical fictions led him to acquire two later works in this genre:
Alexander I and *Der Messias*. The latter (entitled *Akhnaton, King of
Egypt* in the 1927 London and New York editions) was unmistakably
a direct inspiration for Freud's own "novel," *Der Mann Moses und die
monotheistische Religion*, on which he worked throughout his last
decade. A symbolic background for Moses as Egyptian (Freud's
premise) is also richly embroidered in Merezhkovsky's book of

aphorisms, *Die Geheimnisse des Ostens*. This treatise, also in Freud's possession, weaves the image and dicta of Dostoevsky into the fabric of antiquity, as we shall see below. The groundwork for a symbolist Dostoevsky had been laid in Merezhkovsky's famous book *Tolstoi und Dostojewski* (Tolstoy and Dostoevsky), the seventh of his books in Freud's library. Further aspects of Dostoevsky's symbolic configuration were hinted in Merezhkovsky's prefaces to four volumes of the great Munich edition, in Freud's possession.[14]

Now we will attempt to compress some of Merezhkovsky's views of Dostoevsky from these sources familiar to Freud, with emphasis on what might have caught Freud's eye. Our chronological presentation is indeed arbitrary, for there is little certainty about when these books came into his hands or engaged his mind. What is certain is two decades of sustained admiration for Merezhkovsky, the resonance of their historical interests, and the Russian symbolist's cumulative authority as a Dostoevsky critic—down to the time when Freud wrote "Dostoevsky and Parricide." Merezhkovsky's first and most popular book on Dostoevsky, *Tolstoi und Dostojewski* (Tolstoy and Dostoevsky), calls attention to the "enigmatic and tragic nature" of Dostoevsky's father and his certain impact on the character of the son. Only one anonymous source, it is said, had briefly "raised the veil from this family secret ..., instantly dropping it again." In regard to Dostoevsky's epilepsy it had been hinted that "it dates back to his earliest youth, and is connected with a tragic event in their family life."[15] The idea of a tragic event in youth responsible for Dostoevsky's epilepsy (first advanced in O. F. Miller and N. N. Strakhov's authorized Russian biography of Dostoevsky published in 1883), stuck in Freud's memory. He mentioned it to Stefan Zweig in 1920, conjuring up the father's punishment of the son "under very serious circumstances."[16] Obviously he sought a primal scene, as in the case of the Wolf-Man. In Freud's essay, the tragic event becomes blurred with the legendary murder of Dostoevsky's father by family serfs. The essential psychoanalytic quest, in short, was launched by Merezhkovsky (and before him, by the first official biographer, O. F. Miller, reporting a dark hint from an obituary of Dostoevsky by A. S. Suvorin).

Dostoevsky is analyzed into polarities that Merezhkovsky augments by forced comparisons, often embellishing the contrasts with images all his own. For instance, Dostoevsky's spectrum ranges from "the most spiritual passion, bordering on religious enthusiasm" ("the 'angel' Alesha Karamazov") to "the evil insect, 'the she-spider who devours her own mate'."[17] This juxtaposition, not to be found in Dostoevsky, is typically chosen to intensify the erotic content of Dostoevsky's fiction. Merezhkovsky calls attention to the "blood bond" joining the four Karamazovs, their murdered father, and Dostoevsky, "their father in the spirit."[18] This loose identification of author and characters was typical of Freud's method, too. Merezhkovsky exacerbated this identity by attributing to Dostoevsky the extremes of Stavrogin's confession in *The Possessed*, which he knew from the manuscript or hearsay: "I felt an unwholesome thirst for violent moral contrasts, and so I demeaned myself to animality."[19] Dostoevsky's public triumph in 1880 at the Moscow Pushkin Celebration is described, including his mesmerizing declamation of Pushkin's inflammatory lyric "The Prophet," its last line quoted: "And with thy word ignite the hearts of men."[20] Both artistically and politically, Dostoevsky was an artist worthy of Freud, and Freud did not withhold his admiration, in those moments when he managed to separate the genius of the novelist and the pathology of his characters.

Chapter 13 of *Tolstoy and Dostoevsky* is a mytho-historical excursus on antiquity, chiefly the Egyptians and Semites. In the symbolist vein, clear argument yields to obscure art. Judaism had mingled with Hellenism, and "the destructive spirit of Semitism," then infected one branch of the Indo-Europeans with a powerful poison: dread of nakedness, our bodily selves. Through further artifice, Merezhkovsky links the Russian epos to the ancient religion of Ethiopia (Lower Egypt).[21] The scene then abruptly shifts to another legendary era favored by Freud, the Italian Renaissance. Merezhkovsky quotes Leonardo's diary: "Man, you are the king of beasts—*re delle bestie*—for in truth your bestial nature is the greatest."[22] In this context, Dostoevsky's character is remarkable for its extremes of individuality, "from the dark animal roots to the last radiant summits of spirituality."[23] Merezhkovsky extols "the boundless picture of the world's history which is enfolded in *The Brothers Karamazov*."[24] (This was a feature of the work that also engaged Freud, who was impressed and inspired above all by the "Grand Inquisitor" legend.) "One quality of Dostoevsky's muse," said

Merezhkovsky, "cannot be doubted—her intelligence."[25] Amidst all Freud's irritation with Dostoevsky, his admiration for the novelist's intelligence is admitted without reservation (in "Dostoevsky and Parricide"). Merezhkovsky dwells upon the suicide of Svidrigailov (in *Crime and Punishment*), a burlesque crucification "witnessed" by a little fireman wearing "an Achilles helmet" and displaying "the sullen discontent bitterly imprinted on the faces of all Hebrews without exception."[26] This emblematic moment raises the complex question of Dostoevsky and the Jews, framed here by the author himself in a generalized satiric vision of humanity poised on the brink of destruction or salvation. To this issue we shall return, in connection with the parallel problem of Freud's Jewish identity. Dostoevsky "transforms present-day reality into something more mysterious than all legends of past ages. He saw that the most trivial and fleshly goes side-by-side with the most spiritual and 'fantastic'."[27] Clearly, this world view shares certain premises with psychoanalysis.

Dostoevsky, according to Merezhkovsky, shows that Renaissance science and critical thought are approaching completion. "Not only Russia, but all Europe is teetering on the edge of an abyss." Humankind now faced the necessity of a new kind of thought, creative and religious.[28] Here was a signal—if one were needed—for Europe to receive Dostoevsky not as an outlandish alien, but as her prophet. We recall Freud's reservations about the Wolf-Man: "a national character foreign to ours, which made empathy difficult." Dostoevsky represented the Russian character with an imperative to empathize, to grasp aesthetically and to appreciate intellectually, to comprehend politically and morally. Freud, as we shall see, grappled with all these dimensions while asserting himself as physician and analyst. Merezhkovsky compares Leonardo and Dostoevsky: "I love the fantastic after it is carried to the point of realism." Leonardo's diabolically distorted drawings of human faces are counterbalanced by other drawings, full of angelic charm, a contrast that reminds Merezhkovsky of Dostoevsky's "secret of the earth mingling with the mystery of the stars" (in Alesha's vision of the autumn night after the corruption of Father Zosima's corpse).[29] Freud's analyses of Leonardo and Dostoevsky likewise converge in certain respects: their bisexuality and pervasive ambivalence. Merezhkovsky not only helped introduce Freud to a sensationalized ("maximal") Dostoevsky, he also showed Freud the way to a congenial genre of mythologized historical novel, which served him well on several occasions.

In addition to the complete works of Dostoevsky, Freud owned an extra copy of volume 9, in two parts: *Die Brüder Karamasoff*, with introduction by Merezhkovsky, which had appeared in 1908. This brief preface ("Observations on Dostoevsky," composed in 1901) begins by insisting that Russian literature of that time was coming to a natural end of its own, not merely reflecting European degeneration or decadence. Perhaps there was even something "joyous" in this frightful occurrence, for Russian literature had become as great as it could, and still remained smaller than Russian life. Perhaps this ending was the beginning of a great Russian deed? The development of Russian classical literature, from Pushkin's *Onegin* to *Anna Karenina* and *The Brothers Karamazov*, was after all paralleled only in Greek tragedy—from, say, *Prometheus* by Aeschylus to Euripides's *Alcestis*, or in the history of Italian Renaissance painting. (One recalls that before 1900 Freud's models of supreme verbal artistry were *Oedipus Rex* and *Hamlet*. *The Brothers Karamazov* eventually completed his canon.)[30] Zarathustra, noted Merezhkovsky, had said that "Man is something that must be vanquished," which was echoed by Tolstoy: "Human sexuality must be extinguished," and more simply by Dostoevsky (in Merezhkovsky's reiterated interpretation): "The end of the world approaches." But again it was emphasized that Russian "decadence" comes not from the West, but from within. This view of the emergent national character recalls again the "destruction instinct"—Sabina Spielrein's Russian contribution to psychoanalysis in 1912, accepted by Freud in 1920.

Merezhkovsky (and his Dostoevsky) trumpeted the apocalyptic theme. "We accept no average philosophy, for we believe in the end, see the end, desire the end, for we ourselves are the end, or at least the beginning of the end."[31] Small and weak, "we [Russians] almost wither and fade, facing the winds of storms. We rise early when the tops of the oaks are still dark, at earliest dawn. We see what nobody has seen, we are the first who see the sun of a great day, we are the first to say to Him: 'Verily, come, O Lord!'" With these words Merezhkovsky turned the Western reader over to Dostoevsky, whose epigraph (to *The Brothers Karamazov*) from the Gospel of John 12:

24, seemed to promise a lofty discourse indeed, on spiritual death and resurrection.

Merezhkovsky's symbolist view of Dostoevsky takes many a twist and turn. Those which lead us back to ancient Egypt and the legendary past of the Jews we will take up at a later point. Here suffice it to consider one further publication, the popular essay "The Prophet of the Russian Revolution," first published by Merezhkovsky shortly after the 1905 Revolution for the twenty-fifth anniversary of Dostoevsky's death, 28 January 1906. Freud perhaps read it in a collection issued in 1919 by his own publisher, R. Piper of Munich (if not in earlier editions): *Auf dem Wege nach Emmaus*—that is, "On the Road to Emmaus" (the place outside Jerusalem where two disciples met the risen Christ).[32] Dostoevsky's death, said Merezhkovsky, had heralded the advent of revolution in the tsar's assassination a month later (on 1 March 1881). The "cruel truth" was that Dostoevsky's gift "showed us the path of the coming Christ—leading us also to temptation by the Antichrist."[33] This dominant theme of Merezhkovsky's interpretation is here illustrated with material from Dostoevsky's famous, unique, and ostensibly autobiographical story, "Peasant Maréi," published in 1876, which is about an incident from the author's childhood and an episode from his years in prison. Freud must have been struck by the fact that this tale hinges upon a hallucinated cry, "A wolf is coming!"—a pathological symptom reminiscent of the Wolf-Man's dream.[34] Merezhkovsky relates the central moment from "Peasant Marei" as follows:

The cry "A wolf is coming!" heard in childhood, is soothed by the motherly peasant Marei (symbol of "a God-bearing folk"). Dostoevsky had often heard the terrible cry: "The wolf is coming! The beast is coming! The Antichrist is coming!" [Here Merezhkovsky, as usual, plays fast and loose with his sources.]—and always he runs, beside himself with anxiety, to the peasant Marei with his "almost motherly smile," who tells him that Christ is with him. This was Dostoevsky's true christening, not with the holy wafer in a church, but with holy earth in the fields. ... But little Fedia [the boy Dostoevsky] was mistaken. The cry of "Wolf!" was not nearby, but within him. It was the first cry of the final horror: the Beast approaches, the Antichrist is coming! From this horror the peasant Marei could not save him, for the "Russian Christ" had become a Christ-double, had changed into the Beast, the Antichrist who is the double of Christ *[der Doppelgänger Christ]*.[35]

The "Russian mission" attributed to Dostoevsky by Merezhkovsky in 1906 was "suffering freely accepted, along with the political death of free will," which would be "a service to all humanity." Only in this sense could the Russian nation (*Volk*) become "a God-bearing nation." In this sense, "Dostoevsky, despite all his errors, will emerge as the true prophet."[36]

Meanwhile, said Merezhkovsky, Russian reactionaries and revolutionaries alike had failed "to look into themselves."[37] The voice of Dostoevsky was drowned out by the thunder of the immediate revolution, "in which the thunder of the Masters booms, declaring their eternal glory."[38] Finally, Merezhkovsky remarked in passing that "nobody knows whether the waves [of the Russian Revolution] will [also] crush and grind Europe."[39] At this point, his Munich editor reminded the reader in a footnote that these words had been written in 1906. However, in 1919 the Revolution was indeed in full force, and in the West the Red Scare (on the heels of war) was a political reality, lodged in the mass psyche. In this context, Dostoevsky the Prophet achieved his greatest fame among the Germanic reading public. And it was at this moment that Freud began to review the case of Dostoevsky.

As noted above, the immediate occasion for Freud's first recorded dicta on Dostoevsky was Stefan Zweig's presentation of his *Drei Meister* essays on Balzac, Dickens, and Dostoevsky. Zweig, a Viennese born in 1881, was still finding himself as a writer of fiction when he published two short pieces on Dostoevsky, "The Struggle for Truth" (March 1914) and "The Myth of Self-Birth" (January 1915). These were incorporated into his major postwar essay of more than one hundred pages, toward the end of which the author declares: "During the Great War we could not but feel that we owed all our knowledge of Russia to Dostoevsky, and it is he whom we Germans have to thank because, in spite of the fact that Russia was an enemy, we could feel that there existed a brotherland of the soul."[40] This serves to remind us that Russia was in a sense a brotherland, and a lost fatherland, for Freud, whose ancestors had come from Russia and many of whose family still lived there. This must have lent a special ambivalence toward Dostoevsky the artist and psychologist, given to outbursts of xenophobia and anti-Semitism. Zweig seems oblivious of these disturbing traits. It is also curious that his book, presented to the father of psychoanalysis, extols Dostoevsky as "alone responsible for the tremendous widening of our spiritual self-knowledge.... He is the psychologist of psychologists:

> Since Shakespeare lived and wrote we have not learned so much from anyone as from Dostoevsky about the secret sources of the emotions and the magic laws which govern their interaction. And just as Odysseus was the only mortal who ever returned from Hades and told us of his experiences there, so Dostoevsky relates his voyages to the underworld of the soul.
>
> ...
>
> Dostoevsky has delved deeper into the layers of the unconscious than has any physician or lawyer, or criminologist, or psychiatrist. All that science was later to reveal in this field of investigation, all that was subsequently dissected out from this underground region of the human spirit, all the strange phenomena of telepathy, hysteria, hallucination, and perversion, had become known to him, decades in advance, through personal experience, through suffering, and through imaginative insight.[41]

The lavish praise for self-analysis, plumbing the layered depths of the unconscious and revealing the secret sources of the emotions, must have caused some offense to Freud, who is nowhere mentioned! Zweig even praises Dostoevsky for enriching art with "the elements of a new psychology," explaining to the reader that "the science of the mind also has its methodology" which must progress, just as experimental chemistry is constantly discovering new elements.[42] It is as though Zweig had just read Zola (*Roman expérimental*) but never heard of Freud! We shall see that Freud, in replying to Zweig, took pains to describe, ingeniously, the reciprocal relationship between Dostoevsky and psychoanalysis. Unwittingly, Zweig had thrown down a challenge.

Zweig begins his portrait of Dostoevsky with an expressionistic scattering of vague features—boundless expanses, a cosmos, the voyager overwhelmed by alien magic, ideas too vast in range, their message too exotic. All this must be lived from within, testing our powers of compassion to the depths. "The fantastic becomes true, only if we penetrate to the essence of our own personality." Dostoevsky's universe is "suspended between dream and reality."[43] His afflictions awakened "love of suffering in his heart—an almost masochistic yearning."[44] (Freud too accepted the "masochism" diagnosis for Dostoevsky, on the flimsiest of evidence.) Zweig correctly observes that Dostoevsky, "by taking an artistic and scientific interest in his [medical] problems, achieved mastery over them."[45] This indeed was far truer than Zweig could have known.[46] Thanks to Dostoevsky's "duplex nature," he could give to pathological occurrences their metaphysical content.[47] Zweig elaborates Dostoevsky's skill at "laying bare the polarities of the emotions, the perpetual swing from ecstasy to annihilation, the extremes of joy and pain."[48] Love of gambling was symbolic of this duality—a point that Freud elaborated in his own study of Dostoevsky, concluding with an analysis of a short story about gambling by Zweig himself! The abrupt intrusion of Zweig's story into "Dostoevsky and Parricide" caused some amazement among alert readers, which we shall discuss in due course.

Zweig (following Merezhkovsky) noted that Dostoevsky's christlike characters are closely bonded with the unclean sensualists— "God and the beast dwelling side by side in the flesh"—and that every transgression is depicted by Dostoevsky against a background of sexual excitement—a proposition which Freud did not, of course, have to be urged to accept.[49] The development of his heroes comes invariably through self-birth, in Zweig's view, from an idea of love or destruction—bringing forth a primal being out of the contemporary civilized human.[50] Each novel of Dostoevsky ends in emotional catharsis, as in Greek tragedy—an idea applied to Dostoevsky by a number of Russian symbolists, most fully in Viacheslàv Ivànov's *Dostojewski und die Romantragödie*, which was published in Vienna in 1922. Repeatedly Zweig calls attention to the "duplex quality" in Dostoevsky, his characters, and inevitably in his readers. Freud responded directly to this concept, which he termed ambivalence, the dominant feature of the Russian national character, as he had come to understand it by 1920.

Several major ideas about Dostoevsky in these three writers— Brandes, Merezhkovsky, Zweig—had widespread currency in Vienna by 1920. Certain points formed the framework within which Freud's position was assumed. Dostoevsky was a prophet, or symbolic presence, not only for Russia but also for Europe. He represented an "archaic," mainly unconscious, force, linked to the primordial passions and deeds of antiquity (Egypt, the Old Testament world, the Renaissance). He vividly portrayed humanity as *homo duplex*, an inherently ambivalent being, marked for love and destruction (in harmony with the "destruction instinct" thesis of Sabina Spielrein). The creative power of Dostoevsky originated in his pathology, painfully from within, a handicap and a blessing. Creativity under these circumstances required heroic rebirth, and produced an art that was flawed and dangerous: "neurotic," Freud would say. Dostoevsky was somehow connected with the fate of contemporary Europe, particularly the nations of East Europe, in 1920 barely emerging from the war, revolution, and the influenza epidemic that took the life of Freud's daughter Sophie. These were characteristic premises of Brandes, Merezhkovsky, and Zweig, critics of Dostoevsky well known to Freud.

Against this background of popularized ideas with which, we may be sure, Freud was reasonably well acquainted, let us review the discussions of Dostoevsky that occurred in the Vienna Psychoanalytic Society during the same period (1906-20), as reflected in the Society's minutes and occasionally in publications by Freud's followers. By chance the minutes commence in the Society's fifth year, 1906, just when the Dostoevsky vogue began. On 17 October 1906, Adolf Häutler announced a paper on *The Possessed*, to be delivered the following month but not reported in the published record. *The Possessed* (The Devils) was the fifth volume in the edition projected by R. Piper & Co., printed first, out of order, for the timely political sensation of its revolutionary theme. In the 24 November 1906 issue of *Die Nation*, Dostoevsky's novel (in German titled *Dämonen*) was reviewed by Jacob Julius David (1859-1906), an old Viennese acquaintance of Freud's from a village near his birthplace of Freiberg, and who had written a very sensitive and intelligent review of *Die Traumdeutung* (in the same widely known Berlin weekly, *Die Nation*). Several times in 1900 David had visited Freud, who found him "an unhappy man and a not inconsiderable poet."[51] His review of *Die Traumdeutung* Freud pronounced "kind and perceptive, somewhat diffuse."[52] But this was overly modest. It was a lovely review.[53] We may be sure that Freud read David's interesting review of Dostoevsky in 1906, and particularly because the editor of *Die Nation* announced that David had died shortly after submitting this essay. It is prefaced with a warm and deeply appreciative obituary.[54]

The part of David's review that is most important for our purposes is a passage that puts Dostoevsky in the broadest and most intimate perspective, though not without irony.

> Dostoevsky's whole significance consists in being never too weak to think and interpret [*deuten*]. He stood before the miracles of Holy Russia, rich in miracles, as a believer in miracles and as one of the lacerated, given to confession and filled with all the doubts that drift over from the evil West to the devout East. Perhaps the world has never seen, since it came into being or at any rate since we have been following its progress, any such process of disintegration [*Zersetzungsprozess*]. One might compare the ferment [*die Gärung*] within the Jewish community [*das Judentum*]—and indeed they are sufficiently related, since they have sprung from similar roots. But in the case of the Jews it is a small nationality that passionately, with the most secret yearnings, desires the ability to disappear entirely into an Eminent state, an Artistic state, a Human state, in order, however, to assert themselves anew. It is altogether different in the realm of the Tsar and his Mandarin system of bureaucratic ranks.[55]

Russia is described by David as a mighty state and an astonishing thing: all one could do was "stick your nose through the stakes of the border gate and sniff the Russian wind," but little was to be learned except for the views of Dostoevsky.[56] It was not yet possible to tell whether the political awakening of the Russian masses was a blessing or a dire tragedy for the West: "Is it only meaningless howling and mirages of wolves that astound us, and in which we seek prophetic omens?"[57] David thus contrasts the Russian disintegration (*Zersetzung*)—aimed at destruction of a state that has nothing to offer but "miracles," a destructive process with no apparent ideals—and the Jewish ferment (*Gärung*), aimed at assimilation into a condition of artistic or other eminence, in order to rise anew. Nevertheless, similarities between Jews and Russians also struck David: their roots in racial oppression (by the Mongol yoke and "Mongol bureaucracy," in the case of Russia), their lacerations, and their recent political awakening. Freud, whose background as a brilliantly but imperfectly assimilated Viennese Jew from the Slavonic hinterland was identical to that of David, no doubt grasped the measure of truth in this view of Russia and Dostoevsky. Their national character, world view, and psychology had something in common with Freud's own, something that might conjure an illusion of brotherhood in contrast with Western Catholic states. The Jews, like the Russians, might possess a destructive or self-destructive instinct ambivalently mixed with creativity. Jacob David had something to say, and Freud must have read his deathbed message about Dostoevsky with interest.

In February 1907, Paul Federn spoke to the Vienna Psychoanalytic Society about the theme of infantile sexuality in the plays of Frank Wedekind. In passing he referred to other "great psychologists among modern writers," among whom he named "Dostoevsky, Musset, Jacobsen, and others."[58] All but Wedekind overlooked infantile sexuality, so essential for psychoanalytic understanding. Nevertheless, it is important that Dostoevsky was at this date esteemed for his creative psychological insight, not seen chiefly as an unwitting prophet, nor as an "epileptic" diagnostically linked with his own fictional characters.

On 8 April 1908, Dr. Wilhelm Stekel (briefly treated by Freud in 1901) gave a short report to the Society about a paper on epilepsy in the Brussels Journal *Médical*, where various forms of epileptic aura (symptoms heralding seizures) were described. Frequently, observed Stekel, "such cases are hysterias—as, for instance, the case of Dostoevsky."[59] The following year Stekel published a book on the psychology of art and artists, *Dichtung und Neurose*, in which he advanced the same diagnosis of Dostoevsky as a case of hysteria, without evidence. He also notes in passing the opposing opinion of Dr. Timofei Segalov, who argues in his well-informed book that Dostoevsky indeed suffered from epilepsy.[60] Segalov's solid study, *Die Krankheit Dostojewskys*, was not heeded by Freud and his followers who wrote about Dostoevsky. The reason for this is that a diagnosis of epilepsy would have placed the case of Dostoevsky in the realm of "organic" neuropathology, and thus out of the purview of psychoanalysis. On 21 October 1908, Stekel presented a case of "hysterical pseudoepilepsy." Freud commented that "there are hysterias and there are epilepsies; occasionally the two may combine, but all those illnesses that are called hysteroepilepsies are simply hysterias."[61] The editors of the Society *Minutes* here refer without comment to "Dostoevsky and Parricide." As we shall see below, Freud in his study of Dostoevsky deals at length with this problem of differential diagnosis.

At the meeting of 8 April 1908, among books received by the Society was Bernhard Stern's *Geschichte der öffentlichen Sittlichkeit in Russland* (The History of Public Morality in Russia). A sequel to this volume, *Russische Grausamkeit einst und jetzt* (Russian Cruelty Past and Present) illustrated various rumored modes of Russian savagery, such as "a mother throwing her infant to the wolves."[62] Such a report would of course not be credited by Freud and his colleagues. But it calls attention to a popular apprehension of Russian character in Freud's world. In fact, this image of infanticide is linked with notorious murders of sons by the tsars Ivan the Terrible and Peter the Great, deeds assigned symbolic importance by Russian historians, artists, and writers well known in the West (such as Repin and Merezhkovsky). The psychological importance of these historic crimes, as we note below, influenced Freud when he wrote about Dostoevsky.

On 8 March 1911, Bernhard Dattner reported to the Society on "Psychoanalytic Problems in Dostoevsky's *Rodion Raskolnikow* [Crime and Punishment]."[63] No comments by Freud are recorded. However, we recall that in those very years certain aspects of Dostoevsky's most popular novel were being discussed in the Wolf-Man's therapy sessions (notably, Raskolnikov's long dream about a horse being beaten, from which he awoke feeling beaten himself, reminiscent of the Wolf-Man's ambivalent pleasure and pity when animals were beaten). The manifest identification of Raskolnikov with his female victims probably caught Freud's attention, and may have helped persuade him of Dostoevsky's own bisexual nature (another aspect of his dominant ambivalence). On 14 January 1914, toward the end of the Wolf-Man's first analysis, Dr. Hanns Sachs spoke at a Society meeting on Dostoevsky's novella "The Eternal Husband," calling attention to the husband's ambivalent love and hate for his wife's seducer—precisely that problem of "love-hate" about which, as Pankeev claimed decades later, psychoanalysis had nothing to say.[64] The views of Sachs may also have contributed something to Freud's assessment of Dostoevsky's personality as marked by strong bisexual ambivalence. Sachs, incidentally, had gotten to know Freud personally

in 1909, and no doubt at that time told him how his great admiration
for Dostoevsky had led him, in 1904, to a medical career—first
neuropathology (with special interest in epilepsy) and at last
psychiatry. Thus, as with Eitingon (an expert on psychiatric aspects of
epilepsy), a discussion of Dostoevsky's symptoms and diagnosis must
have arisen naturally between Freud and Sachs at an early date, prior
to 1910.

Meanwhile, Dr. Otto Rank, a literary scholar who participated in
Society meetings and became coeditor (with Sachs) of *Imago*,
contributed publications that helped bring Dostoevsky under the
scrutiny of psychoanalysis. In 1912, he mentioned Dostoevsky in
passing in *Das Inzest-Motiv in Dichtung und Sage* (subtitled "Main
Features of a Psychology of Poetic Creativity"). He notes that *The
Brothers Karamazov* is a novel about murder hinging upon Oedipal
conflict, and brings a rather weak command of Dostoevsky's medical
history to bear on the issue.[65] More productive is Rank's stimulating
essay on "Der Doppelgänger," published in *Imago*.[66] Rank devotes
more than ten pages to a discussion of Dostoevsky's early story
dealing directly with the topic in question ("The Double," published in
1845-6), which appeared in volume 14 of the Munich edition. He
indicates the hero's paranoid behavior, mixed with "erotomaniacal
phantasies" and attitudes toward women that draw him into
catastrophic and self-destructive situations.[67] Rank quotes at some
length the passage from Merezhkovsky's *Tolstoy and Dostoevsky*
(originally from Miller's official biography of 1883, later also cited by
Freud), linking the origin of Dostoevsky's illness to the baneful
influence of his father and to some "tragic event in his earliest
childhood."[68] The original Russian source alludes to "something
terrible, unforgettable, tormenting, [which] happened to him in
childhood, a result of which was his falling sickness." This vague
remark, further distorted by memory, led Freud to associate
Dostoevsky's epilepsy with the death of his father, which occurred not
in the Russian writer's early childhood but when he was seventeen.[69]
Rank's slight revision of Dostoevsky's vita of course served to draw
psychoanalytic attention to Dostoevsky's illness. Rank also repeats the
erroneous idea (stemming from an ambiguous remark by Dostoevsky
himself) that during his imprisonment Dostoevsky had been
completely free of seizures.[70] Rank repeats Dostoevsky's attested

accounts of spiritual euphoria preceding his seizures, and of the sense of guilt, of some forgotten crime, that followed his attacks.[71] He quotes Merezhkovsky's insightful remark that Dostoevsky "is perhaps not so much an artist as a doctor of psychic illnesses, moreover a doctor to whom one must say: Physician, first heal thyself!"[72] But Rank also observes that Dostoevsky in his fiction treats paranoia with a suspiciously clinical precision, especially when he treats the theme of the double, which—according to Merezhkovsky—is the central problem of his writing.[73] At the heart of the matter, Rank suggests, is "sexual overvaluation of the ego"—narcissism—from which sublimated homosexuality produces paranoia with "the characteristic paranoid mechanism of projection." The formerly most valued figure (the self and its surrogates) presents a threat toward which a defense is established. A frequent variant of this theme in literature involves the father (or brother) as persecuting surrogate of the self. The great example from Dostoevsky, says Rank, is of course *The Brothers Karamazov*.[74] It is interesting that Rank draws a few minor features of Dostoevsky's clinical profile from Segalov, who insisted that the epilepsy was genuine.[75] But Rank apparently drew no conclusion about the epilepsy diagnosis. On the other hand, his account of the psychodynamics of Dostoevsky's fiction was grist to the mill of psychoanalysis, and anticipates several aspects of Freud's view. One might suppose that Freud, as editor-in-chief of *Imago*, had occasion to discuss this engaging article with Rank. If Rank had not broken with Freud in the mid-1920s, no doubt Freud would have given credit to his ideas in "Dostoevsky and Parricide."

In the meantime, Freud had terminated his first analysis of the Wolf-Man shortly before the outbreak of the war, had written the case history during the first year of war (1914-15), and had at last published it in 1918. By this time Stefan Zweig had already drafted or projected most of his essay on Dostoevsky, the first segment of which—"The Myth of Self-birth"—was published in 1915. (Publication of the anthology *Drei Meister* was announced at this time but deferred until 1920.)[76] The extravagant views of Merezhkovsky were by then widely adopted in the Germanic literature. One further example can suffice here. In 1916 Hermann Hesse published his article "Die Brüder Karamasoff oder der Untergang Europas," which declares that an exhausted Europe longs "to turn homeward"—to the East, to accept "hysteria and neurasthenia" and "all those evils ... which collectively signify the Karamazovs."[77] To Hesse it mattered not whether Dostoevsky was considered a great artist nor whether he was an epileptic or an hysteric. "This sort of sick man, be he called Dostoevsky or Karamazov, has that strange, occult, godlike faculty, the possibility of which the Asiatic venerates in every maniac."[78] And this Asiatic malady had embraced Europe, where "the unconscious of a whole continent and age has made of itself poetry in the nightmare of a single prophetic dreamer."[79] In Hesse's view, "this book of Dostoevsky's has hung a symbol round the neck of mankind, has erected a monument for it just as an individual might in a dream create for himself an image of his warring instinct and forces."[80] Hesse, whose own art had entered a mythologizing mode with psychoanalytic overtones (see *Demian*, published in 1919), represents an extreme of imaginative engagement with Dostoevsky in the Germanic world, sharing many features with the critics and artists most favored by Freud himself.

In these contexts of hyperbole, Freud's first articulated view of Dostoevsky is brief but remarkable. At a meeting of the Society on 19 November 1918, Siegfried Bernfeld presented a paper on "Poetic Writing by Youth."[81] Freud in his commentary suggested a typology of creative writers whose methods are in one way or another "psychological." Dostoevsky, with implicit approval, is named first in a class of his own: "psychological writing that seeks to uncover what is concealed." This would seem to place him on a level with psychoanalysis. By contrast, other types listed by Freud include writers whose psychology amounts to "wish-fulfillment"; those whose psychology is "exhibitionistic description"; yet others who display "secrets" for the type of reader who is an "inexperienced child" (writing known as "realistic"); and finally, lyrical poetry soliciting compassion, sympathy, or love (written out of "instinctual drive"). Despite the extravagance of Dostoevsky's vogue, Freud evidently retained an unqualified admiration for his artistic objectives and methods, and recognized his positive analytic intelligence. Although the evidence is indeed slight, one may say at least that Freud at this point regarded Dostoevsky as a productive artist, not as an alien prophet, pathological case, or evil demon.

Nineteen October 1920 is the date of Freud's response to Stefan Zweig's essay about Dostoevsky—the genesis, it may be, of

"Dostoevsky and Parricide." One further publication may be cited here as a possible stimulus to Freud's views at just that moment. Dr. Tatiana Rosenthal, a student of Jung's, had returned to Russia in 1911.[82] At first driven by political and medical idealism, she became chief clinician at Bekhterev's new Brain Pathology Institute in Petrograd. Toward the end of 1920 a report of her work was relayed by Freud's Berlin colleagues (Max Eitingon and Sara Neiditsch) to the *Internationale Zeitschrift für Psychoanalyse*. Among other things, it included a synopsis of her unfinished essay "The Suffering and Creativity of Dostoevsky—A Psychogenic Study," published a year earlier in a Soviet periodical.[83] Just in time to be included with this account in Freud's journal, a death notice was also received in Vienna: Tatiana Rosenthal, one of the very few didactic analysts in the Soviet medical establishment, an esteemed member of her profession, and the mother of a gifted child, had committed suicide at the age of thirty-six. Her obituary appeared in the *Zeitschrift* just below the detailed review of her work on Dostoevsky.[84]

Rosenthal, like many Russians of the revolutionary era, was attracted to the views of Adler, advocate of a social and rational medicine, who had parted with Freud in 1911. Once the psychiatrist of Trotsky's righthand man Joffe, by 1918 Adler had already spoken out against the violence of the Bolsheviks, correctly predicting a European reaction.[85] In 1920, by the way, Adler also published a lecture (delivered in 1918 in Switzerland) on Dostoevsky. It is rather bland, certainly was not seen by Rosenthal, and was rightly ignored by Freud.[86] No doubt Freud would have said of Adler, as a decade before he had joked about the Russians, that he had "some utopian dream of a world-benefiting therapy" and wanted the work to go faster.[87] Many Russian clinicians of 1920 clung tenaciously, or grimly, to some utopian dream. The dream did not heal Dr. Rosenthal. The résumé of her article on Dostoevsky, which carries his career only to his arrest in 1849 but was to have been continued, concludes by quoting her directly:

> We shall see that the basic tone of [Dostoevsky's] creativity remained unaltered: it is a feeling of self-abasement, and rebellion against this feeling, which intensifies into a diametrically opposite feeling of his own elect predestination [*Auserwähltheit*].The latter is accompanied by an aggressive tendency. (Adler)

The editors of the *Zeitschrift* express uncertainty as to whether the concluding reference to Adler was to have been developed into Rosenthal's "guiding principle."[88] She does state directly that Freud's approach to discussing the psychogenesis of artistic creativity is "a distortion of the psychological perspective" by his "psychosexual monism."

One last preview of Rosenthal's unrealized second installment was given: "The illness of Dostoevsky will be interpreted as an *Affektepilepsie* as defined by Bratz."[89] This reference is no doubt to the study of "affect-epilepsy seizures of neuropaths and psychopaths" published in 1911 by Dr. Emil Bratz, senior physician of a Berlin asylum.[90] Thus, Tatiana Rosenthal's clinical profile of Dostoevsky resembles Freud's in certain respects. The report of her work should have come to Freud's attention a few weeks before he wrote to Zweig about Dostoevsky. Thus, the last contribution of Tatiana Rosenthal may have helped to stimulate Freud's thinking about Dostoevsky, by combining her ideas about the subject with negative views of orthodox psychoanalysis. This volley of criticism may have been all the more effective, fired as it was from the Eastern front by a young woman who might have helped advance the psychoanalytic movement in Russia but who now rejected Freud—from beyond the grave. The situation resembled those cases (described by Freud in 1920) in which the patient's resistance "withdrew to a certain limit, beyond which it then proved to be unconquerable ... —Russian tactics, as they might be called."

It cannot be our task to survey all the German literature on Dostoevsky of Freud's era, although in fact all of it bears upon the complex image of Dostoevsky in Freud's world. Undoubtedly he read much that we cannot identify, and the Dostoevsky vogue defined his frame of reference in subtler ways. Various trends of Dostoevsky's reception by the Germanic readership have been studied—by T. Kampmann in 1930, Leo Loewenthal in 1934, H. Schmidt in 1971, V. Dudkin and K. Azadovskii in 1973, and most recently (1992) by W. J. Dodd. Freud is generally absent or marginal in these accounts, but two of Loewenthal's conclusions seem particularly useful for our purposes. He noted that Dostoevsky's fictions glorified the lower middle classes, and that Freud saw Dostoevsky in the context of world history transformed into a private myth of the bourgeoisie.[91] These facts, one may add, helped bring both Freud and Dostoevsky under attack in the early Stalin era, precisely when Freud wrote his essay on Dostoevsky.

A number of further publications that might have been considered here are simply listed in the Bibliography. To some readers, it may be of interest that several major Russian sources were available to Freud in German translations, in addition to those he is known to have consulted and which will be noted in the next chapter. These books, three of which were probably supplied to Freud by his Munich publisher R. Piper, are the following: Aimée Dostojewski, *Dostojewski, geschildert von seiner Tochter*; A. L. Wolynski, *Das Reich der Karamasoff*; V. Solovjeff, *Drei Reden*; V. Iwanow, *Dostojewski und die Romantragödie*; V. Rosanow, *Dostojewski und seine Legende vom Grossinquisitor*; N. Berdiaev, *Die Weltanschauung Dostojewskis*; A. G. Dostoevsky, *Die Lebenserinnerungen der Gattin Dostojewskis*; and A. G. Dostojewski, *Das Tagebuch der Gattin Dostojewskis*.[92] The books by Volynski and Rozanov, rich though they are in relevant data and ideas, were not indispensable to Freud's work on Dostoevsky, although Rozanov's focus on the "Grand Inquisitor" legend may have helped guide Freud in that direction. The ingenious studies by Ivanov and Berdiaev, which Freud could have read with pleasure but probably did not (beset as he was with duties and illness), had no discernible impact on Freud's work. The memoirs and diary of Anna Grigorievna, Dostoevsky's wife, might have altered his view of Dostoevsky's character and illness, but clearly they did not, and were probably consulted superficially if at all. Other biographical sources were at hand in quantity, above all the official biography by Miller and Strakhov, first published in Russian in 1883. Finally, the book by Dostoevsky's daughter confirmed the family legend of the murder of Dostoevsky's father by his serfs, a crucial element in Freud's understanding.[93] This source also represented the Dostoevsky clan as "Lithuanian nobility," of Pinsk origin, thus sharing the ancestral terrain of Freud's forefathers. This slightly garbled claim would have caught Freud's eye as, to paraphrase Loewenthal, he made of world history his own private myth.

From the hundreds of Dostoevsky critiques remaining to be considered, we conclude with a few words about Paul Natorp's lucid booklet, published in Jena in 1923: *Fedor Dostoevsky's Meaning for the Culture Crisis of the Present, with an Afterword about the Present Spiritual Crisis.*[94] Natorp (1854-1924) was a philosopher associated with the neo-Kantians of the Marburg school. Before turning to medicine, Max Eitingon had studied philosophy at Marburg, so it is likely that he brought Natorp's book to Freud's attention when the Dostoevsky project was undertaken. Eitingon, as the official biography tells us, kept pressing Freud to finish his essay on Dostoevsky "and sent him book after book."[95] Moreover, Natorp was an esteemed philosopher of science, very close to Freud's own age, who published his work on Dostoevsky in the year of his death. Such mortal affinities meant a good deal to Freud, especially once he had begun, in 1923, his long ordeal of operations for cancer of the palate.

Natorp's slim volume on Dostoevsky is in some ways, like Zweig's essay, a cumulative European brief. He builds his case, for example, in part on Merezhkovsky and Hesse. But it is also the original work of a wise and scientifically trained mind, and thus a challenge to Freud to take Dostoevsky seriously, if such a challenge were necessary. Reading Dostoevsky, said Natorp, one encountered a paradox: the unacceptability of reality yet the impossibility of escaping into dreams.[96] There was never just a simple innocence in Dostoevsky's view, but only innocence "that must grow in sin and torment of consciousness, and self-consciousness." Existence for Dostoevsky was "a struggle to assert the self against death and nothingness, to use the life, time, and space on earth to the end." (This reminds one of Tolstoy's pronouncement about the late Dostoevsky, opposing the popular inclination to make a saint of him: "The man was all struggle [*ves' bor'ba*].")[97] In Dostoevsky, thirsting for order and building toward form were counterpoised against eternal destruction. Thus, Natorp (paraphrasing Volynsky's "deep book" on *The Realm of the Karamazovs*) found Dostoevsky's attitude toward world culture "fully affirmative"—a positive orientation often missed by superficial readers.[98] Natorp read "The Grand Inquisitor" with historical literality, as a harsh critique of Roman Catholicism (rather than the sweeping attack against authority that it is—an exposé of church and state, Western and Russian).[99] Dostoevsky's lesson, for the dying Natorp, was that every instant of fully lived life contains the deepest blessedness [*Seligkeit*]. "In this sense of the eternal present, in the presence of eternity, not only the spiritual crisis of the present is dissolved, but even the so-called 'Present' that we believe in, which did not exist yesterday and tomorrow will be no more."[100]

Many features of Natorp's Dostoevsky are aligned with Freud's world view, and Natorp's exposition could have helped Freud see this paradox and struggle as dominant features in a life that is unacceptable, from which escape (into dreams!) is impossible, wherein growth (in sin and torment) from innocence into self-consciousness is the necessary path, precariously balancing "thirst for order" and "building toward form" (both of which psychoanalysis calls "love") against destruction. Thus far, Freud and Dostoevsky might agree. But when we begin to speak of a "fully affirmative" attitude toward world culture, there is ample room for argument both as to whether such was Dostoevsky's position after all and as to Freud's response to such a position. There is also ample room for disagreement on the proposition of *Seligkeit* as to just how such a fully lived life can be lived and what term should really be applied to it, at its best. In the remaining chapters I try to move closer between Freud and Dostoevsky, and I attempt to discover whether such questions of their affinity can be answered.

Notes

1   Theoderich Kampmann, *Dostojewski in Deutschland*.

2   F. Duckmeyer, "Die Einführung Dostojewskis in Deutschland"; Ernst Hanswedell, "Die Kenntnis von Dostojewski"; Leo Loewenthal, "Die Auffassung Dostojewskis im Vorkriegsdeutschland"; H. Schmidt, "Die deutsche Dostojewski-Rezeption"; V. V. Dudkin and K. M. Azadovskii, "Dostoevskii v Germanii."

3   Sigmund Freud, *The Letters of Sigmund Freud*, p. 228.

4   Ibid., p. 75.

5   Letters to Brandes dated 10 October 1888 and 20 November 1888, in Friedrich Nietzsche, *Briefwechsel mit Fr. Nitschl*, pp. 319 and 322.

6   Letter of 16 November 1888, in Friedrich Nietzsche, *Briefwechsel mit Fr. Nitschl*, pp. 319-20.

7   Georg Brandes, *Aus dem Reich des Absolutismus*.

8   Letter of 23 November 1888, in Friedrich Nietzsche, *Briefwechsel mit Fr. Nitschl*, p. 325.

9   Georg Brandes, "Fjodor Dostojewski," pp. 309-10.

10   Ibid., p. 311.

11   Ibid., pp. 338-39.

12   Harry Trosman and Roger Dennis Simmons, "The Freud Library."

13   Sigmund Freud, *The Letters of Sigmund Freud*, p. 296.

14   "Rodion Raskolnikoff," *Sämtliche Werke*, vol. 1, pt. 1, xx-lix; short prefaces to vol. 7, *Jugend*, and vol. 8, *Politische Schriften*; and "Zur Einführung. Bemerkungen über Dostojewski" (originally published in 1901), preface to vol. 9, pt. 1, *Die Brüder Karamasoff*, 1908.

15   Dmitri Mereschkowski, *Tolstoi as Man and Artist*, p. 98.

16   Sigmund Freud, *The Letters of Sigmund Freud*, p. 332.

17   Dmitri Mereschkowski, *Tolstoi as Man and Artist*, p. 147.

18   Ibid., pp. 147-48.

19   Ibid., pp. 148-49.

20   Ibid., pp. 155-6.

21   Ibid., pp. 226-29.

22   Ibid., p. 231.

23   Ibid., p. 239.

24   Ibid., p. 247.

25   Ibid., p. 249.

26   Ibid., pp. 283-84.

27   Ibid., p. 295.

28   Ibid., pp. 295-96.

29   Ibid., pp. 304-305 and 275 See *The Brothers Karamazov*, end of Book Seven.

30   Sigmund Freud, *The Complete Letters of Sigmund Freud to Wilhelm Fliess*, pp. 272-73 (15 October 1897).

31   Dmitri Mereschkowski, "Zur Einführung," p. xv.

32   Dmitri Mereschkowski, *Auf dem Wege nach Emmaus*, pp. 42-92.

33   Ibid., p. 43.

34   James L. Rice, "Psychoanalysis of 'Peasant Marei'." See also James L. Rice, "Beyond Twice-Two."

35   Dmitri Mereschkowski, *Auf dem Wege nach Emmaus*, pp. 44-45 and 64-65.

36   Ibid., p. 92.

37   Ibid., p. 84.

38   Ibid., p. 92.

39   Ibid., p. 90.

40   Stefan Zweig, *Three Masters*, p. 204.

41   Ibid., pp. 204-205.

42   Ibid., pp. 205-6.

43   Ibid., pp. 100-101.

44   Ibid., p. 125.

45   Ibid., pp. 128-29.

46   James L. Rice, *Dostoevsky and the Healing Art*.

47   Stefan Zweig, *Three Masters*, p. 131.

48   Ibid., p. 133.

49   Ibid., pp. 136 and 139-40.

50   Ibid., pp. 158-60 and 162.

51   Sigmund Freud, *The Complete Letters of Sigmund Freud to Wilhelm Fliess*, p. 366.

52   Ibid., p. 398.

53   J. J. David, Review of "Die Traumdeutung."

54   J. J. David, "Dostojewskis 'Dämonen'"; Ernst Heilborn, "Davids künstlerische Lebensbeichte."

55   J. J. David, "Dostojewskis 'Dämonen'," p. 121.

56   Ibid., p. 123.

57   Ibid., p. 121.

58   Herman Nunberg and Ernst Federn, eds., *Minutes of the Vienna Psychoanalytic Society*, vol. 1, p. 117.

59   Ibid., vol. 1, p. 363.

60   Wilhelm Stekel, *Dichtung and Neurose*, p. 41; Timofei Segaloff, *Die Krankheit Dostojewskys*.

61   Herman Nunberg and Ernst Federn, eds., *Minutes of the Vienna Psychoanalytic Society*, vol. 2, p. 19.

62   Bernhard Stern, *Geschichte der öffentlichen Sittlichkeit in Russland*, facing page 273. See illustration.

63   Herman Nunberg and Ernst Federn, eds., *Minutes of the Vienna Psychoanalytic Society*, vol. 3, pp. 189-93.

64   Ibid., vol. 4, p. 225.

65   Otto Rank, *Das Inzest-Motif in Dichtung und Sage*, pp. 190-91.

66   Otto Rank, "Der Doppelgänger," pp. 116-123, 132-35 and 155.

67   Ibid., pp. 117 and 123.

68   Ibid., p. 132.

69   A. S. Suvorin, "O pokoinom" (about the deceased), *Novoe vremia* no. 1771 (1 February 1881), quoting A. S. Dolinin, ed. *F. M. Dostoevskii v vospominaniiakh sovremennikov*, vol. 2, p. 415.

70   James L. Rice, *Dostoevsky and the Healing Art*. Dostoevsky's letter of 22 February 1854 leaves no doubt that his epilepsy had been diagnosed before his arrest, and that his seizures continued in prison, though rarely.

71   Otto Rank, "Der Doppelgänger," p. 133.

72   Ibid., p. 134.

73   Ibid., pp. 133 and 154.

74   Ibid., p. 155.

75   Ibid., p. 132.

76   Stefan Zweig, "Dostojewski. (Der Mythos der Selbstgeburt)," p. 111n.

77   Hermann Hesse, "The Brothers Karamazov," p. 611; Herman Hesse, "Die Brüder Karamasoff oder der Untergang Europas."

78   Hermann Hesse, "The Brothers Karamazov," p. 618.

79   Ibid., p. 616.

80   Ibid., p. 614.

81   Herman Nunberg and Ernst Federn, eds., *Minutes of the Vienna Psychoanalytic Society*, vol. 4, pp. 296-302.

82   See above, chap. 4, note 27.

83   Tatiana K. Rozental', "Stradanie i tvorchestvo Dostoevskogo."

84   Sara Neiditsch, "Die Psychoanalyse in Russland während der letzten Jahre"; James L. Rice, *Dostoevsky and the Healing Art*, index.

85   Henri Ellenberger, *The Discovery of the Unconscious*, p. 594.

86   Alfred Adler, "Dostoevsky," pp. 280-90.

87   Sigmund Freud and C. G. Jung, *The Freud/Jung Letters*, p. 226 (3 June 1909)

88   Sara Neiditsch, "Die Psychoanalyse in Russland während der letzten Jahre," p. 384.

89   Ibid., p. 384.

90   Emil Bratz, "Die affektepileptischen Anfälle der Neuropathen und Psychopathen."

91   Leo Loewenthal, "Die Auffassung Dostojewskis im Vorkriegsdeutschland," pp. 349 and 382.

92   No location of this edition was found in North American libraries.

93   Doubts have lately been raised about the murder of Dostoevsky's father (see G. A. Fedorov, "'Pomeshchik"). We see no compelling reason to believe that Dr. Dostoevsky died a natural death, and no reason to doubt Aimée Dostoevsky's sober and unembellished report of family legend that her grandfather died a violent death at the hands of his serfs (a frequent occurrence in that era). Descendents of the village peasants also confirmed the legend of murder, in interviews with the eminent Soviet scholar Vera Stepanovna Nechaeva. (V. S. Nechaeva, "Iz literatury o Dostoevskom. (Poezdka v Darovoe)."

94   Paul Natorp, *Fjodor Dostojewskis Bedeutung*.

95   Ernest Jones, *The Life and Work of Sigmund Freud*, vol. 3, p. 143.

96   Paul Natorp, *Fjodor Dostojewskis Bedeutung*, p. 4.

97   Tolstoy to Strakhov. In L. N. Tolstoi, Letters to N. N. Strakhov.

98   Paul Natorp, *Fjodor Dostojewskis Bedeutung*, p. 34.

99   Ibid., p. 18.

100   Ibid., p. 41.

Dr. L.O. Darkshevich, Freud's Russian friend in Paris. Photograph from
Bolshaia Sovetskaia Entsiklopediia, 2nd ed. (Moscow 1952), vol. 13.

"Tsar Ivan the Terrible and His Son, Ivan," oil by Ilya Repin, 1885. Reproduced in Igor Grabar, *Repin*, vol. 1 (Moscow: Akademiia Nauk, 1963), facing page 276.

"A [Russian] Mother Throws Her Child to the Wolves" (anon.), from Bernhard Stern, *Russische Grausamkeit einst und jetzt* ["Russian Cruelty of Past and Present"] (Berlin: Hermann Barsdorf, 1908) facing page 273.

Dostoevsky, *Der Doppelgänger*, cover illustration by Alfred Kubin
(Munich: R. Piper & Co. Verlag, 1913). ©1989 Edition Spangenberg,
München 40. Reprinted by permission of the publisher.

Lou Andreas-Salomé, photograph published following page 128 in Sigmund Freud/Lou Andreas-Salomé, *Briefwechsel* (Frankfurt: S. Fischer Verlag, 1966). Reprinted by permission of Frau Dorothee Pfeiffer, Lou Andreas-Salomé Archiv, Göttingen.

Freud with sons Ernst and Martin, in Austrian uniform, Salzburg, 1916.
Photograph reproduced in *The Life and Work of Sigmund Freud* by
Ernest Jones, vol. 2 (New York: Basic Books, 1955), facing page 192. Reprinted by permission of Basic Books and A.W. Freud et al., by arrangement with Mark Paterson & Associates.

The Confession of a Jew in Letters to Dostoevsky, edited by Leonid Grossman, cover of the Munich edition, 1927, in Freud's library.

"Roulette in Hamburg" (anon.), illustration following page 96 in
Dostojewski am Roulette (Munich: Piper Verlag, 1925), in Freud's library.

Freud in Berchtesgaden, 1929. Photograph reproduced in *The Life and Work of Sigmund Freud* by Ernest Jones, vol. 3 (New York: Basic Books, 1957), facing page 143. Reprinted by permission of Basic Books and A.W. Freud et al., by arrangement with Mark Paterson & Associates.

Dostoevsky, 1879. Portrait by the St. Petersburg photographer K.A. Shapiro; frontispiece to Freud's edition of *The Brothers Karamazov*.

7

Russische Innerlichkeit

Freud's view of Dostoevsky, partially outlined in his letter to Stefan Zweig of 19 October 1920, was more fully elaborated in the essay "Dostojewski und die Vatertötung," which appeared in December 1928.[1] Both of these variants need to be considered, along with intervening events of Freud's life and era, as they bear on the case. Finally, in response to criticism, Freud expressed certain disclaimers and revisions of his Dostoevsky portrait, lending another dimension to the whole episode. Despite all of Dostoevsky's admitted greatness, Freud declared in a letter to Theodor Reik on 14 April 1929 that he did not really like Dostoevsky because his patience with "pathological natures" was exhausted in psychotherapy. "In art and life I am intolerant of them."[2] This attitude of clinical condescension is evident in Freud's approach to Dostoevsky, yet he did not conceal his admiration for the writer's genius and intellect. Freud's ambivalence toward his Russian subject dominates our view of their encounter.

Freud's letter to Zweig[3] applauds his success in describing Balzac and Dickens ("straightforward types"), but notes "gaps and unsolved riddles" in the case of Dostoevsky—"the confounded Russian." Here Freud himself claimed a certain advantage over Zweig, since Dostoevsky "has now finally fallen to the lot of the psychopathologist."[4] By this perfectly arbitrary rhetorical conceit ("... der Psychopatholog, dem Dostojewski nun einmal verfallen bleibt") Freud set the stage for his clinical hypotheses. This aggressive mannerism is gracefully balanced by Freud's concluding remark to

Zweig, which abruptly disclaims his "emphasis on the so-called pathological" in Dostoevsky, and denies any intent "to belittle or explain away the splendor of Dostoevsky's creative power." Coming from Freud the clinician, who here began by assuming the role precisely of "psychopathologist," it is doubly disarming that in closing he calls into question the so-called pathological! In fact, such cunning maneuvers are a hallmark of Freud's epistolary style, and frequent enough in his formal prose. Here it has to do primarily with a question of etiquette. How does the Father of Psychoanalysis deal with the giant among psychological novelists? Who is to consult whom? In the letter to Zweig, Freud solves this problem by framing his clinical assertions with casual rhetorical disclaimers (refutatio). Nevertheless, Dostoevsky is here treated chiefly as a pathological case.

Freud faults Zweig for narrowly restricting Dostoevsky's illness to "his alleged epilepsy." Instead, Freud argues that the medical case of Dostoevsky could be diagnosed as hysteria. Unlike hysteria, epilepsy was classed as an "organic brain disease" independent of the "psychic constitution," hence independent of neuroses and inaccessible to psychoanalytic treatment or theory. Epilepsy was then still believed to lead, in most cases, to mental deterioration, though as Freud notes, one great exception was on record: the great physiologist Helmholtz. Thus, Dostoevsky, whose mind was brilliant to the end, did not seem to fit the prevailing clinical stereotype of genuine epilepsy, although exceptions might occur.

Freud's mentor Charcot had studied cases of convulsive disease that seemed to combine the clinical history and symptoms of hysteria and epilepsy. This "mixed form" of illness, known from the late eighteenth century as epileptiform hysteria (Tissot) and later as hysteroepilepsy, is the subject of the final chapter in Charcot's *Leçons sur les maladies du système nerveux*, volume 3, translated by Freud into German and published in 1886.[5] In the Vienna Psychoanalytic Society's meeting of 8 April 1908, a paper on epileptic aura (the final premonitory symptom before convulsion) was criticized for careless diagnosis because it claimed that "frequently such cases are hysterias, as, for instance, the case of Dostoevsky."[6] Perhaps the diagnosis of Dostoevsky was discussed on this occasion, but there is no record of it in the Society's *Minutes*.

Six months later, at the Society's meeting of 21 October 1908, Stekel presented from his own practice a case of hysterical pseudoepilepsy with obsessional neurosis. The patient had claimed to suffer from epileptic convulsions, but Stekel declared that with psychoanalysis such unfortunates could be unmasked for what they usually are, "namely, hysterics." In the discussion, Freud strongly supported this position: "There are hysterias and there are epilepsies; occasionally, the two may combine, but all those illnesses that are called hysteroepilepsy are simply hysteria."[7] On this occasion Freud reminded his colleagues that traumatic family events in early childhood might create a predisposition to hysteria. Cases with such a history came under the purview of psychoanalysis.

Not a great deal was known about Dostoevsky's medical history in Freud's lifetime.[8] One source available to Freud prior to 1920 was Dr. Timofei Segaloff's booklet *Die Krankheit Dostojewskys* (a medico-psychological study), the fifth in a series on "Borderline Questions of Literature and Medicine" edited by Dr. S. Rahmer of Berlin.[9] Segaloff cited the opinion of Dostoevsky's personal physician (Yanovsky) and insisted that the diagnosis of epilepsy could not be doubted, although sudden change of symptoms and occasional apparent influence by psychic suggestion might give rise to speculation about an hysterical malady.[10] Precisely this line of speculation was followed by Rank in writing "Der Doppelgänger," duly noting Segaloff among his sources.[11] Rank called attention to Dostoevsky's remark, out of context, that without catastrophes intervening he would go crazy (recorded by Dostoevsky's wife in her diary).[12] Such circumstances, said Rank, "easy to grasp psychologically," seemed to suggest not epilepsy but rather "an hysterical affliction (with pseudoepileptic seizures)."[13] Rank, who was not medically trained, probably had more than one opportunity to assimilate this "party line" on Dostoevsky from Freud himself. But no attempt is made in "Der Doppelgänger" to elaborate upon the psychoanalysis of Dostoevsky.

In the letter to Zweig of 1920, Freud recalls being shown—possibly by Rank?—a biography of Dostoevsky with a passage "tracing back the late affliction of the man to the boy's having been punished by his father under very serious circumstances—I vaguely remember the word 'tragic,' am I right?" Here Freud superimposes his psychoanalytic fantasy of a threatening father on the vague legend of a tragic family event. There is good evidence that Dostoevsky's father was severely authoritarian, increasingly paranoid and alcoholic, and (in all likelihood) murdered by his family serfs. There is no way to bring these circumstances to bear conclusively on the illness of Dostoevsky the son, nor to say exactly when his illness began. So far as we now know, his grand mal convulsions were first medically diagnosed as epilepsy in July 1847—eight years after his father's death and more than two years before Dostoevsky's sentence to execution before a (mock) firing squad. Freud, however, was speculatively inclined to posit a "childhood scene" (primal, sexual, guilty), which was supposedly reinforced by the mock execution and perpetuated in falling seizures thereafter. "Dostoevsky's whole life is dominated by his twofold attitude to the father-tsar-authority, by voluptuous masochistic submission on the one hand, and by outraged rebellion against it on the other. Masochism includes a sense of guilt which surges toward 'redemption' [*Erlösung*]."[14]

This initial Freudian formulation of Dostoevsky's psychodynamic profile has several points in common with the analysis, posthumously published, by Tatiana Rosenthal, the utopian Marxist revolutionary who had returned to Petrograd after studying with Jung. Her unfinished essay on Dostoevsky probably reached Freud just a month or two before he wrote to Zweig. The brief published preview of her unwritten chapter on Dostoevsky's major fiction states that "the basic tone of Dostoevsky's creativity remained unaltered: it is a feeling of self-abasement and rebellion against this feeling, which intensifies into a diametrically opposite feeling of his own elect predestination [*Auserwähltheit*]."[15] The model appears to be nearly identical with Freud's, except that his sexual etiology of Dostoevsky's illness, and its "voluptuous" (*wollüstig*) component, were not included. A Marxist and Adlerian, Rosenthal had sought a simpler, social explanation for Dostoevsky's condition, until her suicide intervened.

Curiously, Freud declares to Zweig that hysteria (unlike epilepsy) "springs from the psychic constitution itself and is an expression of the same organic elementary power [*Urkraft*] that is revealed in the artistic creativity of a genius." This idea stems from Romantic medicine of the nineteenth century, which tended to link artistic creativity precariously with "nervous constitution," and thus to exalt the concept of disease. However, in that era epilepsy and hysteria had been seen as parallel offshoots from the same schematic "stem" of a purely hypothetical "idiosyncratic hereditary nervous condition"—as represented, for example, by J.-J. Moreau de Tours in his *Psychologie morbide* published in Paris in 1869.[16] Freud evidently relegated epilepsy to a class of purely so-to-speak "mechanical" illnesses, another nineteenth-century clinical view that Dostoevsky himself at times invoked to assure himself and loved ones that the complex epileptic mental symptoms he suffered intermittently were not signs of insanity or some darker spiritual taint.[17] The legendary *morbus sacer* had long been routinely attributed not only to cases of demoniac possession (such as the biblical lunatics), but also to many great historical figures such as Caesar, Muhammad, Peter the Great, and Napoleon.[18] Dostoevsky both in his fictions and in his political life used (but also satirized) these ancient and potent legends, which medical textbooks often still perpetuated. Freud sought to strip Dostoevsky (and epilepsy) of this extravagant psychic charisma and superstition, but endowed hysteria with a trace of the same heroic glamour. Linking hysteria with creative genius was evidently a concession to the creative writer Zweig (whom Freud here hails as the author of *Erste Erlebnisse*), rejecting his view of Dostoevsky as seer of a holy illness but conceding that his talent and pathology were mysteriously intertwined in his "psychic constitution." This Romantic view of hysteria was still commonplace in Freud's time. For example, as we have seen, his old friend Darkshevich published in Russian two essays on hysteria at about this time.[19] He fervently claimed that mankind's spiritual progress would emanate from the same "emotive constitution" that produced hysteria in pathological cases. Saint Paul, said Darkshevich, was the preeminent example of hysteria channeled into historic greatness.[20] Freud and Dostoevsky might have agreed, each with his own ironic reservations.

The "dualism" that Zweig had recognized as Dostoevsky's dominant feature Freud designated psychoanalytically as "ambivalence." In 1928 Freud was to expand his discussion of this point, building upon the theory of primitive "national psychology" expounded in his *Totem and Taboo* (particularly in part 2, "The Ambivalence of Emotions"). Ambivalence, he told Zweig, was "a legacy from the psychic life of primitive races," but "with the

Russians it is far better preserved and more accessible to consciousness than elsewhere." This had been demonstrated, he said, a few years earlier in his "detailed case history of a typical Russian patient" (that is, of course, the Wolf-Man). The strong Russian tendency toward ambivalence, combined with "the childhood trauma," said Freud, may have partly determined "the unusual violence of Dostoevsky's case of hysteria"—that is to say, the violent self-damage that would ordinarily suggest a diagnosis of epilepsy and rule out hysteria. Freud managed to overlook other such symptoms crucial to the differential diagnosis: occurrence of seizures while alone and during sleep (noted by Zweig); and prolonged depressions following seizures.[21] In 1920, Freud did not dwell upon these matters. Observing that Dostoevsky's pathology might stem in part from his primitive racial roots (the Russian psyche), Freud suggested to Zweig that "even Russians who are not neurotic are also very noticeably ambivalent, as are the characters in almost all of Dostoevsky's novels." These ideas are embellished in the essay of 1928.

Most of the peculiarities of Dostoevsky's writing, Freud told Stefan Zweig, can be traced back to his psychic (sexual) constitution, which was "for us abnormal, for the Russian fairly common." This was especially true of "everything annoying and alienating" (*alles Quälende und Befremdende*), of which Freud offers no examples. It followed that Dostoevsky "cannot be understood without psychoanalysis," not that he "needs" it but indeed because he illustrates it in every character and every sentence. *The Brothers Karamazov*, which deals with "Dostoevsky's most personal problem—parricide," is constructed on the psychoanalytic theory that evil intent and evil act are equivalents. (Here Freud shifts his focus to Dostoevsky's last novel and indicates a central issue to which he would return in 1928: *der Vatermord*.) One further aspect of Dostoevsky's kinship with psychoanalysis is "the peculiarity of his sexual love," either blind lust or sublimated compassion, the doubts of his heroes concerning love and hate, the problems of when they love and whom—all of this "shows clearly from what soil his psychology has sprung [auf welch besonderem Boden seine Psychologie erwachsen ist]." Thereupon Freud made his ambiguous disclaimer to Zweig, that "this emphasis on the so-called pathological" was not meant to belittle or explain away "the splendor of Dostoevsky's poetic power of creativity." And so the letter ends, though "not because the material is exhausted."

* * *

Eight years elapsed from the time Freud outlined his ideas on Dostoevsky for Stefan Zweig until the appearance of "Dostoevsky and Parricide" in December 1928. In that interval, certain changes in Freud's life and world modified his view of the subject. The most general and pervasive of these was cancer of the jaw, which from 1923 to the end turned his existence into a stoic physical ordeal. But the experience of chronic pain, the *memento mori*, seems to have allowed a "regressive development" (as he put it) to general cultural problems that had occupied him long before, freeing him from the need to make further contributions to medical science.[22] The treatises that he now produced—*The Future of an Illusion* (published in 1927), *Civilization and Its Discontents* (1930), *New Introductory Lectures on Psychoanalysis* (1933), and *Moses and Monotheism* (1939)—deal with issues of national psychology, religion and patriotism, social revolution, order, and decline.[23] During the 1920s and 1930s the "Russian experiment" was the world's great test case of rapid social change, and it is easy to discern that Freud's major publications of these last two decades actively respond to the violent spectacle of Stalinist Russia. Freud's view of Russia shifted significantly during the very years when he was writing "Dostoevsky and Parricide."

Two points of contact brought the Bolshevik regime home to Freud. In Vienna he followed the intermittent relapses of the Wolf-Man, once a model of psychoanalytic healing, now a paranoid who threatened to shoot the analyst—a living (Russian) reproach to Freud's work. In a seemingly parallel development, Freud witnessed through official bulletins and émigré reports the ill-fated enterprise of the Russian Psychoanalytic Society, newly established after the Revolution, in 1921, by I. Ermakov and Moshe Wolff. At first there had been in fact a good deal to be optimistic about, both in the Moscow Society's intellectual performance and early acceptance by the Soviet scientific establishment, and in the ex-millionaire Pankeev's humble but solid job with an Austrian insurance agency. We recall that the analyst assigned by Freud to Pankeev's case in 1927, Ruth Mack Brunswick, noted her amazement at the rapid adjustment of Russian émigrés.[24] Freud could well appreciate the resilience needed to survive such an exodus. Nevertheless, the serious intermittent deterioration of his Russian patient, coupled with the threat of violence to himself, escalated Freud's ambivalence toward his inherently ambivalent patient. Official Soviet Marxist resistance to the Russian psychoanalytic movement became evident to Freud at the same time. We return to this development below.

In the Wolf-Man's late interviews, he mentions "a certain Schütz," Freud's "relative ... or perhaps an in-law," an Austrian who had studied in Russia apparently during the early 1920s. Pankeev told Schütz that Freud had once advised him to return to Russia, even if the Bolsheviks finally gained control (i.e., at the end of the Civil War in 1920), because "it's better to stay in the country where one was born." Schütz replied: "You know, Freud knows human intelligence very well, but he doesn't seem to know the Bolshevist intelligence." Needless to say, at that time millions of others did not know the Bolshevik mentality particularly well in Russia, let alone the West.

This anecdote suggests some measure of optimism about "the Russian experiment" on Freud's part, at the outset of Lenin's rule. But other sources recall also Freud's skepticism at the utopian extravagance of early Bolshevik propaganda. Hanns Sachs reports that in the early 1920s Freud listened to "a prominent Bolshevist" expounding Lenin's prediction that Europe would experience even greater revolutionary devastation than Russia, followed by unbroken happiness and stability. Freud replied: "Let's make it fifty-fifty. I will accept the first half." Freud told a variant of the same joke to Ernest Jones. When "an ardent Communist" proclaimed that the Revolution would result in years of misery and chaos followed by universal peace, prosperity, and happiness, Freud said he was "half converted to Bolshevism," that is, "I told him I believed the first half."[25] By 1930, when the Russian Psychoanalytic Society had been effectively suppressed, Freud was thoroughly disillusioned with "the Russian dictators" and had "no hope" that Soviet economic policy would lead to improvement. "Indeed any such hope that I may have cherished," he wrote to Arnold Zweig on 26 November 1930, "has disappeared in this decade of Soviet rule."[26] Freud's revolutionary zeal, handed down to him in family legends of 1848, flaring up in 1863 and 1881, expressed fundamentally in *Die Traumdeutung*, inflamed by the rise of Russian anti-Semitism and the First World War, had applauded the fall of the Romanovs and optimistically followed the unfolding of Lenin's New Economic Policy. A shift toward increased skepticism, ambivalence, and irony occurred approximately midway through the 1920s, when Freud was writing "Dostoevsky and Parricide."

In the autumn of 1923, the ranks of the Russian Psychoanalytic Society were strengthened by the arrival of Dr. Sabina Spielrein from Geneva and Dr. A. R. Luria (1902-77), later a leading figure in Soviet psychology. Two colleagues of Luria from Kazan, R. Averbuch and V. B. Friedmann, also joined at this time and proved themselves game advocates of psychoanalysis against attacks by Party journalists. Another friend of Luria, adept at Marxist dialectic, was the gifted literary theoretician L. S. Vygotski, who came to the Society as a guest and soon joined. In 1923, L. D. Trotsky spoke out enthusiastically in defense of psychoanalysis in his *Literature and Revolution*, and on 27 September of that year he wrote a letter to Pavlov urging that psychoanalysis be given serious scientific consideration.[27] These gestures were less propitious than might be supposed, because Trotsky's political career was already on the skids. The Second All-Russian Psychoneurological Congress of 1924 endorsed the use of psychoanalysis.[28] But within a year one senses the defensive polemic in Luria's paper of 26 March 1925, in which he argued that psychoanalysis be placed on the same scientific level as Pavlovian experimental psychology.[29]

On 9 April 1925, Moshe Wulff, president of the Moscow Psychoanalytic Society, spoke about "Freud's more recent critics" in the Soviet Union. Their complaints amounted to "old objections to his theory which have long been refuted.... The feeling against Freud now manifesting itself in Russia is in the main simply a repetition of the controversy long ago concluded in Western Europe, with the addition of some new factors."[30] The nature of those factors is not stated, but clearly it was awkward for the early Marxist-Leninists, beset with major political and economic difficulties, to make room for a hypothetical unconscious in the materialist dialectic.[31] Such an accommodation is what Friedmann was attempting in his talk of 14 May 1925, "Psychoanalysis and Materialistic Monism," insisting that Freud's doctrine was "entirely materialistic."[32] Freud would have agreed, however, that his rhetorical manner often makes it difficult to draw the line between doctrine and speculation. The line all too often vanishes in the writings of Freud's disciples and popularizers. A particularly blatant example is Jolan Neufeld's *Dostojewski. Skizzen zu seiner Psychoanalyse*, published by the International Psychoanalytic Press in 1923 as the fourth volume in a series edited by Freud. In 1925, a Russian translation was published by "Petrograd" Press with the added subtitle: A Psychoanalytic Study Edited by Prof. S. Freud (though he had been only titular editor of the series and was for some years unaware of the book's existence). Neufeld's book is Oedipus run amuck, an unfortunate embarrassment for the Russian Society, particularly because the author attempts to analyze Dostoevsky, a multifaceted and endlessly controversial national figure. A Soviet editor's preface openly sneers at Neufeld's clumsy psychoanalytic excesses. In any event, one may say that by 1925 the handwriting was on the wall, and psychoanalysis had become just one of many embattled styles of thought in Bolshevik Russia. On 3 February 1926, Trotsky continued to support Freud's ideas in his lecture on "Culture and Socialism," repeated on various occasions and published in *Novyi mir* in January 1927. This could hardly help the movement—rather the contrary. A year later Trotsky fell from power and was banished to Alma Ata. His support, it seems in retrospect, may have been a kiss of death for psychoanalysis in Russia.

It was in the spring of 1926 that Freud was invited by R. Piper & Co. of Munich to write an introductory article for a volume that would include notes and drafts for *The Brothers Karamazov*, letters and commentaries, and a detailed study by the Soviet scholar V. L. Komarovich. This publication, dedicated to the memory of another Russian literary historian, D. K. Petrov, did not appear until December 1928.[33] It was edited by René Fülöp-Miller and Friedrich Eckstein, who collaborated in publishing a number of volumes on Dostoevsky and Russia in the 1920s. Freud's official biography tells us that he read "the beginning" of his essay to Max Eitingon at the end of June 1926, but one cannot say whether this draft was incorporated into the finished version. Soon his attention was directed to other projects, and by October 1926 he confessed that his energy and interest had waned.[34] Eitingon, the inveterate Russophile by this time married to a former Moscow Art Theater actress, kept urging Freud to finish the essay on Dostoevsky and took every opportunity to supply him with materials, including a new edition of Dostoevsky's correspondence."[35] Freud's footnotes and the inventory of his library will enable us to identify several other sources at his disposal.

During the interval when Freud set aside his work on Dostoevsky, the Russian Psychoanalytic Society continued to defend itself against escalating attacks by the militant Marxist press.[36] On 28 October 1926, Friedmann read a paper addressing the fateful question: "Does Psychoanalysis Contradict Dialectical Materialism?"[37] A few months later, on 23 February 1927, Freud wrote to Dr. Nikolai Evgráfovich Osipov, a founding editor of the Muscovite prewar psychoanalytic journal *Psikhoterapiia*, who after the Revolution had emigrated to Prague:

> The analysts in Soviet Russia are, by the way, having a bad time. From somewhere the Bolsheviks have caught the opinion that psychoanalysis is hostile to their system. You know the truth, that our science cannot be placed at the service of any party, but that it needs a certain liberal-mindedness in turn for its own development.[38]

That spring, on 7 April 1927, Luria resigned as secretary of the Russian Society, feeling the tide turn and seeking a lucky gambit for professional survival.[39] Sabina Spielrein withdrew to her native Rostov-on-the-Don, and in November 1927 Moshe Wulff emigrated to Berlin, announcing his resignation as Russian Society president effective January 1928.[40] By this time Freud's movement was all but dead in Russia, effectively killed by the new Stalinist order. In these circumstances, Freud returned to his essay on Dostoevsky and completed it, but not until he had written another work on the major philosophical questions that Dostoevsky poses.

On 5 August 1927, Freud wrote to Marie Bonaparte about a problem that occupied him, "the old problem that is raised in a grandiose manner in Dostoevsky's 'Grand Inquisitor', namely, whether mankind is able to profit from its freedom or whether a superior absolutism is most beneficial for it—the problem, yes, but where is the solution? Where do we find the guarantee of the superiority?"[41] In the opening lines of "Dostoevsky and Parricide" Freud extols *The Brothers Karamazov* as "the most magnificent novel ever written," and its "Grand Inquisitor" legend as beyond praise, "one of the peaks of world literature." The novel and its pivotal episode gave Freud the focal themes for his study of Dostoevsky: denial of God, and parricide. However, Freud first addressed the great issues of freedom and authority posed by Ivan Karamazov's "Grand Inquisitor" in a separate booklet, *The Future of an Illusion*.[42] It was written between spring and fall of 1927 and published in November of the same year. In fact, *The Future of an Illusion* and "Dostoevsky and Parricide" are companion pieces, both occupied with problems posed by the Russian novelist and his authoritarian fatherland, past and present. Several times in "Dostoevsky and Parricide" Freud salutes the writer's great intellect, which made it impossible for him "to overlook a single one of the intellectual difficulties (*Denkschwierigkeiten*) to which faith leads." For Freud, this was like saying, "Welcome to the club!" But it is only in *Future of an Illusion* that Freud duly honors the intellect of Dostoevsky, without naming him yet unmistakably and "in a style worthy of the subject": a cosmic dialogue. In "Dostoevsky and Parricide," on the other hand, the subject is presented chiefly as a psychoanalytic case, with results sometimes puzzling and grotesque. Freud's view of Dostoevsky was, in a word, ambivalent. In *Future of an Illusion* his intellectual artistry reaches a peak, an implicit tribute to the philosophical art of Dostoevsky.

A short synopsis of the Grand Inquisitor episode will facilitate what follows. The title figure of Ivan Karamazov's improvisation (book 5, chapter 5) is an atheistic manipulator of society in Seville during the Inquisition, clearly intended as an allegory of modern humanity (and never more aptly so than in Bolshevik Russia of 1927). The tale is told with parody of holy writ, frequent irony, and seeds of doubt: brother Ivan seeks to test and disillusion brother Aliosha. (The novel, *Brothers Karamazov*, is in many respects an attack against faith and illusion: in the actions of the father, the figures of Lise and Smerdiakov, the ordeals of Dmitri, the burlesque of authority in the courtroom, the disintegration and collapse of Ivan himself, whose illusions are not religious but materialistic.) The resurrected Christ is imprisoned by the Inquisitor lest he disrupt sacred doctrine with a single word. He replies to the Inquisitor's diatribe with only a kiss of forgiveness. (But can Christ's passive silence be forgiven, in the face of such godless hypocrisy?)

Man is seen as "an unfinished experimental animal created as a joke." The Inquisitor argues that Christ relinquished power to the Pope, and now he and his brethren have removed the entire burden of freedom from the people, because rebels cannot be happy. He also invokes "science," which denies guilt and sees only the need of feeding the hungry. Rebellion will be defeated by three forces: miracle, mystery, and authority (all rejected by the biblical Christ). Mankind inevitably has had to create new miracles for itself, to bow down (so to speak) before folk quackery and the spells of old women, even if someone is a hundred times over a rebel, heretic, and atheist. Rebels will see that their actions are ludicrous and to no avail. Their main aim on earth is to find somebody to worship, somebody to take charge of the conscience, and a way to merge finally into an indisputably universal and harmonious anthill—or a docile herd. (Dostoevsky's precociously Nietzschean wisdom remained right on target for the emerging Stalinist state of 1927.) Brother Aliosha protests that this is only a distorted image of Rome (not Russian Orthodoxy, nor mankind in general). But the generalizing power of the allegory remains, and as the novel unfolds chinks appear in the rather eccentric faith of Aliosha too. In the unwritten sequel to the novel he was destined to become a revolutionary, perhaps the tsar's assassin.[43] The argument of the Inquisitor may conceal the grander design of Dostoevsky's revolutionary novel: deception in the name of the Ideal, a lie as the nearest approach to Truth. The godless ethic advanced in Ivan's legend is, like psychology itself, "a stick with two ends" because the philosopher destroys himself with his own poisonous skepticism. The outcome, he hints, must be suicide, or else the triumph of the Karamazov force and the doctrine of "all is permitted, since God does not exist."

In *The Future of an Illusion*, Freud addresses the problem of maintaining social order through necessary illusions, be they religious, political, or erotic (for example, the incest taboo). At the close of the first chapter he disclaims any intention of passing judgment on "the great experiment in civilization now in progress in the vast country that stretches between Europe and Asia." But in chapter 9 his interlocutor says that Russia is repeating the French Revolution's experiment, "and we need not feel curious as to its outcome"—indicating that Freud himself now gave a negative prognosis for the

Soviet state. In another passage, after describing an archaic form of cultural illusion, the primitive custom of erasing sin with penance or sacrifice, Freud unexpectedly adds that "Russian spiritual profundity [*Russische Innerlichkeit*] has reached the pitch of concluding that sin is indispensable for the enjoyment of all the blessings of divine grace, so that, at bottom, sin is pleasing to God" (chapter 8). This curiously ironic claim about the Russian national character was to be further developed—and applied to Dostoevsky as well as Ivan the Terrible!—in "Dostoevsky and Parricide." We shall return to it in that context.

The idea of God, argues Freud, has been historically essential for keeping the half-civilized masses from "killing without hesitation." This echoes the concept of the dark Karamazov force, and Dmitri Karamazov's stunned realization (taken up deviously by Ivan) that "if there is no God, then all is permitted."[44] Freud asserts that in the long run it would be better "to leave God out altogether," to admit the purely human origin of all regulations and precepts of civilization.[45] But his interlocutor pleads for maintaining the religious "illusion" as a refined set of sublimated ideas that science cannot disprove.[46] This approximates the Inquisitor's position.

The basic design of *The Future of an Illusion* resembles the"Grand Inquisitor legend in "the grandeur of the plan"—specifically, a dialectic of supreme beings reconstructing civilization, stripping away the masks and illusions that have held the barbaric majority in check.[47] One recalls that as early as 1918, in remarks to the Vienna Psychoanalytic Society, Freud said that Dostoevsky was in a rare class of psychological writers who "seek to uncover what is concealed." Now it becomes clear that the revelations valued by Freud in Dostoevsky's writing were precisely of a psychoanalytic nature, involving the struggle of mankind against authority and the ambiguous role of civilization in determining freedom and destiny. Why, asks Freud, should a child's intellectual growth be blocked by threats of Hell-fire?[48] This is a purely Dostoevskian question, one that each of the Karamazov brothers asks, after his fashion. But it also arises directly from Freud's own early childhood: the vision of sinners burning in Hell taught by his Czech Catholic nanny, his alien "instructress in sexual matters." So it was that Freud valued in Dostoevsky above all his great intellect, struggling against the illusion and authority of religious faith.

Notes

1   Sigmund Freud, "Dostojewski und die Vatertötung"; Gerda Maneval, personal communication.

2   Sigmund Freud, *Standard Edition of the Complete Psychological Works of Sigmund Freud*, vol. 21, pp. 195-96.

3   Sigmund Freud, Letter to Stefan Zweig of 19 October 1920.

4   Sigmund Freud, *The Letters of Sigmund Freud*, p. 332; Sigmund Freud, *Briefe, 1873-1939*, 2nd ed., p. 349.

5   J.-M. Charcot, *Neue Vorlesungen*.

6   Herman Nunberg and Ernst Federn, eds., *Minutes of the Vienna Psychoanalytic Society*, vol. 1, p. 363.

7   Ibid., vol. 2, pp. 13-24 and 19.

8   James L. Rice, *Dostoevsky and the Healing Art*.

9   Timofei Segaloff, *Die Krankheit Dostojewskys*.

10   Ibid., p. 39.

11   Otto Rank, "Der Doppelgänger," pp. 117-23 (on "The Double").

12   Ibid., p. 133.

13   Ibid., p. 133.

14   Sigmund Freud, *The Letters of Sigmund Freud*, p. 333.

15   Sara Neiditsch, "Die Psychoanalyse in Russland."

16   James L. Rice, *Dostoevsky and the Healing Art*, pp. 152-160.

17   Ibid., pp. 85 and 90.

18   Owsei Temkin, *The Falling Sickness*.

19   L. O. Darkshevich, "Moe ponimanie isterii"; L. O. Darkshevich, *Beglye kharakteristiki deiatelei iz vremen Sviashchennogo Pisaniia*.

20   James L. Rice, *Dostoevsky and the Healing Art*, p. 212.

21   Alfred Erich Hoche, *Die Differentialdiagnose*; Pierre Janet, *The Major Symptoms of Hysteria*; Paul Chodoff, "The Diagnosis of Hysteria"; Alan Krohn, *Hysteria: The Elusive Neurosis*; Alec Roy, "Hysterical Seizures."

22   Max Schur, *Freud, Living and Dying*, p. 395.

23   These works were foreshadowed by *Totem and Taboo*, *Beyond the Pleasure Principle*, and passages in earlier writings.

24   S. K. Pankeev, *The Wolf-Man by the Wolf-Man*, p. 303.

25   Karin Obholzer, *The Wolf-Man Sixty Years Later*, p. 48. Hanns Sachs, *Freud. Master and Friend*, p. 140. Ernest Jones, *The Life and Work of Sigmund Freud*, vol. 3, p. 16.

26   Sigmund Freud and Arnold Zweig, *The Letters of Sigmund Freud and Arnold Zweig*, p. 21.

27   L. N. Trotskii, "Pis'mo Akademiku Pavlovu"; L. [N.] Trotskii, *Literatura i revoliutsiia*.

28   Elias Perepel, "The Psychoanalytic Movement in U.S.S.R."

29   A. R. Luria, "Die moderne russische Physiologie."

30   Moshe Wulff, Report of 9 April 1925.

31   M. M. Bakhtin, *Freidism*, pp. 133-224; James L. Rice, "Russian Stereotypes in the Freud-Jung Correspondence"; Martin Miller, "Freudian Theory Under Bolshevik Rule"; Martin Miller, "The Theory and Practice of Psychiatry in the Soviet Union"; Martin Miller, "The Origins and Development of Russian Psychoanalysis"; Gerald Pirog, "The Bakhtin Circle's Freud"; Gerald Pirog, "Bakhtin and Freud on the ego."

32   V. B. Friedmann, *International Journal of Psycho-Analysis* 7 (1926): 295.

33   Gerda Maneval, personal communication.

34   Ernest Jones, *The Life and Work of Sigmund Freud*, vol. 3, p. 143 (letters to Max 3 and 10 October 1926).

35   Ibid., vol. 3, p. 143.

36   Jean Marti, "La Psychanalyse en Russie"; Hans Lobner and Vladimir Levitin, "A Short Account of Freudianism"; George H. Pollock, "Psychoanalysis in Russia and the U.S.S.R."; James L. Rice, "Russian Stereotypes in the Freud-Jung Correspondence"; Martin Miller, "Freudian Theory Under Bolshevik Rule"; Martin Miller, "The Theory and Practice of Psychiatry in the Soviet Union"; Martin Miller, "The Origins and Development of Russian Psychoanalysis."

37   V. B. Friedmann, *International Journal of Psycho-Analysis* 8 (1927): 454.

38   George H. Pollock, "Psychoanalysis in Russia and the U.S.S.R.," p. 274, citing Hans Lobner and Vladimir Levitin, "A Short Account of Freudianism," p. 14. Freud's unpublished letters to Osipov are in the Health Science Library, Columbia University.

39   "Russian Society," *International Journal of Psycho-Analysis* 8 (1927): 455; A. R. Luria, the Making of Mind, p. 211 (Cole).

40 *International Journal of Psycho-Analysis* 20 (1928): 398; *Internationale Zeitschrift für Psychoanalyse* 14 (1928): 295, 432.

41 Max Schur, *Freud, Living and Dying*, p. 404.

42 The connection was first noticed in Max Schur, *Freud, Living and Dying*, p. 404.

43 F. M. Dostoevskii, *Polnoe sobranie sochinenii v tridtsati tomakh* 15 (1976): 485-86.

44 Sigmund Freud, *The Future of an Illusion*, end of chap. 7; beginning of chap. 9.

45 Ibid., chap. 8.

46 Ibid., chap. 10.

47 Ibid., chap. 1, conclusion; chap. 7.

48 Ibid., chap. 9.

8

"Dostoevsky and Parricide"

On 6 May 1926, Freud reached the age of seventy, "the Biblical Age"—as his physician and biographer Max Schur puts it.[1] For three years he had endured frequent surgery on his upper and lower right jaw, removal of cancerous and precancerous tissue, including part of the upper palate, and four refittings of a prosthesis that impaired his speech and caused constant pain.[2] It is remarkable that Freud "could not overcome his addiction and give up smoking," which required special adjustments of the prosthesis to enable him to draw in the cigar smoke and caused the precancerous lesions to proliferate. During 1926 an "endless cycle" of surgical treatments for the condition commenced.[3] On 10 March 1926, he wrote to Max Eitingon that "renouncing the sweet habit of smoking has resulted in a great diminution of my intellectual interests." The solution was to go on smoking and working—for another fourteen years.[4]

This minor yet possibly fatal bit of obsessive behavior has a direct bearing on Freud's view of Dostoevsky. Thirty years earlier he had observed that addiction to alcohol, drugs, or tobacco is a substitute for the "primal addiction" of masturbation (quotes lending irony are his).[5] This concept of addiction was not pursued again in Freud's writing until "Dostoevsky and Parricide," which in fact concludes with a discussion of Dostoevsky's compulsive gambling, seen as yet another form of onanistic obsession. Smoking and gambling have other things in common, besides their hypothetical psychosexual etiology and their symbolically masturbatory "play," of which Freud may have been aware while writing about Dostoevsky. Like roulette, cigars tempt fate, induce euphoria, retard and rechannel one's energy from more vital work (much as the sin of Onan), and promised the obsessive Freud—as gambling had for Dostoevsky—a payoff in intellectual creativity. Thus, Freud shared with his renowned Russian subject a certain degree of addictive neurotic behavior, which was by 1926 an unmistakably self-destructive precondition of creativity. Consciously or unconsciously, this may have contributed to Freud's antipathy for Dostoevsky, an attitude that is plainly evident. When he wrote his essay, Freud probably did not know that Dostoevsky's terminal illness was complicated, like his own, by decades of heavy smoking. This medical opinion, recently confirmed, was first advanced by Erich Ebstein, a Leipzig physician, in the 27 October 1928 issue of *Die Medizinische Welt*, about a month before the belated appearance of "Dostoevsky and Parricide."[6]

Freud divides Dostoevsky's personality into four facets: the artist, the neurotic, the moralist or moral philosopher (*der Ethiker*), and the sinner. Although the artist is initially revered as "unanalyzable," Freud in fact not only subjects *The Brothers Karamazov* to a detailed and favorable comparison with *Oedipus Rex* and *Hamlet*, he also draws upon Dostoevsky's fiction as major evidence of his immoral, sinful, and neurotic character. Dostoevsky's moral shortcomings—above all the allegedly retrograde politics of his later years—Freud explains as "intellectual inhibition due to his neurosis." This opinion (twice stated) introduces yet another dimension of Dostoevsky repeatedly emphasized by Freud—his great intellect. Freud was most struck by this quality in the Grand Inquisitor legend of *The Brothers Karamazov*, which—as shown above—directly inspired *The Future of an Illusion* in the summer of 1927, when the draft of "Dostoevsky and Parricide" had been set aside and Freud confronted the intellect of Dostoevsky directly. The Grand Inquisitor remained for Freud a central problem of Dostoevsky in all his aspects, even the neurotic.

One of Freud's critics (Reik) reproached him for not giving due recognition to Dostoevsky also as psychologist, in fact as the great precursor of psychoanalysis. Freud agreed, saying that he had understood this aspect to be subsumed under the artist.[7] And indeed, insofar as Freud considers Dostoevsky the artist at all, it is Dostoevsky the psychologist that engages him. No doubt, together with the artist and psychologist he would include the intellect—unquestionably that side of Dostoevsky that Freud valued the most.

One difficulty in reading Freud's essay is the interplay of these various "facets" of Dostoevsky's personality, the hierarchy and boundaries of which are not clearly shown. Another difficulty stems from the fact that Freud's article appeared in a connoisseur's edition of drafts and plans for *The Brothers Karamazov*, including a long study of the novel (by V. L. Komarovich) and appended letters and memoirs.[8] This allowed Freud to use his evidence, from Dostoevsky's life and works, in a highly elliptical and allusive fashion, without much by way of documentation. Clearly he made use of extensive sources, but often it is difficult to determine the basis of his pronouncements.[9] Of course he did not know all that is known today; he accepted various judgments of his time, and he made mistakes. The major objective of Freud's essay is to present the case of Dostoevsky in the light of psychoanalytic expertise. His opinions need to be seen in the changing contexts of medical history and in the perspective of Dostoevsky's age, Freud's, and our own. One obligation of our commentary must be to intercede on behalf of Dostoevsky, with the truth as it can be reconstructed now and the truth as he probably knew it, while another obligation is to intercede on behalf of Freud by attesting to his integrity in the use of sources that were available to him.

Freud's essay opens with some provocative remarks about the Russian national character and Dostoevsky's role in the history of civilization. In Dostoevsky's behavior Freud saw a pattern of alternating sin and high morality, unresolved by renunciation (*der Verzicht*). Precisely what he has in mind is not immediately revealed. Instead, without transition Freud shocks us with hyperbole: "He reminds one of the barbarians of the great migrations, who murdered and did penance for it, till penance became an actual technique for enabling murder to be done."[10] And in the next breath: "Ivan the Terrible [*Iwan der Schreckliche*] behaved in exactly this way—in fact, this compromise with morality [*Ausgleich mit der Sittlichkeit*] is a characteristic Russian trait." Thus, in a few sentences Dostoevsky has been associated (like the Wolf-Man) with primitive murderous ambivalence, with the sixteenth-century tsar of legendary violence, and with the Russian national character as perceived by Freud and, no doubt, a portion of his readers in 1928. Let us pause to consider what lies behind such sweeping pronouncements.

From his juvenile cult of Spain to his fascination with Rome and Egyptology, Freud was engaged with problems of "racial psychology"—the subject of his essays published in 1912-13 (during the first analysis of the Wolf-Man) and collected under the title *Totem and Taboo* (published in 1913).[11] The book is subtitled: "Some Points of Agreement between the Mental Lives of Savages and Neurotics." So it followed that Dostoevsky the neurotic, and his morality, should also be considered along these lines. The guilt experienced by obsessive neurotics, Freud had argued, was like that appropriate to mass murderers, because of the intense and frequent death wishes harbored by neurotics toward their fathers.[12] Christian atonement through communion—Freud suggested, following the lead of Frazer's *Golden Bough*—was a reenactment of the father's elimination, "a repetition of the guilty deed."[13] Neurotic guilt creates new restrictions as atonement for psychic crimes committed and as a precaution against committing new ones.[14] In the essay on Dostoevsky, Freud cites *Totem and Taboo*, but not until the eighth page. In fact it is the key to his initial rhetoric, which is concerned primarily not with Dostoevsky's sinful or criminal behavior (such as it was), but with his idiosyncratic faith as a Russian Orthodox Christian. The underlying issue in Freud's analysis is Dostoevsky's supposedly retrograde faith (driven by neurosis), and the great intellect that struggled to free him from that faith but—as Freud believed—failed to do so completely.

For Freud and his readers, the image of Dostoevsky as primitive neurotic Christian was reinforced by Nietzsche's brilliantly ironic portrait in *Der Antichrist*. The true type of the Saviour, said Nietzsche, has come down to us in a greatly coarsened form. One had to imagine the original milieu, "that strange and sickly world into which the Gospels lead us—a world apparently out of a Russian novel, in which the scum of society, nervous maladies and 'childish' idiocy keep a tryst." The self-importance of sectarian veneration has erased or overlooked all the idiosyncrasies ("often so powerfully strange"). Indeed, "it is greatly to be regretted that no Dostoevsky lived in the neighborhood of this most interesting décadent—I mean someone who would have felt the poignant charm of such a compound of the sublime, the morbid, and the childish."[15] Ostensibly introducing

Dostoevsky as an artist neurotically worthy of Christ, Nietzsche subordinates the Christian world to the psychopathological art of Dostoevsky's underground, where neurotic maladies (*Nervenleiden*) predominate. This malevolently comic passage has much in common with Freud's view of Dostoevsky.

Freud's startling comparison of Dostoevsky and Ivan the Terrible strikes one, on the face of it, as an outrageous reversal of historic roles. Ivan was legendary in Russia and the West as a tsar who murdered his own son in a sudden insane rage, whereas Dostoevsky was the victim of a mock execution staged by Tsar Nicholas I. Freud was perfectly aware, as he states much further on, that Nicholas, "the Little Father" (as tsars were traditionally hailed—a forced or wishful term of endearment), "in reality once played with [Dostoevsky] the comedy of killing [*die Komödie der Tötung*]."[16] On the other hand, Freud was convinced that Dostoevsky, like all neurotics, was guilty of a death wish toward his father, compounded first by the fact of his father's murder by his serfs, and second by the "comedy of killing" the tsar had played with him. On the psychic level, Dostoevsky might be reckoned a (wishful) "mass murderer" on a par with Ivan the Terrible. However, Freud nowhere says this in so many words. Finally, this comparison with the violent tsar-father is an ethical injustice to Dostoevsky as political convict and subversive. The image of Ivan perfectly tallies with Freud's political idea of *Russische Innerlichkeit* (reckoning penance just a technique enabling murder to be done), but in fact it is only Freud's ironic euphemism for this national trait—"this compromise with morality " (*dieser Ausgleich mit der Sittlichkeit*)— that properly applies to Dostoevsky. Thus, a key initial trope of Freud's essay, a bit of rhetoric gone wrong, remains something of a puzzle, try as one may to untangle it.

In writing about Ivan the Terrible, Freud had in mind the notorious pattern of his historical behavior: a cycle of violence and public repentance. In 1895 a certain Dr. A. von Rothe published a substantial psychiatric study of "Ivan Vasilievich IV, known as The Terrible." It appeared in the *Jahrbücher für Psychiatrie und Neurologie*, a publication of the Vienna Society for Psychiatry and Neurology. In the same issue there is an advertisement for Freud's translation of Charcot's *Clinical Lectures*. Von Rothe, whose materials include seven Russian historical and medical sources, does mention Ivan's murder of his son in 1582, following which the tsar showed despair and contrition.[17] In another context, Von Rothe speaks of Ivan's repeated efforts to appease God with promises and offerings.[18] He evidently had "a neuropathic constitution" from childhood, suffered abruptly shifting moods, and "even when he laughed his face had a melancholy serious expression."[19] Throughout life his emotions altered abruptly, suggesting "an inhibition of the central nervous system." Even before the first of his seven marriages he was "evidently psychotic."[20] The many murders of his career, says Von Rothe, were symptoms of his illness, links in the chain of psychosis, like his hallucinations and sudden terror.[21] The presumed diagnosis was "neurasthenia and paranoia idiopathica chronica."[22] Yet—and this may have struck Freud—he was revered as the father of his people.[23] Thus, Freud may have concluded that Ivan's repeated acts of penance were cheapened into "a technique to enable murder to be done," and that if such a figure was revered as the father of his people then his compromise with morality became theirs, "a characteristic Russian trait."

Freud's abrupt transition to Dostoevsky's moral struggles, "anything but glorious," implies again the comparison with Ivan. Dostoevsky's struggle "to reconcile individual and community" ended "in a retrograde fashion" (*rückläufig*), that is, in "submission to both temporal and spiritual authority, and a narrow Russian nationalism." Much further on, Freud significantly modifies this statement insofar as Dostoevsky's religious position is concerned. The allusion to Russian nationalism undoubtedly includes the vexed question of Dostoevsky's anti-Semitism, which is not directly addressed by Freud but must lie at the heart of the matter. Other sources can be brought to bear on this question, which will be discussed in the following chapter. Freud wryly notes that Dostoevsky's final position in political and spiritual matters was reached with less effort by inferior minds (*geringere Geister*), thus acknowledging that the genius of Dostoevsky was after all something to be reckoned with. His late politics—reactionary, in Freud's perception—marked "the weak point of the great personality."[24]

Dostoevsky, Freud asserts, did not become the teacher or liberator of humanity, but instead one of its jailers (*Kerkermeistern*). "The future of humanity will have little to thank him for." Leaving this astonishing claim unelaborated, Freud proposes to demonstrate that Dostoevsky was condemned (*verdammt*) to this failure (*Scheitern*) by his neurosis. Here Freud's intricate exordium ends, with a certain ambiguity, by stating that Dostoevsky's loftiness of intellect (*Intelligenz*) and the strength of his love for humanity "should have opened to him another, apostolic way of life [*ein anderer, ein apostolischer Lebensweg*]." The stumbling block in this fine phrase is that one cannot quite imagine Freud's using the word "apostolic" without irony.

More than halfway into his essay, Freud returns to the question of Dostoevsky's faith in a context which at last reveals an essential misunderstanding. Following the ramifications of psychoanalytic theory, Freud declares that Dostoevsky was forever burdened with guilt for the death wish directed against his father, and so ended "in complete submission" to the tsar who had threatened him with death and sent him to Siberia (Nicholas I). Here Freud slips, because it was not Nicholas but his son, Alexander II, who reigned during the last two decades of Dostoevsky's life. But what mattered psychoanalytically was the guilt concentrated on a figure of authority, a guilt that supposedly forced the transgressor to adopt a reactionary posture of contrition.

In the religious sphere, Freud goes on to observe, more freedom was left to the disposal of Dostoevsky's psyche. "His great intelligence made it impossible for him to overlook a single intellectual difficulty to which faith leads."[25] This declaration, indeed the highest praise he could bestow, suggests Freud's genuine rapport with Dostoevsky, especially when we recall that the intellectual difficulties of faith comprise the very subject of *The Future of an Illusion*, which was directly inspired by Dostoevsky's Grand Inquisitor. But Freud supposed that Dostoevsky had unsuccessfully sought escape to freedom in a private Christ-ideal (martyrdom, masochism), and, curiously enough, Dostoevsky's close friend and physician Yanovsky notes that the writer was indeed at times inclined to "play the martyr" after his term in prison.[26] However, that was only a sporadic private weakness, which runs counter to the motivation and power of Dostoevsky's writing and counter to its impact on the Russian readers of his time. In fact, the "martyr's pose" in Dostoevsky's fiction is exclusively satiric, never without a cunning purpose. (Some striking examples are *The Idiot* and "Dream of a Ridiculous Man.") Clearly, the "Christ-ideal" Freud had in mind was the submissive Christ whose only reply to the "Grand Inquisitor" ("the jailer of humanity") is a mute but thoroughly ambiguous kiss, echoed in the kiss that the Christlike Aliosha bestows upon the legend-spinning Ivan. Freud lost sight of the novel's complex plot, the mental deterioration of Ivan, and the growth of Aliosha into subversive freedom. Freud could not have known that Dostoevsky saw Aliosha as a potential revolutionary, or that some early Russian readers of the book saw him as the tsar's future assassin.[27]

Dostoevsky's supposed decline into political reaction is a commonplace of biographical interpretation, clearly stated in at least one of the books in Freud's library.[28] Freud admits that his judgment of the Russian writer reflects a certain political world view: "A conservative would take the side of the Grand Inquisitor and would judge Dostoevsky differently." By this Freud clearly implies that he himself did not take the side of the "Grand Inquisitor"—that is to say, of course, not that he took the side of the mute opponent, Christ, but that he rejected and opposed the "Grand Inquisitor," the "jailer of humanity," the role to which Dostoevsky himself, as Freud asserts at the outset, had been condemned by his neurosis. In short, Freud both here and frequently falls into the error of equating author and character, Dostoevsky and the "Grand Inquisitor." And he repeats that Dostoevsky's final (reactionary) judgment (*Entscheidung*) appeared to have been determined by a neurotic intellectual inhibition (*Denkhemmung*).

Dostoevsky's instinctual disposition, Freud declares, was perversely impulsive and sadomasochistic, marking him as a sinner or criminal.[29] But he rests his case mainly on the writer's choice of material for his fiction—"violent, murderous, egoistic characters." The characters he created indicated "similar tendencies in his own inner being [*in seinem Inneren*]." The biographical evidence of a criminal personality was limited to Dostoevsky's obsessive gambling (discussed separately by Freud in closing) and possibly the sexual abuse of a young girl. Without going into the latter, Freud refers us to the confession of Stavrogin (a suppressed segment of the *The Possessed*) and to scholarship debating its possible autobiographical nature.[30] Suffice it to say that all the sources on this point available then and now lead back only to the novelist's imagination.[31] But the psyche governs imagination, so here too Freud found evidence of Dostoevsky's unusually strong destructive instinct directed inward, his sense of guilt and punishing masochism. His sadistic impulse was restricted to lesser traits, such as irritability and a fondness for tormenting those close to him. With a touch of wit Freud adds that the author treated his readers sadistically, too. Those who recall Dostoevsky's multiple ironies, coy mystifications, unmotivated behavior, false starts, plot suspensions, and ubiquitous trivia may sympathize with this judgment, purely on grounds of technique. Depending on one's taste in books, the level of emotional violence, misery, and pathology in Dostoevsky's plots might also suggest a sadistic design. Answering his first and best critic (Reik), Freud with tongue in cheek admitted not really liking Dostoevsky because "my patience with pathological natures is exhausted in analysis. In art and life I am intolerant of them."[32]

The central part of Freud's essay is devoted to conjecture about Dostoevsky's neurosis. During the last thirty-four years of his life, about once a month on the average, Dostoevsky suffered from epileptic seizures: a brief, intensely exalted, premonitory sensation (clinically known as aura), loss of consciousness, convulsions, and a lingering depression with vague feelings of criminal guilt for three to eight days. Freud, with some medical justification, believed it "highly probable" that Dostoevsky suffered from symptoms of neurosis (hysteria) rather than epilepsy. But he was careful to say that "we cannot be completely certain" because the medical data on Dostoevsky's epilepsy were defective and unreliable, and because clinical understanding of psychopathology combined with epileptiform attacks was imperfect.[33] These caveats still stand today, despite important advances in medical expertise and considerable clarification of Dostoevsky's medical history.[34] Freud observed that "the old *morbus sacer*" (epilepsy) was still an apparent clinical entity, an "uncanny malady" with seemingly unprovoked seizures, progressive change to an irritable and aggressive character, and decline of mental faculties as the usual outcome. Yet the clinical picture blurred, with violent symptoms sometimes replaced by brief absence or occasional behavior out of character and intellectual impairment not inevitable. Freud here cites again the case of the scientific genius Helmholtz, mentioned in his letter to Stefan Zweig of

1920. Nevertheless, the exceptionally strong function of Dostoevsky's intellect to the end of his days was still sufficient reason for Freud at that time to suspect that the writer's chronic illness was not epilepsy. On the other hand, the sheer frequency of Dostoevsky's seizures, their occurrence when he was alone and asleep, the physical damage suffered during attacks, and the debilitating depression that followed, all strongly suggested a diagnosis of epilepsy, not hysteria. These symptoms were noted in sources available to Freud but widely scattered and easily overlooked.

We have already seen that Dostoevsky's symptoms were hypothetically diagnosed as hysteria by Freud's associates, including Stekel in 1908, Rank in 1914, and the Adlerian Tatiana Rosenthal in 1919. Perhaps they were all following the lead of Freud himself, who in 1908 had declared that "all those illnesses called hysteroepilepsies are simply hysterias."[35] In Freud's view, genuine epilepsy was "an organic, alien disturbance of psychic life," while hysteroepilepsy (or simply hysteria) was "an expression of the psychic life itself." So he states the case in the essay on Dostoevsky. In short, if Dostoevsky's epileptic seizures could be diagnosed as hysteria, psychoanalysis might explain their meaning, but not if the illness were in fact epilepsy. To his credit, Freud repeats that although Dostoevsky's seizures were quite probably hysteria, "this cannot, strictly speaking, be proven." One needed to know more about the specific onset of the symptoms and the course of attacks throughout the "psychic life." Having made these clear disclaimers, Freud puts doubt behind him and proceeds on the assumption of Dostoevsky's neurotic hysteria.[36] Ancient medicine held that coitus is "a minor epilepsy." In a short paper of 1909 ("Some General Remarks on Hysterical Attacks"), Freud suggested that the same might be said of violent hysteria, which uses the reflex mechanism of coition, "a mechanism which is ready to hand in everybody" (men and women).[37] The general sexual etiology of hysteria is also of ancient origin, as indicated by the very name of the condition (derived from "uterus"). The mechanism of hysteria, its dramatically violent symptoms, "must to some extent be connected with sexual processes," as Freud now explained the illness of Dostoevsky. The murder of a violent father must have triggered the violent seizures, Freud conjectures. Indeed, Dostoevsky's father was emotionally abusive and sternly authoritarian, sufficiently true to type to have met Freud's conditions. The fear of deathlike sleep and burial alive in Dostoevsky's youth (which actually came much later than Freud thought) must have been a psychic castration, a feminine submission to the father, and at the same time identification with the father, whom he wished dead. Freud had no way of knowing that Russian medical journals of Dostoevsky's day, which he avidly read, gave dire warnings of possible burial alive during trancelike seizures, so this fear was perfectly reasonable.

Freud is wise to admit that symbolic castration and hate-love toward the father must seem "unsavory and incredible" to readers unfamiliar with psychoanalysis, but he insists that a strong bisexual predisposition must have been part of the picture. Dostoevsky's latent homosexuality was evident in the importance of his male friendships, his gentleness toward rivals in love, and the remarkable understanding of repressed homosexuality in his novels. The last point, one may add, is indeed striking in such works as "The Double," "The Eternal Husband," "Peasant Marei," *The Idiot* and *The Possessed*. The frightful seizures of Dostoevsky's maturity, says Freud, mimicked the terrible (*schrecklich*) death of his father. This curiously but aptly echoes the emblematic reference to Ivan the Terrible (*Schrecklich*) several pages earlier, because the serial father figures are as terrible psychologically in their desired death as in their threatening life because of the taboo against parricide and its Oedipal overtones. Freud felt that Dostoevsky's punishment by the tsar (mock execution and penal servitude) should have eliminated his "hysteric" seizures. To Freud's credit, he notes that such was not the case.

"What further [symbolic] content Dostoevsky's seizures absorbed, particularly sexual content, escapes conjecture." Let us add that Dostoevsky's seizures—seen as epilepsy—had a vast weight of diverse symbolic content in legend from antiquity and the Bible, from supposedly afflicted historical figures (such as Alexander, Caesar, Muhammad, Peter the Great, and Napoleon), and from complex characters created by the author in his novels.[38] Dostoevsky consciously pondered and embellished the symbolic values of his illness throughout his career. In this regard, Freud's symbolic analysis of the condition (whether diagnosed as epilepsy or hysteria) is in line with the author's self-image. He observes that the basic, chronic pattern of Dostoevsky's seizures included premonitory aura—

interpreted as a moment of "triumph, liberation" (at news of the father's death), falling seizures ("cruel punishment"), and lingering depression ("guilt and mourning"). This symbolic content of Dostoevsky's seizures came directly from passages in *Totem and Taboo,* cited by Freud, about the brothers of the murderous primal human horde, their triumph and their mourning at the slain father (primal guilt and ambivalence).[39]

Dostoevsky described his own seizures and exploited them in fiction as a complex dialectic of spiritual triumph, euphoria, disintegration, and collapse.[40] His three well-known descriptions of aura have strongly religious overtones, but a fourth, often overlooked though equally reliable, relates the experience differently: "Before the very onset, his body was seized with a kind of inexpressible feeling of voluptuousness"—without a hint of spiritual elevation.[41] This account was available to Freud in his library, conveniently indexed in a volume of letters under the entry *Anfälle, Epileptische* (Epileptic Attacks).[42] The powerfully erotic element (*Wollustgefühl; sladostrastie*) in Dostoevsky's seizures, which he understandably suppressed and sublimated in accounts even to most of those close to him, might appear to anticipate Freud's analysis and to support the theory of "hysteroepilepsy" with a neurotic sexual etiology. Modern medicine diagnoses Dostoevsky's illness as temporal lobe epilepsy, a condition often accompanied by complex psychiatric symptoms.[43] Not infrequently, victims of epilepsy may suffer intermittently from hysterical seizures, and the two conditions can sometimes be difficult even for specialists to distinguish without EEG testing, which was unavailable before 1930.[44] Freud was aware that epileptic and hysterical seizures were sometimes seen in a single patient, but it was then considered to be quite rare, and he did not in any event mention it in connection with Dostoevsky.[45] It seems impossible now to determine whether or not hysteria figured intermittently in Dostoevsky's medical history. But it is clear that many chronic features of his illness—particularly the erotic element of his aura and the depressive guilt following seizures, and perhaps above all the dominant role of psychopathology in his fiction, both invited and accommodated psychoanalysis.

Freud suggests that Dostoevsky's ability to survive imprisonment stemmed from his psychic need for punishment. The novelist of course knew that his sentence as a political offender and the ordeal of his mock execution inflicted by the tsar were unjust, but "he accepted this undeserved punishment at the hands of the Little Father (the tsar)" as a substitute for the punishment deserved from his real father— "deserved," that is, because of the death wish preempted by his father's murder. The need for penitence, writes Freud, gained the upper hand in Dostoevsky's relationship to secular authority, if not altogether to spiritual authority. The theory is shrewd, but there is now convincing evidence that Dostoevsky survived prison by the strength of his pride in the face of class hatred from peasant convicts whom his subversive politics had idealized.[46] A memoir account of his late years convincingly shows that Dostoevsky neither forgot nor forgave the inhuman cruelty of the tsar's mock execution.[47] The evidence of Dostoevsky's mature fiction, above all *The Brothers Karamazov* so admired by Freud in certain respects, eloquently and profoundly proclaims that the great writer remained a subversive to the end. Freud clearly saw this in isolated episodes, but his preoccupation with psychoanalytic conjecture blinded him to the larger political truth. Otherwise he could not have condemned Dostoevsky as humanity's jailer (the "Grand Inquisitor"), nor could he have said that the future of humanity would not be grateful to Dostoevsky. These judgments were mistaken.

In the penultimate passage of his essay, Freud compares *The Brothers Karamazov* with *Oedipus Rex* of Sophocles and Shakespeare's *Hamlet*. Each hinges upon the father's murder and sexual rivalry. Freud is captivated by Dostoevsky's psychoanalytic insight. He notes that, in the novel, murder is enacted by a brother-surrogate (the death wish is negotiable), and that the actual murderer is an epileptic—as though the author confesses that "the epileptic in him was a parricide." Freud seemingly applauds the satiric treatment of psychology itself as "a stick with two ends" (*ein Stock mit zwei Enden*).[48] This metaphoric phrase (which Dostoevsky had employed earlier several times in *Crime and Punishment*) is used by Dmitri Karamazov's defense attorney to discredit the prosecution. Even the most serious people, he concludes, can be tempted by psychology to invent whole novels, and "from psychology you can deduce whatever you like."[49] Rather lamely, Freud says that the real target of the author's satire was not psychology at all but the judicial process. In fact, the satire cuts both ways, like psychology itself—an insight that Freud might have applied to the complex satirical dialectic of the Grand Inquisitor episode. An artful genius of psychology, Freud appears genuinely disarmed by Dostoevsky's psychological creativity.

The scene in which the holy Zosima bows down before Dmitri, who has murder in his heart, reminds Freud of the sacred awe accorded epileptics and the biblical lunatics.[50] The criminal is virtually a Redeemer who assumes the guilt of others and frees them of the need to kill. In this formula, Freud comes full circle to his initial pronouncement about Russian compromise with morality, whereby penance becomes a technique enabling murder to be done. We may see this judgment of the Russian race not only as a reflection of Freud's ancestral experience, but also with reference to the Bolshevik terror and the rising Stalinist state. One last remark on Freud's critique of *The Brothers Karamazov*: although he was particularly intrigued by Dostoevsky's great trial scene, he did not comment on its most strikingly precocious psychoanalytic moment, Ivan Karamazov's challenge to all humanity: "Who does not wish his father's death?"[51]

Freud's essay ends by considering at some length Dostoevsky's compulsive gambling. This obsession is also mentioned briefly at the outset as one fact pointing to the self-destructive "sinner" in Dostoevsky. Freud's interest in gambling, a relatively minor yet striking episodic pathology in Dostoevsky's life, has a number of sources. In May 1926, fending off Otto Rank's belated skepticism about the Wolf-Man case, Freud wrote to Sergei Pankeev out of the blue and without explanation, asking him to verify once more the time and content of the famous wolf dream. Freud's official biographer tells us that confirmation was supplied by Pankeev with "not the slightest doubt in the patient's mind about the early date of that terrifying dream."[52] Contrary to policy, the Freud Archive has published Pankeev's letter to Freud of 6 June 1926, no doubt to support Jones's claim. In a seemingly forthright way, Pankeev does verify Freud's report of his dream. But the bulk of this letter only complicates the issue.

Pankeev now recalled seeing Tchaikowsky's opera *Pique Dame* (based on Pushkin's famous tale of gambling, "The Queen of Spades") either just before or after his dream about wolves. One detail in common was a window opening by itself, to reveal ... wolves in the dream, but the ghost of an old woman with the secret of three winning cards, in the opera. Pushkin's story, published in 1834, which is also cited by Pankeev, playfully eroticizes the old lady's "secret" and the hero's motive in pursuing it. In order to understand the Wolf-Man's letter, Freud must have read or reread Pushkin's masterpiece about gambling at the very time he began his work on Dostoevsky, Pankeev's illustrious countryman. Thirty years later, on 11 June 1957, Pankeev claimed that his attack of paranoia in 1926 had been triggered by Freud's letter to him about the wolf dream, which had abruptly raised questions long since presumed settled between them.[53] If we accept this insight, then Pankeev's letter of 1926—contaminating and obscuring his classic Russian dream with a classic Russian fiction—was a cunning defensive shot at his former analyst. In any event, by October 1926 the genuinely paranoid Pankeev was in therapy again (with Ruth Mack Brunswick), threatening to shoot Freud.[54] Precisely at this time (3-10 October 1926), Freud told Eitingon that his interest in writing about Dostoevsky had waned.[55] Was it not so in part because Freud was now literally "under fire" from Dostoevsky's countryman Pankeev? Both of them, as he had written to Stefan Zweig in 1920, were after all typical Russians in their ambivalence.

In September 1926, when Freud had already written a partial draft of his Dostoevsky study, someone gave him the volume *Dostojewski am Roulette*, published by R. Piper in Munich and edited by René Fülöp-Miller and Friedrich Eckstein. The same editors were also preparing the volume in which Freud's article was to appear. Either they sent him the gift volume on gambling or else it was Eitingon, still supplying "book after book" on Dostoevsky and urging Freud to complete the essay. We cannot say exactly when Freud looked into *Dostojewski am Roulette*, but it is twice cited in his essay, and its materials on gambling (letters of Dostoevsky to his wife, and her diaries) showed him the way to the end of his unfinished article. Freud notes the characteristic pathology of the obsessive gambler, whose need to experience guilt causes a burden of debt to be acquired, and who gambles ostensibly to win but inevitably until all is lost, and with a desperate sense that after all it is only *le jeu pour le jeu*. Dostoevsky perfectly fit this known pattern, abasing himself before his wife, stealing from her to gamble again, losing everything, then resuming his literary creativity when the inhibition was lifted. We may add that

Dostoevsky saw his creative life itself from the beginning as a "noble risk."[56] His gambling was a variant challenge of fate, a biding of time in his existential duel with the tsarist authority, a controlled replay of the "comedy of murder."

The construction of Freud's essay logically needed some concluding words about Dostoevsky's novella *The Gambler* (published in 1866), a work dictated to a young stenographer soon to become his wife. Modern medical authorities on the treatment of compulsive gambling have come to regard this story as a classic case history, perhaps the best account of the condition in fact or fiction.[57] But Freud says nothing at all about this masterpiece from the pen of his Russian subject. Instead, he devotes the final pages (about one-sixth) of his article on Dostoevsky to detailed paraphrase and analysis of a story about gambling by a minor Viennese Jewish writer, his friend Stefan Zweig. Freud's good friend and critic Theodor Reik humorously complained about this "error in proportion," that it seemed "as though a medieval artist painting the Passion of Christ should place in the foreground of the picture the bishop of his native diocese."[58] This good-natured jest aptly insinuated that in Freud's artistry the exalted Russian Orthodox "Christ" Dostoevsky had somehow been upstaged by a minor local Jew ("the bishop of his native diocese"). To the meaning of this displacement we return shortly. First let us consider some of the features of Dostoevsky's displaced *Gambler*, with which Freud was no doubt familiar.

The hero is a minor figure in the suite of a rich Russian general. He gambles at a casino like those known to Dostoevsky in Wiesbaden, Homburg, and Baden. The imaginary name of the setting, "Roulettenburg," helps impart a melodramatic and trivial tone, which matches the gambler's ironically self-destructive abandon. There is a leitmotiv of Russian national inferiority, which seems to drive the hero and to lie at the heart of things. He rails against the Poles and their sympathizers in the French press. He scoffs at Jews who warn him to stop gambling while he is ahead, and sneers at the very idea of "German accumulation by honest toil." Such contempt for ordered existence is recognized as "the Russian ideal," and the hero declares (with irony intended by Dostoevsky but perhaps not readily perceived) that Russians are "too richly endowed and many-sided to evolve a code of manners." This matches Freud's axiom of 1920 that the

Russian character is endowed with extraordinary ambivalence. One dramatic peak in the narrative is the sudden arrival of a rich old lady from Moscow upon whose death the general's fortune depends. She gambles, wins and loses lavishly, and the hero tries to follow her purely whimsical "system." His absurd pursuit of the old woman's "secret" echoes "The Queen of Spades." The gambler 's erotic interest is muted and marginal, an obvious reason for Freud's neglect. The hero loses Polina, the Russian general's poor and neglected stepdaughter, but the general manages to marry the fortune-hunting Mlle. Blanche. Money, as so often in Dostoevsky's fiction, dominates destiny. The hero, who might have served his country, instead simply throws away his life. "Roulette is a game preeminently for the Russians," declares an exasperated English friend. "If it is not roulette it is something similar."

Dostoevsky's classic Russian gambling material, however, was displaced in Freud's essay by Stefan Zweig's tale of Monte Carlo, "Twenty-Four Hours in a Woman's Life," published in the collection *Die Verwirrung der Gefühle* (Confusion of the Emotions, which was published in 1926).[59] This short fiction accommodates psychoanalysis more readily than Dostoevsky's novella. Freud singles out such elements as a middle-aged widow's maternal attraction to a young compulsive gambler, her fascination by the "play" of his hands (a nursery symbol for masturbation), his mistaking her at first for a prostitute ("bringing the unattainable within easy reach"), her determination to "save him from himself" (by the night they spend in bed together), his promise never to "play" again, his backsliding, and his suicide. Underlying this plot Freud sees a universal wish that the mother will initiate her son, saving him from the evils of onanism. The mutual phantasy is acted out here because of the mother's transference of love for her own absent sons, unconscious but vulnerable, her "undefended spot." The boy's gambling brings self-punishment, bad conscience, and self-destruction, in every respect a substitute for masturbation—still considered at the time a neurotic behavior, damaging to the health. Freud concludes that Dostoevsky's bouts of compulsive gambling also repeated the "onanism compulsion" of his puberty because all cases of "serious neurosis" (particularly cases of "hysteroepilepsy" with chronic violent seizures) had an autoerotic component. The connection between efforts to suppress masturbation and fear of the father, Freud says in closing, is so well known that one needs only to mention it. This places the case again, rather abruptly, in the Oedipal perspective, indirectly recalling the dominant concept of "Dostoevsky and Parricide"—father-murder (*die Vatertötung*).

Some features of "Twenty-Four Hours in a Woman's Life" not mentioned by Freud are noteworthy in comparison with Dostoevsky's *Gambler*. Both fictions have cosmopolitan characters and settings, and Zweig's plot, set initially in 1904, carries us back by reminiscence to the Monte Carlo of 1879—the age of Dostoevsky. Zweig's central tale is told by an Englishwoman of sixty-seven to a younger man, about a time when she was forty-two, having an overnight affair with another younger man. Mrs. C's story is triply eroticized: by her own intensely feminine point of view, by the confessional mode, and by her penchant for exotic similes ("hands hairy as wild beasts," "hands damp and writhing like eels," and her lover's hands which "fall apart like two animals killed with one shot" when he loses at roulette). During their night in a cheap hotel, Mrs. C learns that her desperate gambler is a junior diplomat, an Austrian Pole stationed in Vienna. She makes him do penance in a Catholic church and gives him money for a fresh start in his career. Later that day she discovers him back at the roulette table, losing and obsessed with an old Russian general who must have a system—"He could see nothing but the Russian general."

To conclude his story, Zweig has borrowed the old Russian general who financially dominates Dostoevsky's *Gambler*. Instead of the Russian gambler's paranoid fixation on the West (as represented by the French, Poles, and Jews), the Austrian Polish novice diplomat is suicidally obsessed with the illusory but dominant tsarist system. Theodor Reik was right to chide Freud for painting "the bishop of his native diocese" (Zweig) in the foreground of his Dostoevsky "Passion"—thus replacing Russian Orthodox material with Viennese Jewish material. But the truth of the matter goes beyond the jest, because Zweig's Polish hero is psychologically (and allegorically) entangled with a grandiose but fatal Russian system. His role resembles Freud's, as analyst of *Russische Innerlichkeit*, the "system" of Dostoevsky and Pankeev. Zweig's story symbolizes the plight of Freud himself, entangled with the Russian national character for years, for decades, for centuries, in what now had become personal—analysis interminable. Having spent far too long trying to beat

Dostoevsky's system, Freud found in Zweig's story a way to cut his losses and bring the game to an end.

Freud's reply to Reik dated 14 April 1929 is a polite, disarming defense of "Dostoevsky and Parricide," a study that the author now dismisses as "trivial." He claims to have written reluctantly, as a favor to a friend, and agrees that the attention to Zweig's story is out of proportion. Oddly, he complains that Dostoevsky's "insight was so entirely restricted to the workings of the abnormal psyche," forgetting his own denials of sharp boundaries between the normal and abnormal, and his often repeated admiration for the writer's great intellect. Dostoevsky's masochistic subjection and general helplessness in describing love is deplored by Freud, and finally he declares simply that "despite all of my admiration for his intensity and preeminence, I do not really like him. That is because my patience with pathological natures is exhausted in my daily analytic work. In art and life I am intolerant of them."⁶⁰ But such clinically personal remarks—countertransference to Dostoevsky's shade—are offset by Freud's ranking the great novelist as an artist "not far behind Shakespeare" (in the opening lines of his essay), and extolling the great intelligence that "made it impossible for him to overlook a single one of the intellectual difficulties to which faith leads." This insight, we have seen, was confirmed by Freud's careful study of the Grand Inquisitor legend, which was the stimulus for *The Future of an Illusion*. Freud was clearly attached to Dostoevsky, as a psychological genius, and only strove out of duty and self-defense to portray him as a clinical case. In the next chapter we try to reach a deeper understanding of what occurred in Freud's prolonged encounter with Dostoevsky.

Notes

1   Max Schur, *Freud, Living and Dying*, pp. 386-93.

2   Ernest Jones, *The Life and Work of Sigmund Freud*, vol. 3, pp. 468-95, "Surgical Notes"; Max Schur, *Freud, Living and Dying*, pp. 347-85.

3   Max Schur, *Freud, Living and Dying*, p. 364.

4   Ibid., p. 390.

5   Freud to Fliess, 22 December 1897, in Sigmund Freud, *The Complete Letters of Sigmund Freud to Wilhelm Fliess*, pp. 287-89.

6   Erich Ebstein, "Dostojewskijs Krankheit und seine Aertzte"; E. C. Burke, "Dostoevsky's Pulmonary Disease."

7   Theodor Reik, *From Thirty Years with Freud*, pp. 172-73; Sigmund Freud, *Standard Edition of the Complete Psychological Works of Sigmund Freud*, vol. 21, pp. 195-96.

8   F. M. Dostojewski, *Der Urgestalt der Brüder Karamasoff*.

9   In addition to the complete works of Dostoevsky, Freud's publisher R. Piper & Co. (Munich) had by this time brought out twelve supplementary books of journalism, letters, memoirs, and scholarship. These include the memoirs and diary of Dostoevsky's wife; *The Unknown Dostoevsky* (quoted by Freud: drafts, materials, and commentaries for *The Possessed, A Raw Youth*, and the unfinished *Life of a Great Sinner*; the volume to which Freud contributed is a sequel); *Diary of a Writer*, 4 vols.; *The Confession of a Jew in Letters to Dostoevsky* (in Freud's library); Dostoevsky's letters to his wife; his letters to friends, writers, politicians, and others (two volumes); *Paulina Suslova, Dostoevsky's "Eternal Friend"*; his letters to his brother Mikhail; his political journalism; and memoirs by his friends. All of these are listed in the end-papers of F.M. Dostojewskij, *Dostojewski am Roulette*. A good one-volume collection of Dostoevsky's letters was in Freud's London library (a gift from Eitingon), but the five volumes of letters listed above do not appear in the library catalogue. Many of Freud's books were left behind when he emigrated.

10   Sigmund Freud, *Standard Edition of the Complete Psychological Works of Sigmund Freud*, vol. 21, p. 177; Sigmund Freud, *Gesammelte Werke*, vol. 14, p. 400.

11   Ibid., vol. 13 (1955).

12   Ibid., vol. 13, p. 87.

13   Ibid., vol. 13, p. 155.

14   Ibid., vol. 13, p. 59.

15   Friedrich Nietzsche, "Umwerthung aller Werthe, I. Buch: Der Antichrist," in Friedrich Nietzsche, *Werke*, vol. 8, pp. 254-55; Friedrich Nietzsche, "Der Antichrist," sect. 31.

16   Sigmund Freud, *Gesammelte Werke*, vol. 14, p. 411; Sigmund Freud, *Standard Edition of the Complete Psychological Works of Sigmund Freud*, vol. 21, p. 187.

17   A. von Rothe, "Johann Wasiliewitsch IV, genannt der Grausame. Eine psychiatrische Studie," p. 176.

18   Sigmund Freud, *Standard Edition of the Complete Psychological Works of Sigmund Freud*, vol. 21, p. 205.

19   Ibid., vol. 21, pp. 187 and 194.

20   Ibid., vol. 21, p. 196.

21   Ibid., vol. 21, p. 203.

22   Ibid., vol. 21, p. 206.

23   Ibid., vol. 21, p. 156.

24   Sigmund Freud, *Gesammelte Werke*, vol. 14, p. 400.

25   Ibid., vol. 14, p. 411.

26   James L. Rice, *Dostoevsky and the Healing Art*, p. 38.

27   F. M. Dostoevskii, *Polnoe sobranie sochinenii v tridtsati tomakh*, vol. 16, pp. 485-86.

28   L. P. Grossman, *Die Beichte eines Juden*, introduction.

29   Sigmund Freud, *Gesammelte Werke*, vol. 14, p. 401; Sigmund Freud, *Standard Edition of the Complete Psychological Works of Sigmund Freud*, vol. 21, pp. 178-79.

30   F. M. Dostojewski, *Der unbekannte Dostojewski*, pp. 272-75 (notes on *The Possessed* by Dostoevsky's widow).

31   O. F. Miller and N. N. Strakhov, Biografiia, *pis'ma i zametki iz zapisnoi knizhki F. M. Dostoevskogo*.

32   Sigmund Freud, *Standard Edition of the Complete Psychological Works of Sigmund Freud*, vol. 21, p. 196.

33   Sigmund Freud, *Gesammelte Werke*, vol. 14, p. 402; Sigmund Freud, *Standard Edition of the Complete Psychological Works of Sigmund Freud*, vol. 21, p. 179.

34   James L. Rice, *Dostoevsky and the Healing Art*.

35   Herman Nunberg and Ernst Federn, eds., *Minutes of the Vienna Psychoanalytic Society*, vol. 2, p. 19.

36   Norman Geschwind, personal communication, 1 November 1982: Freud's exposition is adequately hedged and medically acceptable for his era.

37   Sigmund Freud, *Standard Edition of the Complete Psychological Works of Sigmund Freud*, vol. 9, p. 234.

38   Owsei Temkin, *The Falling Sickness*; James L. Rice, *Dostoevsky and the Healing Art*.

39   Sigmund Freud, *Standard Edition of the Complete Psychological Works of Sigmund Freud*, vol. 13, pp. 87, 155, 159, and 161.

40   F. M. Dostojewski, *The Idiot*, in F. M. Dostojewski, *Sämtliche Werke*, vol. 3-4; James L. Rice, *Dostoevsky and the Healing Art* (index).

41   A. E. Vrangel', *Vospominaniia*, p. 37.

42   F. M. Dostoevsky, *Briefe*, 2nd ed., p. 266; Harry Trosman and Roger Dennis Simmons, "The Freud Library," p. 679; James L. Rice, *Dostoevsky and the Healing Art*, pp. 83-85.

43   T. Alajouanine, "Dostoevsky's Epilepsy"; Owsei Temkin, *The Falling Sickness*, pp. 373-78 and 393-95; Dietrich Blumer and Kenneth Levin, ed., "Psychiatric Complications in the Epilepsies"; Fabio Cirignotta, "Temporal Lobe Epilepsy with Ecstatic Seizures"; P.H.A. Voskuil, "The Epilepsy of Fyodor Mikhailovich Dostoevsky"; Norman Geschwind, "Dostoievsky's Epilepsy"; James L. Rice, "Russian Stereotypes in the Freud-Jung Correspondence," index; Joseph Frank, *Dostoevsky. The Years of Ordeal 1850-1859*, p. 195n.

44   John N. Mundall, M.D., Neurology Associates of Eugene-Springfield, Oregon, personal communication, 20 May 1981.

45   Herman Nunberg and Ernst Federn, eds., *Minutes of the Vienna Psychoanalytic Society*, vol. 2, p. 19 (21 October 1908).

46   James L. Rice, "Psychoanalysis of 'Peasant Marei," pp. 247-48.

47   Ek. P. Letkova, "O F. M. Dostoevskom," pp. 459-61.

48   Sigmund Freud, *Gesammelte Werke*, vol. 14, p. 413.

49   F. M. Dostoevskii, *Polnoe sobranie sochinenii v tridtsati tomakh* 15 (1976), pp. 152-56 (book 12, part 10, "The Speech for the Defense. A Stick with Two Ends").

50   F. M. Dostojewski, *The Brothers Karamazov*, in F. M. Dostojewski, *Sämtliche Werke*, vol. 9-10 (1908), book 2, p. 6: "Why is such a man alive?"

51   Ibid., book 12, p. 5.

52   Ernest Jones, *The Life and Work of Sigmund Freud*, vol. 3, p. 76; see also Freud's review of the wolf dream in Sigmund Freud, *Inhibitions, Symptoms and Anxiety*, in *Standard Edition of the Complete Psychological Works of Sigmund Freud*, vol. 20, pp. 104-105.

53   S. K. Pankejeff, "Letters Pertaining to Freud's 'History of an Infantile Neurosis'."

54   S. K. Pankeev, *The Wolf-Man by the Wolf-Man*, pp. 263 and 290.

55   Ernest Jones, *The Life and Work of Sigmund Freud*, vol. 3, p. 143, and p. 506 note 119.

56   A.Z. Pistsova, "Neizvestnye pis'ma M.M. Dostoevskogo," p. 155.

57   Richard Rosenthal, "The Gambler and the Poet," p. 2.

58   Theodor Reik, *From Thirty Years with Freud*, p. 172.

59 Stefan Zweig, *Die Verwirrung der Gefühle*. Strachey erroneously dated the appearance of this book in 1927, and suggested that this may have signaled the final stage of Freud's work on Dostoevsky. In fact, Piper & Co. did not publish Freud's essay until December 1928.

60 Sigmund Freud, *Standard Edition of the Complete Psychological Works of Sigmund Freud*, vol. 21 (1961), pp. 195-96;; Theodor Reik, *Freud als Kulturkritiker*. Piper & Co. by this time had brought out not only twenty-two volumes (in twenty-three) of Dostoevsky's collected works, but also twelve supplementary books of journalism, letters, memoirs, and scholarship. These included the memoirs and the diary of Dostoevsky's wife, Anna Grigorievna; *The Unknown Dostoevsky* (drafts, materials, and commentaries for *The Devils, A Raw Youth*, and the unfinished *Life of a Great Sinner*. The volume to which Freud contributed in 1928 is a sequel.); *A Writer's Notebook*, 4 vols.; *The Confession of a Jew in Letters to Dostoevsky* (in Freud's library); Dostoevsky's letters to his wife; his letters to friends, writers, politicians, and others (two volumes); *Paulina Suslova, Dostoevsky's "Eternal Friend"*; his letters to his brother Mikhail; his political journalism; and memoirs by his friends. All of these titles are listed in end papers of *Dostojewski am Roulette* (1925). Few of these publications are catalogued in Freud's London library, though Max Eitingon is said to have "kept pressing Freud to finish the work [on Dostoevsky] and sent him book after book, including a complete set of Dostoevsky's correspondence" (Ernest Jones, *The Life and Work of Sigmund Freud*, vol. 1, p. 143}. A single volume of selected letters (1920) was in Freud's library, but not the five special volumes listed here above.

9

Ein Stock mit zwei Enden

It is to be anticipated that male analysts with feminist views, as well as our women analysts, will disagree with what I have said here. They will hardly fail to object that such notions [about the Oedipus and castration complexes] spring from the "masculinity complex" of the male and are designed to justify on theoretical grounds his innate inclination to disparage and suppress women. But this sort of psychoanalytic argumentation reminds us here, as it so often does, of Dostoevsky's famous "stick with two ends." The opponents of those who argue in this way will on their side think it quite natural that the female sex should refuse to accept a view which appears to contradict their own eagerly coveted equality with men. The use of analysis as a weapon of controversy can clearly lead to no decision.

—Freud, "Female Sexuality"

In Dostoevsky's great novel, The Brothers Karamazov, *the Oedipus situation stands at the focal point of interest. Old Karamazov has made himself detested by his sons through heartless oppression; in the eyes of one of them he is, in addition, a powerful rival for the woman he desires. This son, Dmitri, makes no secret of his intention to avenge himself on his father by force. It is therefore natural that after his father has been murdered and robbed he should be accused as his murderer and, despite all protestations of his innocence, condemned. And yet Dmitri is innocent; another of the brothers has done the deed. A dictum that has become famous occurs during the trial scene in this novel: "Psychology is a stick with two ends."*

—Freud, "The Expert Opinion in the Halsmann Case"

We have traced the emergence of Freud's Russia from the obscure realm of his oppressed ancestors and remote kinsmen, the legendary world of his mother's childhood, to a land of organized pogroms, violent revolution, and open military challenge to the West. Out of the Russian hinterland into Freud's life came cousins, colleagues, patients, and the ever-growing mass of émigré *Ostjude*. His father, Charcot, and Freud himself in fantasy if not in fact, journeyed into the Russian Empire on business. His sons advanced on Russian soil at war.[1] And Freud's embattled followers defended psychoanalysis—his brainchild—in Moscow until 1930, when the Stalinist state put an end to independent professional organizations.[2] The saga of Freud's Russia involves a deep personal involvement and a family drama of archaic origins, exodus, return, and defeat.

In February 1927, Freud was belatedly informed that the Bolsheviks found psychoanalysis "hostile to their system."[3] At almost the same time, Freud's protracted analysis of the Wolf-Man also exploded in hostility. At first Freud had in 1918 claimed Pankeev's case as a model of therapeutic treatment, but now the patient threatened to shoot him! This death threat, a delayed parricidal transference, signaled the violent potential of *Russische Innerlichkeit* and aligned Freud's Russian patient with the central problems of "Dostoevsky and Parricide." No later than 1920 and perhaps a decade earlier, Freud had identified Pankeev and Dostoevsky as examples of "typical Russia ambivalence" toward themselves and toward authority. Now that ambivalence took the form of open aggression against Freud himself. In Freud's analysis, a murderous and self-destructive (sadomasochistic) tendency dominates not only the personality of Dostoevsky but also the Russian national character. The sudden paranoid hostility of the Wolf-Man undoubtedly intensified and personalized Freud's involvement with the "case" of Dostoevsky.[4]

Freud's own ambivalence toward Dostoevsky has been indicated. As he admitted to Theodor Reik in 1929, despite all his deep admiration (*Bewunderung*) for the Russian writer's intensity and excellence (*Intensität und Überlegenheit*), "you are right in your assumption that I do not really like Dostoevsky."[5] The reason given was that his exposure to "pathological natures" in therapy sessions made him intolerant of them "in art and life." In "Dostoevsky and Parricide" it is apparent that Freud wrongly assumed Dostoevsky's identification with the "Grand Inquisitor"—as a "jailer of humanity" rather than its teacher and liberator.[6] This identity, he thought, represented the crux of Dostoevsky's "neurosis": a resolution of filial guilt (the death wish toward his murdered father) through belated submission to the tsar and God, authorities in loco parentis.[7] Despite "violent struggles" for individual liberty, he accepted a "retrograde position" that inferior minds (*geringere Geister*) reached with much less trouble.[8] However, Freud's analysis is significantly hedged midway through the essay, where he states that only Dostoevsky's submission to secular authority was complete, while "in the religious sphere he retained more freedom," reportedly "wavering up to the last moment of his life between faith and atheism."[9]

Freud's uncertainty about Dostoevsky's faith is of paramount importance. Dostoevsky's critique of religion was, after all, the focus of Freud's admiration: "His great intelligence made it impossible for him to overlook any of the intellectual difficulties to which faith leads." Indeed, it is the "Grand Inquisitor", ostensibly the "jailer of humanity," who in this very guise exposes the intellectual difficulties of faith to Christ himself. This legend (closely studied by Freud in the summer of 1927) is invented by the atheist Ivan Karamazov to undermine the faith of his devout brother. In this light, the case against Dostoevsky as a neurotic and retrograde religious fanatic collapses, but with one essential reservation—his anti-Semitism. This, we believe, is what Freud had in mind when he referred ironically to Dostoevsky's "veneration for the God of the Christians" and his "narrow Russian nationalism" as a retrograde position, "which inferior minds have reached with much less trouble."

In order to grasp not only Freud's view of Dostoevky but also, so to speak, what transpired "between" Freud and Dostoevsky, one must reconsider the troubling question of Dostoevsky and the Jews as it may bear upon Freud's Jewish identity. One modern reader of genius, a Russian Jew, once observed that Jews simply did not figure in Dostoevsky's personal world as an issue of much importance.[10] However, this was not the case with his forefathers, first recorded as landowners, soldiers, judges, and clergymen (Orthodox Christians, Catholics, and Uniates) of the Lithuanian Principality, the home of Freud's ancestors. The family seat was an estate—Dostoevo—on the outskirts of Pinsk, where the population was heavily Jewish (two-thirds by the nineteenth century). Dostoevskys traded and sometimes litigated with Jewish merchants.[11] Dostoevsky's father prepared for the Uniate priesthood in Podolian Bratslav, a town of about 5,000 midway between Odessa and Brody on the road once traveled by both of Freud's parents. By the nineteenth century, Bratslav residents were 42 percent Russian Orthodox Christians, 10 percent Russian Old Believers, 40 percent Jews, 7 percent Catholics, and a small number of Lutherans. In 1809, Mikhail Dostoevsky, the writer's father, left the seminary and went to Moscow, where he entered the Surgical Academy, eventually to become a resident in a hospital for the poor. In these humbling urban circumstances, the anti-Semitic reflex of Podolia no doubt came into play and passed from father to son, whose progressive ethical principles kept it in check—for the most part.[12]

In recent years a number of scholars have reconsidered evidence gathered by the late David Goldstein in *Dostoievski et les Juifs*.[13] One overlooked passage, from a letter to Dostoevsky's wife written on 19 July 1876, will give some idea of the habitual private prejudice that underlies the intermittent anti-Semitic outbursts of his late journalism, and figures more problematically in two minor but complex Jewish fictional characters. Here he relates an encounter on the train from Petersburg to Berlin:

> Scarcely had we reached Eydtkuhnen when some Yid who got on at Vilna attached himself to me, a rich upper-class Yid, so to speak, with two sons in Petersburg, one a doctor and the other a lawyer. He kept spitting right there in the coach, frightfully and constantly, and spat whole lakes. With these manners he sat down right across from me and began to expound a long-winded story about how he was going to Karlsbad to take the cure for his hemorrhoids, and described those hemorrhoids, when they healed, what the eruptions were like, and so forth and so on. Out of courtesy I had to listen to all this, and with no possibility of escape, so that he tormented me for about four hours.[14]

This crude anecdote with comic embellishments reminds one of the jokes about untidy *Ostjude* with bad manners, which Freud collected and published in *Wit and Its Relation to the Unconscious*.[15] Of particular interest are the affluence of Dostoevsky's fellow traveler, the professional success of his sons in Petersburg, and the feigned courtesy paid to him for hours on end—by a busy professional writer ever alert for material. Obviously, Dostoevsky could not have remained silent or kept his anonymity (his fame was near its peak and his photo was often published), so the encounter might have been told quite differently. His journalistic treatment of the Jewish Question, despite many unenlightened lapses and combative pejoratives, is not the work of a militant anti-Semite, and at its best rises to the level of genuine dialogue with his Jewish readers, whose letters challenging him were sometimes quoted at length and answered in his journal, *Diary of Writer*. Freud, to whom we will return shortly, was well aware of this.

In Dostoevsky's fiction we find only one Jewish character drawn with some degree of completeness, Isái Fomích Bumstéin, inspired in part by a fellow convict in Siberia. Critics of *The House of the Dead* (published between 1860 and 1862) have frequently seen Dostoevsky's portrayal of Bumstein as "devoid of human traits" and "despicable," a "caricature," expressing "contempt." However, Leonid Grossman, dean of modern Dostoevsky scholars, believed the character was sketched "with no particular animosity and, at times, even with a shade of good-natured humor ... tending toward caricature." Isaiah Berlin argued that the author saw beyond the pitiable or contemptible figure and "began to perceive the Jew as the bearer of an ancient heritage, with its prophets, the long-suffering Job ... and these biblical motifs seemed to stir and reverberate in Bumstein."[16] This positive response is taken a step further by Felix Ingold in *Dostojewski und das Judentum* (published in 1981), a book apparently unnoticed by reviewers in America. He sees a bond between the author and this *born actor*, "an unacknowledged and unprovable connection between the artist Dostoevsky and his Jewish protagonist, as actor," and in fact "a secret *identification* of the Artist and the Jew as social outsiders, in their general existential otherness."[17] Ingold's reading is substantiated by Bumstein's personal closeness to Dostoevsky's narrator-spokesman, each vulnerable in the mass of peasant felons. Isai Fomich not only holds his own with wit and barter, he devoutly prays amidst ridicule, asserts his rights to the prison commandant, and is permitted to attend a prayer house in town each Sabbath—bringing back to the narrator precious news from Petersburg. In one famous scene (the steambath), Isai Fomich seems to triumph, singing, on the highest bench, oblivious of the throng of of the throng of convicts beneath him. The narrative refers to him only as *evrei* (Jew), not with ethnic terms of abuse. Freud could have perceived in this episode some measure of the identification between author and character suggested by Ingold.

Dostoevsky's other Jewish character has only a brief role, but it is essential to the dénouement of *Crime and Punishment* (published in 1866). The hero's villainous alter ego, Svidrigailov, who allegorically represents Despair most Cynical, sums up his impressions of Petersburg society: "The peasants get drunk, educated youth from idleness burn out in unrealisable dreams and fantasies, cripple themselves theorizing; Yids have turned up from somewhere, hiding their money, and everything else sinks into depravity."[18] Soon he commits suicide, choosing as sole witness an anonymous firehouse guard, helmeted like Achilles, with "that eternal peevish grief imprinted on all faces of the Hebrew tribe, without fail."[19] For a reader like Freud, the novel's pointed parallel with the story of Lazarus would not have been missed (John 11: 1-45), wherein Jews witness the miracle with awe, conversion, or betrayal. The suicide of Svidrigailov is a parody of the Gospel and Christ's passion. Freud's novelistic history, *Moses and Monotheism*, portrays the Jews as ambivalent converts, betrayers, and murderers of Moses (not their original "Egyptian" spiritual leader, but a later surrogate). Dostoevsky's eternally embittered Jewish witness, though he speaks with a burlesque Yiddish accent and wears an absurd "Achilles" helmet (symbol of tsarist pretension and domination), may be interpreted as another character with whom the author identified. Dostoevsky's score with authority, both secular and divine, was never quite settled. It is also true that he shared Svidrigailov's jaundiced view of Russia, spiritual anguish, and intermittent paranoia toward the Jews; however, the character he invested with these traits significantly ends in suicide. A parallel case is old Karamazov, whose outburst of vulgar anti-Semitic buffoonery in the early chapters (partly at his own expense) is perfectly in tune with the godless and cynical tirades that follow, making him an ideal victim of parricide. In short, the infrequent but striking treatment of Jews in Dostoevsky's fiction is not calculated to offend Jewish readers, although it has sometimes done so.[20]

The case against Dostoevsky as anti-Semite depends chiefly upon his late journalism and scattered passages in his correspondence.

his late journalism and scattered passages in his correspondence. Freud had access to a good deal of this material, but not in the comprehensive array debated by scholars of our era. Before considering his sources and response, we must take into account Freud's own Jewish identity, and his idiosyncratically hypothetical treatment of the Jews in his last decade. Freud's father, a "lapsed Galician Hasid," raised his precocious son without systematic religious training, and with complete freedom as to choice of profession.[21] Freud's own children were brought up with only two holidays celebrated in their home, the secular festivities of Christmas and Easter. They never went to synagogue and were ignorant of Zionism.[22] Freud himself, "always an unbeliever," joined the B'Nai B'Rith in 1897 to escape his sense of isolation, drawn by "the irresistible attraction of Judaism and the Jews," the congeniality of their "psychological structure," and "many dark emotional powers" that were all the stronger for being inexpressible in words.[23]

Publicly honored on the occasion of his seventieth birthday, he wrote to his follower Marie Bonaparte that "the Jews have celebrated me like a national hero, although my service to the Jewish cause is confined to the single point that I have never denied my Jewishness."[24] Indeed, his capital work, *Die Traumdeutung*, elaborately asserts his Jewishness and studies it, needless to say, in depth. Yet it has been observed that he strove to sever his connections with the *Ostjuden*, "the alien race who were the initial target of German national anti-Semitism."[25] About 1870 he had stopped using his given name, Sigismund, popular in jokes about Polish Jews, replacing it with the Germanic Sigmund. His close personal and professional friends were for the most part Jews, but rarely if ever conservative. To his close gentile colleague Ernest Jones, it seemed that Freud was not at all religious.[26] In his preface to the Hebrew translation of *Totem and Taboo* (published in 1930), Freud admitted that he was completely estranged from the language and religion of his fathers, and alien to their nationalist ideals (as he was alien to all nationalism, and all religions). If, having abandoned these characteristics of his people, he were asked: "What is there left to you that is Jewish?"—he would reply: "A very great deal, and probably the essence." (This coy answer sounds for all the world like Dostoevsky describing the faith of one of his heroes.) That essence could not be expressed clearly in words, "but expressed clearly in words, "but some day, no doubt, it will become accessible to the scientific mind."[27]

There were occasions during his life when Freud challenged and physically attacked anti-Semites in public, when they threatened him or his children.[28] Perhaps the essence of Freud's private Jewish identity could best be summed up in the words he wrote to Martha from Paris in 1886: "I have often felt as though I had inherited all the defiance and all the passions with which our ancestors defended their Temple, and could gladly sacrifice my life for one great moment in history." This Romantic wish, as we have suggested, recalls a yearning of Dostoevsky's heroes throughout his career, to sacrifice all of life for one exalted moment. It has been observed that Dostoevsky, as "a prophet of major political realities," was able to inspire leading Jewish socialists of his generation, such as Moses Hess and Aron Liberman, and as an artist of "critical realism" helped form the revolutionary ethos of Jewish extremists in Freud's era, such as Yosef Aharanovich.[29] Even when Dostoevsky ostensibly satirized utopian socialists and seditious conspirators, he gave his revolutionary characters extraordinary eloquence, unique style, fanatic determination, and grandiose vision. The anti-Semitic Dostoevsky was almost literally nowhere in this dimension of his art.[30] Freud, as a Jew defending the Temple after his fashion, perhaps remained oblivious of the "retrograde" Dostoevsky until he was commissioned to write "Dostoevsky and Parricide" in 1926. By then, the course of history had introduced new variables for assessing the "typical Russian" character, and biographical material of crucial importance had come under Freud's scrutiny, directly addressing the question of Dostoevsky and the Jews. However, Freud himself is another significant variable, if we seek to understand what transpired between him, as a Jew, and Dostoevsky in the years 1926-28, when "Dostoevsky and Parricide" was written.

In Freud's last seven years he was at work on *Moses and Monotheism*, conceived (in 1934) as a "historical novel."[31] One essential element was the hypothetical murder of Moses in a rebellion by his "stubborn and refractory people." This "discovery of decisive importance" ("unmistakable traces of a tradition" in the book of the Prophet Hosea) Freud attributes to the distinguished scholar Ernst Sellin.[32] The idea is developed by Freud in terms of a primordial "brother horde" driven by Oedipal conflict to overthrow the father figure—concepts advanced by Freud in *Totem and Taboo* (published in 1913) and applied both to the Wolf-Man and to Dostoevsky. It is likely that Freud began to imagine a ritual parricide of Moses as early as 1922, when Sellin's book appeared (although Sellin barely hints at such an occurrence). On the last page of *Moses and Monotheism*, Freud says that the Jews who did not admit they had "murdered God"—those who remained Jews—had to suffer reproach from the new religious community through the ages, which in addition to converted Jews included Egyptians, Greeks, Syrians, Romans, and lastly Teutons (Germans). By this time Freud was preoccupied with "the new persecutions" of Jews in the Germanic states.[33] Had he written the passage a decade earlier, when Dostoevsky held his imagination, Freud's list of oppressor nations would have ended with the Slavs, and the Russians in particular. Dostoevsky, he had said, "reminds one of the barbarians of the great migrations, who murdered and did penance for it, till penance became an actual technique for enabling murder to be done.... Indeed this compromise with morality is a characteristic Russian trait."[34]

In *The Future of an Illusion*, we have seen, Freud observed that the balance of murder with penance was in fact a universal trait of religion, but he added that "the Russian spiritual depths" had taken it to an extreme conviction that sin is "indispensable for divine grace" and thus "at bottom pleasing to God."[35] This ironic view of Russian national character combines the historical behavior of Ivan the Terrible with Dostoevsky's heroes, who play devil's advocate in *The Brothers Karamazov*.

Freud's theory of Moses as the victim of his own people unmistakably stems from the same universal psychology argued in "Dostoevsky and Parricide," the archaic psychology of the "brother horde" (but with the Oedipal complex muted or sublimated). *Moses and Monotheism* extends the idea of epic rebellion against authority back to the history of ancient Egypt: "Moses met with the same fate as Ikhnaton, the fate that awaits all enlightened despots." That is, the monumental achievement of Ikhnaton was obliterated after his natural death, while "the savage Semites took their destiny into their own hands and did away with their tyrant."[36] Finally, Freud's "historical novel" made Moses himself an Egyptian, in origin, name, monotheistic faith, and rite of circumcision. Curiously enough, there was in Freud's library a novel entitled *Der Messias* (published in 1927)—*Akhnaton, King of Egypt*, in the English translation—by his favorite Merezhkovsky, and so probably purchased at once when it appeared.[37] The hero's mother was Jewish, his father Egyptian, and he, Issachar, is a priest of the new god Amon. Part of his characterization seems to derive from the Issachar of Genesis, son of Jacob and Leah, by his dying father's prophesy "a strong ass crouching down between two burdens" (Genesis 49: 14). His father, a priest of the old god, has been killed in an uprising against Amon. Issachar's "perpetual torment" is his inability to decide whether he is a Jew or an Egyptian. Moses has already been accepted as a prophet by the Jews, but Issachar discerns that the true Messenger of God will be identical with the slain god-man Osiris. At the conclusion of the novel, wrongly suspected of murdering the high priest, he is transfigured as the Messiah.[38] Here we recall that Merezhkovsky's mystically schematic Egypt was also embellished with aphorisms paraphrased from Dostoevsky (in the treatise *Die Geheimnisse des Ostens*, published in 1924 and part of Freud's library). One may conclude that Merezhkovsky furnished Freud not with a plot but with much of the imaginative wherewithal for his "historical novel" about Moses: above all, a novelistic ambiance, as he had done for Freud's Leonardo and to some considerable degree for his Dostoevsky. It is no more than a hyperbole to say that Freud's Moses came from Freud's Russia as a symbolic embodiment of his forefathers, *die Ostjude*—scapegoats, revolutionaries, tragic heroes and martyrs. The private fantasy of Freud's Moses also emerged from Freud's Russia, that is, from the symbolist world of Merezhkovsky's fiction and treatises, which he evidently found to be civilized, congenial, and intellectually stimulating.

The journalism of Dostoevsky also contributed something to Freud's Russia, but something more elusive than his ideas conveyed in art, or the political legend and psychodrama of his life. Until recently, only the series of Dostoevsky's later articles issued as *The Diary of a Writer* have been reprinted and translated.[39] Here are to be found the anti-Semitic outbursts that so dismayed his admirers, among them Jewish radicals, and that used pejoratives which made liberal Russians wince.[40] Two volumes of selections from *The Diary of a Writer* were part of the Munich edition in Freud's possession (volumes 11 and 13). Also available to him was a separate complete edition of the *Diary* in four volumes (published betwen 1921 and 1924). There is no evidence that he examined these sources with any special care, let alone the systematic and scrupulous judgment applied by David Goldstein in *Dostoievski et les Juifs*.[41]

However, in 1924 the noted Russian scholar Leonid Grossman—a native of Odessa—documented a central episode of Dostoevsky's pugnacious stand on the "Jewish Question." Grossman's book includes the correspondence between Dostoevsky and Abraham Kovner, a convicted embezzler, a detailed account of Kovner's career as publicist and felon, and a deeply thoughtful afterword on "Dostoevsky and Judaism."[42] A German translation, with some additional material and more significant abridgment, was published in 1927 by Freud's own editors at Piper & Co., Munich, under the intriguing title *Die Beichte eines Juden in Briefen an Dostojewski* (The Confession of a Jew in Letters to Dostoevsky). The book actually appeared in December 1926, a few months after Freud had set aside the first draft of "Dostoevsky and Parricide."[43] Freud had a copy in his library, presumably sent to him either by his chief collaborator at Piper & Co., René Fülöp-Miller, or by Max Eitingon.[44] The dust jacket of this edition depicts a shackled prisoner, seated at a desk with pen in hand, and the head of Dostoevsky looking down grimly over the man's right shoulder. Grossman's remarkable book, it seems safe to say, was something Freud could not ignore. In a way stranger than fiction, it dramatizes the complex problem of Dostoevsky and the Jews.

Avraam Uriia Kovner (1842-1909) was born in Vilna, a cultural center of the old Lithuanian Principality and capital of modern Lithuania (Vilnius). Grossman describes the hardship and Jewish traditional life Kovner sought to escape (leaving wife and children behind). He went to Kiev, then Odessa and the Urals, meanwhile publishing two books in Hebrew advocating a complete break with the past of Judaism.[45] In 1871 he found work in Petersburg as a journalist, and published a brief attack against Dostoevsky for betraying his liberal ideals. But financial difficulty forced him to take a job in a bank, and he faded from the literary scene. Burdened with debts and a Dostoevskian obligation to support a widow with four children, the children, the eldest a consumptive daughter named Sonya (like the heroine of *Crime and Punishment*), Kovner resolved on embezzlement. Convinced that his bank—under Jewish management—was an immoral enterprise, he somehow decided it was just and harmless to take precisely 3 percent of the annual net profits, the sum of 168,000 rubles. Swiftly arrested and imprisoned in Moscow, he wrote a letter to Dostoevsky on 26 January 1877 justifying his crime as a noble risk to gain support for "the insulted and injured"—a phrase pointedly borrowed from the title of Dostoevsky's first major novel, published in 1861. The criminal's motive, his meticulous fanaticism (3 percent), and the inept outcome recall Raskolnikov, the hero of *Crime and Punishment* who murders for humanitarian principles. Thus, Grossman referred to Kovner's crime as "the Raskolnikov experiment."[46]

Nevertheless, Kovner was a highly intelligent critic of Dostoevsky's anti-Semitic displays, and at first (in a private letter of 14 February 1877) Dostoevsky praised the astuteness of his reproach. Kovner had pointed out that Dostoevsky's abusive treatment of the *zhid* ("Yid") as "exploiter" made it seem that all Jews were exploiters, and that all exploiters were Jews, whereas Dostoevsky's own published views could be cited to the contrary. Dostoevsky feebly claimed that his use of the pejorative *zhid* had a broader, general referent, that he was never an enemy of the Jews, and even had "Jewish acquaintances." But Kovner had gotten to the heart of the matter, insisting (in his first letter, of 26 January 1877) that Dostoevsky—though he was "a sincere and absolutely honest man"— yet did harm to destitute Jews because he knew "nothing about the Jewish people, its life, its spirit, its four-thousand-year history." In the letter of 22 February, Kovner for his part denied hating the Russians and claimed to love the downtrodden Russians "incomparably more than I do the Jewish people." On the one hand, Kovner as a young refugee from ghetto poverty had embraced a doctrine of assimilation and ultimate Russification for the Jews; something of that remains in his extravagant embrace of the Russian people. On the other hand, he was overwhelmed and disarmed by the personal warmth of Dostoevsky's response. Dostoevsky was, after all, among the greatest literary champions of Russian enlightenment, revered and famous above all as a political convict, a victim of the tsarist authorities, and at that time still under surveillance by the secret police. Not only did he write to Kovner at length, acknowledging his intelligence and—with much hedging—his rightness. He also published a substantial article based on their correspondence, with excerpts directly quoted, in *The Diary of a* Writer.[47] The very act of giving Kovner's strong voice a forum in his journal helps define Dostoevsky's attitude toward the Jews, not to mention that his eloquent correspondent was (unbeknownst to their contemporary readers) a convicted felon writing from jail! Freud, reading their exchange in the Austria of a half-century later, would appreciate those circumstances exquisitely. Finally, Kovner's last response to Dostoevsky's doggedly muddled views—in a private letter published only in Fülöp-Miller's edition—expresses the hope that the great writer may be forgiven for the "thoughtless paradox" of his pronouncements on the Jews: "I say 'thoughtless' because deep down in your heart you are the finest of men."[48]

The exchange between Kovner and Dostoevsky was by no means merely a debate pitting Russians against Jews. Kovner in fact expressed a preferential love for the Russians, a flight from the ghetto that was common enough for the age. Freud, who was of the same generation as Kovner and just a few generations removed from his homeland, knew his ethnic dilemma to perfection and shared his philosophy fully: a complete break with the past and a materialistic world view. Something else that should have caught Freud's eye in Kovner's letter of 3 June 1877 was his response to Dostoevsky's published declaration, "One can't imagine a Jew without belief in God." Kovner told him the obvious, that "many young Jews believe neither in God nor in any organized religion." He went on to pose some very cunning questions: "Would you advise them perhaps to convert to Christianity?... Isn't it better for them to remain 'universal men' [*Allmenschen*]?"[49] The concept of universal men was pointedly taken by Kovner from Dostoevsky's closing chapter in the March 1877 issue of his journal, relating an episode of ethnic harmony in Minsk reported by another Jewish reader.[50]

For Freud, reading in 1927, Kovner's question, whether Jews without faith should convert to Christianity, was clearly ironic and purely rhetorical. And for Dostoevsky the answer was also self-evident. Less than two years later, in the winter of 1878-79, he reminisced at a private gathering about the mock execution he endured in 1849 (two days before Christmas): "We refused to confess our sins, but we did kiss the Crucifix [presented by a priest]. After all, they couldn't be joking with the Crucifix too!" His point was that they *had* been "joking." His host suggested that all of that had by now "passed," but Dostoevsky asked enigmatically: "Has it passed, really?"[51] His grievance against organized religion, as Freud rightly understood, did not pass. Kovner related to Dostoevsky that a Russian general in Kiev once expressed to him regret for the emancipation of the serfs, and his loss of absolute power over them—particularly their wives and daughters.[52] Dostoevsky's own notebooks abound in such anecdotes, and many far more brutal, revealing the Russian national character. Dozens of these harsh parables found their way into *The Brothers Karamazov*. Thus, Kovner's bleak view of the Russian Jews was easily matched by Dostoevsky's grim view of the Russians. Freud, we believe, understood this. No doubt he also shared the editors' conclusion to the German edition, that Kovner despite his apostasy had "served his people gallantly" by invoking Dostoevsky's own vision of universal men in his debate with the great writer.[53]

By designating Freud as presumed reader of the exchange between Kovner and Dostoevsky, we want to imagine a greater degree of rapport between Freud and Dostoevsky as revolutionary psychologists, as critics of religion, and as universal men. Freud saw Dostoevsky as a severely neurotic personality (hypothetically misdiagnosing his epileptic seizures as hysteria). To Dostoevsky's neurosis he attributed his reactionary submission to secular and spiritual authority. But Freud modified this opinion, admitting that in the religious sphere Dostoevsky retained more freedom. Probably Freud was aware (from the German introduction to Kovner's exchange with Dostoevsky) that in 1861 Dostoevsky had published articles defending the Jews.[54] Thus, the later anti-Semitic outbursts might also be understood as part of Dostoevsky's pathology, that (wavering) submission to "the God of the Christians" to which "he was condemned by his neurosis."[55] In the last analysis, so to speak, perhaps no clear line can be drawn between pathological and political anti-Semitism. Dostoevsky exhibited the anti-Semitic reflex common to most goyim under various circumstances. The ill-advised and offensive lapses of his journalism should be weighed against the fact that he welcomed the Jewish convict Kovner to his public forum and modified his own public stance with the doctrine of universal men. For Freud, this behavior should have made *Einfühling* (empathy) less difficult, because Grossman had published the Kovner materials as a unified episode and because Kovner himself represented a social background and a political position close to Freud's own. He was, in fact, a citizen of Freud's Russia.

We have observed that outstanding Jewish politicians of Freud's earlier decades found something to admire in Dostoevsky, qualities such as "political romanticism" and "critical realism"—perhaps squinting to avoid the reactionary streak, ignoring his journalism, or simply reading carelessly in haste, as politicians (and most other readers) generally do. But with the rise of virulent anti-Semitism in Russia soon after Dostoevsky's death, his writings were sometimes unscrupulously used by reactionaries against the Jews. Leonid Grossman, in the Russian afterword to *The Confession of a Jew* (published in 1924), sought to combat this tendency and to eliminate the anti-Semitic taint from Dostoevsky's public image. In "Dostoevsky and Judaism," though acknowledging and citing the anti-Semitic lapses, Grossman persuasively demonstrates "the deep universal traits" bestowed upon Dostoevsky's major Jewish character Isai Fomich, and the author's "latent sympathy" for this figure, whose portrayal is "an unwitting apologia for the Jewish people."[56] Grossman also observes that the mature art of Dostoevsky is imbued with the tone, ideas, and spirit of the Old Testament: the Prophets, legends of the patriarchs, the dreams of Jacob and Joseph, Ecclesiastes, the Psalms, and above all the Book of Job. Grossman emphasizes such Dostoevskian features as protest against suffering, anger at human frailty, grandiose despair and hope, eternal unquiet and soaring indignation, lament, and "aspiration to full flowering of life."[57]

Grossman's inspired apologia for Dostoevsky's creative world was, however, silently omitted from the German edition. The point of including it here is to show how one Jewish reader of Freud's day, an expert biographer of Dostoevsky, understood his fiction in the light of ancient and universal history. Nowhere is Dostoevsky's Old Testament manner more richly displayed than in *The Brothers Karamazov*—the book Freud knew best and the modern fiction that he valued above all others, on a par with Sophocles and Shakespeare.

valued above all others, on a par with Sophocles and Shakespeare. Freud's concern with humanity, like Dostoevsky's, was essentially ecumenical, attuned to biblical antiquity, Egypt, Rome, the Renaissance, and current history.

These two great pioneers of modern psychology had much in common. Each possessed a keen sense of his ethnic vulnerability tempered by a messianic conviction of historical and creative purpose, and by irony. Each—in Freud's view of Dostoevsky (and our own)— was militantly skeptical of religious institutions and doctrine. Both were psychologically burdened by evidence of a hereditary neuropathological taint, and both had a lifelong professional interest in psychopathology. The latter, in Dostoevsky's case, was threefold: as a chronic victim of epilepsy with psychiatric complications; as the son of a physician and nephew of a professor of medicine, always alert to the rapid advances of medical science; and as a creative writer whose every page is haunted by mental illness. Dostoevsky cannot be understood without psychoanalysis, Freud observed, though in a sense he does not "need" it because "he illustrates it himself in every character and every sentence." Finally, both were knowledgeably attentive to scientific progress in general. Dostoevsky, a military engineer by training, perhaps shared the utopian scientific idealism of his day (Comte and his followers), but this soon gave way to skepticism, irony, and the satiric treatment of science that is a hallmark of his fiction. Freud always retained his reverence for rational materialism, rightly predicted that much of his psychoanalytic theory and technique would yield to pharmacology, and spent his last years writing a novel.[58] Perhaps indulging a fantasy, yet plausibly, he was once quoted as saying that "my soul, by its constitution, leans towards the essay, the paradox, the dramatic, and has nothing of the pedantic stiffness which belongs to the true man of science." His books, he said, "more resemble works of imagination than treatises on pathology," and "though I have the appearance of a scientist, I was and am a poet and novelist."[59]

For these several reasons it is not surprising that Freud achieved a good deal of empathy with Dostoevsky despite his initial reservations in 1920, the distortions and contradictions of "Dostoevsky and Parricide," and the rather hollow claim that he just didn't like Dostoevsky because he was a neurotic, like the patients Freud spent so much time treating. The true rapport emerges in Freud's fondness for quoting "a dictum that has become famous," Dostoevsky's definition of psychology as "ein Stock mit zwei Enden" (a stick with two ends—in the orignal Russian: *pálka o dvukh kontsákh*). The defense attorney in *The Brothers Karamazov* uses this trope to counter the prosecution's psychological argumentation, insisting that with psychology you can prove whatever you want to prove. Earlier, in *Crime and Punishment,* Dostoevsky's police inspector uses the same phrase more obscurely and slyly, as if to belittle the significance of his own psychological deductions, or perhaps to reproach himself for reduplicating the criminal psyche—thus proving that anyone might have committed the crime. The psychological "stick with two ends" is thus a bludgeon for coercing a confession, but a dubious instrument of justice and painful for those who wield it.

Freud found it convenient to invoke Dostoevsky's "famous 'stick with two ends'" against feminists who sought to psychoanalyze him! This neat loophole, permitting escape to the sexist hinterlands, was a Russian tactic that Freud gratefully acknowledged. Psychoanalysis employed as "a weapon of controversy" reminded him—"as it so often does"—of Dostoevsky's quip. On another occasion, Freud was called upon to give an opinion when a man accused of parricide was shown to have an "Oedipus complex." Freud gave a synopsis of *The Brothers Karamazov,* explaining how the wrong brother was convicted largely on the basis of "the Oedipal situation." In conclusion Freud adduces his favorite aphorism from the novel's trial scene: "Psychology is a stick with two ends." (See the epigraphs to the present chapter.) It was a joke of which Dostoevsky himself was also fond, judging from the fact that in his two great novels he repeats it six times. In *Wit and Its Relation to the Unconscious* (published in 1905), Freud says that "laughing at the same jokes is evidence of far-reaching psychical conformity."[60] Having witnessed Freud and Dostoevsky laughing at the same joke repeatedly, moreover a joke about psychology, the chief concern of their lives and art, we rest the case for their far-reaching psychic rapport.

Notes

1   Ernest Jones, *The Life and Work of Sigmund Freud*, vol. 2, p. 204; Sigmund Freud, *The Letters of Sigmund Freud*, p. 310.

2   David Joravsky, *Soviet Marxism and Natural Science*; Moshe Wulff, "Zur Stellung der Psychoanalyse in der Sowjetunion"; Elias Perepel, "The Psychoanalytic Movement in U.S.S.R."; Martin Miller, "Freudian Theory Under Bolshevik Rule: The Theoretical Controversy During the 1920s"; Martin Miller "The Theory and Practice of Psychiatry in the Soviet Union"; Martin Miller, "The Origins and Development of Russian Psychoanalysis"; Jean Marti, "La Psychanalyse en Russie"; George H. Pollock, "Psychoanalysis in Russia and the U.S.S.R."; James L. Rice, "Russian Stereotypes in the Freud-Jung Correspondence."

3   In fact their press campaign against him had been launched two years earlier. George H. Pollock, "Psychoanalysis in Russia and the U.S.S.R.," p. 274 (Freud to N. E. Osipov, 23 February 1927); Moshe Wulff, Report of 9 April 1925; Moshe Wulff, Report announcing his resignation, Moshe Wulff, "Zur Stellung der Psychoanlayse"; Elias Perepel, "The Psychoanalytic Movement in U.S.S.R."; Jean Marti, "La Psychanalyse en Russie"; Alex Kozulin, *Psychology in Utopia*; Martin Miller, "Freudian Theory under Bolshevik Rule."

4   William W. Meissner, "The Wolf-Man and the Paranoid Process," 1977 and 1979.

5   Theodor Reik, *Freud als Kulturkritiker*, p. 64; Theodor Reik, *From Thirty Years with Freud*, p. 175.

6   Sigmund Freud, *Standard Edition of the Complete Psychological Works of Sigmund Freud*, vol. 21, pp. 177 and 188.

7   Ibid., vol. 21, p. 187. Dostoevsky himself consciously knew the temptation and psychopathology of submission to authority in loco parentis. See his notes for a revision of "The Double" (1860-64) in F. M. Dostoevskii, *Polnoe sobranie sochinenii v tridtsati tomakh* 1 (1972), pp. 432 and 436. It is interesting that the Russian scholar A. L. Boehm (Bem) rejected this concept as late as 1938: "Even Freud himself did not avoid excesses in applying his doctrine to the field of literature. Introducing the Oedipus complex into the realm of political behavior, with state authority interpreted as a father-figure, is in my opinion an excess of this sort, for which no objective evidence exists" (A. L. Bem, Dostoevskii, p. 11). An essential idea of Dostoevsky's fiction thus escaped him.

8   Sigmund Freud, *Standard Edition of the Complete Psychological Works of Sigmund Freud*, vol. 21, p. 177; Sigmund Freud, *Gesammelte Werke*, vol. 14, p. 400.

9   Sigmund Freud, *Standard Edition of the Complete Psychological Works of Sigmund Freud*, vol. 21, p. 187.

10   Joseph Brodsky, personal communication, 10 May 1982.

11   L. P. Grossman, *Zhizn' i trudy F. M. Dostoevskogo*, pp. 15-19.

12   F. M. Dostojewski, *The Brothers Karamazov*, in F. M. Dostojewski, *Sämtliche Werke*, vol. 9-10 (1908). The father's Odessa anecdote occurs in F. M. Dostoevskii, *Polnoe sobranie sochinenii v tridtsati tomakh* 14, p. 21 (book 1, chap. 4).

13   David I. Goldstein, personal communication; Felix P. Ingold, "Die jüdische Frage im Schaffen F. M. Dostojewskijs"; Robert Alter, response to Robert Alter, Review of *Dostoevsky and the Jews*; Nathan Rosen, Review of *Dostoevsky and the Jews*; Gary Saul Morson, "Dostoevsky's Anti-Semitism and the Critics"; Gary Rosenshield, "Isai Fomich Bumshtein".

14   F. M. Dostoevskii, *Polnoe sobranie sochinenii v tridtsati tomakh* vol. 29, book 2 (1986), p. 90.

15   Elliott Oring, *The Jokes of Sigmund Freud*, pp. 42-51. See also the joke about the poor Jew traveling by train to Karlsbad, "if my constitution can stand it," related by Freud in *The Interpretation of Dreams*, in Sigmund Freud, *Standard Edition of the Complete Psychological Works of Sigmund Freud*, vol. 4, pp. 194-95.

16   David I. Goldstein, *Dostoevsky and the Jews*, pp. 16-17.

17   Felix P. Ingold, *Dostojewski und das Judentum*, p. 67. My emphasis.

18   F. M. Dostoevskii, *Polnoe sobranie sochinenii v tridtsati tomakh* 6, p. 370.

19   Ibid. 6, p. 394.

20   Robert Alter, Review of *Dostoevsky and the Jews*; for other aspects of the issue, see note 13 above. Another controversial moment involves Aliosha Karamazov's reply, "I don't know," to Liza's challenging question of whether Jews murder Christian children at Passover (F. M. Dostojewski, *The Brothers Karamazov*, in F. M. Dostojewski, *Sämtliche Werke*, vol. 9-10, book 11, p. 3). However, Liza is portrayed as a seriously ill hysteric, who crushes her own finger in the door as soon as Aliosha has left. She declares *herself* ready to watch the ritual murder of a child with pleasure, while eating pineapple compote—yet another of her malicious and obvious provocations of Aliosha, who seeks only to avoid agitating her further, certainly not to express the author's "position" on the Jews (Gary Rosenshield, "Isai Fomich Bumshtein," pp. 274-76).

21   Robert S. Wistrich, *The Jews of Vienna*, pp. 541-43; Sigmund Freud, *The Letters of Sigmund Freud*, p. 360 ("To Members of the B'Nai B'Rith Lodge" 6 May 1926).

22   Martin Freud in Josef Fraenkel, ed., *The Jews of Austria*, pp. 203 and 208.

23   Sigmund Freud, *The Letters of Sigmund Freud*, p. 366-7.

24   Ibid., p. 368.

25   Robert S. Wistrich, *The Jews of Vienna*, p. 551.

26   Ibid., p. 571. On Freud's Jewish identity, see Ernest Jones, *The Life and Work of Sigmund Freud*, vol. 1, p. 22; vol. 2, pp. 191 and 427 and Index: "Freud as a Jew"; and vol. 3, pp. 35-51 and 367-69. Also see the Index to this book.

27   Robert S. Wistrich, *The Jews of Vienna*, p. 580. See the foreword "From the Author."

28   Sigmund Freud, *The Letters of Sigmund Freud*, pp. 78-9; Martin Freud in Josef Fraenkel, ed., *The Jews of Austria*, p. 204.

29   Jonathan Frankel, *Prophecy and Politics*, pp. 48 and 406.

30   Robert Alter, Review of *Dostoevsky and the Jews*.

31   Yosef Hayim Yerushalmi, "Freud on the 'Historical Novel'."

32   Ernst Sellin, *Mose und seine Bedeutung*, chap. 5.

33   Sigmund Freud and Arnold Zweig, *The Letters of Sigmund Freud and Arnold Zweig*, p. 91 (30 September 1934).

34   Sigmund Freud, *Standard Edition of the Complete Psychological Works of Sigmund Freud*, vol. 21 (1961), p. 177.

35   Ibid., vol. 21 (1961), pp. 37-38.

36   Ibid., vol. 23, pp. 47-48.

37   Dmitri Mereschkowski, *Der Messias*; Harry Trosman and Roger Dennis Simmons, "The Freud Library," p. 680.

38   Dmitri Mereschkowski, *Akhnaton, King of Egypt*, pp. 8, 43, 144, and 372. See epigraph to the present study, p. vi.

39   F. M. Dostoevskii, *Polnoe sobranie sochinenii v tridtsati tomakh*, vols. 18-27 (1978-1984).

40   Ek. P. Letkova, "O F. M. Dostoevskom," p. 465.

41   David I. Goldstein, *Dostoevsky and the Jews*, pp. 88-163.

42   L. P. Grossman, *Ispoved' odnogo evreia*.

43   Gerda Maneval, personal communication.

44   Ernest Jones, *The Life and Work of Sigmund Freud*, vol. 3, p. 143.

45   David I. Goldstein, *Dostoevsky and the Jews*, p. 107.

46   L. P. Grossman, *Die Beichte eines Juden* in *Briefen an Dostojewski*, p. 62; David I. Goldstein, *Dostoevsky and the Jews*, pp. 106-133.

47   F. M. Dostoevskii, *Polnoe sobranie sochinenii*. 25: 74-88 (*Diary of a Writer*, March 1988, chap. 2).

48   David I. Goldstein, *Dostoevsky and the Jews*, p. 132; L. P. Grossman, *Die Beichte eines Juden* in *Briefen an Dostojewski*, p. 162.

49   L. P. Grossman, *Die Beichte eines Juden* in *Briefen an Dostojewski*, p. 162.

50   F. M. Dostoevskii, *Polnoe sobranie sochinenii v tridtsati tomakh* 25 (1983): 88-92 (*Diary of a Writer* March 1877, chap. 3). It was here that Kovner "for the thousandth time" found proof that Dostoevsky was "der herzensbeste Mensch." (See L. P. Grossman, *Die Beichte eines Juden* in *Briefen an Dostojewski*, p. 162.)

51   Ek. P. Letkova, "O F. M. Dostoevskom," pp. 460-61.

52   David I. Goldstein, *Dostoevsky and the Jews*, p. 115.

53   L. P. Grossman, *Die Beichte eines Juden* in *Briefen an Dostojewski*, p. 237.

54   See preface by Fülöp-Miller, ed., in L. P. Grossman, *Die Beichte eines Juden* in *Briefen an Dostojewski*, p. 10. The anonymous articles in question were attributed to Dostoevsky by Grossman, a view tenuously supported by modern linguistic techniques. G. Khetso, "Avtor stat'i—F. M. Dostoevskii?"; Geir Kjetsaa, *Prinadlezhnost' Dostoevskomu*.

55   Sigmund Freud, *Standard Edition of the Complete Psychological Works of Sigmund Freud*, vol. 21, p. 177.

56   L. P. Grossman, *Confession of a Jew*, p. 143.

57   Ibid., pp. 144-49.

58   Joseph Wortis, *Fragments of an Analysis with Freud*, pp. 110-11 and 138.

59   Giovanni Papini, "A Visit to Freud," pp. 100-101.

60   Sigmund Freud, *Jokes and Their Relation to the Unconscious*; Sigmund Freud, *Standard Edition of the Complete Psychological Works of Sigmund Freud*, vol. 8, p. 151.

Epilogue

Back to Barbarism

I still greatly love the prison from which I have been released.

—Freud to Max Eitingon, 6 June 1938

Freud grew up with the idea of revolution. His uncles had fled from Vienna to Odessa in 1848 under threat of arrest, and Freud in his day was ever alert to the Russian revolutionary movement and ideal. The tsars, models of moribund absolutism everywhere, were "digging their own grave," but the times called for bomb-throwing assassins to hasten them on their way. These earliest dicta (given in 1877) are echoed in some of Freud's last known pronouncements on Russian history, in the *New Introductory Lectures on Psychoanalysis* (published in 1933). Here he rejects Marxist explanations for revolution, which he attributed instead to increased control over forces of nature—at the service of innate aggression between differing groups:

> I really believe that it was gunpowder and firearms that abolished chivalry and aristocratic rule, and that the Russian despotism was already doomed before it lost the War, because no amount of inbreeding among the ruling families of Europe could have produced a race of Tsars capable of withstanding the explosive force of dynamite.[1]

This was a variation on a theme of Feuerbach (an intellectual idol of Freud's youth), who had observed that natural sciences, unbeknownst to reactionary governments, had "long before dissolved the Christian world view in nitric acid."[2]

By 1933 Freud saw that dissolution of the Christian world view in Russia had only created "a prohibition of thought which is just as ruthless as was that of religion in the past." Any skepticism regarding Soviet Marxist orthodoxy was now punished, "just as heresy was once punished by the Catholic Church." The writings of Marx had assumed the place of the Bible and the Koran. Bolshevism now compensated its sufferers with promises of a paradise on earth, as Jews had once expected a Messiah and Christians believed that the Kingdom of God was nigh.[3] In the opening paragraph of "Dostoevsky and Parricide," Freud had portrayed the great Russian writer as a proponent of old illusions, a Christian jailer of humanity like the "Grand Inquisitor." But as his work on this essay progressed, Freud also saw Dostoevsky as a "great intelligence" exposing the illusions of faith. Dostoevsky remained (as Freud had said in 1918) the greatest of psychological poets, a revealer of truth. The finished text of "Dostoevsky and Parricide" does nothing to resolve the paradox of Freud's analysis. Nor does Freud's final view of mankind resolve the paradox of human nature.

The *New Introductory Lectures* go on to acknowledge that, without a fundamental change in human nature, violent control and compulsory education are necessary, a concept that could never be accepted without illusion. People "like me," he said, would shrink from the methods of the Bolshevik experiment. But others, "men of action, unshakable in their convictions, inaccessible to doubt, without feelings for the sufferings of others," would press toward their goals. Then Freud offers a commentary which, one of his ablest interpreters thought, expressed a certain "awe" of the Russian revolutionary achievement, but which strikes us now as characteristically ironic:

> We have to thank men of this kind for the fact that the tremendous experiment of producing a new order of this kind is now actually being carried out in Russia. At the same time, when the great nations [of the West] announce that they expect salvation only from the maintenance of Christian piety, the revolution in Russia—in spite of all its disagreeable

details [*trotz aller unerfreulichen Einzelzüge*]—seems none the less like the message of a better future. Unluckily neither our skepticism nor the fanatical faith of the other side gives a hint as to how the experiment will turn out.[4]

By that time, and unbeknownst to the West, millions of people in Russia knew how the experiment had turned out: badly. From Freud's Viennese distance, one might still have regarded the revolution if not with awe then with some dim hope that Russia would escape the anti-Semitic violence unleashed in the Germanic world. But on this point too one recalls Freud's apprehension in 1930: "One only wonders, with concern, what the Soviets will do after they have wiped out their bourgeoisie."[5] Jewish intellectuals in Russia were equally concerned with what a collapse of Soviet power might bring from the masses: "We would be the first to be hanged from the nearest streetlight."[6]

In May 1933, Freud wrote to his old acquaintance in Switzerland, the Reverend Oskar Pfister: "My judgment of human nature, above all the Christian-Aryan variety, has had little reason to change."[7] Shortly before (on 10 May), his works along with those of Marx (and many others) had been publicly burned by the Nazis throughout Germany. At the end of that year, Max Eitingon left Berlin for Palestine, where his father had purchased land decades earlier. Eitingon, perhaps Freud's most trusted confederate, a Russophile from Freud's ancestral territory, had thus come full circle in the ancient quest for a homeland. Meanwhile, despite some losses, he remained a person of considerable means. The family firm of Eitingon-Schild was solidly established on the New York exchange.

In December 1933, Freud's correspondent Arnold Zweig (no kin to Stefan) also left Berlin for Jerusalem. In their letters we see the genesis of *Moses and Monotheism*, conceived in the face of modern social tragedy: "Faced with the new persecutions, one asks oneself again how the Jews have come to be what they are and why they have attracted this undying hatred. I soon created the formula: Moses created the Jews." Much of Freud's remaining life was devoted to the therapeutic creation of his controversial "historical novel."[8]

Freud had once declared to Arnold Zweig that "mankind on the average and taken by and large are a wretched lot."[9] In the 1930s, as the wretchedness of the human condition enveloped Freud's Vienna and drove him, at last, into a brief and unimagined exile before death, the Bolshevik experiment did not fade from view beyond the eastern front. Among Freud's last known observations on Russia are remarks recorded by the American psychiatrist Joseph Wortis, who underwent a didactic analysis with Freud in 1934-35 and soon afterward introduced insulin shock therapy in the United States. On 14 December 1934, Freud told Wortis:

> All Russia is held together by class hatred [by the proletariat] against other classes and against foreigners. And they have [upper] classes in Russia too. They have their privileged officials who enjoy all sorts of things that the workers haven't got. Go there and see for yourself. They call that progress! They don't know they have gone back thousands of years. In the old days everybody had to live together in huts, as they do now in a single room. What does that mean? It means the end of intellectual work. It's simply going back to barbarism."[10]

In the West, where the descent into barbarism was becoming apparent in other ways, Freud declared that Jews were on a higher plane than the rest of society in their family and intellectual life. But he was implacably opposed to all formal religion. The Jewish and Christian faiths were "equally bad," and "Jews and Christians ought to meet on the common ground of irreligion and humanity."[11] In *Moses and Monotheism* (published in 1939), he reasserted the conclusion he had reached a quarter century before, that psychoanalysis logically reduces religion to "the status of a neurosis in mankind" and explains the grandiose powers of religion as neurotic obsession.[12] This theory had been most thoroughly tested in his analysis of Russian material, chiefly the Wolf-Man and Dostoevsky. These major Russian subjects had, moreover, each revealed a great intelligence allied with Freud's (ambivalently, of course) against religion and the Christian state. Freud's Russia forecast a bleak future for the illusion of faith and for the Bolshevik experiment, based like religion upon new ruthless prohibitions, books of revelation, punishment of heresy, and promises of Paradise—on earth if not after death.

There our story might have ended had not Freud's Russia pursued him, after a fashion, into exile. After the Bolshevik Revolution, the Russian community abroad rapidly grew in such cities as Prague, Berlin, and Paris.[13] Anti-Soviet political activity in the West was countered by NKVD espionage and occasionally by kidnapping and murder. Freud's longtime friend and colleague Dr. Max Eitingon was implicated in one of the most sensational of these incidents, the disappearance of General E. K. Miller, head of the Russian War Veterans Association (ROVS) in Paris. Miller vanished at midday, 22 September 1937, on his way to meet military attachés from the German Embassy. He left a memo casting suspicion upon his second-in-command, Nikolai Skoblín, who also disappeared forever soon after being confronted with the memo. Two years earlier Skoblin had been publicly accused of being a Soviet agent. This old accusation was quickly picked up and embellished by the Russian émigré press. Skoblin's wife, the cabaret singer Nadezhda Plevítskaia, was arrested, charged with complicity in Miller's kidnapping, tried a year later (between 5 and 15 December 1938), and sentenced to twenty years in prison, where she died in 1940.[14] The prosecution alleged that Max Eitingon was a Soviet agent who furnished financial support to Plevitskaia. But, as a resident of Palestine, Max was not subpoenaed to appear in the French court. However circumstantial the evidence, it received sensational press coverage and caused Freud's followers in Paris to rally in support of Eitingon.

In the annals of psychoanalysis, Max Eitingon is portrayed as an invaluable organizer of clinics, training institutes, and publishing activities, whose "Biblical attitude toward Freud's writings" may explain his failure to have made scientific contributions to the movement.[15] We have seen him also as a native of Freud's Russia, a Russophile, for more than thirty years Freud's close confidant, and an active purveyor of Russian culture. The public trial of Nadezhda Plevitskaia provides some insight into the character of Eitingon, revealing his intimate bonds with the Russian émigré community while vilifying him as a Soviet spy and assassin. One recalls how Jung once privately predicted to Freud, half in jest, that Eitingon—an "uninhibited" womanizer and intellectually "impotent gasbag"—might become a member of the Russian Duma.[16] Now rumor again swept Eitingon into the arena of Russian politics—whether rightly or wrongly remained to be seen. Recently, the trial of Plevitskaia has been rediscovered by American scholars and journalists, who sometimes give it a treatment reminiscent of the extravagant newspaper coverage of the time, particularly the Russian émigré press in Paris.[17]

. It is the role of Max Eitingon that intrigues us here, and the question of "what Freud knew"—if in fact there was anything to know of any importance. Max, who as a child had emigrated from Russia to Austrian (later Polish) Galicia, obtained a Polish passport in 1919. That year he married an actress named Mira (Mirra) Raigorodskaia, once associated with the Moscow Art Theater.[18] Thus Max, a native of Russian Mogilev raised in Leipzig, long a citizen of Austria and resident of Berlin, reaffirmed his cultural affinity with Russia through marriage. That same year, Plevitskaia (already a Soviet agent, according to unproven allegations by the prosecution in 1938) married Skoblin in Galipoli. They lived at first in Odessa, then Prague, where she gave concerts, and in 1923 they moved to Berlin. There Max Eitingon, a founding member of the Berlin Psychoanalytic Institute (since 1910), kept a large house on Räuchstrasse. It is reasonable to suppose that the show business connections of the wives brought the two couples together. Max became an occasional benefactor of Plevitskaia, publishing her two volumes of memoirs (*Dëzhkin karagod* and *Moi put' s pesnei*) and once renting a hall for an anniversary benefit concert.[19] On trial, she drew laughter and an ironic inquiry about Russian mores from the judge when she thoughtlessly said that Max dressed her "from head to toe." But she praised his character, denied any romantic involvement, and insisted that nobody who knew Eitingon could believe there had been any "piquante episodes" between them.

Max and Mira had moved to Palestine in December 1933, which would seem to cast doubt on the prosecution's claim that Skoblin and Plevitskaia met Bolshevik sympathizers of the Eurasian movement, as well as Soviet agents, at Eitingon's Berlin home in 1935.[20] The Eitingons, however, did visit Skoblin and Plevitskaia in Paris in the early autumn of 1937, and were seen off by their friends when they departed for Florence on 20 September—two days before the disappearance of General Miller and then Skoblin (already under suspicion as an accomplice in Miller's presumed abduction). Plevitskaia, who claimed to have then wandered about in a daze, purchased two expensive dresses and then spent most of the day before her arrest at the home of Max's brother-in-law, Leonid Raigorodsky. At the trial, Raigorodsky testified that Max was indeed a great patron of the arts and, despite some financial reversals due to the economy, was "worth many millions." (Freud's circle believed that Max had been hit hard by the crash in 1929, and probably he was. But the family assets were diversified, and a solid recovery of his personal situation by 1937 is not unreasonable to suppose.) A key point in the case against Plevitskaia was that the long investigation established no significant savings or income, yet she and Skoblin had lived lavishly, owning, for example, four automobiles (or by some accounts, six). When arrested, Plevitskaia had thousands of francs in her purse, and large amounts in dollars and pounds, but could never explain their source or her reason for carrying such a sum. Her long association with the Russian-born millionaire Eitingon thus came under suspicion.

There was much confusion about the identity of Eitingon, whose name is consistently misspelled Ettingon (sometimes Ettington) in the press. His brother-in-law Raigorodsky vigorously denied that Max was a Soviet agent masquerading as a London fur trader, but he understandably did not volunteer the fact—blurted out by Plevitskaia—that Max had a brother who was in fact a London fur trader. The fur business had long been the major interest of the family's Leipzig firm. Raigorodsky instead put up a smoke screen: "There are many Eitingons in Paris."

Recent scholars investigating the NKVD have raised the stakes fabulously by concluding that the mastermind of subversion in the West was known as Naum (or Leonid) Ettingon (or Eitingon), and some have claimed him as the brother of a Mark Eitingon, alias Max, the honored colleague of Sigmund Freud.[21] Max indeed had a cousin, Naum Isakovich Eitingon, whose life history has not been made public. Even those most strongly disposed to whitewash the Eitingon name, so to speak, have not yet managed, to our knowledge, to divert all suspicion that Max's cousin N. I. Eitingon—who owned textile factories in Lodz (Poland)—was a key organizer of Red terrorism abroad in the 1930s.[22] On the other hand, nobody has proven that it was so, and even if it were, the mystery of Max would remain. At the trial, the prosecutor insisted that Eitingon was a secret agent who had supported Skoblin and Plevitskaia with Soviet funds. This charge was not substantiated, the court ruled. Whether guilty or not, Plevitskaia was convicted of complicity in General Miller's disappearance and sentenced to twenty years on evidence that seems completely circumstantial. She had "failed to account satisfactorily for her movements on the day of the disappearance," as the *London Times* summed up the matter.[23] Given the historical moment and the nature of the charges, one may assume that a hidden diplomatic agenda and perhaps secret evidence governed the outcome. Dozens of Russian émigrés who had been expelled from France were permitted to return in order to testify.

Although Max Eitingon did not appear at the trial, the psychoanalytic establishment of Paris was called upon to attest to his character, and did so. This occurred midway through the proceedings, on 9 December 1938, when the defense requested that Princess Marie Bonaparte be summoned. The reactionary émigré paper *Vozrozhdenie* (*La Renaissance*) was openly hostile to Plevitskaia and given to grotesque distortions of the testimony. Even the editor, Julii Semenov, testified in court against her. *Vozrozhdenie* characteristically claimed that Princess Bonaparte was a "patient" of the psychiatrist Dr. Eitingon, and that "everyone in court laughed" when she was proposed as a witness for her doctor "in order to destroy the legend that he is a Soviet agent."[24] Marie Bonaparte, the leading benefactress of the international psychoanalytic movement, did not appear, however. Instead, the defense read aloud a letter from Dr. René Laforgue, since 1925 the preeminent Freudian psychiatrist in Paris.[25] This was reported on page one of Miliukov's moderate and respected *Poslednie Novosti* (*Les dernières nouvelles*) of 10 December 1938:

The Letter of Doctor Laforgue

At the opening of the session, the defense attorney M. M. Filonenko reads aloud a letter from Dr. René Laforgue, characterizing M. Eitingon in the most favorable light. Dr. René Laforgue is an eminent psychiatrist, well known in international scholarly circles. With amazement he had learned of the suspicions which threaten M. Eitingon, and now he hastens to dispel them. The scholarly contributions of M. Eitingon have been recognized at international congresses, among whose participants he has many personal friends. A person of independent means, M. Eitingon has dedicated himself wholly to science. If because of the economic situation he is not so wealthy now as formerly, still he continues to provide "generous monetary assistance to his unfortunate compatriots."

Dr. R. Laforgue ended his letter by declaring that he considered it "a personal honor to be known as a friend of M. Eitingon."

Vozrozhdenie scarcely mentioned this testimonial in passing and did not even feel obliged to name its eminent author, Dr. Laforgue. In terms of the legal process, of course, and particularly a legal process of this sort, the letter could have little bearing on the verdict. For our purposes, however, it is remarkable to witness the Freudian community thus drawn, if marginally, into the truly nightmarish world of Stalinist terror.

Between the arrest of Plevitskaia in September 1937 and her trial in December 1938, Freud's escape from Vienna to London was arranged by the Princess Bonaparte. En route he spent twelve hours at her home and described the overwhelming emotional climate of those days in a long letter to Max Eitingon, filled with the triumph of his liberation mixed with sorrow, "for in spite of everything I still greatly loved the prison from which I have been released."[26]

It has been reported that Max routinely attended the Psychoanalytic Congress in Paris later that summer, in August, four months before Plevitskaia's trial, while the investigation was in full progress and after it had without any doubt already implicated him.[27] This would seem remarkably risky, even if he was convinced of his innocence, unless he knew something that we do not know—which is of course certain. On this trip he also crossed the Channel to visit Freud in exile. Yet apparently it was not until the trial of Plevitskaia was underway, and Laforgue had submitted his testimonial letter to the court, that Max explained to Freud his involvement in the matter. An unpublished letter from Freud to Eitingon of 12 December 1938 is said to reveal that Max had recently sent word to Freud about his acquaintance with Plevitskaia, who was at that very time on trial as a Soviet agent and assassin.

For the present, the truth of the matter is left to one's imagination.[28] We can be sure that Freud followed the outcome of this courtroom drama with close attention, because it drew his two most loyal and generous followers into the web of Soviet terrorism with all the bizarre logic of a bad dream. No doubt he also pondered the clues of this international crime in the spirit of his favorite Conan Doyle, analyzing the case "Sherlock Holmes-like" as another piece in the puzzle of civilization, and another historic token of *Russische Innerlichkeit*.

"Indeed this compromise with morality is a characteristic Russian trait."[29]

Freud, who had been welcomed as a celebrity in London, remained in contact with the intellectual world he had created. Meanwhile, Nazi Germany took over Austria and eliminated Czechoslovakia, including the pastoral Slavic homeland of Freud's bilingual childhood, the fountainhead of his personal endopsychic myth recaptured in *Die Traumdeutung*. To his historical imagination, this national catastrophe must have recalled the Thirty Years' War and its peasant victims in Bohemia and Moravia, one of the four classic horrors listed in *Civilization and Its Discontents*, the great nightmare of the North rivaling the fate of galley-slaves in antiquity, martyrs of the Inquisition, and Jews beset by pogroms—to the South, West, and Russian East of Freud's now lost Vienna, that "prison" which he had loved to the end.

Freud came full circle to the *Vaterlandslosigkeit* of his lost and recovered dream. We have seen something of Russia's contribution—another lost fatherland—to Freud's creative regeneration of world culture in his extended analysis of Dostoevsky, the Wolf-Man, and diverse "Russian material." Out of Russian absolutism, revolutionary doctrine, and military aggression also came the theory of a destruction instinct, that belated Russian contribution to psychoanalysis. Finally, Freud's "Moses-Novel" explores the Mysteries of the East conjured by Merezhkovsky in his treatises, his many essays on Dostoevsky, and his novel *The Messiah*. Arnold Zweig understood *Moses and Monotheism*, and Freud's own life, as a deeply moving "advance into forbidden territory."[30]

Freud died on 23 September 1939 without witnessing the final horror of the Holocaust but in full understanding of humanity's potential for it.[31] "Freud the man," observed the *London Times*, "was clearly bigger than his detractors are willing to admit. His influence has pervaded the world within the space of but a few years."[32] Freud's intellectual penetration into Russia, however, had been cut off and rejected.[33] That lifelong campaign was his most remarkable advance into forbidden territory, literally into the world of his forefathers and parents, the world of ancient tyranny and modern pogroms, the world of his most valued and challenging patient, the world of Dostoevsky's great intellect and art, a world of parricide, regicide, and revolution that bodied forth from dreams into reality. Freud's involvement in Russian history and *Russische Innerlichkeit* contributed significantly and inevitably to his mature understanding of the human psyche, its illusions and destiny.

Notes

1   Sigmund Freud, *Standard Edition of the Complete Psychological Works of Sigmund Freud*, vol. 22, p. 177.

2   *Die Naturwissenschaft und die Revolution*, 1850, quoted by Hans Küng in his *Freud and the Problem of God*, p. 3.

3   Sigmund Freud, *Standard Edition of the Complete Psychological Works of Sigmund Freud*, vol. 22, p. 185.

4   Ibid., vol. 22, p. 181. See K. R. Eissler, "A Letter to Professor Tandler (1931)," p. 9. K. E. Eissler, personal communications, 11 September 1984 and 24 February 1985.

5   Sigmund Freud, *Standard Edition of the Complete Psychological Works of Sigmund Freud*, vol. 21, p. 115.

6   Collective wisdom attributed to the Russian intelligentsia (perhaps more particularly to the Russian Jewish intelligentsia) by Nadezhda Mandelstam (*Hope Against Hope*, p. 96).

7   Sigmund Freud, *The Letters of Sigmund Freud*, p. 418.

8   Sigmund Freud and Arnold Zweig, *The Letters of Sigmund Freud and Arnold Zweig*, p. 91 (30 September 1934).

9   Sigmund Freud and Arnold Zweig, *Letters*, p. 3 (2 December 1927).

10 Joseph Wortis, *Fragments of an Analysis with Freud*, p. 106 (14 December 1934).

11 Ibid., p. 144 (17 January 1935).

12 Sigmund Freud, *Moses and Monotheism*, pp. 67-68; Sigmund Freud, *Standard Edition of the Complete Psychological Works of Sigmund Freud*, vol. 23.

13 Marc Raeff, *Russia Abroad*.

14 Nina Berberova, *The Italics Are Mine*, pp. 332-33. Theodore Draper, personal communication, 9 July 1988. Plevitskaia reportedly admitted to her lawyer that Skoblin told her of his complicity, but she denied her own. See also Viacheslav Kostikov, *Ne budem proklinat' izgnan'e*," pp. 350-404.

15   Sidney L. Pomer, "Max Eitingon," 59n.

16   Sigmund Freud and C. G. Jung, *Briefwechsel*, p. 90.

17   *Poslednie Novosti* 22 October 1937-15 December 1928; *Vozrozhdenie* 1 July 1938-23 December 1938; Robert Conquest, *The Great Terror. Stalin's Purge of the Thirties*; Boris Prianishnikov, *Nezrimaia pautina*; Vitaly Rapoport and Yuri Alexeev, *High Treason. Essays on the History of the Red Army*, pp. 391-92; John J. Dziak, *Chekisty*; Stephen Schwartz, "Intellectuals and Assassins—Annals of Stalin's Killerati"; Vadim Kondratiev et al., "Stalin's Killerati," p. 2; Theodore Draper, "The Mystery of Max Eitingon," pp. 32-43; Theodore Draper, *A Present of Things Past*; Stephen Schwartz, et al., "'The Mystery of Max Eitingon: An Exchange," pp. 50-55; Robert Conquest, "Max Eitingon: Another View," pp. 22-23; Theodore Draper, personal communication, 9 July 1988; Martin Grotjahn, "Was Max Eitingon One of Stalin's Killerati?," p. 16.

18   No such person has yet been identified in archive records of the Moscow Art Theater personnel (Michael Heim, personal communication, 10 May 1990). Perhaps she used a stage name (or was she a student, or walk-on?).

19   Nadezhda Plevitskaia, *Dëzhkin karagod*; Nadezhda Plevitskaia, *Moi put' s pesnei*.

20   Raeff 1990, 216 note 24 (on the Eurasian movement).

21   Vitaly Rapoport and Yuri Alexeev, *High Treason*, pp. 391-92 (see note 17, above).

22   Theodore Draper, "The Mystery of Max Eitingon," pp. 41-42n, with current Eitingon family tree supplied by the American branch of the family. (See also Theodore Draper, *A Present of Things Past*, p. 290.)

23   *Times* (London), 15 December 1938, p. 15.

24   *Vozrozhdenie* 9 December 1938, p. 6.

25   See E. James Lieberman, *Acts of Will*, p. 259.

26   Sigmund Freud, *The Letters of Sigmund Freud*, p. 446 (6 June 1938).

27   Sidney L. Pomer, "Max Eitingon, 1881-1943," p. 60.

28   Theodore Draper, personal communication, 9 July 1988.

29   Sigmund Freud, "Dostoevsky and Parricide," from the opening sketch of Ivan the Terrible.

30   Sigmund Freud and Arnold Zweig, *The Letters of Sigmund Freud and Arnold Zweig*, p. 179; Moshe Wulff, "An Appreciation of Freud's *Moses and Monotheism*."

31   Four of his sisters perished, in Auschwitz, Treblinka, and Theresienstadt.

32   *Times* 25 September 1939, p. 10.

33   A. I. Belkin, 'Zigmund Freid: Vozrozhdenie v SSSR?"

Bibliography

Anon. "Angriff auf das Reich des König Ödipus." *Der Spiegel* 52 (1964): 116-132.

———. "Botkin, Sergei Petrovich (1832-1889)." In *Bol'shaia sovetskaia entsiklopediia*, 3rd ed., vol. 3, p. 601. Moscow: 1970.

———. "Botkin, Sergei Petrovich." In *Entsiklopedicheskii slovar'*, edited by F.A. Brockhaus and I.A. Efron, chap. 4, pp. 500-501. St. Petersburg: 1891.

———. "Brody." In *Entsiklopedicheskii slovar'*, edited by Brockhaus & Efron, vol. 4, p. 695. St. Petersburg: 1891.

———. "Darkshevich, Liverii Osipovich (1858-1925)." In *Bol'shaia sovetskaia entsiklopediia*, vol. 20, p. 485. Moscow: 1930. 2nd ed. vol. 13, p. 386 (Moscow: 1952). 3rd ed. vol. 7, p. 555 (Moscow: 1972).

———. "Kriegsschauplatz-Karten" (West and East Fronts). *Berliner Tageblatt* 20 October 1914, p. 7.

———. "Missing Leader of White Russians. Paris Trial Opened." *The Times* (London) 6 December 1938, p. 3.

———. "Psycho-Analysis in Russia." *International Journal of Psycho-Analysis* 3 (1922): 513-518.

———. "Russland und das Deutsche Reich." *Ostdeutsche Rundschau* 6 June 1909, pp. 1-2.

———. "Russland. Militärische Antisemitismus. Pogrompolitik in Poland und Galizien." *Frankfurter Zeitung und Handelsblatt (Neue Frankfurter Zeitung)* 4 January 1916 sec. 3, p. 3.

———. "Die slavische Gefahr und das Wiener Deutschtum." *Wiener Rundschau* 22 May 1909, pp. 1-2.

———. "Sentence of Mme Skobline." *The Times* (London) 15 December 1938, p. 15.

237

"100 Reisen durch Europa." Board game produced by Otto Maier Verlag, Ravensburg, in 1898. Photo of 1897 variant supplied by manufacturer. See Sigmund Freud, *The Complete Letters of Sigmund Freud to Wilhelm Fliess, 1887-1904*, p. 307 (3 April 1898).

A.F.S. "Pinsk." In *Entsiklopedicheskii slovar'*, edited by Brockhaus and Efron, vol. 46, pp. 626-8. St. Petersburg: 1898.

———— and V. R-ov, "Mogilev na Dnepre ili Mogilev gubernskii." In *Entsiklopedicheskii slovar'*, edited by F. A. Brockhaus and I. A. Efron, vol. 38, pp. 573-5. St. Petersburg: 1896.

A.V. "Bratslav, ili Braslav (Podolia)." In *Entsiklopedicheskii slovar'*, edited by Brockhaus and Efron, vol. 4, pp. 620-621. St. Petersburg: 1891.

Aberbach, David. "Freud's Jewish Problem." *Commentary* 69 (6) (June 1980): 35-39.

Abraham-Torok, Nicolas and Maria. "Le mot magique de l'Homme aux loups." *Revue française de psychanalyse* 35 (1975): 71-100.

———— and Maria. *Cryptonymie: Le Verbier de l'Homme aux Loups*. Paris: Aubier, 1976.

Adler, Alfred. "Dostoevsky." In *The Practice and Theory of Individual Psychology*. New York: Harcourt, Brace, 1924. Originally a public lecture given in Zurich in 1918. Published in 1920 as *Praxis und Theorie des Individualpsychologie. Vorträge zur Einführung in die Psychotherapie für Aerzte, Psychologen und Lehrer* (Munich and Wiesbaden: J. F. Bergmann).

Alajouanine, T. "Dostoevsky's Epilepsy." *Brain* 86 (2) (June 1963): 209-218.

Aleksandrovskii, B. P. "Istoriia bolezni Ivana Sergeevicha Turgeneva," *Vrachebnoe delo* 8 (1949): 741-44.

Alexander, Franz, Samuel Eisenstadt, and Martin Grotjahn, eds. *Psychoanalytic Pioneers*. New York: Basic Books, 1966.

Allen, Woody. "My Speech to the Graduates." In *Side Effects*, by Woody Allen. New York: Random House, 1980.

Alter, Robert. Review of *Dostoevsky and the Jews*, by David I. Goldstein. *TLS (Times Literary Supplement)* 3 July 1981, pp. 751-2. Response by John Bayley 17 July 1981, p. 813; David Goldstein 28 August 1981, p. 983; John Bayley 11 September 1981, p. 1037; James L. Rice 27 November 1981, p. 1394;

Joseph L. Whelan 15 January 1982, p. 54; Robert Alter 5 February 1982, p. 137.

Andreas-Salomé, Lou. "Der geistliche Russe." *Der neue Merkur* (Munich) November 1919, pp. 380-386.

———. "Physische Liebe" (Physical Love). *Die Zukunft* 29 October 1898, pp. 218-222.

———. "Die Russen." *Die Schaubühne* 5 (39) (23 September 1909): 305-308.

———. "Russische Dichtung und Kultur." *Cosmopolis* 20 (August 1897): 571-580; 21 (September 1897): 872-885.

———. "Russische Geschichten." *Die Zeit* 9 December 1899, pp. 152-157.

———. "Russische Philosophie und semitischer Geist." *Die Zeit* (Vienna) 172 (15 January 1898): 40-43.

———. "Zum Typus Weib," *Imago* 3 (1) (1914): 1-14.

———. *Die Erotik*. Frankfurt/M.: Rütter & Loening, 1910.

———. *The Freud Journal of Lou Andreas-Salomé*. New York: Basic Books, 1964.

———. *Lebensrückblick*, edited by Ernst Pfeiffer. Frankfurt/M.: Insel, 1968. Published as *Looking Back* in 1992 (London: Paragon House).

Anzieu, Didier. *Freud's Self-Analysis*. London: Hogarth Press, 1986.

Aron, Willy. "Notes on Sigmund Freud's Ancestry and Jewish Contacts." *Yivo Annual of Jewish Social Studies* 11 (1956/57): 286-295.

Aronson, M. "Geographical and Socioeconomic Factors in the 1881 Anti-Jewish Pogroms in Russia." *The Russian Review* 39 (1) (1980): 18-31.

Auerbach, Elias. *Moses*. Detroit: Wayne State University, 1975.

Azadowski, Konstantin, ed. *Rilke und Russland: Briefe, Erinnerungen, Gedichte*. Frankfurt/M.: Insel Verlag, 1986. Reviewed by George Cheron, *Slavic and East European Journal* 32 (4) (1988): 656-7.

Baedeker, Karl. *Austria, Including Hungary, Transylvania, Dalmatia, and Bosnia. Handbook for Travelers*. Leipzig: Karl Baedeker, 1900.

———. *Austria-Hungary with Excursions to Cetinje, Belgrade, and Bucharest. Handbook for Travelers*. Leipzig: Karl Baedeker, 1911.

————. *Russland nebst Teheran, Port Arthur, Peking.* Leipzig: Karl Baedeker, 1912.

Bahr, Hermann, O.J. Bierbaum, and Dmitri Merezhkovsky. *Dostojewski.* Munich: R. Piper, 1911.

Bakan, David. *Sigmund Freud and the Jewish Mystical Tradition.* Boston: Beacon, 1958.

Bakhtin, M. M. *Freidizm.* Moscow-Leningrad: Gosudarstvennoe Izdatel'stvo, 1927. There is disagreement on who is the author of this volume, some saying it was really written by V. N. Voloshinov. Reprinted New York: Chalidze Publications, 1983 (with an afterword by Anna Tamarchenko, "Mikhail Mikhailovich Bakhtin," pp. 225-280).

Bakunin, Mikhail. *Bakunin on Anarchy.* Edited by Sam Dolgoff. New York: Knopf, 1972.

Baron, Salo W. *The Russian Jews under Tsars and Soviets.* New York: Macmillan, 1964.

Bassin, F. V. "Freidizm v svete sovremennykh nauchnykh diskussii. Soobshchenie pervoe." *Voprosy psikhologii* (Moscow) 5 (1958): 133-145. Continued as "Soobshchenie vtoroe" (*Voprosy psikhologii* 6 [1958]: 140-153).

Belkin, A. I. "Zigmund Freid: vozrozhdenie v SSSR?" In Z. Freid,*Izbrannoe*, edited by A. I. Belkin. Moscow: Vneshtorgizdat, 1989, pp. 5-35.

————, ed. *Rossiiskii psikhoanaliticheskii vestnik* (Moscow) No. 1 (1991).

Bem (Boehm), A. L. *Dostoevskii. Psikhoanaliticheskie etiudy.* Berlin: Speer & Schmidt, 1938. Dedicated to the memory of Nikolai Evgrafovich Osipov.

Benedikt, Moritz. "Oesterreich als slawische Vormacht," *Die Zukunft* (Berlin) 27 March 1915, pp. 387-390.

Benjamin, Walter. "'Der Idiot' von Dostojewskij [1921]." In his *Gesammelte Schriften*, vol. 2 (1), pp. 237-241. Frankfurt/M.: Suhrkamp, 1977.

Berberova, Nina. *The Italics Are Mine.* New York: Harcourt, Brace & World, 1969. 2nd ed., London: Chatto and Windus, 1991; New York: Knopf, 1992,

Berdiaev, N. A. *Die Weltanschauung Dostojewskis.* Munich: C. H. Beck, 1925.

Bernays, Anna Freud. "My Brother, Sigmund Freud." *The American Mercury* 51 (203) (November 1940): 335-342.

Bernays, Hella Freud. Personal communications, 18 October 1984 and 9 November 1984. Letters from one of Freud's nieces.

Bernfeld, Siegfried. "Freud's Scientific Beginnings." *American Imago* 6 (1949): 163-196.

————. "Sigmund Freud, M.D., 1882-1885." *International Journal of Psychoanalysis* 32 (July 1951): 204-217.

————. "An Unknown Autobiographical Fragment by Freud." *American Imago* 4 (1) (August 1946): 3-19.

————, and Suzanne Cassirer Bernfeld. "Freud's Early Childhood." *Bulletin of the Menninger Clinic* 8 (July 1944): 107-115. Reprinted in Hendrik M. Ruitenbeek, ed., *Freud As We Knew Him*. Detroit: Wayne State University, 1973, pp. 188-196.

————, and Suzanne Cassirer Bernfeld. "Freud's First Year in Practice." *Bulletin of the Menninger Clinic* 16 (2) (March 1952): 37-49.

Bernfeld, Suzanne Cassirer. "Freud and Archaeology." *American Imago* 8 (2) (June 1951): 107-128.

Bettelheim, Bruno. *Freud's Vienna & Other Essays*. New York: Knopf, 1990.

Bierbaum, Otto Julius. "Dostojewskij." *Die Zukunft* 69 (1909): 186-197.

Binswanger, Otto. *Die Epilepsie*. 2nd ed. Vienna/Leipzig: Alfred Hölder, 1913.

————. *Die Hysterie*. Vienna: Alfred Hölder, 1904.

Bloom, Harold, ed. *Sigmund Freud. Modern Critical Views*. New York: Chelsea House, 1985.

Blumer, Dietrich, and Kenneth Levin, ed. "Psychiatric Complications in the Epilepsies: Current Research and Treatment." *McLean Hospital Journal* June 1977. Special issue.

Boehm, M. H. "Die Geschichtsphilosophie Dostojewskis und der gegenwärtige Krieg." *Preussische Jahrbücher* 159 (1915): 193-215.

Bonaparte, Marie. Unpublished notebook. 1925. Copies are in private circulation; the original manuscript not located. An edition is said to be in preparation by Frank Hartman.

Botkin, S. P. "Mnenie S. P. Botkina o khode bolezni I. S. Turgeneva (chitano v obschchestve russkikh vrachei, 27-go oktiabria)," *Novosti* (St. Petersburg) 29 October 1883.

Bottome, Phyllis. *Alfred Adler*. New York: G. P. Putnam's, 1939.

Brandes, Georg. "Fjodor Dostojewski." In *Menschen und Werke*, pp. 309-344. Frankfurt/M.: Rütten und Loening, 1894.

————— (Georg Morris Cohen). *Aus dem Reich des Absolutismus: Charakterbilder aus Leben, Sitten, Kunst und Literatur Russlands*. Leipzig: Siegismund & Volkening, 1896.

—————. *Ferdinand Lassalle*. New York: Bergman, 1968. First German edition, translated from the Danish, Berlin: F. Duncker, 1877. Contains the epigraph from Vergil "Flectere si nequeo Superos, Acheronta movebo"; cf. Freud's *Die Traumdeutung*.

—————. *Friedrich Nietzsche*. New York: Macmillan/London: Heinemann, 1909. Includes correspondence between Brandes and Nietzsche from 26 November 1887 to 4 January 1889, with commentaries and two retrospects by Brandes.

—————. *Jesus. A Myth*. New York: Albert & Charles Boni, 1926.

—————. *Menschen und Werke*. Frankfurt/M.: Rütten & Loening, 1894.

—————. *Moderne Geister. Literarische Bildnisse aus dem neunzehnten Jahrhundert*. Frankfurt/M.: Rütten & Loening, 1882.

Bratz, Emil. "Die affektepileptischen Anfälle der Neuropathen und Psychopathen." *Monatsschrift für Psychiatrie und Neurologie* 29 (1911): 45-76. This article was cited by T.K. Rozental' in "Stradanie i tvorchestvo Dostoevskogo. Psikhogeneticheskoe issledovanie" (*Voprosy izucheniia i vospitaniia lichnosti* 1 (1919): 88-107).

Breger, Louis. *Dostoevsky. The Author as Psychoanalyst*. New York: New York University, 1989.

Brodsky, Joseph. Personal communications. 30 October 1976; 10 May 1982; 6 April 1984.

Brodsky, Patricia Pollock, *Russia in the Works of Rainer Maria Rilke*. Detroit: Wayne State University, 1984.

Brome, Vincent. *Freud and His Early Circle*. New York: William Morrow, 1968.

Brooks, Peter. "Fictions of the Wolfman: Freud and Narrative Understanding." *Diacritics* Spring 1973: 72-81.

————. "The Wolf Man" (letter). *TLS* (*Times Literary Supplement*) 24 October 1986, p. 1191.

Brueckner, Peter. "Sigmund Freud's Privatlecture," *Psyche* 15 (1961): 881-902; 16 (1962): 721-743 and 881-895.

Brunswick, Ruth Mack. "Ein Nachtrag zu Freuds 'Geschichte einer infantilen Neurose'." *Internationale Zeitschrift für Psychoanalyse* 15 (1) (1929): 1-43.

————. "A Supplement to Freud's 'History of an Infantile Neurosis'" and "The Wolf-Man in Later Life." In S.K. Pankeev, *The Wolf-Man by the Wolf*-Man, edited by Muriel Gardner, 263-307 and 309-366. New York: Basic Books, 1971.

Bruss, Neal. "The Sons Karamazov: Dostoevsky's Characters as Freudian Transformations." *The Massachusetts Review* 26 (4) (Spring 1986): 40-67.

Burke, E. C. "Dostoevsky's Pulmonary Disease." *Minnesota Medicine* 2 (1969): 685-7.

Bülow, Frieda Freiin von. "Dostojewski in Deutschland." *Das literaturische Echo* 9 (1906/07): 203-206.

Byr, Robert (Karl Beyer). "Kleinere Erzählungen von Turgenjew." *Das Magazin für die Literatur des In-und Auslandes* (Leipzig) 101 (January-June 1882): 10-12. Contains reviews of "A Quiet Backwater," "Faust," and "First Love."

C.J.F. "Morelli, Giovanni (Ivan Lermolieff)." In *Encyclopaedia Britannica*, 10th ed. (1902), vol. 7, pp. 830-2.

Carotenuto, Aldo, ed. *Diario di una segreta simmetria. Sabina Spielrein tra Jung e Freud.* Rome: Astrolabio, 1980.

————, ed. *A Secret Symmetry. Sabina Spielrein between Jung and Freud.* Foreword by William McGuire; commentary by Bruno Bettelheim; postscript, with report on Spielrein's fate, by Magnus Ljunggren. New York: Pantheon, 1984.

Carter, Geoffrey. "Freud and *The Brothers Karamazov.*" Literature and Psychology 31 (3) (1981): 15-32.

The Century Atlas. New York: Century Company, 1897. Contains useful maps of Russia and Austria.

Charcot, J.-M. "Le foi qui guérit." *Archives de Neurologie* 20 (73) (January 1893): 72-87.

————. *Lectures on the Diseases of the Nervous System.* Philadelphia: Henry C. Lea, 1879.

————. *Neue Vorlesungen über die Krankheiten des Nervensystems imbesonders der Hysterie*. Leipzig/Vienna: Toeplitz und Deuticke, 1886. Translated by Sigmund Freud.

Chekhov, A. P. *Polnoe sobranie sochinenii i pisem*. Vols.1-20. Moscow: 1944-51. Volume 4, published in 1946, is titled "Psikhopaty."

Chernyshevskii. *Chto delat'? Iz rasskazov o novykh liudiakh*. Leningrad: Nauka, 1975.

Chickering, Roger. *We Men Who Feel Most German: A Cultural Study of the Pan-Germanic League, 1886-1914*. Boston: Allen & Unwin, 1984.

Chodoff, Paul. "The Diagnosis of Hysteria: An Overview." *American Journal of Psychiatry* 131 (10) (October 1974): 1073-1078.

Cirignotta, Fabio. "Temporal Lobe Epilepsy with Ecstatic Seizures (so-called Dostoevsky Epilepsy)" *Epilepsia* 21 (1980): 705-710.

Clark, Ronald W. *Freud. The Man and the Cause*. New York: Random House, 1980.

Cocks, Geoffrey. *Psychotherapy in the Third Reich. The Goering Institute*. New York/Oxford: Oxford University, 1985.

Cohen, Ralph, ed. "Psychology and Literature: Some Contemporary Directions." *New Literary History* 12 (1) (Autumn 1980).

Cole, Michael. "Alexander Romanovich Luria: 1902-1977." *American Psychologist* November 1977: 969-971.

Conquest, Robert. "Max Eitingon: Another View." *New York Times Book Review* 3 July 1988. Reply to Schwartz et al., "'The Mystery of Max Eitingon': An Exchange."

————. *The Great Terror. Stalin's Purge of the Thirties*. Rev. ed. New York: Macmillan, 1973. 3rd ed. Oxford: Oxford University Press, 1990.

Crews, Frederick. *Skeptical Engagements*. New York: Oxford University, 1986.

Crowley, Aleister. *The Book of Thoth (Egyptian Tarot)*. York Beach, Maine: Samuel Weiser, 1984.

Dahl, Per, and John Mott. "Georg Brandes—a bibliographical survey." *The Activist Critic* (Copenhagen), edited by Hans Hertel and Sv. Möller Kristensen: 1980.

Dalton, Elizabeth. *Unconscious Structures in "The Idiot" : A Study in Literature and Psychoanalysis.*, Princeton, N.J.: Princeton University Press, 1979.

Darkshevich, L. O. "Moe ponimanie isterii." *Russkii vrach* 41 (1915): 961-967; 42: 991-999; 43: 1013-1027.

————. *On the Question of Hysteria in the History of Nations: The Apostle Paul* (in Russian: Beglye kharakteristiki deiatelei iz vremen Sviashchennogo Pisaniia. K voprosu ob isterii v istorii narodov. I: Apostol Pavel). Berlin: Otto Kirchner & Co., 1923.

David, J. J. "Dostojewskis 'Dämonen'." *Die Nation* (Berlin) 24 November 1906, pp. 121-124. See Ernst Heilborn, "Davids künstlerische Lebensbeichte" (J. J. David obituary).

————. Review of *Die Traumdeutung* by S. Freud. *Die Nation* 17 (1900): 238-239.

Decker, Hannah S. *Freud in Germany. Revolution and Reaction in Science,1883-1907.* New York: International Universities, 1977. Special supplement to *Psychological Issues* 11 (1), monograph 41.

Deutscher, Isaac. *The Prophet Armed.* New York: Oxford University, 1954.

Diller, Jerry Victor. *Freud's Jewish Identity.* Rutherford, N.J.: Fairleigh Dickinson University Press, 1991.

Dinnage, Rosemary. "Declaration of Dependence." *TLS* (*Times Literary Supplement*) 10 December 1982, pp. 1351-1352. Review of *Diario di una segreta simmetria. Sabina Spielrein tra Jung e Freud*, edited by Aldo Carotenuto, and *Gespräche mit dem Wolfsmann*, by Karin Obholzer.

Dodd, W. J. *Kafka and Dostoyevsky.* New York: St. Martin's Press, 1992.

Dolinin, A. S., ed. *F. M. Dostoevskii v vospominaniiakh sovremennikov.* 2 vols. Moscow: Khudozhestvennaia Literatura, 1964.

Dostoevskii, F. M. *Polnoe sobranie sochinenii v tridtsati tomakh.* 30 vols. in 33. Edited by G. M. Fridlender et al. Leningrad: Nauka, 1972-1990.

Dostoevsky, A. (Anna Grigorievna Dostoevskaia). *The Diary of Dostoevsky's Wife.* Edited by R. Fülöp-Miller and F. Eckstein. New York: Macmillan, 1928.

————. *Die Lebenserinnerungen der Gattin Dostojewskis.* Edited by Fülöp-Miller and Eckstein. Munich: R. Piper & Co., 1925.

————. *Das Tagesbuch der Anna Grigorjewna Dostojewski.* Munich: R. Piper, 1925.

Dostojewski, Aimée (Liubov' Fedorovna Dostoevskaia). *Dostojewski, geschildert von seiner Tochter.* Munich: Reinhardt, 1920.

————. *Fyodor Dostoevsky. A Study.* London: William Heinemann, 1921.

Dostojewski, F. M. *Raskolnikoffs Tagebuch, mit unbekannten Entwurfen, Fragmenten und Briefen zu "Raskolnikoff" und "Idiot."* Edited by Fülöp-Miller and Eckstein. Munich: R. Piper & Co., 1925.

————. *Sämtliche Werke* [Collected Works]. Vols. 1-22. Edited by D. Merezhkovsky and Moeller van der Bruck, translated by E. K. Rahsin. Munich: R. Piper & Co., 1906-1919. Part of Freud's library as a gift from Max Eitingon in February 1910; later volumes added as they appeared. Vols. 1-2 *Crime and Punishment* (1908), 3-4 *The Idiot* (1909), 5-6 *The Possessed* (The Devils) (1906), 7-8 *A Raw Youth* (The Adolescent) (1915), 9-10 *The Brothers Karamazov* (1908), 11 *Autobiographical Works* (1919), 12 *Writings on Literature* (1913), 13 *Political Works* (1907), 14 *Poor Folk & The Double* (1910), 15 "White Nights" and other novellas (1911), 16 "The Manor Stepánchikovo" (1909), 17 "Uncle's Dream" and other humoresques (1909), 18 *Notes from the House of the Dead* (1908) 19 *The Insulted and Injured* (1909), 20 *From the Dark of the Metropolis* ("Notes from Underground," and eight other tales (1907), 21 *The Gambler & The Eternal Husband* (1910), and 22 "The Little Hero" (8 tales) (1912). Vols. 11 and 12 also contain the authorized biography *Biografiia, pis' ma i zametki iz zapisnoi knizhki F. M. Dostoevskogo* by O. F. Miller and N. N. Strakhov that was first published in Russian in 1883.

————. *Schuld und Sühne* [Guilt and Atonement, i.e., Crime and Punishment]. Leipzig: Reclam, 1888. Later in Freud's era was known by the title *Raskolnikoff.*

————. *Der unbekannte Dostojewski* [The Unknown Dostoevsky]. Edited by Fülöp-Miller and Eckstein. Munich: R. Piper & Co., 1926.

———. *Der Urgestalt der Brüder Karamasoff. Dostojewskis Quellen, Entwürfe und Fragmente, erläutert von V. Komarowitsch.* Edited by Fülöp-Miller and Eckstein, Munich: R. Piper, 1928. Includes a long essay by V. L. Komarovich and Freud's introductory article *"Dostojewski und die Vatertötung,"* pp. xi-xxxvi.

———. "Der Bauer Marei." In *Von der Kinderseele. Beiträge zur Kinderpsychologie und Biographie,* edited by Gertrud Bäumer and Lili Droescher, 88-90. Leipzig: R. Voigtländer, 1908. The authors present the core anecdote stripped of context.

———. (Fedor Mikhailovich Dostoevskii). *Aufzeichnungen aus einem Totenhaus.* Berlin: Th. Knaur, 1861-62; Dresden: n.p., 1886; Munich: R. Piper & Co., 1908.

———. *Briefe.* Translated by Eliasberg. Munich: Piper & Co., 1914; 2nd ed. 1920. Part of Freud's library as a gift from Max Eitingon in 1926.

———. *Die Briefe Dostojewskis an seine Gattin.* Munich: R. Piper, 1922.

———. *Die Brüder Karamasoff.* 2 vols. Translated by E. K. Rahsin (pseud. of Less Kaerrick, the Russian-born sister-in-law of the coeditor, A. Moeller van den Bruck). Preface by D. Merezhkovsky. Munich: R. Piper & Co., 1908. Part of Freud's library.

———. *Die Brüder Karamazow.* Leipzig: n.p., 1884.

———. *Der Doppelgänger.* Munich: R. Piper & Co., 1913. Includes sixty sketches by Alfred Kubin.

———. *Dostojewski am Roulette.* Edited by Fülöp-Miller and Eckstein. Munich: R. Piper & Co., 1925. Part of Freud's library. Cited in "Dostojewski und die Vatertötung" (Dostoevsky and Parricide).

Draper, Theodore. "The Mystery of Max Eitingon." *New York Review* 14 April 1988, 32f. Reprinted in Theodore Draper, *A Present of Things Past* (New York: Hill & Wang, 1990). This article led to a response titled "'The Mystery of Max Eitingon': An Exchange," by Stephen Schwartz and Vitaly Rapoport. The exchange is also to be found in *Chekisty. A History of the KGB,* by John J. Dziak.

———. Personal communication. 9 July 1988.

Drouilly, Jean. "Freud et Dostoïevski." *Evolution psychiatrique* (Toulouse) 4 (1977): 127-140.

Duckmeyer, F. "Die Einführung Dostojewskis in Deutschland." *Die Funken* 3 (22) (1906): 685-688.

Dudkin, V. V., and K. M. Azadovskii. "Dostoevskii v Germanii (1846-1921)." In *F. M. Dostoevskii. Novye materialy i issledovaniia*, edited by I. S. Zil'bershtein and L. M. Rozenblium, 659-740. Moscow: Nauka, 1973.

Dziak, John J. *Chekisty. A History of the KGB*. Lexington, Mass.: Lexington Books (D. C. Heath), 1988. This volume was reviewed by Stephen Schwartz ("Intellectuals and Assassins—Annals of Stalin's 'Killerati'"). See also Robert Conquest, *The Great Terror. Stalin's Purge of the Thirties*; Robert Conquest, "Max Eitingon: Another View"; Theodore Draper, "The Mystery of Max Eitingon"; and Martin Grotjahn, "A Letter by Freud with a Recollection of His Adolescence."

Ebstein, Erich. "Dostojewskijs Krankheit und seine Aertzte." *Die medizinische Welt* 43 (27 October 1928): 1623-5. Ebstein lived in Leipzig at the time.

Eisner, Pavel. "Masaryk a Dostojevski." *Nase doba* 1938, pp. 333-336.

Eissler, K. R. "A Letter to Professor Tandler (1931)." *International Review of Psychoanalysis* 10 (1983): 9.

———. "Bericht über die sich in den Vereinigten Staaten befindenden Bücher aus S. Freuds Bibliothek." *Jahrbuch des Psychoanalyse* 11 (1979): 10-50.

———. Personal communications. 11 September 1984 and 24 February 1985.

Eissler, Ruth S., and K.R. Eissler. "A Letter by Freud to Professor Tandler (1931)." *International Review of Psychoanalysis* 10 (1) (1983): 1-12.

Eitingon, Max. *Über die Wirkung des Anfalls auf die Assoziationen der Epileptischen*. Leipzig: Alexander Edelmann, 1909. Dissertation. The degree was granted in Zurich. Author's residence given as Buczacz.

Eliasberg, Aleksandr. *Bildergalerie zur russische Literatur*. Preface by Thomas Mann. Munich: Orchis, 1922. This is a bilingual edition with excellent illustrations.

Ellenberger, Henri. *The Discovery of the Unconscious.* New York: Basic Books, 1970.

Ermakov, I. D. "Dvoistvennost." Chapter 7 of his unpublished monograph "F. M. Dostoevskii. / On i ego proizvedeniia." About 1920. 13 pages.

Etkind, Alexandre M. "Russkaia kul'tura moderna mezhdu Edipom i Dionisom." Unpublished manuscript. 1991.

Farrell, B. A.*The Standing of Psychoanalysis.* Oxford: Oxford University Press, 1981.

Fedorov, G. A. "'Pomeshchik. Ottsa ubili.', ili istoriia odnoi sud'by," *Novyi mir* 10 (1988): 219-238.

Feuer, Lewis S. "Freud's Ideas in the Soviet Setting: A Meeting with Alexander Luriia (1963)." *Slavic Review* Spring 1987: 106-112.

Fischman, Susan C. "Sigmund Freud and the Case of the Underground Man." *Dostoevsky Studies* 8 (1987): 209-218.

Fish, Stanley. "Withholding the missing portion: Power, meaning, and persuasion in Freud's 'The Wolf-man." *Times Literary Supplement* 29 August 1986, pp. 935-8.

———. Personal communication. 20 January 1987.

Forel, Auguste. *Die sexuelle* Frage. N.p. 1905. Cited in *Die Erotik,* by Andreas-Salomé.

Fraenkel, Josef, ed. *The Jews of Austria. Essays on Their Life, History and Destruction.* London: Vallentine & Mitchell, 1967.

Frank, Joseph. "Freud's Case-History of Dostoevsky." In *Dostoevsky. The Seeds of Revolt 1821-1849*, 379-392. Princeton, N.J.: Princeton University Press, 1976. First published in *Times Literary Supplement* 18 July 1978.

———. *Dostoevsky. The Years of Ordeal 1850-1859.* Princeton, N.J.: Princeton University Press, 1983.

Frankel, Jonathan. *Prophecy and Politics. Socialism, Nationalism, and the Russian Jews, 1862-1917.* Cambridge: Cambridge University Press, 1981.

Freeman, Lucy, and Herbert S. Strean. *Freud and Women.* New York: Frederick Ungar, 1981.

Freud, Martin. "Who Was Freud?" In *The Jews of Austria. Essays on Their Life, History and Destruction*, edited by Josef Fraenkel, 197-211.

————. *Sigmund Freud: Man and Father*. London: Angus and Robertson, 1958.

Freud, Sigmund. Letter to W. Fliess on "primal addiction" and alcohol, morphine, tobacco, etc. 22 December 1897. See *The Complete Letters of Sigmund Freud to Wilhelm Fliess, 1887-1904*, by Sigmund Freud; *Briefe an Wilhelm Fliess, 1887-1904*, by Sigmund Freud; and *Standard Edition of the Complete Psychological Works of Sigmund Freud*, by Sigmund Freud, vol. 1, pp. 272-73.

————. Letter to Theodor Reik, 14 April 1929. In *Standard Edition of the Complete Psychological Works of Sigmund Freud*, by Sigmund Freud, vol. 21, 195-96. See also Theodor Reik, *Freud als Kulturkritiker*.

————. Letter to Stefan Zweig of 19 October 1920. In *The Letters of Sigmund Freud*, by Sigmund Freud, pp. 191-193.

————. "An Autobiographical Portrait" (*Selbstdarstellung*). In *Standard Edition of the Complete Psychological Works of Sigmund Freud*, by Sigmund Freud, vol. 20, pp. 3-74. This piece was written in 1925.

————. "Dostoevsky and Parricide," *The Realist* 1 (4) (July 1929): 18-33.

————. "Dostoevsky and Parricide." In *Standard Edition of the Complete Psychological Works of Sigmund Freud*, by Sigmund Freud, vol. 21, 175-196.

————. "Dostojewski und die Vatertötung" (Dostoevsky and Parricide). See *Der Urgestalt der Brüder Karamasoff. Dostojewskis Quellen, Entwürfe und Fragmente, erläutert von V. Komarowitsch*, by F.M. Dostojewski, pp. xi-xxxvi. Written in 1928.

————. "Dostojewski und die Vatertötung." In *Gesammelte Werke*, by Sigmund Freud, vol. 14 (1963), 397-418.

————. "The Expert Opinion in the Halsmann Case." In *Standard Edition of the Complete Psychological Works of Sigmund Freud*, by Sigmund Freud, vol. 21, 251-253. Also published in *Gesammelte Werke*, by Sigmund Freud, vol. 14 (1961), 541-2, 582n.

————. "Frau Emmy von N., Age 40, from Livonia." In "Studies on Hysteria," *Standard Edition of the Complete Psychological*

Works of Sigmund Freud, by Sigmund Freud, vol. 2, 48-105. This study describes the case of a patient treated ca. 1888-90, possibly at her Baltic estate in the Russian Empire.

————. "The Future of an Illusion." In *Standard Edition of the Complete Psychological Works of Sigmund Freud*, by Sigmund Freud, vol. 21 (1961), pp. 1-56. Written in 1927.

————. "Hysteria." In *Standard Edition of the Complete Psychological Works of Sigmund Freud*, by Sigmund Freud, vol. 1, 39-59.

————. "Hystero-Epilepsy." In *Standard Edition of the Complete Psychological Works of Sigmund Freud*, by Sigmund Freud, vol. 1, 58-59.

————. "Jugendbriefe Sigmund Freuds" (to Emil Fluss, 1872-74). Edited by E. L. Freud. *Psyche* 24 (1970): 766-784.

————. "The Moses of Michelangelo." *Imago* 3 (1914): 15-36. First published anonymously. Authorship acknowledged in 1924.

————. "Psycho-Analysis and Telepathy." In *Standard Edition of the Complete Psychological Works of Sigmund Freud*, by Sigmund Freud, vol. 18, 177-192. The manuscript was written 2 August 1921 but not published until 1941.

————. "Some General Remarks on Hysterical Attacks." In *Standard Edition of the Complete Psychological Works of Sigmund Freud*, by Sigmund Freud, vol. 9, 227-234.

————. *Beyond the Pleasure Principle.* London: International Psychoanalytic Press, 1922.

————. *Briefe an Wilhelm Fliess, 1887-1904.* Edited by Jeffrey Moussaieff Masson. Frankfurt/M.: S. Fischer, 1986.

————. *Briefe, 1873-1939.* Edited by Ernst L. Freud and Lucie Freud. 2nd ed. 1968. 3rd ed. 1980. Frankfurt/M.: S. Fischer.

————. *The Complete Letters of Sigmund Freud to Wilhelm Fliess, 1887-1904.* Edited by Jeffrey M. Masson. Cambridge: Harvard University Press, 1985. See also *The Origins of Psycho-Analysis*, by Sigmund Freud, with indispensable complementary notes to the corrrespondence with Fliess.

————. *The Concordance to the Standard Edition of the Complete Psychological Works of Sigmund Freud.* 6 vols. Edited by Samuel A. Guttman. New York: International Universities, 1984.

————. *Cocaine Papers*. Edited by Robert Byck. New York: Meridian, 1974.

————. *Finding Guide*. Sigmund Freud Archives, Library of Congress, Manuscript Division, Washington, D.C.

————. *Gesammelte Werke*. 18 vols. Edited by Anna Freud. Hamburg: S. Fischer, 1952-1961.

————. *The History of the Psychoanalytic Movement*. New York: The Nervous and Mental Disease Publishing Company, 1917. Also published in Sigmund Freud, *Standard Edition of the Complete Psychological Works of Sigmund Freud*, vol. 14, pp. 1-66 under the title *On the History of the Psychoanalytic Movement*.

————. *Jokes and Their Relation to the Unconscious*. New York: W. W. Norton, 1960.

————. *Jugendbriefe an Eduard Silberstein 1871-1881*. Edited by Walter Boelich. Frankfurt/M.: S. Fischer, 1989.

————. *The Letters of Sigmund Freud*. Edited by Ernst L. Freud. Introduction by Steven Marcus. New York: Basic Books, 1975.

————. *Moses and Monotheism*. New York: Vintage Books, 1955. Also published in vol. 23 of *Standard Edition of the Complete Psychological Works of Sigmund Freud*, by Sigmund Freud.

————. *The Origins of Psycho-Analysis: Letters to Wilhelm Fliess, Drafts and Notes, 1887-1902*. Edited by Marie Bonaparts et al. New York: Basic Books, 1954. The complete edition is to be found in *The Complete Letters of Sigmund Freud to Wilhelm Fliess, 1887-1904*, by Sigmund Freud.

————. *Standard Edition of the Complete Psychological Works of Sigmund Freud*. 24 vols. Edited by James Strachey. London: Hogarth Press and Institute of Psycho-Analysis, 1953-1974.

————. *Die Zukunft einer Illusion*. In *Gesammelte Werke*, by Sigmund Freud, vol. 14, 323-380.

————, and Karl Abraham. *A Psycho-Analytic Dialogue* (correspondence between Freud and Abraham 1907-1927). Edited by Hilda S. Abraham and Ernst L. Freud. New York: Basic Books, 1965.

————, and Lou Andreas-Salomé. *Letters*. Edited by W. and E. Robson-Scott. New York: Harcourt, Brace Jovanovich, 1972.

————, and C. G. Jung. *Briefwechsel*. Edited by William McGuire. Frankfurt/M.: S. Fischer, 1974.

————, and C. G. Jung. *The Freud/Jung Letters*. Edited by William McGuire. Princeton, N.J.: Princeton University Press, 1974.

————, and Oskar Pfister. *Psychoanalysis and Faith. The Letters of Sigmund Freud and Oskar Pfister*. Edited by Heinrich Meng and Ernst L. Freud. London and New York: Basic Books, 1963.

————, and Arnold Zweig. *The Letters of Sigmund Freud and Arnold Zweig* (1927-1939). Edited by Ernst L. Freud. New York: Harcourt, Brace & World, 1970.

Fridlender, G. M. "Estetika Dostoevskogo." *Voprosy filosofii* 11 (1971): 91-102.

————. *Dostoevskii i mirovaia literatura*. Moscow: Khudozhestvennaia Literatura, 1979.

Friedberg, M. "The Jewish search in Russian literature." *Prooftexts* 4 (1) (1984): 93-106.

Fritsch, Theodor. *Handbuch der Judenfrage*. Hamburg: Hanseatische Druck- und Verlags-Anstalt, 1907.

Fülöp-Miller, René. "Dostojewskis 'Heilige Krankheit'." *Neue Schweizer Rundschau* 17(2) (1924): 1184-1191. This journal's title was *Wissen und Leben* until 1919, which explains why it was cited as such by Freud in "Dostoevsky and Parricide."

————. *Geist und Gesicht der Bolschewismus. Darstellung und Kritik des kulturellen Lebens in Sowjet. Russland*. Zurich: Amalthea, 1926. This work includes 500 photographic plates from an exhibit organized in Vienna in 1926 by Fülöp-Miller, Freud's principle editor at R. Piper & Co. The Epilog on pages 451-53 includes passages from Eikhenvald and Lunacharsky on Dostoevsky as the prophet of revolution. It also has passages on Shigalev's program for social reform from Dostoevsky's *The Possessed*, and on the "Grand Inquisitor" from *The Brothers Karamazov* ("millions of happy children for only a hundred thousand martyrs").

Gay, Peter. *Freud. A Life for Our Time*. New York: W. W. Norton, 1988.

————. Personal communication. 22 June 1988.

Gedo, John E., and Ernest Wolf. "Die Ichthyosaurusbriefe." *Psyche* 24 (1970): 785-797.

Geha, R. "Dostoevsky and 'The Gambler'." *Psychoanalytical Review* 57 (1970): 95-123 and 289-302.

Gelfand, Toby. "'Mon Cher Docteur Freud': Charcot's Unpublished Correspondence to Freud, 1888-1893, Annotation, translation, and commentary." *Bulletin of the History of Medicine* 62 (1988): 563-588.

————. "Charcot's Response to Freud's Rebellion." *Journal of the History of Ideas* 1 (2) (April-June 1989): 293-307.

————. "Fathers and Sons in Charcot's Paris." Unpublished manuscript. 56 pages. 1990.

Gerber, Jane. *The Jews of Spain. A History of the Sephardic Experience.* New York: The Free Press, 1992.

Gershenzon, M. O."Tvorcheskoe samosoznanie." In *Vekhi,* 70-96. 2nd ed. Moscow: V. M. Sablin, 1909.

Gershon, David Hundert, and Gershon C. Bacon. *The Jews in Poland and Russia. Bibliographical Essays.* Bloomington: Indiana University Press, 1984.

Geschwind, Norman. "Dostoievsky's Epilepsy." In *Psychiatric Aspects of Epilepsy,* edited by Dietrich Blumer, 325-333. Washington, D. C.: American Psychiatric Publications, 1984.

————. Personal communication. 1 November 1982.

Gesemann, Wolfgang. "Nietzsches Verhältnis zu Dostojewski auf europäischen Hintergrund der 80er Jahre." *Die Welt der Slaven* 6 (2) (1961): 129-156.

Gicklhorn, Renée. *Sigmund Freud und der Onkeltraum—Dichtung und Wahrheit.* Vienna: Ferdinand Berger & Söhne, 1976.

Gifford, Sanford. Personal communication. 7 December 1984.

Goldstein, David I. Personal communication. 24 September 1981.

————. *Dostoevsky and the Jews.* Austin: University of Texas, 1981.

————. *Dostoievski et les* Juifs. Paris: Gallimard, 1976.

Goldstein, Jan. "The Wandering Jew and the Problem of Psychiatric Anti-Semitism in Fin-de-siècle France." *Journal of Contemporary History* 20 (4) (1985): 521-552.

Goleman, Daniel. "Lost Paper Shows Freud's Effort to Link Analysis and Evolution." *New York Times* 10 February 1987, pp. 19 and 22.

Gombrich, E. H. Review of Carlo Pedtrotti and Sigmund Freud on Leonardo. *New York Review of Books* 11 February 1965: 2-3

Grabar', Igor'. *Repin.* 2 vols. Moscow: Akademiia Nauk, 1963.

Gray, Eden. *A Complete Guide to the Tarot.* New York: Bantam, 1972.

Greenberg, Louis. *The Jews in Russia.* New Haven: Yale University, 1944.

Grigg, Kenneth A. "All Roads Lead to Rome: The Role of the Nursemaid in Freud's Dreams." *Journal of the American Psychoanalytic Association* 21 (1973): 108-126.

Grinstein, Alexander, et al., eds. *The Index of Psychoanalytic Writing.* 9 vols. New York: International Universities, 1952-59.

———, et al., eds. *Sigmund Freud's Dreams.* 2nd ed. New York: International Universities, 1980.

Grollman, Earl A. *Judaism in Sigmund Freud's World.* New York: Appleton-Century, 1965.

Grossman, L. P. *Die Beichte eines Juden in Briefen an Dostojewski.* Munich: R. Piper, 1927. Part of Freud's library.

———. *Confession of a Jew.* New York: Arno, 1975.

———. *Ispoved' odnogo evreia.* Moscow: L. Frenkel', 1924. Reviewed by M. Klevenskii in *Pechat' i revoliutsiia* 6 (1924): 227-8.

———. *Zhizn' i trudy F. M. Dostoevskogo. Biografiia v datakh i dokumentakh.* Moscow/Leningrad: Academia, 1935.

Grotjahn, Martin. "A Letter by Freud with a Recollection of His Adolescence." *Journal of the American Psychoanalytic Association* 4 (1956): 644-652.

———. "Was Max Eitingon One of Stalin's Killerati?" *Bulletin of the Southern California Psychoanalytic Institute* 81 (Fall 1988): 16.

———. *Beyond Laughter. Humor and the Subconscious.* New York: McGraw-Hill, 1957.

Grubman, G. B. "Turgenev i 'russkii Parizh' v romane Genri Dzhemsa 'Amerikanets'." In *I. S. Turgenev. Voprosy biografii i tvorchestva*, edited by M. P. Alekseev, 108-114. Leningrad: Nauka, 1982.

Guillain, Georges. *J.-M. Charcot 1825-1893: His Life—His Work.* New York: Paul B. Hoeber (Harper & Brothers), 1959.

Hanswedell, Ernst. "Die Kenntnis von Dostojewski und seinem Werke im deutschen Naturalismus und der Einfluss seines 'Raskolnikoff' auf die Epoche von 1880-95." Dissertation. Ludwig-Maximilians-Universität 20 May 1924.

Hardin, Harry T. "On the Vicissitudes of Freud's Early Mothering." *Psychoanalytic Quarterly* 57 (1988): 209-223.

Harms, E. "A Fragment of Freud's Library." *Psychoanalytic Quarterly* 40 (1971): 491-5.

Harris, H. J. "Dostoevsky: the writer as anti-semite." *Midstream*, 28 (2) (February 1982): 50-53.

Hárnik, J. "Dostojewski, 'Njetotschka Neswanowa', Bruchstück eines Romanes." *Imago* 1 (1913): 530-534. This is a review of Dostoevsky's works in volume 22 of the Munich edition.

Heer, Friedrich. "Freud, the Viennese Jew." In *Freud. The man, his world, his influence*, edited by Jonathan Miller, 1-20.

Heilborn, Ernst. "Davids künstlerische Lebensbeichte" (J. J. David obituary). *Die Nation* 24 November 1906, pp. 120-121. See J.J. David, "Dostojewskis 'Dämonen'."

Heim, Michael. Personal communication. 20 May 1990.

Heller, Judith Bernays. "Freud's Mother and Father. A Memoir." *Commentary* 21 (1 April 1956): 418-421.

Hemmings, F. W. J. *The Russian Novel in France 1884-1914*. London: Oxford University, 1950.

Herlihy, Patricia. *Odessa: A History, 1794-1914*. Cambridge: Harvard Ukrainian Research Institute and Harvard University Press, 1986.

Hess, Edward. "Dostojewski über seine epileptischen Anfälle." *Allgemeine Zeitschrift für Psychiatrie und psychisch-gerichtliche Medicin* (Berlin). 55 (1898): 117-119. The editorial board included Krafft-Ebing of Vienna.

Hesse, Hermann. "The Brothers Karamazov—The Downfall of Europe." *The Dial* 72 (June 1922): 607-618.

———. "Die Brüder Karamasoff oder der Untergang Europas." *Der Zwiebelfisch* (Munich) 7 (1916): 376-388. Reprinted in *Die neue Rundschau* (Frankfurt) 31 (1920): 376-388; in *Blick ins Chaos*, by Hermann Hesse, 1-20 (Bern: Seldwyla, 1922).

Hoche, Alfred Erich. *Die Differentialdiagnose zwischen Epilepsie und Hysterie*. Berlin: August Hirschwald, 1902.

Hoefert, Sigfrid. "Stefan Zweigs Verbundenheit mit Russland und der russischen Literatur." *Modern Austrian Literature* 14 (3/4) (1981): 251-270.

Hoffmann, Camill. "Immoralisten als Romanhelden." *Das literarische Echo* 1 January 1906, 171-72. She resided in Vienna at the time.

Hoffmann, Nina (Matscheko). *Th. M. Dostojewsky. Eine biographische Studie*. Berlin: E. Hoffmann, 1899.

Ingold, Felix P. "Die judische Frage im Schaffen F. M. Dostojewskijs." In *Kritik und Gegenkritik in Christentum und Judentum*, edited by S. Lauer, 119-164. Frankfurt/M: Peter Lang, 1981. Third title in series called "Judaica et Christiana."

Ingold, Felix P. *Dostojewski und das Judentum*. Frankfurt/M.: Insel, 1981.

Ioffe, A. A. "Po povodu 'bezsoznatel'nogo' v zhizni." *Psikhoterapiia* (Moscow) 4 (1913): 234-238.

Ivanov-Natov, Anatolii. *Ikonografiia F. M. Dostoevskogo*. Bayville, N.J.: G. Homjakow/Tovarishchestvo Zarubezhnykh Pisatelei, 1981.

Ivask, Iu. "Savly, ne stavshie Pavlami." *Vestnik russkogo khristianskogo dvizheniia* 133 (1961): 95-104.

Iwanow, W. *Dostojewski und die Romantragödie*. Leipzig-Vienna: n.p., 1922.

Jaffe, Ruth. "Moshe Woolf. Pioneering in Russia and Israel." In Alexander et al., *Psychoanalytic Pioneers*, 200-209. Woolf is Wulff in German and Vulf in Russian.

Janet, Pierre. *The Major Symptoms of Hysteria*. New York: Macmillan, 1920.

Janik, Allan, and Stephen Toulmin. *Wittgenstein's Vienna*. New York: Simon & Schuster, 1973.

Jászi, Oscar. *The Dissolution of the Habsburg Monarchy*. Chicago: University of Chicago, 1929.

Johnston, Thomas. *Freud and Political Thought*. New York: Citadel, 1965.

Jones, Ernest. "Freud's Early Travels." In *Freud As We Knew Him*, edited by Hendrik M. Ruitenbeek, 275-282. Detroit: Wayne State University, 1973.

————. *The Life and Work of Sigmund Freud*. 3 vols. New York: Basic Books, 1953-57.

Joravsky, David. "A Great Soviet Psychologist." *New York Review* 16 May 1974, pp. 22-25. The article is about A. R. Luria.

————. "The Stalinist Mentality and the Higher Learning." *Slavic Review* 42 (4) (Winter 1983): 575-600.

————. *Russian Psychology. A Critical Study*. Oxford: Basil Blackwell, 1989.

————. *Soviet Marxism and Natural Science, 1917-1932*. New York: Columbia University, 1961.

Jung, C. G. "The Phenomenology of the Spirit in Fairy Tales." In *Psyche and Symbol*, edited by Violet S. Laszlo, 61-112. Garden City, New York: Doubleday Anchor, 1945. Presented as a lecture in 1945. In the Postcript (p. 99) are the words, "Only after the completion of my manuscript was my attention drawn by a friend to a Russian variant of our story."

————. *Memories, Dreams, Reflections*. New York: Random House, 1963.

————. *The Psychology of the Transference*. Princeton, Princeton University Press, 1966.

Kampmann, Theoderich. *Dostojewski in Deutschland*. Wilhelms-Universität: Münster in Westfalen, 1930. This dissertation was defended 6 June 1930 and has the most extensive bibliography on the subject.

Kann, Robert A. A *Multinational Empire. Nationalism and National Reforms in the Habsburg Monarchy, 1848-1918*. 2 vols., New York: Columbia University, 1950.

Kanzer, Mark. Personal communications. 7 September 1985; 5 October 1985.

————. Review of *The Wolf-Man by the Wolf-Man*, by S.K. Pankeev. *International Journal of Psycho-Analysis* 53 (1972): 419-422.

————, and Jules Glenn, eds. *Freud and His Patients*. New York: Jason Aronson, 1980. Includes five essays on the Wolf-Man.

Kashina-Evreinova, A. (Anna Aleksandrovna). *Podpol' e geniia. (Seksual'nye istochniki tvorchestva Dostoevskogo)*. Petrograd: Tret'ia Strazha, 1923. Reprint: St. Petersburg, 1991. Reviewed in *Russkaia mysl'* 7 (1912); S.V. Belov, *Knizhnoe obozrenie* 9 (12 February 1992): 6. Freud is applied, with moderation.

Kaus, Otto. "Flaubert und Dostojewski." *Die Weissen Blätter* 1 (7) (March 1914): 646-671.

————. "Der Irrtum Dostojewskis." *Frankfurter Zeitung* 4 January 1916, p. 1.

————. *Dostojewski und sein Schicksal*, Berlin: E. Laub, 1923. Kaus resided in Vienna at the time.

———. *Dostojewski. Zur Kritik der Persönlichkeit.* Munich: R. Piper, 1916.

———. *Die Träume in Dostojewskys "Raskolnikoff."* Munich: J. F. Bergmann, 1926. Fourth in a series called "Individuum und Gemeinschaft: Schriften der Internationalen Gesellschaft für Individiualpsychologie," edited by Alfred Adler et al.

Kenez, Peter. *The Civil War in South Russia, 1918.* Berkeley: University of California, 1971.

———. *The Civil War in South Russia, 1919-20.* Berkeley: University of California, 1977.

Kerr, John. Personal communication. 7 August 1990.

Khetso, G. (Kjetsaa). "Avtor stat'i—F. M. Dostoevskii?" *Dostoevskii. Materialy i issledovaniia* (Leningrad) 6 (1985): 207-224.

Kjetsaa, Geir. *Prinadlezhnost' Dostoevskomu: K voprosu ob atributsii F. M. Dostoevskomu anonimnykh statei v zhurnalakh "Vremia" i " Epokha."* Oslo: Solum Forlag A.S., 1985. Fourth in a series called "Slavica Norvegica." Reviewed by Martin P. Rice in *Dostoevsky Studies* 8 (1987): 240-41.

Klein, Dennis B. *Jewish Origins of the Psychoanalytic Movement.* New York: Praeger, 1981.

Klein, Richard, ed. "The Tropology of Freud." *Diacritics* Spring 1973. This special issue included articles by Derrida and others.

Kochan, Lionel. *The Jews in Russia since 1917.* 3rd ed. London: Oxford University Press in collaboration with the Institute for Jewish Affairs, 1978.

Kohn, Hans. *Pan-Slavism. Its History and Ideology.* New York: Random House, 1953.

Kolb, Laurence, ed. *Noyes' Modern Clinical Psychiatry.* 7th ed. Philadelphia: W. B. Saunders, 1968.

Kondratiev, Vadim, Sidney Hook, Peter Gay, Simon Karlinsky, and Vitaly Rapoport. "Stalin's Killerati" (letters). *New York Times Book Review* 6 March 1988.

Kopal, Pawel (Dr. Ladislav Josef Stěhule). *Das Slawentum und der deutsche Geist. Problem einer Weltkultur auf Grundlage des religiösen Idealismus.* Jena: Eugen Diederichs, 1914. Dostoevsky as spokesman of Eastern Urtiefe, Goethe's counterpart.

Kostikov, Viacheslav. *Ne budem proklinat' izgnan'e... Puti i sud'by russkoi emigratsii.* Moscow: Mezhdunarodnye Otnosheniia, 1990.

Kozulin, Alex. *Psychology in Utopia. Toward a Social History of Soviet Psychology.* Cambridge: MIT Press, 1984.

Krauss, F. S. "Der Doppelgängerglaube im alten Aegypten und bei den Suedslawen." *Imago* 1920: 387-392.

Kravchenko, Maria. *Dostoevsky and the Psychologists.* Amsterdam: Adolf M. Hakkert, 1978.

Kravchinskii, S. M. See Stepniak.

Krieger, Hans. "Der verlorene Sohn. Briefwechsel Sigmund Freuds mit Carl Gustav Jung." *Die Zeit* 30 (26 June 1974): 13.

Krohn, Alan. *Hysteria: The Elusive Neurosis.* New York: International Universities Press, 1978. Also published in *Psychological Issues* 12 (1/2) (monograph 45/46).

Krüll, Marianna. *Freud and His Father.* New York: W. W. Norton, 1986.

————. *Freud und sein Vater.* Munich: C. H. Beck, 1979.

Küng, Hans. *Freud and the Problem of God.* New Haven: Yale, 1979.

Laqueur, Walter. *Russia and Germany. A Century of Conflict.* Boston: Little, Brown, 1965.

Leppmann, Wolfgang. Personal communication. 28 August 1984.

————. *Rilke.* New York: Fromm International, 1984.

Letkova, Ek. P. (Sultanova). "O F. M. Dostoevskom." *Zven'ia* (Moscow-Leningrad) 1 (1932): 459-477.

Lewis, Nolan D. C., and Carney Landis. "Freud's Library." *Psychoanalytic Review* 44 (1957): 327-8. Also published in a catalogue issued in 1939 by a Viennese book dealer.

Lieberman, E. James. *Acts of Will. The Life and Work of Otto Rank.* New York: Macmillan, 1985.

Likhtenshtein, E. I. "Istoriia bolezni I. S. Turgeneva," *Klinicheskaia meditsina* 46 (9) (1968): 134-42.

Likierman, Meira. "Re-translating Freud." *Times Literary Supplement* 4501 (7-13 July 1989): 744. Paul Roazen's response to Likierman was published in *TLS* 4-10 August 1989: 847.

Liubimov, A. *Professor Sharko. Nauchno-biograficheskii etiud.* St. Petersburg: Suvorin, 1894.

Ljunggren, Magnus. "The psychoanalytic breakthrough in Russia on the eve of the First World War." *Russian Literature and Psychoanalysis*. Edited by Daniel Rancour-Laferriere, 173-191. Amsterdam: John Benjamins, 1989.

Lobner, Hans. "Some Additional Remarks on Freud's Library." *Sigmund Freud House Bulletin* 1 (1975): 18-29.

————, and Vladimir Levitin. "A Short Account of Freudianism. Notes on the History of Psychoanalysis in the USSR." *Sigmund Freud House Bulletin* 2 (1978): 5-30.

Loewenthal, Leo. "Die Auffassung Dostojewskis im Vorkriegsdeutschland." *Zeitschrift für Sozialforschung* 3 (1934): 343-82.

Lombroso, Cesare. *Neue Fortschritte in den Verbrecherstudien*. Gera: C. B. Griesbach, 1899. See especially the short chapter about Dostoevsky as criminal type on pages 301-314.

Lubin, Albert. "The Influence of the Russian Orthodox Church on Freud's Wolf-Man: A Hypothesis (with an Epilogue Based on Visits with the Wolf-Man)." *The Psychoanalytic Forum* 2 (2) (Summer 1967): 146-162. This is a discussion by Willi Hoffer, Muriel M. Gardner, Henry Edelheit, Arthur A. Clinco, and Leon Ferber, followed by the author's response on pp. 163-174.

Lukács, Georg. *The Theory of the Novel*. Cambridge: MIT Press, 1971. Dostoevsky "did not write novels," "belongs to the new world" (pp. 152-53).

Lunacharskii, A. V. "O 'mnogogolosnosti' Dostoevskogo. Po povodu knigi M. M. Bakhtina 'Problemy tvorchestva Dostoevskogo'." In *Sobranie sochinenii v vos'mi tomakh*, vol. 1, pp. 157-78. Moscow: Khudozhestvennaia literatura, 1963. This review article first appeared in *Novyi mir* 10 (October 1929).

————. "Vstupitel'noe slovo na vechere, posviashchennom F. M. Dostoevskomu, 20 noiabria 1928 g." In *Neizdannye materialy*, 149-67. Moscow: Nauka, 1970. Volume 82 of series "Literaturnoe nasledstvo."

Lunatscharsky (Lunacharskii), A. "Dostojewski als Künstler und Denker." *Vivos voco* 12 June 1922, pp. 659-669.

Luria, A. R. "Die moderne russische Physiologie und die Psychoanalyse." *Internationale Zeitschrift für Psychoanalyse* 12 (1926): 40-53.

————. *The Making of Mind. A Personal Account of Soviet Psychology*. Edited by Michael Cole and Sheila Cole. Introduction and Epilogue by Michael Cole. Cambridge: Harvard University Press, 1979. See Michael Cole, "Alexander Romanovich Luria: 1902-1977."

Luxemburg, Rosa. "Über Dostojewski." *Die Aktion* 11 (1921): 663-665.

Mackey, Ilonka Schmidt. *Lou Salomé. Inspiratrice et interprète de Nietzsche, Rilke et Freud*. Paris: Librairie A. J. Nizet, 1956.

Maenchen, Anna. Personal communication. 21 April 1984.

Mahony, Patrick. *Cries of the Wolf Man*. New York: International Universities, 1984.

Malcolm, Janet. *Psychoanalysis: The Impossible Profession*. New York: Knopf, 1981.

Malcolm, Norman. *Ludwig Wittgenstein. A Memoir*. London: Oxford, 1962.

Mallory, J. P. *In Search of the Indo-Europeans*. London: Thames and Hudson, 1989. "The Aryan Myth" is on pages 266-270.

Mandelstam, Nadezhda. *Hope Against Hope*. New York: Atheneum, 1979.

Maneval, Gerda. Personal communication. 26 July 1985. Ms. Maneval represents the Literary Department of the Munich publishing house R. Piper & Co.

Marti, Jean. "La Psychanalyse en Russie et en Union Soviétique de 1909 a 1930." *Critique* 32 (346) (March 1976): 199-236.

Marx, Karl. *Communist Manifesto*. New York: Washington Square Press, 1964.

————, and Friedrich Engels. *The Communist Manifesto*. Edited by Francis B. Randall. New York: Washington Square, 1977.

Masaryk, Thomas G. "Dostojewski und Europa." *Nord und Sud* 50 (1) (1927): 8-11.

————. "Die Revolution in Russland." *Oesterreichische Rundschau* 2 (February 1905): 1-8.

————. *Russland und Europa*. 2 vols. Jena: Eugen Diederichs, 1919.

————. *The Spirit of Russia*. 3 vols. London: George Allen & Unwin, 1967. "Part One. Dostoevsky" is on pages 3-157. The quote "Dostoevsky, of course, always does have a tendency to play with fire..." appears on page 148.

Masson, Jeffrey Moussaieff. Personal communication. 18 January 1985.

———. Review of *Gespräche mit dem Wolfsmann,* by Karin Obholzer. *The International Review of Psycho-Analysis* 9 (1982): 116-119. Important archival materials are included in this review.

———. *The Assault on Truth. Freud's Suppression of the Seduction Theory.* New York: Farrar, Straus and Giroux, 1984.

May, Arthur J. *The Hapsburg Monarchy, 1867-1914.* Cambridge: Harvard University, 1951.

Mayer, Sigmund, ed. *Lotos. Naturwissenschaftlische Zeitschrift.* (Prague). Published 1851-1942.

———. *Gesetzgebung und die Medizin des Thalmuds.* Translated from the French by I. M. Rabbinowicz. Trier: F. Lintz/Paris: Selbstverlag des Verfassers, 1881. 2nd ed. Leipzig: Schulze, 1883.

———. *Die thalmudischen Principien des Schächtens und die Medicin des Thalmuds, verglichen mit Hippokrates und der modernen Wissenschaft.* Translated from the French by Israel Michel Rabbinowicz. Trier: Selbstverlag des Verfassers, 1881.

McGrath, William J. "Freud as Hannibal. The Politics of the Brother Band." *Central European History* 7 (1974): 31-57. See Stanley Rothman and Phillip Isenberg, "Sigmund Freud and the Politics of Marginality."

———. *Freud's Discovery of Psychoanalysis. The Politics of Hysteria.* Ithaca: Cornell University Press, 1986. "The Dream of Joseph" is on pages 26-58.

Meir, Heinrich. "Galician Jews in Vienna." In *The Jews of Austria. Essays on Their Life, History and Destruction,* edited by Josef Fraenkel, 361-373. London: Vallentine & Mitchell, 1967.

Meissner, William W. "The Wolf-Man and the Paranoid Process." *Annual of Psychoanalysis* 5 (1977): 23-74.

———. "The Wolf-Man and the Paranoid Process." *Psychoanalytic Review* 66 (2) (Summer 1979): 155-171.

———. *The Paranoid Process.* New York: J. Aronson, 1978.

———. *Psychoanalysis and Religious Experience.* New Haven: Yale University Press, 1984.

Mereschkowski, Dmitri. "Rodion Raskolnikoff." Preface to *Sämtliche Werke*, by F.M. Dostoevsky, vol. 1, part 1, pp. xx-lix.

————. "Zur Einführung. Bemerkungen über Dostojewski." In *Sämtliche Werke*, by F.M. Dostojewski, vol. 9, part 1 (*Die Brüder Karamasoff*), xi-xvi. Munich: R. Piper, 1908. Mereschkowski's introduction was originally published in 1901.

————. *Auf dem Wege nach Emmaus. Essays.* Munich: R. Piper, 1919. "Der Prophet der russischen Revolution" (abridged) appears on pages 42-92. "Wer ist der Mörder" (Kiev "ritual murder" trial of 1912) is on pages 243-6.

————. *Die Geheimnisse des Ostens.* Berlin: Welt, 1924. Part of Freud's library. Russian edition is *Taina trekh. Egipet—Vavilon* (mystery of the three. Egypt—Babylon). Prague: Plamia, 1925.

————. *Der Messias.* Leipzig: Grethlein, 1927. Originally published in Russian as *Messiia* (Paris: 1927). Part of Freud's library.

————. *Peter der Grosse und sein Sohn Alexei.* Leipzig: Schulze, 1905. This book, with *Julian the Apostate* and *Leonardo da Vinci*, completed the trilogy Christ and Antichrist. All were part of Freud's library.

————. *Das Reich des Antichrist: Russland und der Bolschewismus.* Munich: Drei Masken, 1921.

————. *Tolstoi as Man and Artist, with an Essay on Dostoevsky.* New York: G. P. Putnam's Sons, 1902.

————. *Tolstoi und Dostojewski als Menschen und Künstler.* Leipzig: Schulze, 1903. Part of Freud's library. Other editions include St. Petersburg, 1902; Leipzig, 1903; and Berlin, 1919 and 1924.

————. *Vom Krieg zur Revolution. Ein unkriegerisches Tagebuch.* Munich: R. Piper, 1919. "Die Judenfrage als eine russische Frage" is on pages 106-110.

Merezhkovsky, Dmitry. *Akhnaton, King of Egypt* (Der Messias).Translated by Natalie A. Duddington. New York: E. P. Dutton, 1927.

————. *L'âme de Dostoïewsky, le prophète de la révolution russe.* Paris: Bossard, 1922.

Mikhailov, Vladimir. "Psikhoanaliz—novaia religiia?" *Literaturnaia gazeta* 12 (November 1969): 13.

Miller, Jonathan, ed. *Freud. The man, his world, his influence.* Boston: Little, Brown, 1972.

Miller, Martin. "Freudian Theory under Bolshevik Rule: The Theoretical Controversy During the 1920s." *Slavic Review* 44 (4) (Winter 1985): 625-646.

————. "The Origins and Development of Russian Psychoanalysis, 1909-1930." *Journal of the American Academy of Psychoanalysis* 14 (1) (1986): 125-135.

————. "The Theory and Practice of Psychiatry in the Soviet Union." *Psychiatry* 48 (February 1985): 13-24.

Miller, O.F., and N.N. Strakhov. *Biografiia, pis'ma i zametki iz zapisnoi knizhki F. M. Dostoevskogo*. Saint Petersburg: A. S. Suvorin, 1883. This is the authorized biography and was published in German in vols. 11 and 12 of Dostojewski's *Sämtliche Werke*. Part of Freud's library.

Morelli, Giovanni (Ivan Lermolieff). *Italian Painters. Critical Studies of Their Works*. London: John Murray, 1892.

Morson, Gary Saul. "Dostoevsky's Anti-Semitism and the Critics: A Review Article." *Slavic and East European Journal* 27 (3) (1983): 302-317.

Mundall, John N. Personal communication. 20 May 1981.

Murashkintsev, A. "Odessa." In *Entsiklopedicheskii slovar'*, vol. 21, pp. 726-729. Edited by F. A. Brockhaus and I. A. Efron. St. Petersburg: Efron, 1897.

Murray, Robert K. *Red Scare: A Study in National Hysteria, 1919-1920*. New York: McGraw-Hill, 1964.

Mühsam, Erich. "Bohême." *Die Fackel* 202 (30 April 1906): 4-10. The editorial preface "Ein Vorschlag" is signed "Reformator."

Münzer, Arthur. "Dostojewski als Psychopathologe. I. Die Brüder Karamasow." *Berliner Klinische Wochenschrift* 21 December 1914, pp. 1943-1945.

Nathan, Paul. "Duma und Bureaukratie." *Die Nation* 26 (30 March 1907): 406-8.

Natorp, Paul. *Fjodor Dostojewskis Bedeutung für die gegenwärtige Kulturkrise, mit einem Anhang zur geistigen Krisis der Gegenwart*. Jena: Eugen Diederichs, 1923.

Nechaeva, V. S. "Iz literatury o Dostoevskom. (Poezdka v Darovoe)." *Novyi mir* 3 (1926): 128-144.

Neiditsch, Jeanne. "Über den gegenwärtigen Stand der Freudschen Psychologie in Russland." In *Jahrbuch für psychoanalytische und psychopathologische Forschungen*, vol. 2 (August 1910), part 1, 347-349. Leipzig/Vienna: Franz Deuticke, 1910.

Neiditsch, Sara. "Dr. Tatiana Rosenthal, Petersburg" (obituary). *Internationale Zeitschrift für Psychoanalyse* 7 (1921): 384-5.

————. "Die Psychoanalyse in Russland während der letzten Jahre." *Internationale Zeitschrift für Psychoanalyse* 7 (1921): 381-4. Includes a synopsis of "Stradanie i tvorchestvo Dostoevskogo. Psikhogeneticheskoe issledovanie," by T.K. Rozental'. Nieditsch lived in Berlin at the time.

————, and N.E. Osipov. "Psycho-Analysis in Russia." *International Journal of Psycho-Analysis* 3 (1922): 513-520.

Neifel'd (Neufeld), Iolan. *Dostoevskii. Psikhoanaliticheskii ocherk pod redaktsiei Prof. Z. Freida.* Leningrad-Moscow: "Petrograd," 1925.

Nettau, Max. *Michael Bakunin; eine biographische Skizze.* Berlin: P. Pawlowitsch, 1901.

Neufeld, Jolan. *Dostojewski. Skizze zu seiner Psychoanalyse.* Leipzig: Internationaler Psychoanalytischer Verlag, 1923. Fourth volume in series titled "Imago - Bücher." Cited, with excessive praise, in "Dostojewski und die Vatertötung" (Dostoevsky and Parricide), by Sigmund Freud.

Nietzsche, Friedrich. *Briefwechsel mit Fr. Nitschl, J. Burckhardt, I. Taine, G. Keller, F. von Stein, G. Brandes.* Edited by E. Förster-Nietzsche and Kurt Wachsmuth. Berlin/Leipzig: Schuster & Loeffler, 1904.

————. *Gesammelte Briefe.* Vol. 3, part 1, Berlin/Leipzig: Schuster & Loeffler, 1904; vol. 3, part 2, Berlin/Leipzig: Schuster & Loeffler, 1905; vol. 4, Leipzig: Insel, 1908.

————. *Werke.* Leipzig: Alfred Kröner. Vol. 8 (1919), vol. 9 (1922).

Noveck, Simon, ed. *Judaism and Psychiatry.* New York: National Academy for Adult Jewish Studies, 1956.

Nötzel, Karl. *Dostojewski und wir.* Munich: Musarion, 1920.

Nunberg, Herman, and Ernst Federn, eds. *Minutes of the Vienna Psychoanalytic Society.* 4 vols. New York: International Universities, 1962-1975.

Obholzer, Karin. *Gespräche mit dem Wolfsmann.* Reinbek bei Hamburg: Rowohlt, 1980.

————. *The Wolf-Man Sixty Years Later*. New York: Continuum, 1982.

Oring, Elliott. Personal communication. 29 September 1984.

————. *The Jokes of Sigmund Freud. A Study in Humor and Jewish Identity*. Philadelphia: University of Pennsylvania Press, 1984.

Osman, Ahmed. *Moses: Pharaoh of Egypt*. London: Grafton Books, 1990.

Osokin, N. E. "L. O. Darkshevich kak uchenyi i pedagog," *Zhurnal nevropatologii i psikhiatrii imeni S. S. Korsakova* 5 (1948): 49-53.

Ossipow, N. (Nikolai Evgrafovich Osipov). "Neue Wege in der Dostojewskij-Forschung. Die Arbeiten von A. L. Boehm." *Slavische Rundschau* 2 (4) (April 1930): 253-259.

————. (Nikolai Evgrafovich Osipov). "Zur psychoanalytischen Bewegung in Moskau." *Internationale Zeitschrift für Psychoanalyse* 7 (1921): 385-7.

Pachmuss, Temira. *D. S. Merezhkovsky in Exile*. New York: Peter Lang, 1990.

Pankeev, S. K. *The Wolf-Man by the Wolf-Man*. Edited by Muriel Gardner. New York: Basic Books, 1971. Contains "The Memoirs of the Wolf-Man" (1938); "My Recollections of Sigmund Freud," by the Wolf-Man (1952); "From the History of an Infantile Neurosis," (1914-1918, 1923); "A Supplement to 'The History of an Infantile Neurosis'," by Ruth Mack Brunswick" (1928); and "Meetings with the Wolf-Man" (1938-1949).

Pankejeff, S. K. (Pankeev, Sergei Konstantinovich; the Wolf-Man). "Letters Pertaining to Freud's 'History of an Infantile Neurosis'." *The Psychoanalytic Quarterly* 26 (October 1957): 449-460. Contains letters to Freud (6 June 1926) and to K. Eissler (11 June 1957).

Papini, Giovanni, "A Visit to Freud." In *Freud As We Knew Him*, edited by Hendrik M. Ruitenbeek, 98-102. Detroit: Wayne State University, 1973.

Pawel, Ernst. *The Labyrinth of Exile. A Life of Theodor Herzl*. New York: Farrar, Straus & Giroux, 1990.

Perepel, Elias. "The Psychoanalytic Movement in U.S.S.R." *The Psychoanalytic Review* 26 (1939): 299-300.

Peters, H. F. *My Sister, My Spouse. A Biography of Lou Andreas-Salomé*. New York: W. W. Norton, 1962.

Piaget, Jean. Personal communication. 23 February 1976. Piaget had lost contact with Sabina Spielrein, his former student analysand, despite all efforts, since 1924.

Piper, Reinhold. *Vormittag. Erinnerungen eines Verlegers*. Munich: R. Piper Verlag, 1947.

Pirog, Gerald. "Bakhtin and Freud on the ego." In *Russian Literature and Psychoanalysis*, edited by Daniel Rancour-Laferriere, 401-415. Amsterdam: John Benjamins, 1989.

———. "The Bakhtin Circle's Freud. From Positivism to Hermeneutics." *Poetics Today* 8 (3-4): 1987, 591-610.

Pistsova, A.Z. "Neizvestnye pis'ma M.M. Dostoevskogo o brate-znamenitom pisatele." *Vestnik Leningradskogo Universiteta* no. 2, vyp. 1 (1972): 152-155 (Istoriia/Iazyk/Literature).

Plevitskaia, Nadezhda. *Dëzhkin karagod*. Paris/Berlin: Tair, 1925.

———. *Moi put' s pesnei*. Paris: Tair, 1930.

Poesche, Theodor. *Die Arier. Ein Beitrag zur historischen Anthropologie*. Jena: H. Costenoble,1878.

Pollock, George H. "Psychoanalysis in Russia and the U.S.S.R.: 1908-1979." *Annals of Psychoanalysis* 10 (1982): 267-279.

Pomer, Sidney L. "Max Eitingon, 1881-1943, The Organizer of Psychoanalytic Training." In *Psychoanalytic Pioneers*, edited by Alexander, Eisenstein, and Grotjahn, pp. 51-62.

Popova, Marta Anatol'evna. *Freidizm i religiia*. Moscow: Nauka, 1985.

Poslednie Novosti (Les dernières nouvelles) (Paris), edited by P. N. Miliukov, 22 September 1937-15 December 1938.

Prianishnikov, Boris. *Nezrimaia pautina*. Silver Springs, Md.: Boris Prianishnikov, 1978.

Psikhoterapiia. Obozrenie voprosov psikhicheskogo lecheniia i prikladnoi psikhologii (Moscow), edited by N. A. Vyrubov with M. M. Asatiani, A. N. Bernshtein, Iu. V. Kannabikh, and N. E. Osipov, 1910-1914.

Raeff, Marc. *Russia Abroad. A Cultural History of the Russian Emigration, 1919-1939*. New York: Oxford University, 1990.

Ramani, S. Venkat, et al. "Diagnosis of Hysterical Seizures in Epileptic Patients." *American Journal of Psychiatry* 137 (6) (June 1980): 705-9.

Ramm, Agatha. *Germany 1789-1919. A Political History.* London: Methuen, 1967.

Rancour-Laferriere, Daniel. "Freud Returns to Russia." *Report on the USSR* (RFE/RL Research Institute) 3 (38) (1991): 4-11.

———, ed. *Russian Literature and Psychoanalysis.* Amsterdam/Philadelphia: John Benjamins, 1989.

Rank, Otto. "Der Doppelgänger." *Imago* 3 (2) (1914): 97-164.

———. "Der Doppelgänger." Leipzig/Vienna: Internationale Psychoanalytische Verlag, 1925.

———. *The Don Juan Legend.* Edited by David G. Winter. Princeton, N.J.: Princeton University Press, 1975.

———. *Das Inzest-Motif in Dichtung und Sage.* Leipzig: Franz Deuticke, 1926. (1st ed. 1912) Draft read to Vienna Psychoanalytic Society in 1907.

Rapoport, Vitaly, and Yuri Alexeev. *High Treason: Essays on the History of the Red Army 1918-1938.* Durham, N.C.: Duke University Press, 1985.

Reich, Wilhelm. "Dialectical Materialism and Psychoanalysis" (1927-28), and "Psychoanalysis in the Soviet Union" (1929). In *Sex-Pol. Essays 1929-1934*, 1-74 and 75-78. New York: Random House, 1972.

———. *Reich Speaks of Freud.* New York: Farrar, Straus & Giroux, 1967.

Reik, Theodor. "Freud and Jewish Wit." *Psychoanalysis* 2 (1954): 15-20.

———. "Freuds Studie über Dostojewski." *Imago* 15 (1929): 232-242.

———. "The Study on Dostoevsky." In *From Thirty Years with Freud*, by Theodor Reik, 158-176.

———. *Freud als Kulturkritiker.* Vienna: Dr. Max Präger, 1930.

———. *From Thirty Years with Freud.* Westport, Conn.: Greenwood Press, 1940.

———. *Geständniszwang und Strafbedürfnis. Problem der Psychoanalyse und der Kriminologie.* Leipzig/Vienna/Zurich: Internationaler Psychoanalytischer Verlag, 1925.

————. *Listening with the Third Ear*. New York: Farrar, Straus, 1948.

Rice, James L. "Beyond Twice-Two." *Times Literary Supplement* 4,413 (30 October 1987): 1188. Letters in response were published in *TLS* 4 December 1987: 324; 8 January 1988: 37; 12 February 1988: 163.

————. "Dostoevsky's Doctor." In *Proceedings of the Kentucky Foreign Language Conference 1983*, edited by Boris Sorokin, Slavic Section, vol. 1, no. 1, 26-31. Lexington, Ky.: University of Kentucky, Dept. of Slavic and Oriental Languages.

————. "Dostoevsky's Medical History: Diagnosis and Dialectic." *Russian Review* 42 (2) (April 1983): 131-161.

————. "Freud and Dostoevsky." Edited by Gil Latz and Laurence Kominz. *Proceedings Prepared for the Second Portland State University/Hokkaido University Faculty Research Symposium*, 79-86. Portland, Oregon: Portland State University, 1989.

————. "Psychoanalysis of 'Peasant Marei': Some Residual Problems." Edited by Daniel Rancour-Laferriere. In *Russian Literature and Psychoanalysis*, 245-261. Amsterdam: John Benjamins, 1989.

————. "Russian Stereotypes in the Freud-Jung Correspondence." *Slavic Review* 41 (1) (Spring 1982): 19-34.

————. *Dostoevsky and the Healing Art*. Ann Arbor, Mich.: Ardis, 1985.

Rieff, Philip. *Freud: The Mind of a Moralist*. Garden City, N.Y.: Doubleday, 1961.

Rilke, Rainer Maria. *Das Stunden-Buch*. Frankfurt/M.: Insel Verlag, 1972. The 1905 edition carried the dedication "Gelegt in die Hände von Lou."

Roazen, Paul. Personal communications. 8 February 1988; 16 March 1988; 6 April 1988; 4 October 1990.

————. "Encountering Freud." *Society* May/June 1989: 77-82.

————. "The Wolf Man and the Rat Man." *Partisan Review* Fall 1987: 650-653. Review of *Cries of the Wolf Man, by Patrick Mahony*.

————. *Brother Animal. The Story of Freud and Tausk*. New York: Knopf, 1969.

————. *Encountering Freud*. New Brunswick: Transaction, 1990.

————. *Freud and His Followers*. New York: Knopf, 1975.

————. *Freud: Political and Social Thought*. New York: Knopf, 1968.

Robert, Marthe. *From Oedipus to Moses. Freud's Jewish Identity*. New York: Doubleday, 1976.

Roberts, Thomas. Personal communications. 4 August 1988; 14 September 1990. Roberts represents Sigmund Freud Copyrights in Wivenhoe, England.

Rodin, Ernst. "Epileptic and Pseudoepileptic Seizures: Differential Diagnostic Considerations." In *Psychiatric Aspects of Epilepsy*, edited by Dietrich Blumer, 179-195. Washington, D.C.: American Psychiatric Press, 1984.

Rogger, Hans. *Jewish Policies and Right-Wing Politics in Imperial Russia*. Los Angeles/Berkeley: University of California, 1986.

Roith, Estelle. *The Riddle of Freud. Jewish Influence on His Theory of Female Sexuality*. London: Tavistock, 1987.

Rosanow, W. *Dostojewski und seine Legende vom Grossinquisitor*. Berlin: n.p., 1924. Cited in Theoderich Kampmann, *Dostojewski in Deutschland*, 236. Apparently not available in any North American library.

Rosen, Nathan. Review of *Confessions of a Jew*, by Leonid Grossman. *Slavic Review* December 1976: 153-54.

————. Review of *Dostoevsky and the Jews*, by David I. Goldstein., *Dostoevsky Studies* 3 (1980): 200-203. Actually published in 1982.

————. "Freud on Dostoevsky's Epilepsy: A Revaluation." Paper presented at International Dostoevsky Symposium, Ljubljana, July 1989.

Rosenfeld, Eva M. "Dream and Vision. Some Remarks on Freud's Egyptian Bird Dream." *International Journal of Psycho-Analysis* 37 (1) (1956): 97-105.

Rosenshield, Gary. "Dostoevsky's Jewish Portraits: The Function of the Stereotype in Dostoevsky's Fiction." Unpublished manuscript. 1982.

————. "Isai Fomich Bumshtein: The Representation of the Jew in Dostoevsky's Major Fiction." *Russian Review* 43 (1984): 261-276.

Rosenthal, Richard J. "Dostoevsky's Experiment with Projective Mechanisms and the Theft of Identity in *The Double*." In *The*

Anxious Subject. Nightmares and Daymares in Literature and Film, edited by Moshe Lazar, 13-40. n.d. Part 2 of the series "Interplay."

—————. "The Gambler and the Poet: Notes on Dostoevsky, Illness and Creativity." Unpublished manuscript. May 1989.

—————. "The Poetics of Gambling: False Beauty and the Aesthetics of Perversity." Unpublished manuscript. March 1979.

—————. "The Psychodynamics of Pathological Gambling: A Review of the Literature." In *The Handbook of Pathological Gambling*, edited by T. Galski, 41-70. Springfield, Illinois: Charles C. Thomas, 1987.

Rosenthal, Tatiana K. See Rozental', T. K.

Rothe, A. von. "Johann Wasiliewitsch IV, genannt der Grausame. Eine psychiatrische Studie." *Jahrbücher für Psychiatrie und Neurologie* (Leipzig/Vienna) 13 (1895): 145-207.

Rothman, Stanley, and Phillip Isenberg. "Sigmund Freud and the Politics of Marginality." *Central European History* 7 (1974): 58-78. This is a reply to William J. McGrath, "Freud as Hannibal. The Politics of the Brother Band."

Roy, Alec. "Hysterical Seizures." *Archives of Neurology* 36 (July 1979): 447.

Rozental', Tatiana K. (Rosenthal). "Stradanie i tvorchestvo Dostoevskogo. Psikhogeneticheskoe issledovanie." *Voprosy izucheniia i vospitaniia lichnosti* 1 (1919): 88-107. Actually appeared February 1920, according to Sara Neiditsch in her 1921 obituary of Rozental', "Die Psychoanalyse in Russland während der letzten Jahre."

Ruitenbeek, Hendrik M., ed. *Freud As We Knew Him.* Detroit: Wayne State University, 1973.

Sachs, Hanns. *Freud. Master and Friend.* Cambridge: Harvard University Press, 1945.

Sajner, Josef. "Sigmund Freuds Beziehung zu seinem Geburtsort Freiberg (Příbor) und zu Mähren." *Clio Medica* 3 (1968): 167-180

Schmidl, Fritz. "Freud and Dostoevsky." *Journal of the American Psychoanalytic Association* 13 (1965): 518-532.

Schmidt, H. "Die deutsche Dostojewski-Rezeption der 20er Jahre." *Zeitschrift für Slawistik* 16 (6) (1971): 871-879.

Schmidt, Wera. "Russian Psycho-Analytical Society, Second Quarter 1927-First Quarter 1928." *International Journal of Psycho-Analysis* 9 (1928): 397-299.

———. "Russian Psycho-Analytical Society First Quarter, 1930." *International Journal of Psycho-Analysis* 11 (1930): 34.

———. "Russian Psycho-Analytical Society." *International Journal of Psycho-Analysis* 5 (1924): 122.

———. "Russische Psychoanalytische Vereinigung. II. und III. Quartal 1927." *Internationale Zeitschrift für Psychoanalyse* 14 (1928): 294-5.

Schorske, Carl E. "Politics and Patricide in Freud's Interpretation of Dreams." *American Historical Review* 78 (April 1973): 328-347. Reprinted in *Fin-de-siècle Vienna*, by Carl E. Schorske, 181-207 (New York: Knopf, 1980).

Schröter, Michael. "'Freud-Schüler als Geheimagent Stalins entlarvt'. Zur Entstehung einer Schimpflegende." *Merkur* (Stuttgart) 9 (1988): 890-95.

Schur, Max. "Some Additional 'Day Residues' of the Specimen Dream of Psychoanalysis." In *Psychoanalysis. A General Psychology: Essays in Honor of Heinz Hartmann*, edited by Rudolph M. Löwenstein et al., 45-85. New York: International Universities, 1966.

———. *Freud, Living and Dying*. New York: International Universities, 1972. The author was Freud's physician after 1929.

Schwartz, Stephen. "Intellectuals and Assassins—Annals of Stalin's 'Killerati'." Review of *Chekisty: A History of the KGB*, by John J. Dziak. *New York Times Review of Books* 24 January 1988, p. 1. This review elicited responses by Vadim Kondratiev, Sidney Hook, Peter Gay, Simon Karlinsky, and Vitaly Raporport, whose letters were printed in the *New Times Review*, with an author's reply published 6 March 1988.

———, and Vitaly Rapoport. "'The Mystery of Max Eitingon': An Exchange." *New York Review* 16 June 1988, 50f. This article was in reply to "The Mystery of Max Eitingon," by Theodore Draper. See *Nezrimaia pautina* by Boris Prianishnikov; "The Mystery of Max Eitingon" by Theodore Draper; and *Chekisty. A History of the KGB* by John J. Dziak.

————, Vitaly Rapoport, Theodore Draper, and Walter Laqueur, "'The Mystery of Max Eitingon: An Exchange." *New York Review* 16 June 1988.

Schweisheimer, W. "Die Krankheit Dostojewskis." *Neue Schweizer Rundschau* 15 (1921): 176-182.

Seduro, Vladimir. "The Problem of F. M. Dostoevski's Origin." *Zapisy* (New York: Byelorussian Institute of Arts and Sciences) 16 (1978): 44-60.

Segaloff, Timofei. *Die Krankheit Dostojewskys. Eine ärzlich-psychologische Studie.* Munich: Ernst Reinhardt, 1907.

Sellin, Ernst. *Mose und seine Bedeutung für die israelitisch-jüdische Religionsgeschichte.* Leipzig/Erlangen: A. Deichert, 1922. The quotation "Mit ihm haben vielleicht seine 'Söhne' den Tod erleiden müssen. Das Ganze ist eine tragische, ergreifende Schilderung sondergleichen" appears on page 50.

Seton-Watson, R. W. *A History of the Czechs and Slovaks.* London: Hutchinson, 1943.

Shengold, Leonard. "Freud and Joseph." In *Freud and His Self-Analysis*, edited by Mark Kanzer and Jules Glenn, 67-86. New York: Jason Aronson, 1979.

Shepherd, William R. *Shepherd's Historical Atlas.* Totowa, N.J.: Barnes and Noble, 1980.

Slochower, Harry. "Incest in *The Brothers Karamazov.*" *The American Imago* 16 (1) (Spring 1959): 127-145.

Sokel, Walter H. "The Wolfman and the Castle." *Journal of the Kafka Society of America* 1/2 (June/December 1988): 64-68.

Solovjeff, Wladimir [Solov'ev]. "Dostojewskis religiöse Grundidee." *Seele* (Regensburg) 1 (2) (1919): 45-48.

———— [Solov'ev]. *Drei Reden. Dem Andenken Dostojewskis gewidmet.* Mainz: 1921. Cited by Theoderich Kampmann in his *Dostojewski in Deutschland*, p. 227. No North American locations have this book.

———— [Solov'ev]. *Russland und Europa.* Jena: Eugen Diederichs, 1917.

Spector, Jack J. *The Aesthetics of Freud. A Study in Psychoanalysis and Art.* New York: Praeger Publishers, 1973.

Spielrein, Sabina. "Die Destruktion als Ursache des Werdens." *Jahrbuch für psychoanalytische und psychopathologische Forschungen* (Leipzig/Vienna) 4 (1912): 465-503.

———. "Russische Literatur." In *Bericht über die Fortschritt der Psychoanalyse in den Jahren 1914-1919*, 356-365. Leipzig/Vienna/Zurich: 1921. Vol. 3 of the series "Beihefte der *Internationalen Zeitschrift für Psychoanlyse*," edited by Sigmund Freud.

Stammler, Heinrich A. "Julianus Apostata Redivivus. Dmitrij Merezhkovskij: Predecessors and Successors." *Die Welt der Slaven* 11 (1966): 180-204.

Stanescu, Heinz. "Unbekannte Briefe des jungen Sigmund Freud an einen rumänischen Freund." *Neue Literatur* (Bucharest) 16 (3) (June 1965): 123-132.

———. "Young Freud's Letters to His Rumanian Friend Silberstein." *The Israel Annals of Psychiatry and Related Disciplines* 7 (3) (December 1971): 195-207.

Steinberg, A. S. "Dostoevsky and the Jews." In *History As Experience: Aspects of Historical Thought—Universal and Jewish*, 247-260. New York: KTAV Publishing House, 1983.

———. "Dostoevsky and the Jews." In *The Jew: Essays from Martin Buber's Journal "Der Jude," 1916-1928*, edited by A. A. Cohen, 158-170. University of Alabama Press, 1980.

Stekel, Wilhelm. "Die psychische Behandlung der Epilepsie." *Zentralblatt für Psychoanalyse* 1 (5-6) (1911).

———. *The Autobiography of Wilhelm Stekel*. New York: Liveright, 1950. The author says he met Pankeev's mother April-August 1913 in Ischl. Says her son's sessions with Freud were twice daily (pp. 125-26).

———. *Dichtung und Neurose. Bausteine zur Psychologie des Künstlers und des Kunstwerkes*. Wiesbaden: J. F. Bergmann, 1909. Vol. 64 of the series "Grenzfragen des Nerven-und Seelenlebens," edited by L. Loewenfeld.

———. *Nervose Angstzustände und ihre Behandlung*. 3rd ed. Berlin/Vienna: Urban & Schwarzenberg, 1921 Chapter 33 has "Die psychische Behandlung der Epilepsie" on pp. 523-546.

———. *Sadism and Masochism. The Psychology of Hatred and Cruelty*. 2 vols. New York: Liveright, 1953. Vol. 1, chap. 15, is called "Polyphony of Thought"; vol. 2, chap. 18 (pp. 331-375) is "The Epileptic Symptom Complex and Its Analytic Treatment.". The first edition was published in 1929.

————. *Sadismus und Masochismus für Ärzt und Kriminologen dargestellt*. Berlin/Vienna: 1925.

Stepansky, Paul E. "Feuerbach and Jung as Religious Critics—with a Note on Freud's Psychology of Religion." In *Freud. Appraisals and Reappraisals*, edited by Paul E. Stepansky, vol. 1, pp. 215-239. Hillsdale, N.J.: Analytic Press, 1986.

Stepniak (S. M. Kravchinskii). *Underground Russia. Revolutionary Profiles and Sketches from Life*. Westport, Conn.: Hyperion, 1973. The original Russian edition was published in 1883.

————. *Das unterirdische Russland (La Russie sotterrances). Porträts und Skizzen aus der Wirklichkeit*. Bern: R. Jenni, 1884.

Sterba, Richard F. "Discussions of Sigmund Freud." *The Psychoanalytic Quarterly* 47 (2) (1978): 173-191.

Stern, Bernhard. *Geschichte der öffentlichen Sittlichkeit in Russland. Kultur, Aberglaube, Kirche, Klerus, Sekten, Laster, Vergnügungen, Leiden* (The History of Public Morality in Russia). 2 vols. Berlin: Hermann Barsdorf, 1907. Among books received by the Vienna Psychoanalytic Society in 1908.

————. *Russische Grausamkeit einst und jetzt* (Russian Cruelty Past and Present) (Ein Kapitel aus der Geschichte des öffentlichen Sittlichkeit in Russland). Berlin: Hermann Barsdorf, 1908.

Stern, Fritz. "Moeller van den Bruck and the Third Reich." In *The Politics of Cultural Despair. A Study in the Rise of the Germanic Ideology*, 189-191. Berkeley: University of California Press, 1961. About Dostoevsky's complete works, see pp. 189-191.

Storr, Anthony. *Freud*. Oxford: Oxford University Press, 1989.

Strobl, Karl Hans (Brünn). "Dostojewski, Russland und die Revolution." *Die Gegenwart* 6 (1907): 87-88; 7 (1907): 103-104.

Sulloway, Frank J. *Freud, Biologist of the Mind. Beyond the Psychoanalytic Legend*. New York: Basic Books, 1979.

Swales, Peter J. Personal communications. 18 July 1990; 11 August 1990.

————. "Freud, Minna Bernays, and the Conquest of Rome. New Light on the Origins of Psychoanalysis." *The New American Review* Spring/Summer 1982: 1-23.

————. *Freud, Fliess, and Fratricide; The Role of Fliess in Freud's Conception of Paranoia.* N.p.: Peter J. Swales, 1982.

————. *Freud, Martha Bernays, & the Language of Flowers.* N.p.: Peter J. Swales, 1983.

Tartakower, Arieh. "Jewish Migratory Movements in Austria in Recent Generations." In *The Jews of Austria. Essays on Their Life, History and Destruction,* edited by Josef Fraenkel, 285-310.

Temkin, Owsei. *The Falling Sickness. A History of Epilepsy from the Greeks to the Beginnings of Modern Medicine.* 2nd ed. Baltimore: Johns Hopkins University, 1971.

Thun, Alphons. *Geschichte der revolutionären Bewegung in Russland.* Leipzig: Duncker & Humblot, 1883. The author was a professor in Basel from 1854 to 1886.

Tolstoi, L. N. Letters to N. N. Strakhov, 30 November-1 December 1883. In *Polnoe sobranie sochinenie,* vol. 63, pp. 142-43, edited by V. G. Chertkov. Moscow-Leningrad: GIKhL, 1934.

Treitschke, Heinrich von. *Treitschke's History of Germany in the Nineteenth Century.* Vol. 4 Edited by W. H. Dawson. New York: Robert M. McBride, 1918. "Radicalism and the Jews" is on pp. 553-568.

Trilling, Lionel. Review of *The Freud/Jung Letters (Briefwechsel),* by Sigmund Freud and C.G. Jung. *New York Times Book Review* 21 April 1974, p. 1.

Trosman, Harry, and Roger Dennis Simmons. "The Freud Library." *Journal of the American Psychoanalytic Foundation* 21 (1973): 646-687.

Trotskii, L. N. "Kul'tura i sotsializm." In *Sochineniia,* vol. 21, 423-446. Moscow-Leningrad: 1927. Also published in *Novyi mir* January 1927. First presented as a public address on 2 February 1926 and also on various later occasions not specified by the author, but alluded to, in vol. 21 (1927) of his works.

Trotskii, L. [N.], *Literatura i revoliutsiia.* Moscow: Izdatel'stvo politicheskoi literatury, 1991. First published 1923.

Trotsky, Leon [L. N. Trotskii]. "Pis'mo Akademiku I. P. Pavlovu 27 sentiabria 1923 g." In *Sochineniia,* vol. 21, 260, 488n-491. Moscow-Leningrad: 1927. On psychoanalysis.

————. *My Life.* New York: Pathfinder, 1970. Written in 1929.

Tschuppik, Karl. *The Reign of the Emperor Francis Joseph 1848-1918*. London: G. Bell & Sons, 1930.

Tur-Sinai, N. H. "Viennese Jewry." in *The Jews of Austria. Essays on Their Life, History and Destruction,* edited by Josef Fraenkel, 311-318.

Tyrras, Nicholas. "On Dostoevsky's Funeral." *Slavic and East European Journal* 30 (2) (1986): 271-277.

Vassilyev, A. T. (Vasil'ev). *The Ochrana. The Russian Secret Police.* Edited and with introduction by R. Fülöp-Miller. London: George G. Harrap, 1930. The Introduction cites Freud on "human trait of cruelty" and aggression, now confirmed in "the institution of the Russian state" (pp. 14-15). Chapter 6 ("The Jewish Question," pp. 98-107) blames Jews for the Revolution "for profit and revenge."

Vekhi. 2nd ed. Moscow: V. M. Sablin, 1909.

Vitz, Paul C. *Sigmund Freud's Christian Unconscious.* New York: Guilford, 1988.

Vogel, Léon. "Freud and Judaism: An Analysis in the Light of His Correspondence." *Judaism* 24 (2) (Spring 1975): 181-193.

Vogüé, E. M. de. *Le Roman russe.* 2nd ed. Paris: E. Plon, Nourrit, 1888. Chapter 5, pp. 203-277, is called "La religion de la souffrance—Dostoïevsky" and was first published in *La Revue des Deux Mondes* 15 January 1885.

Voloshinov, V. N. See *Freidizm,* by M.M. Bakhtin.

Völsche, Wilhelm. *Das Liebesleben in der Natur.* Not located. Cited by Andreas-Salomé 29 October 1898.

Volynski, A. L. *Das Reich der Karamasoff.* Munich: R. Piper, 1920.

Vorst, Hans. *Das bolschewistische Russland.* Leipzig: Der Neue Geist, 1919. The author's preface is signed "January 1919, Berlin." The author was the Moscow correspondent from late summer to autumn 1918 for *Berliner Tageblatt.* In this volume, the penultimate chapter describes the Cheka as "the organ of active class war and terror" (see p. 221). The last chapter ends with two passages from *The Idiot* (pp. 261-63).

Voskuil, P. H. A. "The Epilepsy of Fyodor Mikhailovich Dostoevsky (1821-1881)." *Epilepsia* 24 (1983): 658-67.

Vozrozhdenie (La Renaissance). Iuli Semenov was the editor from 23 September to 16 December 1938, during which the Plevitskaia trial résumé and sentence took place.

Vrangel', A. E. *Vospominaniia o F. M. Dostoevskom v Sibiri 1854-56 gg.* St. Petersburg: 1912. This volume was first serialized in *Novoe vremia*, 1908-9.

Vyšný, Paul. *Neo-Slavism and the Czechs, 1898-1914.* Cambridge: Cambridge University Press, 1977.

Wallace, Edwin R., IV. "The Primal Parricide." *Bulletin of the History of Medicine* 54 (2) (Summer 1980): 153-165.

Winters, Stanley B. "Hramář, Kaizl, and the Hegemony of the Young Czech Party, 1891-1901." In *The Czech Renascence of the Nineteenth Century*, edited by Stanley B. Winters, 282-313. Toronto: University of Toronto, 1970

Wiskemann, Elizabeth. *Czechs and Germans. A Study of the Struggle in the Historic Provinces of Bohemia and Moravia.* 2nd ed. New York: St. Martin's, 1967.

Wistrich, Robert S. *The Jews of Vienna in the Age of Franz Joseph.* Oxford: Oxford University Press, 1989. Chapter 16 (pp. 537-582) is titled "The Jewish Identity of Sigmund Freud."

Wittfogel, Karl August. "Dostojewski und der Bolschewismus." *Vivos voco* 2 (1922): 674-681.

Wolynski (Volynskii), A. L. (A. L. Flekser). *Das Reich der Karamasoff.* Munich: R. Piper, 1920.

Wortis, Joseph. *Fragments of an Analysis with Freud.* New York: Simon and Schuster, 1954. The analysis took place in 1934-35.

Wrangel [Vrangel'], A. E. "Dostojewski in Sibirien (Persönliche Erinnerungen)." *Hamburger Fremdenblatt* nos. 70, 72, 73 (1909).

Wulff [Woolf], Moshe. "An Appreciation of Freud's *Moses and Monotheism*." In *Max Eitingon In Memoriam*, 124-142. Jerusalem: Israel Psycho-Analytic Society, 1950.

———. "Zur Stellung der Psychoanalyse in der Sowjetunion. Bemerkungen zu dem Artikel von W. Reich." *Psychoanalytische Bewegung* 2 (1929) 70-75, 195-6.

———. Report announcing his resignation from the Russian Psychoanalytic Society beginning first quarter 1928. *International Journal of Psycho-Analysis* 9 (1928): 398.

————. Report of 9 April 1925, from the president of the Russian Psychoanalytic Association, on Russian Marxist criticism of psychoanalysis. *International Journal of Psycho-Analysis* 8 (1926): 295.

Yerushalmi, Yosef Hayim. "Freud on the 'Historical Novel': From the Manuscript Draft (1934) of *Moses and Monotheism.*" *International Journal of Psycho-Analysis* 70 (1989): 375-395.

————. Personal communication. 21 January 1991.

————. *Freud's Moses: Judaism Terminable and Interminable.* New Haven: Yale, 1991.

The Wolf-Man (*der Wolfsmann*). See Pankeev, S.K., *The Wolf-Man by the Wolf-Man.*

Zanuso, Billa. *The Origins of Psychoanalysis in Late Nineteenth-Century Viennese Culture.* Oxford: Basil Blackwell, 1986.

Zipperstein, Steve J. "Jewish Enlightenment in Odessa: Cultural Characteristics, 1794-1871." *Jewish Social Studies* 44 (1) (Winter 1982): 19-36.

————. *The Jews of Odessa. A Cultural History, 1794-1881.* Stanford: Stanford University, 1985.

Zohar, Zvi. "Dostoevsky as Seen by the Father of Psychoanalysis." *Ofakim le-hinukh ule-tarbut* (Perspectives on Education and Culture) 10 (1956): 290-294. Published in Hebrew.

Zweig, Arnold. *The Case of Sergeant Grischa.* New York: Viking,1928. Originally published in 1927 in German as *Der Streit um den Sergeanten Grischa.*

————, and Sigmund Freud. *Briefwechsel* [1927-1939]. Edited by Ernst L. Freud. Frankfurt/M.: Fischer, 1968. See Freud, Sigmund, and Arnold Zweig.

Zweig, Stefan. "Dostojewski: Der Kampf um die Wahrheit." *Österreichische Rundschau* 40 (1914): 199-203.

————. "Dostojewski. (Der Mythos der Selbstgeburt)." *Die Zukunft* 23 January 1915, pp. 111-117.

————. Review of *The Diary of Dostoevsky's Wife,* by Anna Grigorievna Dostoevsky. *Die Literatur* 27 (1924/25): 581-3.

————. *Conflicts.* New York: Viking, 1927. Includes "Four-and-Twenty Hours in a Woman's Life," analyzed in "Dostoevsky and Parricide".

————. *Drei Meister. Balzac, Dickens, Dostojewski.* Leipzig: Insel, 1920. Incorporates "Dostojewski: Der Kampf um die Wahrheit" and "Dostojewski. (Der Mythos der Selbstgeburt)."

————. *Erstes Erlebnis.* Leipzig: Insel, 1917.

————. *Three Masters. Balzac, Dickens, Dostoevsky.* New York: Viking, 1930.

————. *Die Verwirrung der Gefühle.* Leipzig: Insel, 1927. Includes "Vierundzwanzig Stunden aus dem Leben einer Frau."

————. *The World of Yesterday.* New York: Viking, 1945.

Index

Abraham, Karl, 74, 75-76, 81, 102
Addiction, 169
Adler, Alfred, 68, 71-73, 142-143
Adler, Raisa (nee Epstein), 68
Adler, Victor, 69
Akhnaton, King of Egypt (Merezhkovsky), 202
Alexander II (tsar), 175
Ambivalence (Russian), 114-117, 138, 163-164, 202
Amsterdam Congress, 75-76
Andreas-Salomé, Lou (1861-1937), 83-87
Antichrist, The (Nietzsche), 180-181
Anti-Semitism, 19, 21, 48, 100-101, 167, 203-215
Aptekmann, Esther, 73-74
Archaic regression, 104-106
Asatiani, M.M., 79
Austro-Prussian War, 14
Averbuch, R., 167

Bakunin, Mikhail (1814-1876), 17-18, 82, 109
Bazhenov, Dr. Nikolai (1857-1923), 106
Berlin, Isaiah, 205

Bernhardt, Sarah, 28-29
Beyond the Pleasure Principle (Freud), 109
Bismarck, Otto von (1815-1898), 14
Bolsheviks, 202
Bonaparte, Marie (princess), 169, 207, 230, 241
Botkin, Dr. Sergei Petrovich (1832-1889), 30
Brandes, Georg, 61, 113, 123-126
Bratz, Dr. Emil, 143
Brothers Karamazov, The (Dostoevsky), 4, 20, 114-115, 123, 128, 140, 164, 168, 171, 178-179, 189-190, 214, 215, 216-217
Brunswick, Dr. Ruth Mack, 94, 110-113, 115, 116, 165-166

Chalewsky, Fanny, 73
Charcot, Jean-Martin (1825-1893), 2, 14, 15, 25-26, 31-40, 160
Chekhov, Anton, 31
Chernyshevsky, 36
Chizh, Dr. Vladimir, 38
Civilization and Its Discontents (Freud), 11, 20, 232

Clinical Lectures (Charcot), 31

Cocaine, 25, 32-33

Colosseum, 38

Communist Manifesto, The (Marx), 17

Confession of a Jew in Letters to Dostoevsky, The (Grossman), 211-215

Count Thun dream, 50-52, 54-56

Course on Nervous Illnesses, A (Darkshevich), 36

Crime and Punishment (Dostoevsky), 114, 129, 206, 217

Darkshevich, L.O. (1858-1925), 17, 26-31, 35-36, 38, 163

Dattner, Bernhard, 138

David, Jacob Julius, 135-137

Death instinct, 18-19, 130, 180

De Vogüé, 37

Diary of a Writer (Dostoevsky), 205, 210

Die Erotik (Andreas-Salome), 85-86

Die Fackel, 82

Die Nation, 135-136

Dostoevsky, Aimee, 144

Dostoevsky, Anna G., 144

Dostoevsky, Feodor, 1-5, 11, 30, 34, 35, 37, 38, 71, 105, 113-117, 138-146; anti-Semitism and, 203-215; compulsive gambling of, 190-195; Dmitry Merezhkovsky on, 126-132; epilepsy of, 185-188; Georg Brandes on, 123-126; Jocob

David on, 135-137; psychoanalytic nature of writing, 159-172; Stefan Zweig on, 132-134

"Dostoevsky and Parricide" (Freud), 3-5, 114-116, 165, 170, 177-185, 208, 216, 224

"Double, The" (Dostoevsky), 139

Dream therapy, 81

Drosnes, Dr. Leonid, 101, 102

Ebstein, Erich, 170

Eitingon, Max, 11, 69-70, 73, 75, 139, 145, 168-169, 177, 225, 227-230

Eitingon, Mira (nee Raigorodskaia), 228

Endopsychic mythology, 72, 80

Engels, Friedrich, 16-17

Epilepsy, 34, 35, 137, 185-188

Ermakov, I., 165

"Eternal Husband, The" (Dostoevsky), 138

Fathers and Sons (Turgenev), 82

Federn, Paul, 137

Fedor Dostoevsky's Meaning for the Culture Crisis of the Present (Natorp), 144-146

Feuerbach, Ludwig, 17

"First Love" (Turgenev), 37

Fliess, Dr. Wilhelm, 21, 43, 48, 59

Frank, S.L., 82

"Frau Emmy von N.," 68

Freud, Emanuel, 45-47

Freud, Jacob, 13, 17, 46, 47

Freud, Josef, 43-45, 46-48

Freud, Martha (nee Bernays), 15, 25-26
Freud, Martin, 57
Freud, Moriz (1857-1920), 12-13
Freud, Philipp, 45-47
Freud, Sigmund:; ancestors of, 9-22; correspondence with Jung, 72-81; death of, 232-233; "Dostoevsky and Parricide," 177-185; in Paris, 25-40; The Interpretation of Dreams, 43-61; Wolf-Man analysis and, 93-117
Friedmann, V.B., 167
Future of an Illusion, The (Freud), 4, 170-172, 178, 183, 195, 209

Gambler, The (Dostoevsky), 192-194
Gardiner, Muriel, 94
Gershenzon, M.O., 80
Goethe, Johann, 38
Goldstein, David, 204, 211
Grossman, Leonid, 211-215

Hautler, Adolf, 113, 135
Hesse, Hermann, 140-141
House of the Dead, The (Dostoevsky) 205
Hysteria, 35, 36, 68, 186

Imago, 124, 139
Infantile sexuality, 137
Ingold, Felix, 205
International Journal of Psycho-Analysis, 74
Interpretation of Dreams, The

(Freud), 1, 5, 6, 12, 14, 19, 21, 33, 34, 43-61, 207, 232
Irma's injection dream, 59
Ivan the Terrible, 178, 181-182

Joffe, Adolf, 68-69
Jones, Ernest, 4, 13, 32, 207
Jung, Carl, 2, 5-6, 72-81, 104, 227

Kampmann, Theoderich, 124
Klikovich, Dr., 29-30
Koller, Carl, 32
Kovner, Uriia Avraam (1842-1909), 211-215
Kravchinskii, Sergei Mikhailovich. *See* Stepniak
Kropotkin, Peter, 82
Kuchin, 36

Laforgue, Dr. Rene, 230-231
La Revue des Deux Mondes, 37
Latent homosexuality, 187
Leonardo da Vinci and a Memory of His Childhood (Freud), 99
Leontieva, Tatiana, 71
Lermolieff, Ivan, 100
Le roman russe (DeVogüé), 37
Literature and Revolution (Trotsky), 167
Lithuania, 9-11
Loewenthal, Leo, 143
Lotos, 56
Luria, Dr. A.R., 167, 169

Marx, Karl, 71-72, 223-224
Masterbation, 177, 193-194
Mayer, Sigmund, 56

Memoirs of a Revolutionist
(Kropotkin), 82
Memoirs (Pankeev), 114
Merezhkovsky, Dimitry, 99-100,
115, 123, 126-132, 210, 232
Mikado (Gilbert & Sullivan), 40
Miller, General E.K., 227, 228,
229
Morelli, Giovanni, 100
Moser, Fanny, 68
Moses and Monotheism (Freud),
21, 39, 206, 208-210, 225,
226, 232
"Moses of Michelangelo, The"
(Freud), 99, 100
"Mourning and Melancholia"
(Freud), 5
Mythic symbolism, 104-106
"Myth of Self-Birth, The"
(Zweig), 132

Nathansohn, Amalie (1835-1930),
11
Nathansohn, Hermann
(1822-1895), 11-12, 13
Nathansohn, Nathan, 11
Nathansohn, Sara (nee Wilenz),
12
Nathansohn, Simon, 12
Natorp, Paul, 144-146
Nazis, 225, 232
Neue Freie Presse, 45
Neufeld, Jolan, 168
*New Introductory Lectures on
Psychoanalysis* (Freud), 223
Nicholas, Grand Duke, 14
Nicholas II (tsar), 39
Nicholas I (tsar), 181

Nietzsche, Friedrich, 125,
180-181
Nihilist models, 82
NKVD, 229

Obholzer, Karin, 94
"On a Case of Infantile Neurosis"
(Freud), 94, 102
"On the History of the
Psychoanalytic Movement"
(Freud), 106
*On the Question of Hysteria in
the History of Nations*
(Darkshevich), 36-37
Origins of Psycho-Analysis, The
(Freud), 43
Osipov, Dr. Nikolai E., 169

Pankeev, Konstantin
(1858-1908), 95
Pankeev, Sergei (Wolf-Man,
1886-1979), 1-3, 58, 71, 73,
80, 86, 93-117, 129, 138,
165-166, 190-191, 202
Pankeev, Therese, 97, 99,
100-101, 108
Papini, Giovanni, 38
"Peasant Marei" (Dostoevsky),
131-132
Peter and Alexis
(Merezhkovsky), 99-100, 115
Pique Dame (opera), 190-191
Plevitskaia, Nadezhda, 227-231
Pogroms, 10, 21
Possessed, The (Dostoevsky),
113, 135
Prague dream fragment, 57
Prague Fortress dream, 105-106

Psikhoterapiia, 79
"Psychogenesis of a Case of
    Homosexuality in a Woman"
    (Freud), 107
"Psychopaths" (Chekhov), 31

Racial psychology, 172
Rank, Dr. Otto, 69, 139-140, 161
    190
Recollections of Sigmund Freud
    (Pankeev), 114
Reik, Theodor, 192, 194, 202
Rilke, Rainer Maria, 84
*Romance of Leonardo da Vinci,
    The* (Merezhkovsky), 99
Rosenthal, Tatiana, 73-74,
    142-143, 162
R. Piper & Co. (Munich
    publisher), 123, 124, 131, 168,
    211
Russian Psychoanalytic Society,
    101, 166-167
Russian Revolution, 109, 132,
    165-166, 223-224
Russian stereotype, 71, 75, 79-82,
    86-87
Russkii Vestnik, 38

Sachs, Dr. Hanns, 138-139, 166
Schorske, Carl, 4, 60
Schur, Max, 4, 55, 177
Segaloff, Dr. Timofei, 137, 160
"Self Portrait" (Freud), 10
Sellin, Ernst, 208
Sephardim, 100
Sexual repression, 70, 72
Silberstein, Eduard, 13-14
Skoblin, Nikolai, 227, 228

Spielrein, Sabina, 19, 70, 73-83,
    86, 104-105, 109, 130, 167,
    169
Stekel, Dr. Wilhelm, 137, 161
Stepniak (Sergei Kravchinskii),
    18
Stern, Bernhard, 138
"Struggle for Truth, The"
    (Zweig), 132

Tchaikowsky, Peter Illich,
    190-191
Theodora (Sardou), 28-29
Tolstoy, Count Leo, 130
Tolstoy and Dostoevsky
    (Merezhkovsky), 115, 127,
    128, 139-140
Totem and Taboo (Freud),
    104-106, 163-164, 180, 188,
    207, 208-209
Trotsky, Leon, 2, 68-69, 167, 168
Turgenev, Ivan, 37, 82
"Twenty-Four Hours in a
    Woman's Life" (Zweig),
    193-195

Uncle Josef dream, 44, 58-61
University of Vienna, 15

Vekhi, 82
Vienna Psychoanalytic Society, 2,
    68, 135
von Rothe, Dr. A., 181-182
Vozrozhdenie 230, 231
Vygotski, L.S., 167

Weimar Congress, 85
Werther (Goethe), 38

What To Do? (Chernyshevsky),
    36
Wiener Zeitung, 45
*Wit and Its Relation to the
    Unconscious* (Freud), 203, 217
Wittels, Dr. Fritz, 71
Wolf-Man (1886-1979, Sergei
    Pankeev), 1-3, 58, 71, 73, 80,
    86, 93-117, 129, 138,
    165-166, 190-191, 202
Wolf-Man by the Wolf-Man, The
    (Pankeev), 6

Wortis, Joseph, 226
Wulff, Dr. Moshe, 1, 102, 106,
    110, 165, 167, 169

Zola, Emile, 38
Zweig, Arnold, 225, 232
Zweig, Stefan, 113, 123,
    132-134, 140, 159-160, 163,
    192, 193-195